# Congress

## Process and Policy

**FOURTH EDITION**

# Congress

## Process and Policy

**Randall B. Ripley**

*THE OHIO STATE UNIVERSITY*

**FOURTH EDITION**

W·W·Norton & Company   New York·London

Library of Congress Cataloging in Publication Data

Ripley, Randall B.
   Congress: process and policy/by Randall B. Ripley. —4th ed.
      p.   cm.
   Bibliography: p. 423
   Includes index.
   1. United States. Congress.   I. Title.
JK1061.R55   1988
328.73—dc19                                                          88-12434

W. W. Norton & Company, Inc., 500 Fifth Avenue, New York, N. Y. 10110
W. W. Norton & Company Ltd., 37 Great Russell Street, London WC1B 3NU


ISBN 0-393-95617-2


1 2 3 4 5 6 7 8 9 0

To G.A.F.

# Contents

# List of Tables

# List of Figures

# Preface

Congress always has been and will remain central to self-government in the United States. This volume, a basic analysis of Congress, presents many fundamental facts about the institution and the way it works. My aim, however, is to interpret the nature of Congress and its involvement in policy-making, not just describe it.

Congress is the most systematically studied of all American governing institutions. Scholars, journalists, and other commentators have produced a vast literature, which I have mined. I also present original data relevant to a number of points. My goal is to analyze Congress systematically so as to present an accurate picture of Congress as it enters its third century. At the same time, I hope to make clear the nature of change in Congress, which is an institution that is remarkably stable in some ways and constantly changing in other ways. I draw on systematic political science in dealing with many points and seek to enrich the findings of that work with specific illustrations of Congress at work, including a number of self-contained vignettes, both by me and by others, that are scattered throughout the book. I have studied, taught, and written about Congress continuously throughout the 1960s, 1970s, and 1980s. Many of my illustrations are drawn from these three decades. I have taken full account of the sizable scholarly literature on Congress produced during that same period. Where appropriate, I have also used some illustrations and literature from before 1960.

Short-term, contemporary changes in Congress can be important, but they do not turn the institution inside out or upside down. Constant patterns of behavior persist and underlie congressional dynamism. Proclamations of "new eras" in the nature or behavior of Congress are usually misleading.

Some consider Ronald Reagan's presidency revolutionary by American standards. In terms of the nature and function of Congress, however, the Reagan era has produced changes that are neither revolutionary nor necessarily permanent.

The largest impact of the Reagan period has come from the substance of the administration's agenda. The 1960s were a decade of the politics of creation in Congress. New domestic policies and programs proliferated. Although some creation continued into the 1970s, the brakes began to be applied. In 1981, with the coming of Ronald Reagan to the White House, the brakes were suddenly jammed on. The Reagan era is best characterized as one of the politics of adjustment.

The adjustments for individual policies ranged from termination, through severe retrenchment, to continuation with only modest change, to substantial growth in the defense realm. For domestic policy the center of gravity was somewhere between severe retrenchment and modest change.

In the first eight years of the 1980s, Congress could no longer realistically pursue the creation of new domestic programs or large-scale expansion of existing domestic programs. Suddenly, many congressional committees with full agendas in the previous decades had much smaller agendas. Simultaneously, budget matters—including spending, deficit reduction, and tax policy—became the centerpiece of domestic policy-making. The lion's share of congressional domestic-policy activity flowed from the committees dealing with these matters: the budget and appropriations committees in both houses, the House Ways and Means Committee, and the Senate Finance Committee.

At the same time that deficit-mania was taking hold of Congress, Reagan's aggressiveness in foreign and defense policy—his urge to expand our military establishment, his unwavering commitment to the Strategic Defense Initiative, his support of anti-communist rebels in places like Nicaragua and Angola, his hard line toward accommodation with the Soviet Union—forced Congress to get more involved in the details of foreign policy. Congressional involvement did not change the relative dominance of the president in the realm of foreign policy. Budget considerations did, however, produce congressional restraint on presidential proposals for military growth.

Congress can be observed from many perspectives. In this volume the focus is on two related aspects: first, the characteristics and performance of Congress as an institution; and, second, the disparate and often fragmented membership of Congress. A reader of this volume should come away with a good sense of Congress as an institution, of congressional relations with key portions of its environment, and of the importance of Congress as a policy-maker. Above all, he or she should come away with a sense that the members of Congress are not caught up in some ritual with inevitable endings. Instead, they have a number of options open to them in relation both to personal behavior and the collective behavior of the institution. Congress is neither immutable nor is it moribund. Like many institutions, it appears conservative much of the time. But it is also important and influential as a policy-maker even in its most conservative mood and can enlarge that influence in periods of aggressiveness.

The organization of the book is straightforward. In Part I Congress is presented in broad strokes. Chapter 1 paints a general picture of Congress in its environment and discusses the position of Congress in relation to policy making. Chapter 2 summarizes the development of Congress. Chapter 3 deals with the elections that provide the members of the House and Senate.

Part II investigates the internal environment for policy-making by Congress. Chapter 4 presents an overview of how members of Congress are socialized into certain patterns of making decisions and how those decisions get made. Chapter 5 focuses on committees and subcommittees. Chapter 6 examines the party leadership. Chapter 7 deals with a variety of other internal influences such as state delegations, ideologically based groups, personal and committee staffs, and support agencies for Congress as a whole.

Part III focuses on the external relations of Congress that are critical to determining both the nature and the scope of its policy impact. Chapter 8 explores congressional relations with interest groups and constituents. Chapter 9 discusses congressional relations with the president and the institutional presidency. Chapter 10 examines congressional relations with the bureaucracy.

Part IV draws together the policy-related themes introduced in earlier chapters and focuses on two broad facets of congressional influence over American public policy: congressional access to policy-making (Chapter 11) and congressional impact on policy (Chapter 12).

It is good form to state an author's overriding biases before allowing the reader to plunge into the book. My central belief can be stated simply: genuinely representative legislative assemblies, with all of their foibles, can and should play a central role in making modern government and its policies relatively humane and intelligent. Congress, as a specific case of a representative legislative assembly, has this potential and is valuable because of it. I have always taken Congress seriously as a maker of public policy and continue to do so.

I also harbor the prejudice that before meaningful discussion of "reform" can occur, the discussants must have a thorough knowledge of how Congress works, and this can come only from serious study. The literature of reform is too often marked by a great deal of emotion and not enough attention to reality. I believe systematic analysis must precede prescriptions for change. This prejudice does not mean that I am an apologist for all that Congress is and does. There is much in congressional practice and performance that distresses me as a citizen and as a political scientist, but that makes me even more eager to analyze it as objectively as possible as a necessary prelude to making sound normative judgments.

Like anyone who studies a subject for a long time, I owe many debts to many people. Several individuals wrote helpful critiques of the third edition before I began work on the fourth edition: William Buchanan, Kenneth P. Hayes, Lawrence Hough, Burdett Loomis, and Leroy Rieselbach. As always, everyone at W.W. Norton has performed his or her task with a high degree of professional competence. The editor for this edition, Roby Harrington, was especially helpful. Over the years, several friends and fellow students of Congress have proved to be particularly insightful and stimulating: the late D.B. Hardeman, Charles O. Jones, Samuel C. Patterson, Roger H. Davidson, and Theodore J. Lowi.

Above all, I am grateful to my friend Grace A. Franklin. She provided specific help in doing the research and first draft of six of the original case vignettes that appear in the book. More important, she has been a fine and generous colleague in a number of explorations of American institutions and policies, including this one.

# I

## Congress in the American Political System

# 1

## The Nature of Congress

The American Congress is the most powerful national legislature in the world. It possesses four characteristics that, combined, make it unique. First, it is the single most important institution for determining the substance of American public policies. Second, it serves as a forum for the expression of genuine disagreements over those policies. Third, its members are chosen by routinely recurring free, honest, competitive elections. Fourth, vigorous national print and electronic media subject the institution and its members to constant scrutiny.

Within this context of great power, Congress has demonstrated both continuity and change. In the last few decades, for example, the basic method of organizing work through committees and subcommittees has persisted, the openness of the institution to lobbying and the pleas of interest groups has remained constant, and the central (but not dominant) role of the party leaders in both houses has remained quite stable. However, at the same time, a variety of external and internal forces led Congress to shift the basic nature of its policy activity from one of creation of new programs to one of adjusting past policies and programs to new realities. In the 1960s Congress participated in creating a variety of new programs, a stance that meshed well with the preferences of Presidents John Kennedy and Lyndon Johnson and also responded to a number of developments in society. By the 1980s, however, Congress was primarily involved in adjusting a variety of past policies and programs to deal with the agenda of President Ronald Reagan, a more conservative public mood, and a massive federal deficit. The budget, and related questions of tax policy, became the focus of a great deal of congressional activity. Congress ceased fashioning new programs. Instead it shifted to adjusting the size and cost of existing programs to newly perceived budget constraints. This change, like virtually all Congressional changes, will itself give way to some other mode of behavior in the future.

The general public has two quite different impressions of Congress, each derived from a different sort of media coverage.[1] At the institutional level the national media (the few newspapers with national readership, the news magazines, the wire services, and the radio and television networks) cover congressional participation in major policy-making ventures. They also give considerable coverage to scandals and wrongdoing, both alleged and real. The tone of this coverage is generally negative and enhances public cynicism or skepticism about Congress as an institution. Unedited television coverage of both chambers on C-SPAN television does not change the public image of Congress as disorganized and somewhat confused.

On the personal level, however, most members of the House and Senate receive their principal coverage from an uncritical local set of media (newspapers, radio stations, and television stations within their districts). Incumbent members are in a strong position to dominate what these local organs of public information present in the way of coverage. Such domination leads to the creation of a favorable image of the individual member in his or her home state or district. A number of observers of Congress have remarked that the general public seems to be very wary of and cynical about Congress as an institution but still respects individual members. This news coverage situation helps explain that seemingly inconsistent division of opinion.

[1]See Michael J. Robinson, "Three Faces of Congressional Media," in Thomas E. Mann and Norman J. Ornstein (eds.), *The New Congress* (Washington, D.C.: American Enterprise Institute for Public Policy Research, 1981): Chapter 3; Michael J. Robinson and Kevin R. Appel, "Network News Coverage of Congress," *Political Science Quarterly* 94 (1979): 407–18; and Roger H. Davidson and Walter J. Oleszek, *Congress and Its Members,* 2nd ed. (Washington, D.C.: Congressional Quarterly Press, 1985): Chapter 6.

Congress shares its policy-making powers principally with the executive branch—both the president and the vast bureaucracy that has developed. The interaction between Congress and the executive, often with spokespersons for private interests also involved, is responsible for most of the detailed decisions about what specific policies to pursue and what specific programs to implement.

This chapter introduces Congress in three ways. First, it explores the tensions in Congress between aspects of fragmentation and aspects of integration. Second, it discusses the principal functions Congress performs. Third, it begins the treatment of the relationship between Congress and the executive branch, the core relationship in the American policy process.

## FRAGMENTATION AND INTEGRATION

There are two principal dimensions to fragmentation and integration as they are defined in this volume. One involves the organizational state of Congress. The second involves the degree of coherence or coordination between individual policies and programs contained in legislation. Fragmentation is characterized by a decentralized organization and by a lack of planned coherence (and only limited random coherence) between individual policies. Integration is characterized by a centralized organization and by the potential for planned coherence between individual policies. It should be added that "fragmentation" and "integration" are used analytically throughout this book, not as code words for "bad" and "good."

In a highly fragmented situation there are no forces and mechanisms that allow for the planned achievement of policy coherence and integration. The results stemming from such a situation usually include specific policies and programs that have no planned relationship to one another. In fact, they may be inconsistent, or even flatly contradictory, when viewed together. Different specific goals are articulated or at least implicit for individual policies, and there are no overriding goals that bind the individual policies together.

In a highly integrated situation there are forces and mechanisms that at least provide Congress with the opportunity of producing policies and programs characterized by a high degree of coherence and coordination. Collectively, individual policies can be linked in a broad program aimed at achieving some concrete overriding goals. Naturally, Congress may not grasp the opportunity or make the most of it.

Policy coherence is impossible when the organization is highly decentralized. Policy coherence is not guaranteed when the organization is highly centralized, but such coherence is possible.

The two situations described above are representative of a range of possibilities that lie along a spectrum from fragmentation to integration. Most of the time Congress falls somewhere between the extremes.

Two situations earlier in this century illustrate opposite points on the spectrum between fragmentation and integration and suggest the range of possibilities even when the White House and Congress are controlled by the same party. (Divided party control usually results in the appearance of policy fragmentation for partisan reasons.) At the integration end of the spectrum stands the period of 1913 and 1914. Woodrow Wilson was president and had a coherent domestic-policy agenda. He was abetted by strong, able, centralized leadership in both the House and Senate. The key individuals used considerable skill in pushing relentlessly for the Wilsonian program. The result was a series of major policies such as the Clayton Antitrust Act, the Federal Reserve Act, and the Federal Trade Commission Act. Congress, in this case, was relatively well integrated organizationally and also responded to policy proposals that presented a coherent vision of the American economy when taken together.

The 1925–26 period serves as a good example of the other end of the spectrum. Calvin Coolidge was president. He showed little desire to be a legislative leader. The Republican leaders in both houses had to contend with sizable dissident blocs in their own party (the "progressive Republicans" of the era) and were not especially forceful leaders. Organizationally they were also dependent on reaching agreements with many other members of their own party before movement was possible. The policy results were few, not satisfying to either Coolidge or the Republican congressional leaders. They were related to no integrated domestic or foreign policy agenda but simply stood as isolated ventures.

Similar examples involving degrees of fragmentation and integration throughout the rest of the book will come from the period since World War II, especially the last three decades. However, these examples from earlier in the century suggest that the basic tension between forces pushing for fragmentation and forces pushing for integration is not timebound but represents a continuing theme in analyzing Congress.

## Conditions Favorable to Fragmentation

There are eight major aspects of congressional life that foster greater fragmentation. Each will be discussed in some detail in this chapter.

- members are popularly elected from specific geographical constituencies in which they must reside.
- there are two separate, and quite different, houses of Congress.
- the federal government has a large and diverse agenda.
- Congress shares powers with a large and disaggregated bureaucracy.
- Congress is open to the activities and influence of a large number of diverse organized interest groups.
- Congress organizes itself into a very large number of committees and subcommittees in order to process its business.
- the national political parties are generally weak, although they do offer significant campaign finance help, especially in the case of Republicans.
- many members are ambitious primarily in terms of personal influence, re-election, and/or advancement to more prestigious elective office.

POPULAR ELECTION. Members of the Senate are popularly elected from individual states in which they must reside. Members of the House of Representatives are popularly elected from individual districts in which they must reside. The consequences of these simple facts for both the individual members and for the institution are enormous. Of necessity, members are concerned much of the time with the locally-oriented interests of their constituents. This necessity in turn helps shape the general policy orientation of Congress. Because members attend to the needs of 435 districts and 50 states there are only rare incentives or opportunities to assert congressional primacy in large national policy areas.

Also, given the diversity of interests in the various districts and states, natural impetus is given to a bargaining and compromising style of decision-making by the members of Congress. Many major bills are simply aggregates of specific provisions designed to benefit specific constituency interests. They often do not have a clear goal or set of goals from which specific provisions logically stem.

Another result of constituency focus is that the diversity of interests to be satisfied generally prevents any single voice emerging as "the" congressional spokesman. The internal organization of Congress reflects this fact.

TWO HOUSES. The House and Senate, equal in power, have some important similarities and differences. The fact of having two houses that must agree on every detail before legislation can emerge is a force favoring fragmentation (and relatively slow action) much of the time.

Many major differences between House and Senate stem from the basic facts of size, both of chamber and of constituency: a Senate of 100 members, each of whom represents an entire state; and a House of 435 members, each of whom represents a district with about half a million persons. Senators are more visible than representatives and more frequently play to a national audience. Senators also more frequently make broad policy pronouncements. Representatives tend to concentrate much more on the details of committee and subcommittee legislative work, in part because they have fewer committee assignments and fewer opportunities to make nationally visible pronouncements. The larger size of the House also leads to internal rules that facilitate more efficient consideration of legislation on the floor of the full chamber. Majority party leaders in the House have more control over more tightly constructed rules than do Senate leaders. The latter face looser rules that require both more agreement between the majority and minority and, frequently, a reliance on the consent of all Senators.

LARGE SUBSTANTIVE AGENDA. In the two centuries of our national existence the agenda of the entire federal government, and therefore the agenda of Congress, has increased enormously in size and complexity. Over that period of time the congressional workload has increased dramatically whether measured by time in session, bills processed, bills enacted, or hearings conducted. In the period since World War II there have been some fluctuations and simple, linear growth is not an appropriate image.[2] The size and complexity of the congressional agenda has helped lead to a highly developed specialization of labor for individual members in committees and subcommittees and to increased use of staff both by individual members and committees and subcommittees.

The large workload has also contributed to the development of elaborate rules that facilitate the processing of a large amount of business in reasonably good order. The rules are not impartial. They facilitate the legislative process but can also be used to substantive advantage by skillful legislators seeking specific outcomes. They also allow for relative invisibility in handling issues if visibility is not

[2]Roger H. Davidson, "The Legislative Work of Congress," unpublished paper presented at the annual meeting of the American Political Science Association, Washington, D.C., August 28–31, 1986.

demanded by a sizable group of members. The rules do not promote disciplined political parties in Congress that might tamper with the freedom of individual members to follow their own policy preferences.

The rules ensure that any piece of legislation must go through several committee and floor processes in both houses. This means that the opportunities for defeating or amending proposals are numerous. Typically, a bill will be considered by two subcommittees (one in each house), by two full committees (one in each house), the House Rules Committee, by a conference committee to iron out differences between the versions passed in the two houses, and in separate meetings of both houses (perhaps two—once for initial passage and once to consider the handiwork of the conference committee). This complexity necessitates bargaining and compromise between members representing differing points of view and competing interests.

POWER-SHARING WITH THE BUREAUCRACY. The federal bureaucracy is divided into a seemingly infinite number of bureaus, administrations, offices, divisions, and branches, each with its own piece of the policy world as its turf. The numerous congressional subcommittees parallel the organization of the bureaucracy in most instances. A situation is created whereby a few individuals in each house with their counterparts "downtown" (that is, in the bureaucratic offices scattered around Washington) are at the center of policy-making in each of numerous small—but often important—substantive areas.

OPENNESS TO ORGANIZED INTEREST GROUPS. Both Congress and the bureaucracy are permeable. They are open to influence from outside interests and individuals. Organized interest groups are able to be particularly effective in representing their points of view both in Congress and in the bureaucracy. This fact helps create the opportunity for the emergence of "subgovernments"—small groups composed of a few key bureaucrats, interest group members, and senior members of subcommittees who, in effect, make policy. Subgovernments do not dominate in all policy situations, but where they exist they make coordinated policy almost impossible to achieve.

COMMITTEES AND SUBCOMMITTEES. The establishment, growth, and entrenchment of congressional committees and subcommittees has been primarily a response to a strong executive branch and to a large workload. Congress, with many of its members desiring important influence over policy, hit on a strong committee system as the device for retaining influence in the face of a growing substantive workload (both in amount and in scope) and a growing bureaucracy. The device has worked to achieve that purpose. But it has also become the cornerstone of both organizational and policy fragmentation in Congress. Each committee and particularly each subcommittee has its own niche in the policy world and is rarely challenged in it. More to the point, there is little coordination on the substance of legislation between committees in the two houses, between committees in the same house, or even between subcommittees of the same committee. There are occasional readjustments of jurisdictions (usually to reflect changes in the structure of the bureaucracy), but the general thrust of the committee and subcommittee system supports fragmentation.

WEAK NATIONAL PARTIES. National political parties in the United States are wraithlike. Often they are primarily constructs in the minds of people who think of themselves as Democrats or Republicans. Organizationally their main function is to prepare for a national convention every four years in order to nominate candidates for president and vice-president and adopt a party platform. They have nothing to do with congressional nominations and are involved in congressional elections only marginally through some provision of campaign funds. This situation also lends itself to helping create policy fragmentation in Congress. In some countries, the United Kingdom being the best-known example, national parties help frame national policy and enforce support of that policy in the legislature through active and authoritative participation in nominations and elections. That potential source of policy integration or centralization is missing in the United States.

PERSONAL AMBITION OF MEMBERS. Most of the time most members of the House and Senate are concerned with their own careers. This means that they are primarily interested in re-election to their seats. In order to enhance their chances of re-election they are interested in receiving credit in their constituencies for their work in Congress. They are likely to concentrate on helping their constituents who are having trouble with parts of the bureaucracy ("casework") or with getting credit for constituency-oriented legislation or actions by the bureaucracy. Concern with broad, integrated national policies is likely to be secondary.

If the members are not interested primarily in re-election to their present seats, they may well have their eyes on other elective offices: governorships or Senate seats or even the presidency in the case of House members; governorships or the presidency in the case of senators. Those aspiring to the presidency may take more interest in broad, integrated policy, but those individuals are relatively few in number.

These concerns mean that individual members have a stake both in organizational decentralization—so they are relatively free to pursue their interests without interference—and in low coordination between policies—so that their pet interests will not be held up by the necessity of considering other policies simultaneously.

## Conditions Favorable to Integration

Although not as numerous or as compelling, there are also some major aspects of congressional life that can push in the direction of greater integration:

- members take pride in Congress as an institution and seek to increase its policy impact.
- there are well-developed party organizations inside the House and Senate that have potential for providing centralized leadership.
- some members have strong, broad substantive policy commitments.
- Congress shares power with a strong president, who is buttressed by a well-developed institutional presidency; the president and presidency have the potential for providing centralized leadership and focusing congressional attention on at least a few broad policy areas.

INSTITUTIONAL PRIDE AND AMBITION. Although personal ambition tends to predominate, there are also members who worry about the institutional place of Congress in the American governing scheme. These individuals want to make sure that Congress as an institution is important. One way of enhancing congressional importance is to create visible legislation in one or more broad policy areas.

PARTY ORGANIZATION IN CONGRESS. Party leaders and party machinery operate continuously for both Democrats and Republicans. They represent a constant potential for increased integration. This potential is greater in the House than in the Senate.

BROAD SUBSTANTIVE POLICY COMMITMENTS BY MEMBERS. Despite the strength of personal ambition and the various forces pulling members to consider mainly bits and scraps of policy, much of it constituency-oriented, there are a number of members that have policy commitments that go well beyond constituency interests. Some are concerned, for example, with broad-gauged, coherent Foreign policy. Others articulate comprehensive visions of the nature of the U.S. economy and how best to enhance its performance through legislation. This number varies from time to time. As the number grows the chances for integration are enhanced.

POWER-SHARING WITH THE PRESIDENT. The fact that the president is constitutionally an important legislative actor provides an opportunity for some integrating leadership both organizationally and in terms of policy coherence. Some observers claim Congress and the president are competing for a fixed amount of power or influence over legislation and policy. If this were true, as one gained the other one would lose. When Congress was thought to be "strong," the president would be "weak," and vice versa.

This view of zero-sum competition for influence between Congress and the president is, however, misleading. By virtue of the constitutional structure in which they both must work, Congress and the president are more realistically viewed as "partners" who share power—power that, in fact, has grown over time and is not limited to a fixed sum.[3] To be sure, they compete with each other on some matters, but they also cooperate with each other on a large number of other matters. At some points in history both have seemed weak and ineffectual; at other points both have seemed strong and aggressive.

The presence of an aggressive legislative leader in the presidency does not guarantee integration. But such a leader in that office, working with aggressive congressional leaders of his own party, can bring considerable organizational integration to Congress and can create conditions allowing a fair amount of programmatic integration. In the first year of the Reagan presidency (1981) Ronald Reagan provided such integration, both by setting the major agenda (budget cutting and a tax cut) and by working closely with the leaders of his party in both the Senate (where the Republicans were in the majority) and in the House (where they were still in the minority but could count on a number of conservative Democrats as allies). In fact, for much of the first six years he was such an integrating force, although neither he nor the Republican leaders in Congress were again as consistently effective as they had been in 1981. Only after the Democrats recaptured the Senate in the 1986 election, and especially after the revelations

[3]See Ralph K. Huitt, "Congress: Retrospect and Prospect," *Journal of Politics* 38 (1976): 209–27.

about arms sales to Iran with diversion of the proceeds to the Nicaraguan contras in late November 1986, did President Reagan cease to be an important integrating force in relation to congressional business.

## Policy Consequences of Fragmentation and Integration

Fragmentation pushes toward the following policy consequences:

- stability of policy content; changes that occur are slow and small.
- a tendency to define most domestic policy as distributive (providing only subsidy and support for private activity) rather than as protective regulatory or redistributive.
- a low degree of concern in Congress with the oversight of bureaucratic performance and with the evaluation of the impact of policies and programs.
- a generally passive stance toward the policy role of Congress on the part of the members.

Integration pushes toward the following policy consequences:

- a willingness to change some existing policies, including some major changes.
- a willingness to define some domestic policy as protective regulatory or redistributive (and to consider changes in established sanctions for certain kinds of private activity and in benefit distribution patterns that have an impact on the nature of equality and inequality for various social classes).
- a higher degree of concern in Congress with the oversight of bureaucratic performance and with evaluation of policy impact.
- a more aggressive stance toward the policy role of Congress on the part of the members.

STABILITY OF POLICY. Change in policies is difficult in a highly fragmented situation. Each policy tends to be produced within its own subgovernment and by and large those subgovernments are happy with what they have wrought. There is no incentive to change very much or very fast.

When there is organizational centralization and more concern with policy coherence, there are more forces pushing for more change. Greater integration does not guarantee that such change will occur, but the conditions are present to allow it.

TYPE OF POLICY. There are three major types of domestic policy in which Congress is constantly and heavily involved: distributive, protective regulatory, and redistributive.[4]

Distributive policies and programs are aimed at promoting private activities that, in theory, would not or could not otherwise be undertaken and are thought to be desirable for society as a whole. These policies and programs provide subsidies for those private activities. Examples include land grants for railroad companies in the nineteenth century to build western railroads; direct cash payments for agricultural commodity purchases; tax benefits for home owners; and grants to companies and inventors. Much defense policy also involves heavy subsidies to defense contractors and to localities through decisions about where to locate military facilities in the United States.

Protective regulatory policies and programs are designed to protect the public by setting the conditions under which various private activities can be undertaken. Some conditions are prohibited; others are required. Examples of such policies include requirements that banks, stores, and other grantors of credit disclose true interest rates, prohibitions of unfair business and labor practices, prohibition of harmful additives to food, and licensing of medical drugs before they can be put on the market.

Redistributive policies and programs are intended to alter the allocation of wealth, property, rights, or some other value among socioeconomic classes or racial groups. The redistributive feature enters because a number of actors perceive that there are "winners" and "losers" in the policies and some value is being transferred from one class or group to another class or group *at the expense of* the first class or group. Many policies in fact redistribute items of value from the less privileged to the more privileged, but most political debate is over policies perceived to run in the other direction: redistributing items of value from the more privileged to the less privileged.

Examples of redistributive policies include setting progressive income tax rates so that affluent people pay a higher percentage in taxes than less affluent people, requirements that housing, public accommodations, and public education be available without racial discrimination, provision of food stamps for the disadvantaged, and government-sponsored health insurance to help the elderly meet the costs of medical care.

---

[4]These policy types are treated fully in Randall B. Ripley and Grace A. Franklin, *Congress, the Bureaucracy, and Public Policy,* 4th ed. (Chicago: Dorsey Press, 1987). The pioneering work on this typology appears in Theodore J. Lowi, "American Business, Public Policy, Case-Studies, and Political Theory," *World Politics* 16 (1964): 677–715.

The easiest of these types of policy for Congress to work with is distributive because it threatens no one. In principle, all claimants for support in the form of one or more subsidies can be satisfied. The policies are disaggregated and resources to satisfy requests are not perceived to be tightly limited.

The most difficult issues are those perceived to be protective regulatory or redistributive. In both of these instances some actors' interests are directly threatened. There are "losers" in the cases of these decisions, as well as "winners"—and even the "winners" might not know it or be particularly happy or particularly grateful to individual members of the House and Senate.

Fragmentation in Congress lends itself to supporting a situation in which almost all issues are considered to be distributive and are handled as such. Integration does not guarantee that protective regulatory and redistributive issues will be handled in a straightforward fashion, but it increases the chances that that will happen.

CONCERN WITH OVERSIGHT AND EVALUATION. In a fragmented situation, in which most policy is distributive and in which most decisions are made by subgovernments, few members of Congress see any necessity of much oversight of the bureaucracy. Members and bureaucrats and beneficiaries have all agreed ahead of time what should be done. It is in the bureaucrats' self-interest to follow through with implementing policies in the ways that all parties find congenial. Similarly, policies in this fragmented situation are usually simply assumed to be effective and to be having the desired impact. Even if systematic evaluation showed little or no impact, that finding would be perceived mainly as a threat to an entrenched set of interests rather than as a cue to scrap the policy or alter it in a major way.

Integration does not guarantee systematic attention to oversight or evaluation but does enhance the chances that both will be taken seriously, since there is more chance that some significant policies will not be distributive and will not simply be the product of subgovernments with a stake in maintaining existing policies without the implicit threats contained in both systematic oversight and evaluation.

PASSIVENESS VS. AGGRESSIVENESS. Members of Congress have two particularly important general choices they are free to make: (1) how vigorously to assert substantive policy preferences, and (2) whether to support the institutional status quo in Congress or whether to advocate and pursue institutional change. Both choices are important in helping determine the policy importance of Congress at any given time.

In many ways the easiest choice for individual members to make is to adopt a passive stance in terms of pushing for specific policy preferences on broad issues and a conservative role in terms of supporting the institutional status quo. Members making such choices do not renounce all impact on public policy—rather they opt for highly specific, marginal impact most of the time. Such an option is attractive in general terms because it is immediately workable within the highly complex process by which legislation makes its way through Congress. It also allows many members to maximize their interests in re-election, projects and services for their constituencies, and amicable relations with the bureaucracy. Likewise, it helps members process the vast array of information potentially available to them by simply ignoring much of it and thus saving time to be used for other purposes.

Members who opt for a more aggressive stance with regard to their personal impact and the collective congressional impact on the substance of policy and for a more change-oriented position toward the congressional institution take a difficult route. They are likely to run head-on into frustrations generated by the slowness and complexity of the legislative process and may also jeopardize amicable relations with the bureaucracy and interest groups and thereby lessen their ability to produce projects and services for their constituencies.

A passive member of Congress tends to be principally interested only in the work of his or her committee and especially of a few subcommittees. Within that province the member usually supports the policies advocated by the bureaucrats and the leading interest groups appearing before the committee or subcommittee and will suggest only small changes. His focus is narrow and his manner is accommodating.

An aggressive member of Congress tends to have interests beyond the jurisdiction of his or her particular committee and subcommittee assignments. He is more willing to question the judgments of the bureaucrats and interest group representatives with whom he comes in contact. He will work for the adoption of wide changes from existing statutes when he thinks them necessary and useful. He is not willing to compromise on those issues about which he feels strongly.

A relatively passive congressional stance offers numerous benefits to members. It maximizes committee and subcommittee autonomy and, thus, the influence of committee members. The nature of most issues before Congress is likely to be non-controversial, which enhances members' perceptions of electoral safety. Proceedings can be relatively invisible, especially if the agenda contains few controversial items.

Available time for members to spend on constituency-oriented business, including frequent trips to the state or district, is maximized by a passive congressional stance. Likewise, good relations with bureaucrats, who facilitate servicing constituency interests, are more likely. Good relations with the president are valuable, at least for members of the president's party, because White House good will can influence the allocation of tangible benefits to members' states or districts. Good relations with the president are more likely to occur with a Congress that is relatively passive. Finally, members benefit from a low-profile, passive congressional stance because, given the fact of weak congressional parties, they are free to take policy stances of their own different from the majority of their party without fear of meaningful sanctions.

The costs of passivity are that Congress as an institution has little unified impact on national policy. Members who envision broad national policy goals have little opportunity to see their goals realized in a passive Congress. Consequently there is not likely to be any feeling of pride among members toward the institution they serve. The most costly disadvantage of congressional passivity is that Congress leaves itself open to domination by the executive branch, a development that not only further weakens Congress but that may make passivity an entrenched characteristic, difficult to overcome.

Relative aggressiveness, on the other hand, generates a mirror image of the costs and benefits of relative passivity. The major benefits are that members increase their potential for seeing the adoption of national policy important to them and that they can take pride in the institution as an important participant in policy-making. By exercising its power, an aggressive Congress is much more likely to resist domination by the executive branch.

If a large number of members pursue policy aggressiveness, the possibility of diminished committee and subcommittee autonomy exists because members will freely cross jurisdictional lines in terms of their interests and proposals. Such a situation also enhances the possibility that more controversial issues will come before Congress in a more visible way because of the lessened importance of usually quiet and unreported committee meetings. This may pose a threat to perceived electoral safety on the part of a number of members.

If members increase the scope of their legislative interests and their willingness to pursue ends different from those proposed by bureaucrats and interest-group representatives, they may also reduce the time they have available to spend on constituency matters or in the constituency. They may antagonize parts of the bureaucracy, thereby reducing the desire of the bureaucrats to respond favorably to con-

stituency-oriented requests. They run an increased risk of antagoniz-
ing the president, thereby reducing the desire of the White House to
cooperate in providing a variety of tangible benefits for specific states,
districts, and constituents.

Finally, if the desire to be aggressive about policy preferences
spreads to the party leaders in Congress, they may begin to work to
strengthen party mechanisms that will allow the imposition of greater
"discipline" on members, thereby reducing the freedom of those members to take whatever policy positions they choose without much
regard for a party position.

It is clear that the average member of Congress is likely to find
passivity more attractive than aggressiveness. However, this is not an
inevitable and unchangeable situation. At given points in the past
Congress has, for a variety of reasons, opted for an aggressive stance.
This option is still very much alive. Thus, although there is considerable pressure to be relatively passive, conditions can emerge that produce quite a different response. One central argument in this book is
that Congress is free to choose various courses of action. Pressures will
be described that push more strongly in one direction than in another.
But the ability of the men and women who constitute Congress to
oppose these prevailing pressures successfully is specifically and vigorously affirmed.

## The Frequency of Fragmentation and Integration

Fragmentation is the "natural" condition of Congress. Most of the
supporting conditions for fragmentation are simply givens, a number
of them contained in the Constitution. It requires no act of will to
promote fragmentation. Even in periods of relatively high integration,
elements of fragmentation remain.

Integration, on the other hand, is difficult to achieve and requires
deliberate choice and acts of will. Important aspects of integration
can, however, be achieved. There is nothing "inevitable" about fragmentation as all-encompassing. Its "naturalness" does not mean that
"unnatural" elements of integration cannot be introduced and maintained for considerable periods of time, even though they are likely to
be under continual attack.

Table I–I contains a summary of fragmentation and integration in
terms of the organizational state within Congress, the degree of policy
coherence, supporting conditions within Congress, principal policy
consequences, and the likelihood of occurrence.

**Table 1–1.** Fragmentation vs. Integration in Congress: A Summary

|  | HIGH DEGREE OF FRAGMENTATION | HIGH DEGREE OF INTEGRATION |
|---|---|---|
| Organizational State | Decentralized | Centralized |
| Degree of Policy Coherence | No possibility of planned coherence; limited random coherence at most | Possibility of planned coherence; no guaranteed coherence |
| Supporting Conditions | Popular election Two houses Large substantive agenda Power-sharing with the bureaucracy Openness to organized interest groups Well-developed committee system Weak national parties Personal ambition of members | Institutional pride and ambition Party organization in congress Broad substantive policy commitments by members Power-sharing with the president |
| Principal Policy Consequences | Stable policy Policy primarily defined as distributive Low concern with oversight of bureaucracy Low concern with evaluation of policy results Policy passiveness on part of members | Chance of important policy change Some policy defined as protective regulatory or redistributive More concern with oversight of bureaucracy More concern with evaluation of policy results More policy aggressiveness on part of members |
| Likelihood of Occurrence | Most likely; the "natural" state of congress; requires little or no deliberate action to create or sustain | Difficult, but not impossible to achieve; an "unnatural" state; requires considerable deliberate action |

# CONGRESSIONAL FUNCTIONS AND SOCIAL IMPACT

Congress performs a variety of functions, but one can be viewed as broadest and most important: it helps, or at least tries to help, resolve differences of opinion about public policy between different individuals and groups in society. These differences can be narrow or broad. They can be pursued peacefully through argument or they can be pursued in a more physical manner through such measures as strikes, lockouts, demonstrations, and both planned and unplanned violence.

If Congress is largely successful in the performance of this function and if the other institutions of society are also largely successful in performing the same function, then society is likely to be relatively stable. If Congress and the other institutions of government are unsuccessful in resolving conflict, then social instability may develop. Failure is, of course, possible; the Civil War is the most extreme American example of what happens when the most fundamental social conflict cannot be resolved through normal institutional channels.

In performing this important function of conflict resolution Congress engages in deliberation. Much of what Congress does is based on bargaining between different interests. But in the course of that bargaining there is also opportunity for solutions to problems to emerge that are based in part on "community-oriented responses" as well as on narrower and more specific interests.[5]

Congress performs four more concrete policy-relevant functions that are all related, ultimately, to conflict resolution: lawmaking, oversight of administration, education of the public, and representation. Congressional performance is not predetermined or immutable. It varies as the environment varies and as the membership of Congress changes. Although environmental factors can have an important influence on the way Congress performs its functions, Congress nonetheless has a great deal of latitude in choosing its direction. The wishes and preferences of the collection of individuals happening to serve in it at any particular time are a principal internal variable that influences the performance of basic congressional functions.

## Congress and Lawmaking

Prior to the Civil War, congressional lawmaking activity in the domestic sphere was basically limited to promoting the development of the nation by subsidizing a large number of private activities (for example, building turnpikes and canals). This sort of interest has persisted to the present day. Congress is still heavily involved in the subsidy of a wide range of private development activities.

Once the Civil War had demonstrated that the federal government

[5]For good treatments of the deliberative aspects of congressional behavior see Joseph M. Bessette, "Is Congress a Deliberative Body?" in Dennis Hale (ed.), *The United States Congress: Proceedings of the Thomas P. O'Neill, Jr., Symposium* (Boston: Boston College, 1982); Arthur Maass, *Congress and the Common Good* (New York: Basic Books, 1983); and David J. Vogler and Sidney R. Waldman, *Congress and Democracy* (Washington: Congressional Quarterly Press, 1985). The phrase "community-oriented responses" comes from Maass, p. 28.

was also a national government, new problems, largely associated with the rapid industrialization of the nation, began to arise that involved public discussion of what the government should do. Corporate wealth, which rapidly made the Republican party its political handmaiden, began to alter the dimensions of American opportunity. The end of the homesteading era and the massive waves of immigration from Eastern and Southern Europe compounded the new problems.

The political system took about twenty years to frame even the beginnings of a coherent response. The response came in the form of involving the government—including Congress—in regulation. In the late nineteenth century Congress began the long development of regulation of railroads and corporations with the passage of the Interstate Commerce Act in 1887 and the Sherman Antitrust Act in 1890. In the first fifteen years of the twentieth century other regulatory laws, such as the Hepburn Act of 1906, the Clayton Act of 1914, and the Federal Trade Commission Act of 1914, were enacted. Since then, congressional concern with regulation has expanded greatly to include such matters as unfair business practices, all modes of transportation, power, radio and television, food and drugs, labor relations, and the securities market.

It took the catastrophe of an economic depression seemingly irreversible by normal means to legitimize the activity of conscious and planned redistribution of economic and social benefits in society. The economic disaster of the 1930s revealed the corresponding social disaster that had been developing for a number of decades. Congress made some attempts to redraw more equitably the social and economic lines that the mythical "free market" had produced. In the last five decades the congressional agenda has included a great number of topics involving debates over equality or inequality and degree and direction of redistribution; wages and hours, social security, medical care for the aged, national health insurance, aid to depressed geographic areas, public housing, aid to inner city public education, and job training serve as examples.

In the period after the Second World War—and in large part as a result of social forces unleashed by the domestic impact of the War—the congressional agenda of redistributive questions was expanded to include questions about racial discrimination.

Congress occasionally surrenders some of its lawmaking activities in the domestic realm. For example, the adoption of the Reciprocal Trade Agreements Act in 1934 diminished the congressional role in the making of tariffs and increased the role of the executive branch, especially the president. Congress can also be aggressive in seeking out new areas of endeavor. Congressional initiatives were responsible for the development of water and air pollution policy in the 1950s and 1960s, for example. Similarly, congressional entrepreneurial activity in the 1960s and 1970s was responsible for the rapid proliferation and expansion of Federal grant programs for states and localities. Congress was the principal agent that produced the major change in the tax code in 1986.

Congressional performance of the lawmaking function in the realm of foreign affairs has varied from relatively passive to relatively aggressive. Congress can never absolutely control foreign policy. It is constitutionally prevented from doing so because of the powers specifically allocated to the president. It can put itself in a genuinely subservient role, however, as it did at the time of the passage of the 1964 Gulf of Tonkin Resolution, which gave the president a virtual carte blanche to proceed in Vietnam as he saw fit. In that resolution Congress responded to President Johnson's report on North Vietnamese attacks on two U.S. ships and the retaliatory air strike he ordered against North Vietnamese Naval bases by declaring their support for the President's "determination . . . to take all necessary measures to repel any armed attack against the forces of the United States and to prevent further aggression." Only two senators and no representatives voted against this broad grant of authority that President Johnson used to justify rapid and massive escalation of the Vietnam War. Congress repealed the resolution in 1970, although the repeal was more important symbolically than in terms of any real impact on American involvement in Vietnam.

In the Reagan years Congress was much more active in foreign-policy matters. It engaged in extended consideration of such matters as sales of arms and military technology to middle eastern countries, U.S. aid to the anti-Sandinista forces in Nicaragua, creation of the Strategic Defense Initiative ("star wars") space-based defense, sanctions on the Republic of South Africa, and the sale of arms to Iran. The president prevailed, at least in part, on these matters but only after considerable delay and/or modification in some cases. And, in the case of South African sanctions, Congress and the president met head on in September and October of 1986 with the result that Congress passed a fairly stringent sanctions bill over a Reagan veto.

If Congress is relatively aggressive, it can work jointly with the president and bureaucracy in a number of foreign policy areas to develop policy. This has been true in recent years in the consideration of some treaties and in the treatment accorded some aspects of foreign aid and immigration. In the making of war, Congress has become concerned about reasserting its constitutionally granted powers. In November 1973 Congress passed a war-powers bill over a Nixon veto. This provided that the president must report commitments of American troops to foreign combat within forty-eight hours. He must order the cessation of such combat after sixty days unless Congress has given its approval (although he can extend that period by thirty more days if he determines that American troops are endangered). There is no evidence yet, however, that presidential behavior has been effectively curtailed in this area.

## Congress and Oversight of Administration

Congress has the responsibility of determining if its programs are being executed as it intended and if the money it has appropriated is being spent on the purposes for which it was authorized. Oversight is the method of supervising both the programs Congress has created and the bureaucrats who administer them.

The General Accounting Office (GAO), the official watchdog arm of Congress, is vital in the oversight function, but its activities are necessarily limited by the limited number of its personnel and the large number of programs run by the bureaucracy. Congress supplements the reports and information coming from the GAO with the oversight activities of its committees and subcommittees. In effect, almost all appropriations and authorization hearings become forums for Congress to oversee the activities of the bureaucracy as they administer programs.

An important feature of oversight, which is also tied to the lawmaking function, is the inclusion of standards for administration of programs and for program performance in original authorizing legislation. When standards are specified, Congress has a tool to use later in oversight hearings to assess how well a program is being administered.

Some programs have very specific standards included. For example, the Social Security Act of 1935 contained remarkably clear standards to guide subsequent administration of the law. Other programs have poorly defined standards. For example, the phrase "maximum feasible participation" (of the poor) contained in the Economic Opportunity Act of 1964 (an act designed to combat poverty in a variety of ways) proved to be confusing to most persons who came in contact with the law—federal administrators, city officials, and actual or potential beneficiaries. Some thought it meant only token formal participation of the poor. Others thought it meant genuine program control by a majority of the poor. Many took a middle position somewhere between the extremes. Congress never provided an authoritative interpretation.

The inherent nature of a program affects the kind of evaluation criteria, if any, that can be specified in authorizing legislation. In general, it is more difficult to devise measures of success for programs in human resource fields such as education, health, and rehabilitation, which attempt to improve the quality of individual lives. Evaluation criteria in areas such as defense seem to be more easily devised because the area deals with quantifiable items rather than with qualitative changes in education, health care, career opportunities, racial equality, and similar aspects of human lives.

Congress can pursue its oversight activities in a variety of moods. It can be intent on very narrow questions, for example, "What did you do with the $10,000 for new downspouts at Fort Sill?"; or pursue very broad questions, for example, "What should the role of the federal government be in relation to the development of the nation's urban areas?" Much oversight approaches the "Fort Sill" end of the spectrum—in fact, some members of Congress seem intent on becoming day-to-day managers of specific programs. But a good deal of the other kind of oversight also takes place.

Individual members and subcommittees also get involved sporadically in the implementation of programs. Such involvement is related to oversight, but the purpose is not immediately to work toward formal legislation. The purpose, rather, is to push bureaucracy into making specific implementation decisions favored by the individuals or subcommittees who care. Even infrequent congressional interventions can be important. In general, members and subcommittees are more likely to intervene under one or both of two conditions: 1) if tangible benefits going to constituents are at stake in implementation decisions, and 2) if federal bureaucrats are dealing with constituents in a personal, hands-on sense.

## Congress and Education of the Public

Perhaps inevitably, Congress as an institution has never devised an appropriate mode of communicating its views about public policy to the public. As a multi-headed institution composed of members with differing party affiliations and policy views it is hard to imagine "the

Congress" ever appearing as a single entity to the public. There is no one spokesman for Congress, even on relatively noncontroversial issues, and especially not on controversial ones. When members of Congress have locked horns with the president over some issue, the natural advantage lies with the president. He can state his position clearly in public with immediate and thorough coverage by the mass media. The leaders of the congressional majority on an issue can try to counteract it, but the congressional posture is almost always muddied because there will always be a vocal minority in Congress supporting the presidential position.

Individual members of Congress, however, can and do engage in educating the public. Indeed, most of the time that they spend in contact with the public, particularly constituents, is an attempt to educate (and usually to influence votes, but the two activities are not incompatible). Speeches, appearances, and newsletters to home states and districts are all opportunities for congressmen to convey informed views on issues important to the nation or some part of it.

Members take different stances with respect to education, and their stance is usually tied to their individual conception of representation. Some can play it safe by trying to take only positions they gauge to be popular. By following "the voice of the people" they try to maximize their chances for continued electoral success. In large part, of course, the "voice" they hear may be an echo of what they themselves have said and want to believe that "the people" support. Others, perhaps more courageous, may try to lead the public, taking positions they know may be unpopular.

## Congress and Representation

The nature of representation is both a practical and philosophical question of great importance to those who write about government and to those practitioners who contemplate the deeper meaning of what they do. Numerous conceptions of representation have been advanced for the last several thousand years. At root, Congress can be called representative because it is an elected body and because a system of periodic free elections can remove from office any member judged by his constituents to be unrepresentative. It cannot be labelled representative in a variety of precise senses, however. For example, the characteristics of the members are different from the characteristics of the population as a whole. Members of Congress are better educated, wealthier, and more likely to be lawyers, white, and males than the general population. Nor can Congress be said to be representative in terms of exactly reproducing "public opinion" on a variety of issues. Senators and representatives clearly have and use freedom of judgment in acting on issues without, in most instances, specific instructions from the people they represent. Nor can Congress be said to represent all interests in society simultaneously. On some issues some individuals and classes of individuals are "losers" and, in a sense, their losses provide the benefits that are redistributed to other individuals and classes of individuals (the "winners").

But the fact of free elections coupled with the fact that most citizens acquiesce or consent to the legitimacy of Congress by accepting the results of those elections, seem sufficient to establish a case for Congress as a valid representative institution. Even more important, it is evident that members of the House and the Senate think of themselves as representatives and worry about their behavior in that light. They are very conscious of being representatives of their districts or states. They are aware that conflict may exist between the demands of the district and the demands of party. They cite constituency and conscience as legitimate reasons for deserting party stands.[6] They use this language in explaining defection to the party leaders, who usually accept the explanation. Conversely, they occasionally cite the demands of party or the unaminity of their fellow party members from their state or region in explaining votes to questioning constituents.

Members of Congress are genuinely concerned with their constituencies' attitudes. But their perceptions may be incorrect, in part because they may take their cues from a very small and biased sample.[7] Some may conduct polls to determine sentiment. Some of these polls are professionally constructed and produce accurate results. Most members rely on a combination of intuition and discussion with individual constituents whose views they trust and respect or at least those with enough political influence to make consultation prudent. Members who come from highly competitive districts or states are especially likely to worry about representing with some precision the views

---

[6]Randall B. Ripley, *Party Leaders in the House of Representatives* (Washington, D.C.: Brookings, 1967): 140–41.

[7]Warren E. Miller and Donald E. Stokes, "Constituency Influence in Congress," *American Political Science Review* 57 (1963): 45–56; and George R. Boynton, Samuel C. Patterson, and Ronald D. Hedlund, "The Missing Links in Legislative Politics: Attentive Constituents," *Journal of Politics* 31 (1969): 700–21.

of their district.[8] They may, however, badly misinterpret real feelings in their district.

A well-established fact—recognized by some members much more clearly than others—is that most constituents have no clear opinions on most issues with which senators and representatives must deal.[9] This means that an aggressive and self-confident member has wide latitude. It also means that when a member claims to be representing the opinion of his district he or she is, on most issues, representing the opinion of only a minority of the constituents. Most constituents don't know or care about the issue at hand. Even few of those with opinions communicate them to the representative.

Individual members of the House and Senate undertake a number of different kinds of activities that can be considered representative. First, they support the interests of individuals in a variety of "casework" activities. These cases typically involve deportation and immigration, selective service, social security, and tax matters. Casework activities may involve so-called "private legislation"—for example, a bill to exempt named individuals from immigration quotas. They may also involve non-legislative congressional inquiries into various bureaucratic proceedings—for example, pursuing the question of the eligibility of a specific individual for social security or medicare benefits.

Members of the House and Senate also pursue casework for corporate entities. Typically, these cases involve enforcement and interpretation of the tax code or exemptions from various regulatory provisions. For example, when strict enforcement of federal safety standards threatened the last steamboat on the Ohio River with extinction, interested members of Congress from the region were successful in getting different standards applied to this particular boat. Defense contractors involved in cost overrun disputes with the government can regularly count on some congressional intervention on their behalf.

Members are also concerned with intervening in the division of federal largesse. Here they pursue not only such tangible and visible items as new post offices and dams for given localities and contracts

---

[8]See John C. Wahlke, Heinz Eulau, William Buchanan, and Leroy Ferguson, *The Legislative System* (New York: Wiley, 1962); and Heinz Eulau, John C. Wahlke, William Buchanan, and Leroy C. Ferguson, "The Role of the Representative," *American Political Science Review* 53 (1959): 742–56, for evidence at the level of the state legislature.

[9]John C. Wahlke, "Policy Demands and System Support: The Role of the Represented," *British Journal of Political Science* 1 (1971): 271–90.

for certain companies but also assist local units of government in seeking federal funds for such things as education, health, pollution control, job training, and housing.

Senators and representatives can also seek to represent entire classes or races. For example, some black members consider themselves representatives of the interests of all blacks; some conservative white southerners consider themselves representatives of the interests of all southern whites and perhaps all whites. Some members consider themselves spokesmen for all the poor or for some segment of the poor—perhaps urban, Appalachian, Indian, or Mexican-American.

Finally, senators and representatives can seek to represent "the national good." This applies to most members at least some of the time. In this mood some members are even led to take stands that are unpopular and endanger their seats. The early opposition of Senators Wayne Morse (D-Oregon) and Ernest Gruening (D-Alaska) to the war in Vietnam provides a case in point. Their position on this issue—and their visibility in pushing it—contributed to their subsequent defeats at the polls.

Most members of Congress pursue a mixture of these representative activities, although different members weight the activities differently. It was not at all unusual to see the same Senator Morse who opposed Vietnam on grounds of national interest extremely vigorous in support of high tariffs to protect Oregon cherries. Nor was it unusual to see Senator J. William Fulbright (D-Ark.) simultaneously pursuing "national interest" concerns as chairman of the Foreign Relations Committee and promoting the welfare of Arkansas chicken and rice farmers.

Fulbright himself commented on the balancing act he felt most legislators, including himself, had to undertake between constituency interests and broader national interests:

The average legislator early in his career discovers that there are certain interests, or prejudices, of his constituents which are dangerous to trifle with. Some of these prejudices may not be of fundamental importance to the welfare of the nation, in which case he is justified in humoring them, even though he may disapprove. The difficult case is where the prejudice concerns fundamental policy affecting the national welfare. . . .

As an example of what I mean, let us take the poll-tax issue and isolationism. Regardless of how persuasive my colleagues or the national press may be about the evils of the poll-tax, I do not see its fundamental importance, and I shall follow the views of the people of my state. . . . On the other hand, regardless of how strongly opposed my constituents may prove to be to the creation of, and participation in, an ever stronger United Nations Organization, I could not follow such a policy in that field unless it becomes clearly hopeless.[10]

# RELATIONS WITH THE EXECUTIVE BRANCH: A BROAD PERSPECTIVE

Congress responds to a number of outside forces as well as to the dynamics of the institution itself in making policy choices. Its relationship with the executive branch is central to the policy process. This relationship is examined in considerable detail in later chapters, but because of its centrality we will also look at it in broad terms in this introductory chapter.

Both the executive branch and Congress can be seen as three-level institutions. The executive branch has the president, the institutional presidency, and the vast bureaucracy (peopled mostly by civil servants). Congress has party leaders, a committee and subcommittee structure, and rank-and-file senators and representatives. Eight two-way relationships between these six institutional participants are especially important. They are portrayed in Figure 1–1.

Within the executive branch, relationships are relatively hierarchical in that the direct relationship between the president and the bureaucracy is not very strong. Instead, the institutional presidency—particularly the White House office, the Office of Management and Budget, and cabinet and sub-cabinet officials appointed by the president—plays a critical mediating role between the president and his policy preferences and the various parts of the bureaucracy. The president often experiences a great deal of difficulty in getting what he wants from the bureaucracy. Within Congress all of the possible relationships are consistently important in determining the legislative results emerging from the institution as a whole.

The relationship between the two branches has two levels. The president and institutional presidency relate mostly to the party leaders of the president's party. They rely on the leaders to relay their preferences both to committees and subcommittees and to rank-and-file members. On a few matters of special importance, the president

[10]Quoted in David J. Vogler, *The Politics of Congress,* 4th ed. (Boston, Mass.: Allyn and Bacon, 1983), 79.

**Figure 1–1.** Most Important Policy-Relevant Relationships between and within the Executive Branch and Congress

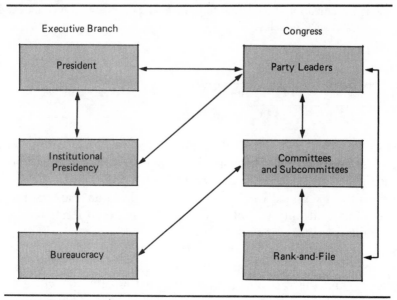

and his top advisors will try to influence some rank-and-file members directly.

Members of the House and Senate look to the leaders to carry information and preferences back to the president and presidency. Individual organizations within the bureaucracy, however, primarily relate directly to the committees and subcommittees responsible for substantive decisions involving them. The reason that central direction of policy is so difficult to achieve is the weakness of the link between the party leaders and the committees and subcommittees. They tend to be much more responsive to the parts of the bureaucracy than to the party leaders. Given that the parts of the bureaucracy are also imperfectly responsive to the president and institutional presidency there is often little central direction to policy decisions.

## Policy-Relevant Relationships: Cooperation or Conflict?

The Constitution created a governmental scheme in which virtually nothing new can be started unless Congress and the president find some mutually acceptable level of cooperation. The incentives for cooperation are great.

A president has many reasons for wanting to get along with Congress. His image as a masterful leader is enhanced if no senator or representative creates conditions that make him look inept. He can give more attention to his public and press relations, or even his influence within the executive branch of the government, if strong opposition emanating from the Capitol does not constantly threaten him. He can comfortably leave the country for diplomatic ventures if he knows that a group of "barons" a mile or so southeast of the White House will not seize the occasion to aggrandize themselves at the expense of the sojourning "chief."

None of these reasons for wanting amicable relations with Congress is ignoble, but one practical motive is more important. Simply to keep the government functioning, a president must be concerned with at least some congressional legislative activity, especially when it involves raising and spending money.

Members of the House and Senate also have many reasons for wanting to get along with a president, although their reasons are probably not as great as his. Nevertheless, members with broad programmatic aspirations stand a greater chance of realizing some of those aspirations if the president can be induced to support or initiate some of their ideas. For example, Congressional initiators of anti-air-pollution legislation in the late 1950s and early 1960s made a major stride forward only when they finally induced President John Kennedy to support their views. Similarly, in the mid-1980s, proponents of tax reform such as Senator Bill Bradley (D-N.J.) sought to reach accommodation with the Reagan administration so that their initiatives could succeed. Even members with few legislative ambitions will find White House support useful as they seek new post offices, dams, and defense contracts for their districts.

There are also conditions that promote conflict between president and Congress. These include genuine disagreement over policy goals (disagreement that may be magnified for partisan reasons); the almost inevitable jealousies of individuals each responsible to their own constituencies; and the natural desire of potential competitors to maintain some information not available to the other party (this helps explain the continuing debate over "executive privilege" with regard to the sharing of information). Disagreement over policy goals is the most important source of conflict. Examples include the basically hostile reaction by Congress to much of President Kennedy's New Frontier program in the early 1960s, to President Nixon's initiatives in welfare and housing in the early 1970s, to many of President Carter's proposals during his term, and to the most conservative proposals of the Reagan administration.

The relationship between Congress and the bureaucracy is less visible to the public because of the relative lack of media coverage when compared to the attention given the relationship between Congress and the president. But it too is vital in determining the shape of national policy. The policies that emerge from this relationship are not as dramatic as some emerging from the presidential-congressional relationship, but they are collectively important. Equally important, although less glamorous, the nexus between bureaus and subcommittees determines some central details of how ongoing programs will be implemented. These seemingly routine and dull decisions can shape programs in ways very different from what the proponents in the White House and in Congress originally envisioned.

In much of the writing on the relations between Congress and the bureaucracy (and, surprisingly, the literature on this subject is scarce) the element of conflict is stressed. Not only is conflict depicted as a normal condition, but the discussions of these relations are usually cast in polemical terms. Typically, bureaucrats are portrayed as either trying to administer programs in the public interest despite the limitations imposed by parochial-minded congressmen, or else as trying to avoid the attentive eyes of public-spirited congressional watchdogs who insist on economy and efficiency instead of the normal "bureaucratic" (that is, wasteful) methods of administration. Discussions of congressional oversight of administration usually focus on congressional aggressiveness in oversight and bureaucratic resistance to it. Depending on the point of view, congressional aggressiveness is either praised or condemned, and the bureaucratic resistance is described as dastardly or heroic.

By contrast, it is here argued that the bureaucratic-congressional relationship is at the center of public policy development in the United States and that cooperation characterizes this relationship far more than conflict. Members of Congress and members of the bureaucracy have valuable items to trade and, unless the terms of trade strike one party or the other as outrageous, there are strong incentives to keep the relations smooth, cooperative, and devoid of disruptive conflict. Conflict can be costly to both sides and so both sides are reluctant to initiate it. Conflict does arise and should be noted, but the more usual situation is one of relative harmony.

It has been suggested that even some of what seems to be conflict is symbolic only and, in fact, is indicative of a continuing implicit arrangement between Congress and the bureaucracy that give both of them what they want: the bureaucracy receives increased authority, staff, and budget, and members of Congress are able to provide additional important services to their constituents. This argument is elaborated in a provocative short book by Morris Fiorina. His central point is best summarized in his own words:

> Congressmen (typically the majority Democrats) earn electoral credits by establishing various federal programs (the minority Republicans typically earn credits by fighting the good fight). The legislation is drafted in very general terms, so some agency, existing or newly established, must translate a vague policy mandate into a functioning program, a process that necessitates the promulgation of numerous rules and regulations and, incidentally, the trampling of numerous toes. At the next stage, aggrieved and/or hopeful constituents petition their congressmen to intervene in the complex (or at least obscure) decision processes of the bureaucracy. The cycle closes when the congressman lends a sympathetic ear, piously denounces the evils of bureaucracy, intervenes in the latter's decisions, and rides a grateful electorate to ever more impressive electoral showings. Congressmen take credit coming and going. They are the alpha and the omega.
>
> The popular frustration with the permanent government in Washington is partly justified, but to a considerable degree it is misplaced resentment. *Congress is the linchpin of the Washington establishment.* The bureaucracy serves as a convenient lightning rod for public frustration and a convenient whipping boy for congressmen. But so long as the bureaucracy accommodates congressmen, the latter will oblige with ever larger budgets and grants of authority. Congress does not just react to big government—it creates it. All of Washington prospers. More and more bureaucrats promulgate more and more regulations and dispense more and more money. Fewer and fewer congressmen suffer electoral defeat. Elements of the electorate benefit from government programs, and all of the electorate is eligible for ombudsman services. But the general, long-term welfare of the United States is no more than an incidental by-product of the system.[11]

As members of a congressional committee or subcommittee and officials of a bureau interact, mutual support can be offered in several forms. The committee or subcommittee can provide the bureau with favorable decisions on budget, authority, jurisdiction, procedure, organization, and reorganization. Committee members also provide bureaucrats with rewards in the form of public praise for jobs well done. Bureaus can provide committee members with "good" policy (that is, policy in accord with the preferences of the committee mem-

---

[11]Morris P. Fiorina, *Congress: Keystone of the Washington Establishment* (New Haven: Yale University Press, 1977): 48–49.

bers) and with special treatment for the states, districts, and constituents of committee members on matters involving the application of regulations, the location of facilities, or the priority given a specific matter. Bureaucrats can also provide public support for senators and representatives by deferring to them as experts in given areas. The instances of conflict that do occur usually stem from genuine differences of opinion over what is good policy, disputes motivated by partisan considerations, or personal dislikes.

From the congressional point of view, the danger of close cooperation is that it may, in fact, amount to cooptation by a bureau with a more numerous staff and more complete information about the subject matter of its own programs. The danger of generating programmatic conflict is that the benefits that the bureau can offer to committee members may be withheld or withdrawn.

In general, then, influence over the development of public policy is shared (unevenly, in most instances) by the president and individuals in the institutional presidency, members of the House and Senate, civil servants in the bureaucracy, and lobbyists representing various interests. In any specific policy area various coalitions may emerge involving these basic participants. One particularly strong link is that between Congress and the bureaucracy—specifically, between a subcommittee or two and the top officials in a specific bureau. When this nexus adds a few supportive interest-group representatives it becomes exceptionally powerful and can often withstand even pressure from the White House.

## The Reagan Years: Change and Continuity

The complicated, but extremely important nature of the relationship between Congress and the executive branch (both the president and the bureaucracy) was well illustrated during the Reagan years. In essence, Reagan tried to change the substantive agenda of the federal government—both bureaucracy and Congress. He had some success. Congress paid attention to some new issues, dropped some old issues, and came out with results that differed rather dramatically from the 1960s and considerably from the 1970s. Specifically, Reagan led Congress in dropping serious consideration of new domestic policy initiatives, in cutting taxes and shifting more of the burden onto the upper middle class and away from both the poorest and the richest citizens, and building up the armed might of the United States with greater rapidity. However, the basic institutional tensions between Congress and the president and executive branch did not vanish. Nor did the normal tensions between fragmenting and integrating influences. An analysis of the Reagan years and examples from them will appear in a number of later chapters. However, an overview of the essence of that relationship is useful here to underscore the general point that congressional change always takes place in the context of considerable continuity. This 200-year-old institution is never transformed fully by any president, no matter how dynamic and popular he is.

In the 1960s Congress worked with (and sometimes against) President John Kennedy and President Lyndon Johnson to create a number of new domestic programs such as the various parts of the War on Poverty, a large program of aid to elementary and secondary education, the Model Cities program aimed at resuscitating inner cities, and a number of initiatives in the civil-rights and voting-rights fields. In the foreign-policy realm, Congress, without much apparent thought, cooperated with these same presidents, especially Johnson, in expanding the war in Vietnam. But, by the end of the decade and into the 1970s the creation of new domestic programs had ceased. The Vietnam war wound down in the midst of political acrimony, both in society and in the institutions of government. Congress became preoccupied with the notion of "no more Vietnams." Domestically, President Jimmy Carter tried a few initiatives, especially in the field of energy policy, that went beyond the holding action and modest expansion of the Nixon and Ford years, but he was inept in his leadership. Congress, for a variety of reasons, was only sporadically responsive and little was accomplished. By the last few years of the decade the rate of inflation had increased rapidly and had become the dominant domestic issue. In the realm of defense policy Carter began to have some impact, with a willing Congress, in increasing defense spending in relative terms as well as in absolute terms.

When Ronald Reagan assumed the presidency in January 1981 his agenda represented some important changes from the past, but it also represented some continuities. Naturally, his agenda has changed during the course of his two terms, but the central thrusts have remained much the same. One thrust—building on developments from the late 1970s—was to insist on the need for dramatically increased defense spending. This insistence was tied to an aggressive stance toward the Soviet Union and areas in which the Soviet Union was perceived as the hidden adversary, as in Nicaragua. A second thrust was to cease creation of domestic programs, scrap some existing programs, and cut back substantially on a number of others. This position had not been espoused by any president since 1933. A third thrust was to reduce taxes dramatically—both to force the shrinkage of federal government programs and the federal government itself and, so the theory went, to release resources that would stimulate economic growth.

Reagan insisted on his agenda. Congress bought some of it, but far from all of it. And the reaction varied over time. In broad strokes, Congress restrained military growth (and at least slowed down the aggressive and automatic nature of the global anti-Soviet campaign); in effect, it agreed to stop creating domestic programs, but successfully resisted the elimination of some existing programs. It also funded some programs more generously than the administration wished. It helped fashion major tax cuts in 1981 and 1986, although it supported a partially offsetting tax increase in 1982.

The failure of the economy to grow as rapidly as predicted by the administration, coupled with growth in defense spending, restraints in shrinkage in domestic spending, and tax cuts, resulted in large and rapidly increasing annual federal deficits. They soared to well over $200 billion annually by the mid-1980s and threatened to remain at least that large or even get larger. Congress, the president, the media, and—seemingly—the public all responded by creating an add-on layer to national policy concerns. The Reagan years had from day one featured a preoccupation with budget and taxes. Now an overlay of what can reasonably be called deficit-mania was added, and one result was the Gramm-Rudman bill, which had a formula for inducing Congress to reduce the deficit on a schedule leading to a balanced budget by 1991 or face automatic cuts that presumably no one wanted. But Gramm-Rudman showed quick signs of becoming a dead letter. The Supreme Court declared part of the act unconstitutional in the early summer of 1986 (the act had passed in December 1985). The replacement passed by Congress in September 1987 seemed unlikely to provide more than symbolic help in deficit reduction. It postponed to 1993 the goal of a balanced budget. More important, Congress showed no desire to conform to the provisions of the act. The so-called reductions for Fiscal 1986 (a relatively modest amount required in early calendar year 1986) and the reductions for Fiscal 1987 (adopted in the autumn of 1986) were mostly accounting tricks and did not represent serious, genuine cuts. Cuts for Fiscal 1988 fell far short of original goals. Thus, Gramm–Rudman and deficit-mania did not change policy dramatically nor did they change the mix of conflicting pressures and motives to which Congress responds. Nor did they change the basic congressional relationship with the executive branch.

Details of the Reagan years, as well as of other instances of congressional interaction with the bureaucracy, the president, the impact of Congress on policy, and the congressional role in federal budgeting appear throughout later chapters—especially Chapters 9 through 12. But this preview is a signal to the reader that short-term events and personalities are important but are overshadowed by more basic forces that shape the congressional institution and its performance.

## SUMMARY

Several broad generalizations emerge from this chapter:

First, Congress is important in terms of its policy impact. Its actions affect the daily life of all American citizens. It performs four principal functions that can and do have major effects on society.

Second, Congress is a dynamic institution that changes both in response to outside events *and* in response to the deliberate plans and choices of its members. It is not a museum featuring relics of the past. Rather, it is a complex institution in a constant state of change— sometimes slow and occasionally rapid.

Third, the key relationship in determining the congressional policy impact at any given time is that between Congress and the executive branch—both the president and the bureaucracy.

Fourth, it is useful to think about Congress at any given time as lying somewhere along a spectrum between fragmentation and integration in terms of both its internal organization and its impact on the policies of the federal government. Congress' position on the spectrum changes over time, although there are more "natural" forces leading it to gravitate toward the fragmentation pole than toward the integration pole. Achieving integration takes more deliberate will and effort than achieving fragmentation. Any specific mix of fragmentation and integration promotes different values.

# 2

# Congressional Development

How did Congress come to be the way it is? The framers wanted a powerful institution. But they also wanted its powers limited, as they wanted all governmental powers limited. Therefore, they also created major elements of what we call fragmentation. This chapter highlights some of the developments in Congress throughout our national history that have helped produce the institution of today.

Although Congress has changed over time—especially in response to a developing presidency, the growth of the bureaucracy, and the vast expansion of the tasks undertaken by the federal government—it has always been an important force in governing the nation. In this it was following a tradition well-rooted in the colonial period of the seventeenth and eighteenth centuries as well as in British antecedents.

The development of a representative and powerful legislature in Great Britain (Parliament) evolved through at least four stages.[1] First, beginning late in the thirteenth century and for a few centuries the-

---

[1] See Charles A. Beard and John D. Lewis, "Representative Government in Evolution," *American Political Science Review* 26 (1932): 223–40.

reafter the king called Parliaments to meet for his own purposes, primarily to levy taxes. Second, this body called by the king to vote taxes also gradually acquired other legislative power. Third, by the seventeenth century Parliament had evolved to the stage where it could put definite limits on what the king could do, both in lawmaking and in raising revenues. These gains were cemented by the Puritan Revolution of the mid-seventeenth century and especially by the Glorious Revolution of 1688. From that point until the late nineteenth century in Great Britain the representative and electoral base for Parliament was very limited, however. Only the relatively well-to-do in society were effectively heard in Parliament. The fourth stage of development came in the late nineteenth century when the representative and electoral base was broadened.

American legislative development, stemming from the state of Parliament in the early seventeenth century, began immediately and took a different course than did that in Great Britain. The colonial legislatures, beginning with the Virginia House of Burgesses in 1619, became important very quickly. Whereas in Great Britain the contest between Parliament and the Crown for power was not resolved until 1688 (and even after 1688 there were some shaky moments for parliamentary supremacy for at least a hundred years), legislative power in the colonies grew immediately. Furthermore, although a broad electorate did not develop in Great Britain until the late 19th century, in some of the colonies such an electorate was present even before independence was achieved.

The American Congress created at the Constitutional Convention in Philadelphia in 1787 was virtually automatically a powerful body and a body that was assumed to be broadly representative by the standards of the eighteenth century. Any other decisions would have run counter to the dominant traditions of specifically American legislatures (as contrasted to the British Parliament) that had begun to develop in 1619.

These twin characteristics of a national American legislature—powerfulness and representativeness—were a foregone conclusion in Philadelphia. The dominant political thinking in the country and at the convention accepted them as necessary and as proper. The strength of these views was reinforced by the fact that one of the most successful claims the rebellious colonists had made before and during the War of Independence was that they were not receiving adequate representation in the government of Great Britain. Therefore, they argued, they could not be expected to support that government through taxes and in other ways.

## THE CONSTITUTIONAL MANDATE

Much lively debate and many detailed compromises characterized the decisions made by the members of the Constitutional Convention in 1787 that stated the powers Congress would possess.[2] But the principle that there would be a powerful national legislature was never jeopardized. The numerous provisions and clauses throughout the Constitution that refer to Congress, especially those in Article I, section 8, make evident the intent of the framers to have such a legislature. In that section Congress is given a variety of specific powers, including the power to tax, borrow and coin money, regulate foreign and interstate commerce, establish a post office, establish federal courts in addition to the Supreme Court, declare war, and provide for the creation and maintenance of armed forces. And, in the event that these grants did not prove sufficient, the framers of the Constitution also granted Congress the power "To make all Laws which shall be necessary and proper for carrying into Execution the foregoing Powers, and all other Powers vested by this Constitution in the Government of the United States, or in any Department or Officer thereof."

The members of the Constitutional Convention made several assumptions that most closely affected the place of Congress in the American scheme of government. First, as already indicated, they assumed that the legislature should and would be powerful and important. No other course was ever seriously considered. Second, they assumed that the government in general needed substantial restraints as well as substantial power. Third, they assumed that the legislature in particular needed to be restrained. The decisions made on the basis of these assumptions produced the mix of powers and restraints that characterize the entire government.

The thoughts of those who took the lead in creating the new government, including Congress, are revealed best in the *Federalist* papers. Two of those papers, numbers 10 and 51, are especially worth careful attention as a key to understanding the convention's vision of Congress.

In number 10 James Madison outlined the dangers of what he called "faction" and sought a cure. That cure is alleged to be present in the proposed new governing scheme. Madison's analysis can best be summarized in his own words:

[2]On the Constitutional Convention's decisions about Congress and for "founding fathers" interpretations of those decisions see Max Farrand, *The Framing of the Constitution of the United States* (New Haven: Yale University Press, 1913); and Alexander Hamilton, John Jay, and James Madison, *The Federalist* (New York: Random House).

Among the numerous advantages promised by a well-constructed Union, none deserves to be more accurately developed than its tendency to break and control the violence of faction. . . .

By a faction, I understand a number of citizens, whether amounting to a majority or minority of the whole, who are united and actuated by some common impulse of passion, or of interest, adverse to the rights of other citizens, or to the permanent and aggregate interests of the community.

There are two methods of curing the mischiefs of faction: the one, by removing its causes; the other, by controlling its effects. . . .

The inference to which we are brought is, that the *causes* of faction cannot be removed, and that relief is only to be sought in the means of controlling its *effects.*

If a faction consists of less than a majority, relief is supplied by the republican principle, which enables the majority to defeat its sinister views by regular vote. It may clog the administration, it may convulse the society; but it will be unable to execute and mask its violence under the forms of the Constitution. When a majority is included in a faction, the form of popular government, on the other hand, enables it to sacrifice to its ruling passion or interest both the public good and the rights of other citizens. To secure the public good and private rights against the danger of such a faction, and at the same time to preserve the spirit and the form of popular government, is then the great object to which our inquiries are directed. Let me add that it is the great desideratum by which this form of government can be rescued from the opprobrium under which it has so long labored, and be recommended to the esteem and adoption of mankind.

By what means is this object attainable? Evidently by one of two only. Either the existence of the same passion or interest in a majority at the same time must be prevented, or the majority, having such coexistent passion or interest, must be rendered, by their number and local situation, unable to concert and carry into effect schemes of oppression.

Madison concludes number 10 by showing that the proposed government will allow control over the evil effects of faction and will prevent the tyranny of the majority.

In number 51, also written by Madison, the guarantees against tyranny of the majority (recall that a majority was defined as but a special kind of faction in number 10) are made more explicit. These guarantees are embodied in an elaborate scheme of separated powers enhanced by checks and balances. The place of Congress in this scheme of limited power is clearly shown, again most succinctly in the words of the author:

To what expedient, then, shall we finally resort, for maintaining in practice the necessary partition of power among the several departments, as laid down in the Constitution? The only answer that can be given is, that as all these exterior provisions are found to be inadequate, the defect must be supplied, by so contriving the interior structure of the government as that its several constituent parts may, by their mutual relations, be the means of keeping each other in their proper places. . . .

In framing a government which is to be administered by men over men, the great difficulty lies in this: you must first enable the government to control the governed; and in the next place oblige it to control itself. A dependence on the people is, no doubt, the primary control on the government; but experience has taught mankind the necessity of auxiliary precautions. . . .

But it is not possible to give to each department an equal power of self-defence. In republican government, the legislative authority necessarily predominates. The remedy for this inconveniency is to divide the legislature into different branches; and to render them, by different modes of election and different principles of action, as little connected with each other as the nature of their common functions and their common dependence on the society will admit. It may even be necessary to guard against dangerous encroachments by still further precautions. As the weight of the legislative authority requires that it should be thus divided, the weakness of the executive may require, on the other hand, that it should be fortified. . . .

There are, moreover, two considerations particularly applicable to the federal system of America, which place that system in a very interesting point of view.

*First.* In a single republic, all the power surrendered by the people is submitted to the administration of a single government; and the usurpations are guarded against by a division of the government into distinct and separate departments. In the compound republic of America, the power surrendered by the people is first divided between two distinct governments, and then the portion allotted to each subdivided among distinct and separate departments. Hence a double security arises to the rights of the people. The different governments will control each other, at the same time that each will be controlled by itself.

*Second.* It is of great importance in a republic not only to guard the society against the oppression of its rulers, but to guard one part of the society against the injustice of the other part. Different interests necessarily exist in different classes of citizens. If a majority be united by a common interest, the rights of the minority will be insecure. There are but two methods of providing against this evil: the one by creating a will in the community independent of the majority—that is, of the society itself; the other, by comprehending in the society so many separate descriptions of citizens as will render an unjust combination of a majority of the whole very improbable, if not impracticable. The first method prevails in all governments possessing an hereditary or self-appointed authority. This, at best, is but a precarious security; because a power independent of the society may as well espouse the unjust views of the major, as the rightful interests of the minor party, and may possibly be turned against both parties. The second method will be exemplified in the federal republic of the United States. Whilst all authority in it will be derived from and dependent on the society, the society itself will be broken into so many parts, interests and classes of citizens, that the rights of individuals, or of the minority, will be in little danger from interested combinations of the majority.

In short, when Federalist numbers 10 and 51 are read together, a formula for a fragmented Congress is quite clear. It is to be a powerful Congress but one that will be limited by (1) being composed of two houses with different constituencies, (2) the powers of other branches of the federal government, (3) the powers of state governments, and (4) the necessities imposed by representing a large and diverse set of interests ("factions" or potential "factions") that will have trouble agreeing on any scheme that might be oppressive to a minority.

Within this general institutional and philosophical framework—to which all of the specific decisions of 1787 were faithful—several concrete decisions stand out as most important in the subsequent development of Congress: (1) the decision to create a separate and independent judiciary that could serve to check both the president and Congress; (2) the decision to make the legislature bicameral, with equal houses representing different constituencies; and (3) the decision to interweave the powers of the president and Congress thoroughly while maintaining their very distinct institutional identities. The latter two decisions have been much more consistently important than the first. Judicial power has been an important potential check, even though not often used with major impact. Each of the three decisions will be considered in turn.

## Judicial Power

The policy interaction between the federal courts and Congress has been sporadic and has mainly involved congressional statutes struck down by the Supreme Court as unconstitutional (beyond the power of Congress according to the constitution) in whole or in part. Between 1789 and 1985 the Supreme Court made 134 declarations that all or part of a federal statute was unconstitutional. Prior to 1864 this occurred only twice. Between 1864 and 1936 the Court became much more aggressive and made 71 such declarations. A short period of reticence set in and the Court made only three such declarations between 1936 and 1953. Since 1954 the Court has again been more active in declaring congressionally-passed statutes unconstitutional. It did so 54 times between 1954 and the autumn of 1985.[3]

The courts also have had a major impact on Congress through their role in redistricting since 1962 (treated in Chapter 3). In principle, the Supreme Court staked out a major claim to influence congressional behavior when, in 1983, it declared the legislative veto unconstitutional. That practice required congressional approval (or at least lack of disapproval) of specific executive branch actions within a specific time period before they could take effect. However, little has happened following the Supreme Court ruling. Both Congress and the executive branch chose to ignore the broadest implications of the 1983 decision. Congress amended some legislative-veto provisions in ways that presumably met the Court's objection. New legislative-veto provisions have been enacted since 1983. Most important, both Congress and the executive branch have continued to observe the provisions of the various legislative-veto provisions in several hundred statutes.

## Bicameralism

The decision to have two houses of the national legislature followed the precedent set by the British Parliament and ten of the thirteen colonies. The convention opted for a two-house national legislature with little debate.

There was debate, however, over the basis on which the two houses should be organized and elected. There was only minimal sentiment against having at least one house popularly elected (a "popular" electorate by the standards of the eighteenth century included a large proportion of all adult white males, although some white males might be denied the vote on the grounds of not having sufficient property). The delegates also assumed that the House of Representatives (as the popularly elected branch was called) would represent "democratic" interests—that is, measures favored by the majority of the voters that were widely expected to be "radical." The institution of slavery was protected even in the House, however, because representatives were

[3]Henry J. Abraham, *The Judicial Process*, 5th ed. (New York: Oxford University Press, 1986): 291–308.

apportioned to the states on the basis of their white population plus three-fifths of their slave population, even though slaves could not vote. Thus southern states received extra seats in the House because of their large populations of black slaves. This compromise marked the first attempt to deal with a subject that would eventually tear the Union apart.

The Senate (as the second house of the legislature was called) was expected to serve as a check on the impetuosity of the House. How the Senate should be organized and elected was a subject of some debate, although there was virtually no sentiment for having it popularly elected. It was expected to be representative of more privileged interests in society that presumably would be badly treated in the House. But the delegates could not find a way of defining interests other than in terms of states. Thus every state was given two senators and the power to elect them was lodged in the state legislatures.

The overly simple assumption that individuals elected by what passed for a mass electorate in 1787 to represent "the people" would be radical and that individuals elected indirectly to represent states would be more conservative and solicitous of economic interests was not borne out in practice.

In 1913 the seventeenth amendment to the Constitution changed the mode of election of senators so that they too would be elected by a mass electorate. The electoral system had been moving toward popular election for some time. Even during the period of election by state legislatures, senatorial candidates had often involved themselves in the campaigns of candidates for the state legislatures so that citizens were informed who their senator might be when they made their choice among state legislative candidates.[4]

In theory, the Constitution made the two chambers equal partners in the making of laws, although some special functions were reserved for each house: the Senate was given sole power to try impeachments, ratify treaties, and approve presidential nominations; the House was given the sole power to bring impeachments and to initiate tax bills (by custom this has also included the power to initiate appropriations bills). In practice, the two houses have remained generally equal, although at various points in American history one house has seemed to overshadow the other one. Throughout most of congressional his-

---

[4]On the interweaving of senatorial campaigns and state legislative campaigns see William H. Riker, "The Senate and American Federalism," *American Political Science Review* 49 (1955): 452–69.

tory it has also been true that as individuals senators have had more prestige than representatives. Many representatives have willingly left the House to run for the Senate while virtually no one has gone the reverse route. Nevertheless, prestige is not "power" or "influence." Equality may vary between substantive fields and over time, but the fact of equality is real: both bodies are jealous of their independence and their impact on public policy. This means that both houses will usually seek to have an impact in virtually all important areas of legislation. No substantive fields become the exclusive property of one house or the other. Relative importance of the two houses varies, but both houses are always important.[5]

## Congress and the President

The second crucial decision made by the Constitutional Convention involved the nature of the relationship envisioned between Congress and the executive. The two were formally separated, each with particular "checks and balances" on the other, yet there are also some shared functions, and policy-making on a large scale is impossible without sustained close cooperation between Congress and the president. In Article II, section 3, the Constitution formally charges the president to give "to the Congress Information of the State of the Union, and recommend to their Consideration such Measures as he shall judge necessary and expedient." The president is also given the power to call special sessions of either or both houses. Finally, he can veto a measure passed by both houses if he feels it is unsound or otherwise improper.

Congress, however, is responsible for either passing or rejecting various proposals for laws—proposals coming from the president or from any other source. Although the president is commander-in-chief of the armed forces, only Congress can formally declare war. All operations of the executive branch are dependent on money that can be provided only by Congress. And the resources from which that money comes are derived from taxes that are imposed only after congressional action. Two-thirds of the voting members of both houses can override a presidential veto. Treaties and nominations made by presidents require congressional approval.

[5]For evidence of vacillations in relative impact of the two chambers on legislation, see David J. Vogler, *The Third House* (Evanston: Northwestern University Press, 1971): 110–11.

A president can be removed from office by Congress. This is extremely difficult to do because most members fear the negative consequences for the stability of the political system and a majority of the House and two-thirds of the Senate must agree in separate actions in order to effect the removal of the president. Only two serious attempts have been made to impeach presidents in the whole course of American history. In 1868 President Andrew Johnson was impeached by the House but the Senate fell one vote short of conviction.

In 1974 Congress was well on the way to impeaching and convicting President Richard Nixon when he resigned. The House Judiciary Committee spent a number of months sifting the evidence against Nixon, and committee members from both parties recommended impeachment of the President on three different counts (articles) to the full House. These articles involved obstruction of justice, abuse of presidential powers, and contempt of Congress—all in connection with the attempt by Nixon to cover up the White House role in the break-in at the Watergate headquarters of the Democratic National Committee in June 1972, and, in the case of the second article, with the attempt by the president to use federal agencies to harass political "enemies." It seemed very likely that the House would support at least the first two articles and that the Senate would vote to convict on at least those two articles. The case became moot when Nixon, in effect, admitted to ordering a cover-up of Watergate activities six days after the break-in by releasing information not previously available to the Judiciary Committee. The reaction to this admission was so overwhelmingly negative that it took only three days (from the admission on 5 August 1974, until 8 August 1974) for Nixon to decide that resigning would be preferable to certain impeachment and conviction.

Article II, section 4 of the Constitution provides that "The President, Vice President and all Civil Officers of the United States, shall be removed from Office on Impeachment for, and Conviction of, Treason, Bribery, or other high Crimes and Misdemeanors." There is no specific definition either in law or precedent of what constitutes "other high crimes and misdemeanors." In the case of a president it seems likely that offenses against the Constitution and oath of office to support it as interpreted by a majority of the House and two-thirds of the Senate could bring impeachment and conviction even though those offenses might not literally involve acts for which the president could be tried and convicted in a court of law. Before Nixon's final disastrous admission, his defenders on the House Judiciary Committee had argued that impeachable offenses should be narrowly defined as only those for which criminal conviction could be obtained in a court. But their position was in a minority of about two-to-one in the Committee. In general, Congress has used its impeachment power rarely. The Senate has held only 13 trials (10 involved judges) and convicted only five men (all judges).

Presidents are chosen by the House if the electoral college does not provide a majority. This happened after inconclusive elections in 1800 and 1824. In the first instance the House chose Thomas Jefferson over Aaron Burr and in the second John Quincy Adams over several rivals, including Andrew Jackson. On another occasion, following the election of 1876, Congress created an Electoral Commission that, in effect, determined the results of the election, probably contrary to the will of the majority of the electorate—Rutherford B. Hayes became president instead of Samuel Tilden. The Senate is responsible for choosing the vice-president following an inconclusive election. This has happened only once, in 1837. When the vice-presidency is vacant, a majority of both the House and Senate must confirm the president's nominee. If a president declares himself able to resume his duties after a period of disability and the vice-president and a majority of the cabinet disagree, Congress must settle the issue.

In effect, no matter what vision the president has about the shape of public policy, the implementation of that vision is dependent on Congress. Congress can take considerable initiative in shaping public policy according to some collective vision possessed by a large number of its members. Congress is also deeply involved when those policies are implemented through the bureaucracy. Both Congress and the president legislate, and both Congress and the president influence administration. Yet they are part of a governmental system in which, in some important ways, they are kept separate and distinct. They are mutually interdependent in producing results; but they are separate and independent in defending institutional prerogatives.

## THE EMERGENCE OF THE MODERN CONGRESS

In the early part of the nineteenth century Congress bore only a partial resemblance to the institution with which we are familiar today. The electorate for representatives had not yet stabilized (in some states restrictions on voting on the basis of property continued through the first few decades) and state legislatures elected senators. Not all representatives were elected from specific districts; until 1842 states were free to elect all representatives on a statewide basis and many did. Congress dealt with only a few aggressive presidents (chiefly Washington, Jefferson, and Jackson) before the Civil War. Even more important, the workload of the government was not very demanding. The main business of Congress consisted of debates on tariff policy every decade or so and two major efforts to preserve the federal union without civil war in 1820 and 1850.

By mid-century and particularly following the Civil War new conditions emerged. The remaining restrictions on voting based on property disappeared and black male citizens were added to the electorate by the fourteenth and fifteenth amendments to the Constitution. Virtually all representatives now came from districts that were only part of a state. Lincoln revived the tradition of a consistently aggressive president that had been dormant since the days of Jackson. His successful prosecution of the war left little doubt that the government could be mobilized to pursue national policy. His immediate successors did not appear aggressive—in part because Congress had adopted an aggressive stance, particularly with regard to Reconstruction. By late in the century Cleveland and McKinley began to revive the presidency and, in a sense, prepare it for the burst of activity that would come in the twentieth century. Following the Civil War, the government—both executive and legislature—had a great deal more to do as the nation industrialized rapidly and the government sought to cope with the consequences of that development.

Before the immediate post-Civil War period of the 1870s and 1880s Congress was in a "pre-modern" phase. After the 1870s and 1880s the "modern" Congress emerged. Naturally, change existed before the 1880s and has continued since then. But the process of emergence was rapidly accelerated for a few decades in the late nineteenth century.

The difference between the pre-modern Congress and the modern Congress can be illustrated in seven important areas: (1) turnover of membership; (2) finality of electoral decisions; (3) workload and length of sessions; (4) orderliness of floor proceedings; (5) stability of committee memberships and criteria for assignments to committees; (6) appointment criteria for committee chairs; and (7) the level of party development within the House and Senate. Table 2–1 summarizes the differences. Discussions of each follow.

These features were chosen because, collectively, their impact in the modern Congress has been to promote professionalism and stability in contrast with the relative amateurism and instability in the pre-

**Table 2–1.** Primary Differences between Pre-Modern Congress and Modern Congress

| PRE-MODERN CONGRESS | MODERN CONGRESS |
| --- | --- |
| High turnover of membership | Low turnover of membership |
| Many contested elections | Few contested elections |
| Short sessions, relatively light workload | Long sessions, heavy workload |
| Chaotic floor proceedings | Orderly floor proceedings |
| High turnover of committee personnel; shifting criteria for assignment | Low turnover of committee personnel; stable criteria for assignment |
| Numerous criteria for appointment of committee chairs | Seniority the dominant criterion for appointment of committee chairs |
| Undeveloped political party structures | Well-developed political party structures |

modern era.[6] As indicated in Chapter I, institutional stability has both costs and benefits in terms of maximizing substantive congressional policy impact. Congress can still consciously promote internal, institutional change, but it cannot recreate the radical instability of the pre-modern period.

## Turnover of Membership

In the pre-modern Congress, members came and went rapidly. There were few senior members. Life in Washington was not pleasant, Congress did not seem very important, and the unstable party situation often made re-election difficult to achieve. In the modern Congress, members began serving for much longer periods of time. They became wedded to the notion of a career in Congress. This new desire stemmed from several factors: the strengthening of the parties and the emergence of one-party states and districts after the Civil War made re-election easier; the emergence of national problems raised a legislative career to a new level of importance; and Congress demonstrated after Lincoln's death that it intended to be an aggressive part of the government.

[6]Another difference between the pre-modern Congress and the modern Congress is the nature and amount of congressional pay, perquisites, and allowances for staff and other kinds of support such as travel and office rental in the districts. In the modern Congress all of these supports and rewards have increased constantly, with a large burst coming in the last several decades. In the pre-modern Congress such supports and rewards were minimal. This difference is not given full treatment in this chapter mainly because it does not seem to be a cause of the emergence of the modern Congress. The increase of staffing is important and is treated separately in Chapter 7. Incumbents use some of the supports to enhance their chances of re-election (see Chapter 3).

Until the 1880s the length of service of the average senator and representative remained at a low and fairly constant level—representatives averaged two years (after a higher level of around three years during a peak of House influence on national policy in the 1810s and 1820s) and senators around four years. Members of both chambers, especially the House, routinely left Congress for other opportunities, both governmental and private. Mid-term resignations were common.

Beginning about 1880 the average years of service rose dramatically in both houses, doubling in the Senate in less than two decades and almost tripling in the House in three decades. The upward trend continued, with breaks for political turnovers, until the late 1960s. Since then the trend has been gradually downward in both houses, although the average years of service remain high (over 7 in both houses) when viewed in historical perspective.

The increase in length of service after 1880 was produced by two factors: the desire on the part of members to seek re-election and the decreasing competitiveness of many districts (and some states) so that re-election became relatively easy to achieve for the incumbent. Both the desire for long service and the requisite condition for fulfilling the desire emerged in the late nineteenth century.[7]

The critical factor in helping to produce decreasing electoral competitiveness in individual districts (safe seats) was a strengthening of the party system in that period and a geographical division of party strength. The major reason for these developments was the Civil War, which produced an aggressive Republican party in the north that retained its aggressiveness after the war and was countered by a revived Democratic party, with a strong southern and border state base.[8]

In the pre-modern Congress there were always large numbers of new (freshmen) members in both houses. In fifteen of the first forty-eight Congresses (from 1789 until 1883) over half of all members of the

[7]See H. Douglas Price, "The Congressional Career—Then and Now," in Nelson W. Polsby (ed.), *Congressional Behavior* (New York: Random House, 1971). On the general point of the development of a "career" in Congress see Nelson W. Polsby, "Institutionalization in the U.S. House of Representatives," *American Political Science Review* 62 (1968): 144–68; Samuel P. Huntington, "Congressional Responses to the Twentieth Century," in David B. Truman (ed.), *The Congress and America's Future,* 2nd ed. (Englewood Cliffs, N.J.: Prentice-Hall, 1973); T. Richard Witmer, "The Aging of the House," *Political Science Quarterly* 79 (December 1964): 526–41; H. Douglas Price, "Congress and the Evolution of Legislative 'Professionalism'," in Norman J. Ornstein (ed.), *Congress in Change* (New York: Praeger, 1975); and Robert Struble, Jr., "House Turnover and the Principle of Rotation," *Political Science Quarterly* 94 (1979–80): 649–67.
[8]See Eric L. McKitrick, "Party Politics and the Union and Confederate War Efforts," in William N. Chambers and Walter D. Burnham (eds.), *The American Party Systems* (New York: Oxford University Press, 1967).

House of Representatives were freshmen. During the same period of time (in fact, until 1901) the percentage of freshmen was never below 30 percent and was usually well above 40 percent.[9] Between 1789 and 1899 an average of over 45 percent of all House members were freshmen in each Congress. From 1901 through 1987 the average number of freshmen in each Congress has been about 20 percent.

Figures 2–1 and 2–2 summarize the percentage of representatives and senators coming for the first time to their respective chambers since 1791 (the Second Congress) through the One Hundredth Congress (1987–89). The First Congress is not included, of course, because all members were freshmen. The elections of 1980, 1982, 1984, and 1986 produced 17, 18, 10, and 11 percent freshmen in the House and 18, 5, 7, and 13 percent freshmen in the Senate.

Figures 2–1 and 2–2 show a dramatic and continuing drop in turnover in the House beginning in the 1870s and continuing for a hundred years. In the Senate the major drop in turnover occurred in the 1870s and 1880s and has continued somewhat sporadically since. Before the Civil War the turnover in both houses was very high: between one-quarter and one-third of every Senate was composed of freshmen senators and close to half of every House was composed of freshmen representatives. In the last several decades those figures have generally been somewhere between one in every five to one in every eight in both houses. The emergence of relatively strong parties with different geographical bases in the late nineteenth century is a powerful factor helping to explain the initial change.

## Finality of Electoral Decisions

In the pre-modern Congress, members were subject to challenges to their election. These challenges, on the grounds of electoral irregularities, were especially frequent from the end of the Civil War to the turn of the century. Virtually all contests were decided by the House and Senate on strictly partisan grounds.[10] Each seat was particularly valuable in the late nineteenth century because it was a period of close competition between the parties. Partisan election contests in both houses dropped dramatically around the turn of the century, and have continued to decline since. In the last two decades, for example, there

[9]Polsby, "Institutionalization," 146.
[10]Price, "Congressional Career," reports that only 3 of 382 contested seats in the House were given to the minority party candidate from 1789 to 1908.

**Figure 2–1.** Percent of New Representatives, 1791–1987

SOURCE: Adapted from data contained in Nelson W. Polsby, "Institutionalization in the U.S. House of Representatives," *American Political Science Review* 62 (1968): 146. Updated from raw data.

**Figure 2-2.** Percent of New Senators, 1791–1987

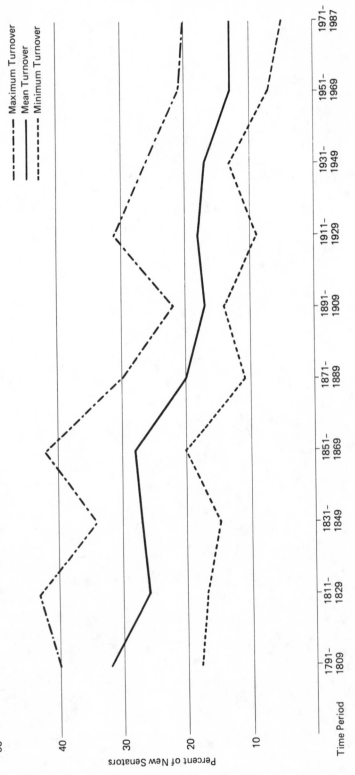

have been only two contested House seats. Members who wanted to make careers in Congress—now a majority instead of a small minority—could no longer afford to tolerate arbitrary threats to their goal.

## Workload and Length of Sessions

The pre-modern Congress did not meet much of the time because it did not have a great deal to do. Until early in the twentieth century Congress met less than twelve months out of every two years. Except for the First Congress, which met seventeen months for the purpose of creating a governing apparatus, and the Civil War and Reconstruction Congresses, which met between ten and twenty-two months, the length of sessions remained consistently short until about 1911. Since that time Congress has met over twelve months out of every twenty-four. In the last four decades Congress has been in session most of the time. This feature of the modern Congress has required that a large proportion of the members become full-time legislators. The reason for this change is primarily that the workload of the entire national government has increased steadily since the Civil War. Since Congress is a central unit in the governing apparatus its workload has also increased steadily.[11]

## Orderliness of Floor Proceedings

In the pre-modern Congress, particularly in the House, floor proceedings were chaotic. H. Douglas Price described the House of the nineteenth century: "Members often used bitter and outrageous language, scathing ridicule, and sarcasm. Outbreaks of physical violence were not infrequent, and guns and knives were on occasion carried into the chamber." Neil MacNeil reports a number of instances of violence on the House floor and duels outside the House between members. In one famous encounter before the Civil War, Preston Brooks, a South Carolina representative, beat Charles Sumner, a Massachusetts sena-

[11]For various statistical measures of congressional activity, see Norman J. Ornstein and others, *Vital Statistics on Congress,* 1984–1985 Edition (Washington, D.C.: American Enterprise Institute, 1984): 138–52; Donald L. Eilenstine, David L. Farnsworth, and James S. Fleming, "Trends and Cycles in the Legislative Productivity of the United States Congress, 1789–1976," *Quality and Quantity* 12 (1978): 19–44; and Roger H. Davidson, "The Legislative Work of Congress," unpublished paper prepared for the annual meeting of the American Political Science Association, August 28–31, 1986.

tor, senseless on the Senate floor. Even more important, the rules of the House and Senate did not allow the orderly conduct of business.[12]

In the modern Congress decorum replaced raucousness. Rules evolved that allowed Congress to dispatch large amounts of business on the floor rapidly. The development of such rules in the House was particularly important. The major developments came between 1876 and 1899 and were largely the result of the work of four Speakers: Samuel J. Randall (1876–1881), John G. Carlisle (1883–1889), Thomas B. Reed (1889–1891; 1895–1899), and Charles F. Crisp (1891–1895). Randall made the power of recognition absolute and not subject to appeal, obtained a general revision of the rules, and strengthened the Rules Committee, of which he was chairman. Carlisle was particularly astute in using the power of recognition and he further developed the Rules Committee as an instrument of party government. Reed had the House pass rules effectively outlawing dilatory motions and filibustering in the House. He also continued to use the power of recognition for party ends. Crisp extended the jurisdiction of the Rules Committee to bills still pending in standing committees. The Rules Committee also began to grant special orders or "rules" that would allow legislation to be brought to the floor more systematically.

The Speaker himself was shorn of some of his power acquired during this period in a House revolt against Speaker Joseph Cannon (1903–1911) that took place in 1909–1911 and reached a dramatic peak on the House floor on 19 March 1910. In 1909 the House established a consent calendar (which provided for the orderly consideration of bills to which there was no important opposition) and agreed to call the standing committees every Wednesday for consideration of business on the Union or House calendars (calendars are simply lists of bills ready for floor action; different calendars include different types of bills). These changes limited the Speaker's arbitrary power to control the flow of business. In the March 1910 revolt the Speaker was removed from the Rules Committee, which was enlarged and made elective rather than appointive. Later that year, a method of discharging bills from standing committees was approved that gave the majority of the House the right to bring a bill to the floor even if it was opposed by a committee chairman and the Speaker. In 1911 the rules were changed to provide for the election by the full House of all standing committees and their chairmen. In practice, this led to the establishment of committees on committees (see Chapter 5).

[12]Price, "Congressional Career," 18; Neil MacNeil, *Forge of Democracy* (New York: McKay, 1963): 306–9.

The Senate, which established decorum earlier than the House, has continued to take a more leisurely pace on the floor. But even in the Senate the wasting of time on the floor has declined. In the pre-modern period Congress could afford to waste time because the workload was so light. Once the workload grew and was attended to by professional legislators, time became valuable and procedures were invented to prevent gross waste of it.

## Committee Membership: Stability and Assignment Criteria

In the pre-modern Congress there were shifting processes for assigning members to standing committees, and no consistent criteria were applied when such assignments were made. High turnover occurred in the membership of specific committees every two years, in part simply because turnover in Congress itself was so high. In the House the appointment power early gravitated to the Speaker, but it was not used with any consistency to promote policies he favored. Henry Clay, for example, the Speaker for eight years between 1811 and 1824, seems to have used this power merely to make friends and continue his tenure in the Speaker's chair.[13]

In the Senate even the location of appointment authority kept changing. The Senate had no standing committees until 1816 when eleven were authorized. Until 1823 the members of these committees were chosen by ballot by the whole Senate. From 1823 to 1833 the method of choice alternated between ballot, appointment by the president pro tempore of the Senate, and, for one short period, appointment by the vice-president. During much of the period before 1833 seniority for initial assignments and for rank on committees was so unimportant that chairmanships were rotated.

After 1833 the Senate again resorted to balloting for all members. Chairmanships ceased to rotate, and party control of assignments began to appear. Committees began to divide on predictable ideological lines, and minority reports were written, whereas previously only majority reports were written. Party control was firm enough by 1846 that, although the formal requirement of balloting remained, the committee assignment lists supplied by the parties were routinely approved.

As the parties split under the strain of dealing with the slavery

[13]James S. Young, *The Washington Community, 1800–1828* (New York: Columbia University Press, 1966): 132–33.

question, the Senate found committee assignments more difficult to make. From 1849 to 1857 the president pro tempore again became the appointing agent, although the parties did not relinquish their influence. The southern Democrats dominated the committee chairs because of their number in the party. They supported the hardening of seniority to protect their position so that they could defend slavery. Democrats defended a version of the principle of seniority (not removing sitting committee members because of their experience) in an 1857 debate over proposed committee assignments. The Republicans had challenged the assignments as unfair; they had not been consulted by the Democrats when the assignments were made. When the Republicans became the majority in the Senate in 1861 they consulted the Democrats in that year but then ceased consulting them, instead filling all committee places themselves. This situation prevailed until the Democrats became numerous enough after the Civil War to force, in effect, the adoption of a seniority criterion.[14] Since then memberships on committees have been relatively stable—the same members tend to serve on the same committees term after term and develop both their own legislative career and the capacity of Congress to cope with the professionalism of the bureaucracy. Long service on specific committees has accompanied long service in the House and Senate as a whole.

## Committee Chairs: Appointment Criteria

In the pre-modern Congress chairmen were selected by the same variety of methods by which other committee members were selected. And a variety of criteria for choice were used—including personal loyalty to the appointing authority. Turnover of chairmen was frequent.

In the modern Congress seniority developed as a virtually automatic rule for apportioning committee chairmanships.[15] In the Senate, seniority became well-established very quickly in 1877, when the Senate again had a minority party large enough to pose a threat to the

[14]See George Lee Robinson, "The Development of the Senate Committee System" (Ph.D. dissertation, New York University, 1954).

[15]On this subject see Barbara Hinckley, *The Seniority System in Congress* (Bloomington: Indiana University Press, 1971); Michael Abram and Joseph Cooper, "The Rise of the Seniority System in the House of Representatives," *Polity* 1 (1968): 53–85; Nelson W. Polsby, Miriam Gallaher, and Barry Spencer Rundquist, "The Growth of the Seniority System in the U.S. House of Representatives," *American Political Science Review* 63 (1969): 787–807; and George Goodwin, Jr., "The Seniority System in Congress," *American Political Science Review* 53 (1959): 412–36.

policy preferences of the majority party. Between 1865 and 1877, when vacancies occurred in the chairs of ten of the most important standing committees in the Senate, the Republican party filled those vacancies only about one-quarter of the time on the basis of seniority. Since 1877 the seniority rule for chairmanships has been basically sacred, with only scattered violations. The evidence suggests that the Democrats had begun to use seniority in the four Congresses preceding the Civil War (at which time most of them left the Senate). In the period after the war, until 1875, there were only a few Democrats in the Senate. When they reappeared in sizable number seniority was rarely violated.[16]

In the House the development of seniority occurred more gradually. Speakers were struggling to get control of the House in the 1880s and 1890s and they frequently ignored seniority in the appointment of committee chairmen and ranking minority members in order to assure that individuals personally loyal to them and in general agreement with their policy views would hold key committee positions. (It should also be noted that, at least in formal terms, the Speaker made minority appointments as well as those from his own party until 1903, when he formally delegated the power to the minority leader.) The members who were removed or passed over in these non-seniority appointments were sometimes compensated by receiving better assignments, equal or better chairmanships, or positions of party leadership. However, a number of seniority violations went uncompensated—that is, a member eligible to become chairman or ranking minority member on the basis of seniority was effectively demoted and someone else with less seniority got the desired position; the senior member received no compensating assignment.

There was a high level of uncompensated violations of seniority in the House in the 1880s and early 1890s. This level declined rapidly. There was another burst of such violations in the years surrounding the drastic reduction of the power of the Speaker in 1910. By 1921 uncompensated violations had virtually disappeared. Only twelve have occurred between 1921 and 1986. The last four of these came after the House Democrats had changed their rules to allow for meaningful election: three cases in 1975 and one case in 1985. In each of these cases the incumbent chairman lost to a challenger because of a combination of age, unresponsiveness to the members of their committees, and ideological and policy disagreements with the majority of their party. In the 1985 case, Les Aspin (D–Wisc.), who was seventh-ranking

---

[16]Randall B. Ripley, *Power in the Senate* (New York: St. Martin's, 1969): 43–45.

Democrat on the Armed Services Committee, defeated the incumbent chairman, Melvin Price (D.–Ill.). Aspin himself was almost defeated (not by Price, however) in 1987 but hung on to the chairmanship after pledging to moderate his behavior in the committee that aggravated some of his Democratic colleagues. Since 1975 chairpersons of full committees tend to be more careful about behaving in ways acceptable to their members.

The seniority criterion is also dominant in the choice of subcommittee chairmen in the House. In the Eighty-sixth through Ninety-sixth Congresses (1959–1981), for example, just over five percent of the subcommittee chairmanship appointments involved uncompensated violations of seniority.[17] The changes in Democratic caucus rules before the Ninety-second Congress (1971–1973) did not alter that low percentage.

The rise of seniority as virtually the single criterion for advancement toward committee chairmanships is explained principally by the emergence of a large number of career legislators. Because committee work is an important factor in the creation of a congressional reputation, career legislators could not tolerate arbitrariness in this area. Therefore, they supported—or perhaps demanded—an automatic rule of advancement that would protect orderly career development.

## Development of Party and Leadership Structures

PRE-MODERN CONGRESS. In the pre-modern Congress there were few identifiable party leaders or institutions in either House. Members would occasionally rise to prominence in one House or the other, but this was usually a result of personal accomplishments, not of position holding. The one institutional position that did have a number of influential incumbents was the speakership of the House (the only congressional office specified in the Constitution), but a large number of Speakers were figureheads[18]—either serving as pawns for others or purposely apolitical. There were no majority leaders or minority lead-

[17]Thomas E. Cavanagh, "The Deinstitutionalization of the House," paper prepared for a Dirksen Center/Rayburn Library Conference on Understanding Congressional Leadership, June 10–11, 1980. See also Thomas R. Wolanin, "Committee Seniority and the Choice of House Subcommittee Chairmen: 80th–91st Congresses," *Journal of Politics* 36 (1974): 687–702; and Jack A. Goldstone, "Subcommittee Chairmanships in the House of Representatives," *American Political Science Review* 69 (1975): 970–71.

[18]See Mary P. Follett, *The Speaker of the House of Representatives* (New York: Longmans, Green & Co., 1896).

ers or whips—positions that evolved well after the Civil War, either late in the nineteenth or early in the twentieth centuries. The few individuals who were widely recognized in their time as leaders came and went quickly, were often very junior at the time of their rise to eminence, and often voluntarily left Congress for other pursuits. Pre–Civil War Speakers such as Henry Clay and a host of individuals long since forgotten serve as examples.

The speakership changed quite quickly in the 1870s from a short-term job for relatively junior members of the House who usually left the House to pursue other jobs to one representing the pinnacle of a House career. Table 2–2 summarizes relevant data on the 27 men who were Speakers between 1789 and 1875 and the 21 men who were Speakers between 1875 and 1987. After 1875 Speakers were suddenly much more experienced in the House than before 1875. They served as Speaker almost twice as long, even though they were older when they assumed office. After 1875 they rarely left the House or the speakership for any reason save death, retirement, or loss of the majority in the House by their party. Three-quarters of them were "career Speakers," that is, they finished their careers as Speaker. Prior to 1875 only two individuals met the criteria needed to qualify as "career Speakers."

With one exception before 1875 and one afterwards, individuals who left the speakership for other jobs took other public offices. But before 1875 these offices were not likely to be very important by our standards: a receiver-general of the Pennsylvania land office, a state treasurer of Virginia, and a minister to Russia were all men fresh from the speakership. Sixteen of the 24 men who left the speakership before 1875 for other public offices took lesser offices. Only eight went to a higher office (president, vice president, or U.S. senator). After 1875, however, four of the five non-career speakers went on to one of the higher offices. The only individual who left to engage in private business was Thomas B. Reed, in most ways a career Speaker, who quit when he

**Table 2–2.** The Professionalization of the Speakership

| | MEAN YEARS OF HOUSE SERVICE PRIOR TO BECOMING SPEAKER | MEAN YEARS OF SERVICE AS SPEAKER | NUMBER OF CAREER SPEAKERS | NUMBER OF NON-CAREER SPEAKERS |
|---|---|---|---|---|
| 1789–1875 (N=27) | 6.5 | 3.2 | 2 | 25 |
| 1875–1987 (N=20) | 20.1[a] | 5.6 | 15 | 5 |

[a]The N for this figure is 21 since the individual elected Speaker in 1987 is included.

became disgusted with the policies and personality of President William McKinley.[19]

It needs to be underscored that this change was not gradual. The year 1875, in fact, marks a clear watershed. The changes in the nature of American politics following the Civil War came rapidly and transformed the Speakership into one of the most reliably powerful political offices in the nation. Patterns of partisan competition, relatively weak presidents, and the new domestic agenda tied to rapid industrialization help explain this rapid change. In this century the Speaker has become a very senior figure. Fourteen individuals have been elected to the speakership since 1903. The average age of these fourteen is almost 64. Only two were less than 60 years old and three were 70 or older. These fourteen individuals had served an average of over 25 years in the House prior to election; only one individual had less than 20 years of service. Four had 28 years of service. Two had 30 or more years.

Partisan patterns of voting on roll calls on the floor appeared from time to time in the pre-modern House and Senate. But at other times there appeared to be little partisan voting.[20] On the whole, the party system was not well developed in the pre-modern House and Senate. Formal organization and consistent party leadership were missing until late in the nineteenth century. One student of the early Congress offers an accurate description of congressional parties in the era just before Jackson became president:

> If the party did not meet, neither did it attain, but momentarily, the status of an organized group in the congressional community. What degree of

[19]See Polsby, "Institutionalization." Some of the data in Table 2–2 are adapted from that source.
[20]There is disagreement in the scanty historical literature on the pre-modern Congress on how much party unity there was in contrast to unity "caused" by other factors, such as region or rooming together in Washington. There is agreement, however, that little is known about how unity that does appear to be related to party was generated. It seems to have been at least partially spontaneous, not the result of any presidential leadership or party leadership or party organization, all of which were missing all or most of the time.

For empirically based discussions of these questions in different periods of the pre-modern Congress see Thomas B. Alexander, *Sectional Stress and Party Strength* (Nashville: Vanderbilt University Press, 1967); Rudolph M. Bell, *Party and Faction in American Politics: The House of Representatives, 1789–1801* (Westport, Conn.: Greenwood Press, 1973); Allan G. Bogue and Mark Paul Marlaire, "Of Mess and Men: The Boardinghouse and Congressional Voting, 1821–1842," *American Journal of Political Science* 19 (1975): 207–30; John F. Hoadley, "The Emergence of Political Parties in Congress, 1789–1803," *American Political Science Review* 74 (1980): 757–79; David J. Russo, "The Major Political Issues of the Jacksonian Period and the Development of Party Loyalty in Congress, 1830–1840," *Transactions of the American Philosophical Society* 62 (1972): part 5; Joel H. Silbey, *The Shrine of Party* (Pittsburgh: University of Pittsburgh Press, 1967); and Young, *Washington Community.*

formal organization the party did achieve was only for the brief duration of its convocation as a nominating caucus [for President]. . . . In the periods intervening between caucuses the party had no officers, even of figurehead importance, for the guidance or management of legislative processes. Party members elected no leaders, designated no functionaries to speak on their behalf or to carry out any legislative task assignments. The party had no whips, no seniority leaders. There were no Committees on Committees, no Steering Committees, no Policy Committees: none of the organizational apparatus that marks the twentieth-century congressional parties as going enterprises.[21]

The same description, with minor alterations, could serve for any period in the pre-modern Congress.

Party membership was a loose concept. It did not bind self-identified members to any particular behavior. There was little party cohesion even in voting for Speaker.[22] Party labels changed. Before the Civil War the Whigs, National Republicans, Democratic Republicans, and Federalists came and went as major parties. In some Congresses there were no readily identifiable parties at all but merely pro-administration and anti-administration groups of members. In the period between 1830 and 1870, there were often sizable numbers of minority (third-party) party members in Congress. After the Civil War the two-party system crystallized both nationally and congressionally.

MODERN CONGRESS. In the modern Congress, parties emerged as much more structured parts of the congressional apparatus, although their policy importance has fluctuated.[23] In the period between the Civil War and the present, both parties in both houses have identified formal leaders and established a variety of party committees. The sequence varied in the two houses, however. Since 1789 the Speaker of the House had been at least a nominal leader of the majority party; he became consistently important after 1869 (with the single major exception of 1919–1925, when internal politics in the House Republican

---

[21]Young, *Washington Community,* 126–27.

[22]See Appendix C of Follett, *The Speaker of the House of Representatives.* See also Gerald R. Lientz, "House Speaker Elections and Congressional Parties, 1789–1860," *Capitol Studies* 6 (1978): 63–89.

[23]For studies, based on roll-call votes, that show a powerful party leadership in the House achieving a high degree of unity, and therefore a high degree of party impact on policy, see David W. Brady, *Congressional Voting in a Partisan Era* (Lawrence, Kans.: The University Press of Kansas, 1973); and David W. Brady and Phillip Althoff, "Party Voting in the U.S. House of Representatives, 1890–1910: Elements of a Responsible Party System," *Journal of Politics* 36 (1974): 753–75.

party produced a Speaker explicitly elected because he agreed to be a figurehead). A formal minority leader emerged in the early 1880s and has been a consistently important figure in his party. In terms of status and function he has been parallel to the Speaker for his own party.[24]

In the period between 1897 and 1911 both parties in the House added additional central leadership positions as partisan conflict became more intense and the maintenance of party unity more difficult. Both the Speaker and the minority leader needed assistance. The majority leader became a formal and important leader in 1899 and has been generally influential in both parties since then. Both parties appointed their first whips in the last few years of the nineteenth century. Men in these positions were sporadically active until the 1930s. In the early 1930s both parties developed large whip organizations that have helped to make most chief whips more important figures. These organizations are heavily involved in the distribution and collection of information for the central leaders and in securing the most favorable attendance on the floor from a partisan standpoint. Their emergence in the 1930s was related to the vast increase in the congressional agenda as the New Deal responded to the Depression. (The name "whip" itself comes from the British Parliament and is derived from a fox-hunting term: the "Whipper-in" of the hounds.)

Both parties created important party committees after 1910–11, when the speakership was substantially reduced in terms of potential influence. Chairpersons of some of these committees have occasionally been prominent figures in the party.

In the Senate the development was reversed and the timing changed. The party committees and organizations emerged in both parties after the Civil War and became important in the decade between 1885 and 1895. No easily identifiable formal central leadership positions were created until the period between 1911 and 1915, although powerful leaders began to emerge after 1885.

The difference in the timing of Senate and House developments is largely explained by the development of the "career senator" several

---

[24]There are, inevitably, some ambiguities in dating developments that evolved and did not just happen overnight. In some cases the selection of a single date to mark the "beginning" of a given office is necessarily arbitrary and plausible arguments can be made for alternative dates. For example, I use the year 1899 as the *unambiguous* beginning of the modern majority leadership in the House. But either the Ways and Means chairman or the Appropriations chairman tended to play that role from the Civil War until 1899. Similarly, an argument can be made that the House Minority Leadership began during the Civil War. Again, I think the relatively *unambiguous* beginning of the modern position can be dated in 1883. For a careful study arguing the plausibility of some different dating see Garrison Nelson, "Leadership Position-Holding in the United States House of Representatives," *Capitol Studies* 4 (1976): 11–36.

decades before the development of the "career representative." The professionalization of the Senate career occurred simultaneously with the centralization of power, whereas in the House the centralization of power preceded career professionalization. Thus, in the Senate there was a reluctance on the part of senators to trust single powerful leaders because their decisions could be so important (and so potentially harmful) to individual senators who wanted to stay in the Senate for the rest of their political lives. Seniority hardened at the time in the Senate in order to offer some protection to career senators. Party committees and organizations were thought to be less threatening than single leaders and they were first entrusted with leadership functions. Only after the Senate went through a period of leaderlessness in the early years of the twentieth century were senators willing to admit the need for strong single leaders.

In the House, power was centralized in the hands of the Speaker and minority leader before most members aspired to House careers. When that development occurred, the members of the House demanded restrictions on the central leaders (symbolized by the revolt against Speaker Cannon in 1910), and seniority and party committees were established as protections for the career-oriented House members.

Table 2–3 summarizes the chronology of the two separate developmental histories.

The majority leader in the Senate emerged as a formal and readily identifiable party leader in both parties in the period between 1911 and 1915. The minority leader emerged at the same time. After some dominant personalities left the Senate in the first few years of the twentieth century, the Senate experienced a period during which arriving at decisions had become very difficult. It also had experienced an aggressive president in the person of Theodore Roosevelt. Both party leaders have remained influential in the affairs of their respective parties since then. The majority and minority whips were created in the same

**Table 2–3.** Party Development and Related Events in House and Senate

| EVENT | HOUSE | SENATE |
|---|---|---|
| Centralization of power | 1875–95 | 1885–95 |
| Professionalization of career | 1890–1910 | 1875–95 |
| Hardening of seniority as criterion for advancement on committees | 1911–25 | 1885–95 |
| Creation of central leadership positions | 1897–1900 | 1911–15 |
| Creation of party committees and organizations | 1919–present | 1885–95 |

period to aid the floor leaders, but these individuals have not been major figures in their parties until the last several decades. From 1935 to 1944, in fact, the Republicans did not bother to fill the position because they were such a small minority in the Senate.

Important party committees—the equivalents of policy committees and committees on committees—developed in both parties during the 1870s and were the vehicles used to centralize power in both parties in the Senate in the 1880s and 1890s by men who did not bear formal leadership titles but who were highly influential and effective leaders.

Table 2–4 summarizes the establishment of various formal leadership positions and party committees on a continuing basis in both houses. The activities of these leaders and committees in the modern House and Senate will be discussed in Chapter 6.

By the beginning of the twentieth century, parties were an obvious, influential, and permanent feature of life in Congress. The development of strong parties in the electorate following the Civil War was reflected in Congress. When the national parties weakened again in the twentieth century, the congressional parties also weakened. However, given the vital procedural role of the leaders in providing order for a busy legislature, the pre-modern situation was not recreated.

Since the late nineteenth century, members have been very clear about which party they belonged to and the identity of their formal

**Table 2–4.** The Establishment of Formal Party Leadership Positions and Committees in Congress

| | YEAR OF CREATION ON A CONTINUING BASIS | |
|---|---|---|
| | REPUBLICANS | DEMOCRATS |
| *House*[a] | | |
| Majority Leader | 1899 | 1911 |
| Minority Leader | 1883 | 1889 |
| Whip | 1897 | 1900[b] |
| Policy Committee | 1919 | 1933 |
| Committee on Committees | 1917 | 1911 |
| *Senate* | | |
| Floor Leader (Majority Leader and Minority Leader) | 1913 | 1911 |
| Whip | 1915 | 1913 |
| Policy Committee | 1874 | 1879 |
| Committee on Committees | 1865 | 1877 |

[a]Positions in addition to the Speakership.
[b]The identity of the Democratic Whip between 1908–13 and 1915–21 is not clear, however, and the position itself may have disappeared temporarily.

party leaders. Third parties have almost vanished. Speakers have been elected by a straight party vote. There were still some major centrifugal forces in both houses—particularly the orientation of members to serving constituency interests before party interests when the two were perceived to clash—but well-organized parties became firmly enough entrenched to counteract such forces at least some of the time.

Much of the debate over "reform" in Congress centers around the role of parties and party leadership. Parties clearly have the apparatus to centralize much of the policy-making in the Senate and particularly in the House; whether their leaders have the will or the opportunity to develop such centralization as a prelude to policy integration is always an open and important question.

## SUMMARY

The above analysis points to one conclusion: on all of the criteria discussed, the modern Congress has become both professional and stable. The professionalism has allowed Congress to cope with its large workload and also to face the fact of a powerful executive branch in such a way as to keep a considerable amount of legislative influence. The stability has permitted the processing of the workload in reasonably good and timely order.

On the other hand, stability also has its costs. It may be deemed necessary by a group of career-oriented professionals—such as most senators and representatives—but it may also lead to seemingly permanent alliances on major questions of public policy between the professionals in Congress and the professionals in the executive branch and in the interest groups. These alliances may result in good policy or bad policy, in programs that work or in programs that fail. But, in any event, such alliances are not likely to view dramatic changes in policy as necessary or useful. Such changes might threaten the existence of the alliances themselves and thus threaten the security of the members of those alliances, including the congressional members. Some argue this is a wise way to make public policy—with any changes widely agreed on and only relatively minor in scope. Others argue that such excessive stability and concern with preserving the status quo inhibits the government's ability to meet pressing national problems.

# 3

# Congressional Elections

Congressional elections usually contribute in a major way to the fragmentation that typifies Congress. First, they serve to keep Congress permeable *and* concerned with representation. Permeability and attention to representation come both in the form of challengers ousting incumbents in elections and in the responsiveness of members to communications from at least some of their constitutents.

Second, the character of the American party system, when coupled with elections for all seats in both houses, pushes in the direction of fragmentation through providing little stress on agreement on national issues among members professing the same party identification. The stress instead tends to be on local issues. One of the leading students of American political parties, the late V.O. Key, makes several observations underscoring this point:

> Observation of the nomination of candidates for the House and Senate brings forcibly to attention at least two peculiar characteristics of the

American party system. First is the odd mixture of centralization and decentralization in the organization of American parties. . . .

In the national conventions a consensus is sought among the divergent interests within the party; in the nominations for House and Senate those same interests are free to impose their special policy coloration on the party's local candidates. The differences compromised in the national convention are perpetuated, even accentuated, in the party's congressional slate.

A focus on nominations also brings to the fore another feature of the American system, namely, the fact that much of our politics is intraparty, not interparty, politics. . . .

Despite the capacity of the party system to confront the nation's electorate with great alternatives, the independence of the choice of executive and legislature assures that elections will produce a mixed mandate. To some extent the affairs of senatorial politics in each state and of congressional politics in each district are governed, not by the great considerations of national politics, but by questions peculiar to the locality. . . .

This mixture of nationalism and parochialism in elections contains the roots of the conflicting tendencies of amalgamation and cleavage in executive-congressional relations. . . .

The fundamental characteristics of the American parties—their diversity of composition, their dominant policy orientations, their inner contradictions—manifest themselves in bold relief in the membership of the party groups in the House and Senate.[1]

The nature of elections to the House and Senate can be summarized another way: *they are local events with national consequences and (sometimes) are influenced by national events.*[2] Thomas P. ("Tip") O'Neill, who retired in 1986 after 34 years in the House, the last 10 as Speaker, puts this proposition more succinctly: "All politics is local." Local candidates by and large are responsible for their own electoral fates and yet, when they win, they are automatically national policy actors. But the ties between electoral success and the directions of policy preference, although present, are tenuous, general in nature, and shifting.

The point here is not that national forces are unable to influence congressional elections, but rather that there are many forces, often

[1] V. O. Key, Jr., *Politics, Parties, and Pressure Groups,* 5th ed. (New York: Crowell, 1964): 434–35, 545–46, 665.
[2] See Thomas E. Mann, *Unsafe at Any Margin: Interpreting Congressional Elections* (Washington, D.C.: American Enterprise Institute, 1978); and Thomas E. Mann, "Elections and Change in Congress," in Thomas E. Mann and Norman J. Ornstein (eds.), *The New Congress* (Washington, D.C.: American Enterprise Institute, 1981): 32–54.

vaguely and sporadically influential, which are mediated through local events and personalities.[3] The impact of short-term party evaluations, economic conditions, and policy preferences of voters[4] as well as party organizations at all territorial levels[5] varies by contest.

In many ways members of Congress are always running for re-election. As one House member put it: "You should say 'perennial' election rather than 'biennial.' It is with us every day."[6] Members perceive virtually everything they do as affecting re-election, and much of their behavior is shaped by that perception. "The electoral connection" is central in explaining what goes on inside Congress.[7] That fact is perhaps ironic when one considers that many potential or actual voters do not share the overriding interest in elections exhibited by members. Many individuals will not vote. Of those who do vote a large proportion will have little precise knowledge about the behavior of their senators or representatives. Many will not even recognize their names. Fewer still will know anything about the challengers.

There are, however, some voters in every district and state who do pay attention to the behavior of their representatives and senators. Members try to be particularly responsive to these individuals and to groups in which they are active.

Elections provide the main occasion of authoritative contact between constituents and members. Constituents control the ultimate sanction or reward for a member or an aspiring member through the electoral process. This fact motivates much of the contact that occurs between members and constituents between elections.

Elections are also the mechanism linking weak national political

[3]See Gary C. Jacobson, *The Politics of Congressional Elections,* 2nd ed. (Boston: Little, Brown, 1987): Chapter 5; and Gary C. Jacobson, "National Forces in Congressional Elections," unpublished paper prepared for the annual meeting of the American Political Science Association, August 28–31, 1986.

[4]On these influences see, for example, Alan I. Abramowitz, Albert D. Cover, and Helmut Norpoth, "The President's Party in Midterm Elections: Going from Bad to Worse," *American Journal of Political Science* 30 (1986): 562–76; Amihai Glazer and Marc Robbins, "Congressional Responsiveness to Constituency Change," *American Journal of Political Science* 29 (1985): 259–73; John R. Owens, "Economic Influences on Elections to the U.S. Congress," *Legislative Studies Quarterly* 9 (1984): 123–50; Lynda W. Powell, "Issue Representation in Congress," *Journal of Politics* 44 (1982): 658–78; and Gerald C. Wright, Jr. and Michael B. Berkman, "Candidates and Policy in United States Senate Elections," *American Political Science Review* 80 (1986): 567–88.

[5]Paul S. Herrnson, "Do Parties Make a Difference? The Role of Party Organizations in Congressional Elections," *Journal of Politics* 48 (1986): 589–615.

[6]Quoted in Charles L. Clapp, *The Congressman: His Work as He Sees It* (Washington, D.C.: Brookings, 1963): 330.

[7]See David R. Mayhew, *Congress: The Electoral Connection* (New Haven: Yale University Press, 1974).

parties, constituency parties that are usually weak organizationally, and congressional parties that have considerable influence over the agenda and policy results produced by Congress.

Congressional elections will be analyzed here by considering the voters, electoral districts, candidates and campaigns, election results, and the implications of elections for congressional behavior.

## THE VOTERS

From its beginning, the House of Representatives was conceived to be a popular body—representing "the people" and chosen by them. The Senate did not formally become a popular body until the ratification of the seventeenth amendment to the Constitution in 1913. In practice, however, the Senate was well on its way to becoming a popular body before 1913.[8]

The opportunity for direct popular impact on both the House and Senate is present, but it is an opportunity that is never fully exercised by the electorate. Turnout for elections of representatives has never reached 60 percent and often is much less. For all senatorial elections aggregated turnout is rarely more than 60 percent and is usually much lower. Turnout has gone steadily down for all national elections since the early 1960s. The 1986 turnout for House elections was the lowest since 1942 for a non-presidential year. If 1942 is eliminated as unusual because of the absence of millions of people in military service, 1986 was the lowest off-year turnout for House elections since 1930. The 1984 turnout for House elections was the lowest since 1924 in a presidential year. In 1984 almost 48 percent of eligible voters voted in contests for the House. Just over 33 percent voted in 1986.

---

[8]This was true for two basic reasons: (1) state legislatures had only infrequently tried to bind their senators' voting and policy positions in the Senate, a practice that virtually disappeared after the Civil War, and (2) several events occurred that introduced popular control, albeit indirectly, prior to adoption of the seventeenth amendment. These included the active involvement of senatorial candidates in the campaigns for state legislatures (so that voting by the populace for state legislators was in effect a referendum on U.S. senatorial candidates). The development of the primary election system after 1888 also offered popular control. Finally, shortly before the seventeenth amendment was adopted, a system was invented and used in Oregon that provided for direct popular vote on senatorial candidates in connection with the regular election, even though formal electoral power remained in the state legislature.

On all of these developments and their impact see William H. Riker, "The Senate and American Federalism," *American Political Science Review* 49 (1955): 452–69.

Low turnout has been interpreted in several different ways. Some suggest that it indicates satisfaction with the governmental system. Others argue that it is a sign of alienation from the system, that people are cynical and do not believe that their vote will make any difference. Still others argue that it is merely a sign of apathy, that a large number of people just do not much care about the political system and are neither supportive nor hostile.[9]

Figure 3–1 illustrates the relationship between turnout for presidential elections and turnout for congressional elections for the years 1932–86. In presidential election years, almost as many people voted for representative as for president; the average dropoff between presidential voting and voting for representatives was about 4 percent for this period. In 1984 it was just over five percent. In years when there was no presidential election to act as a stimulant to bring voters to the polls, the turnout rate for congressional elections was considerably lower. The average dropoff was about 13 percent for the period between 1932 and 1986. That is, of every 100 eligible voters, 13 who voted for a representative in a presidential year did not vote for that office two years later in the off-year election.

One persistent factor related to the different levels of turnout is the public's awareness of different elections. Presidential elections have a much higher visibility than congressional elections. Other factors affecting turnout include the level of competition in the contests, the voter's sense of political efficacy, sense of duty, strength of partisan preference, and interest in the campaign.[10]

Why do voters make the individual choices for members of the House and Senate that they do? The best evidence is that most vote on the basis of general party identification or simply for the incumbent.[11] The incumbency "cue" for voting is much more potent for House elections than for Senate elections.[12] Issues play a distinctly minor role in most individual voting decisions in elections for the

[9]On some of these issues see E. E. Schattschneider, *The Semi-Sovereign People* (New York: Holt, Rinehart, and Winston, 1960).

[10]Angus Campbell, Philip E. Converse, Warren E. Miller, and Donald E. Stokes, *The American Voter* (New York: Wiley, 1964).

[11]Political scientists in the U.S. have produced a considerable and rapidly growing literature on congressional elections. For two recent overviews and good bibliographies see Barbara Hinckley, *Congressional Elections* (Washington, D.C.: Congressional Quarterly Press, 1981); and Gary C. Jacobson, *The Politics of Congressional Elections.*

[12]See Alan I. Abramowitz, "A Comparison of Voting for U.S. Senator and Representative in 1978," *American Political Science Review* 74 (1980): 633–40; and Thomas E. Mann and Raymond E. Wolfinger, "Candidates and Parties in Congressional Elections," *American Political Science Review* 74 (1980): 617–32.

**Figure 3–1.** Participation in Elections for President and U.S. Representative, 1932–1986

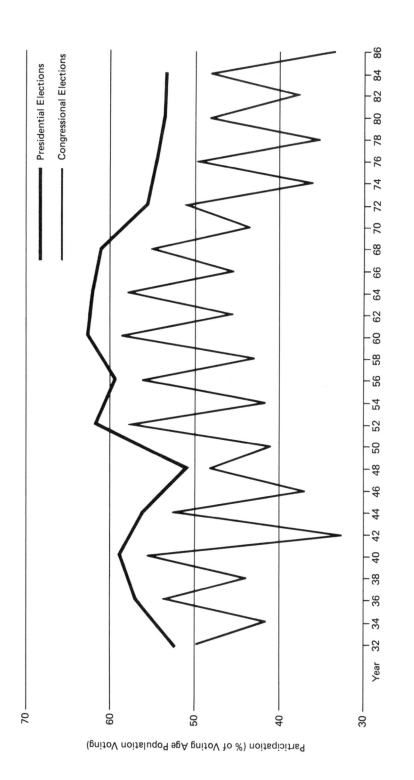

Participation (% of Voting Age Population Voting)

- Presidential Elections
- Congressional Elections

70

60

50

40

30

Year   32   34   36   38   40   42   44   46   48   50   52   54   56   58   60   62   64   66   68   70   72   74   76   78   80   82   84   86

SOURCE: Norman J. Ornstein and others, *Vital Statistics on Congress, 1984–1985 Edition* (Washington: American Enterprise Institute, 1984): 40 through 1982. *Statistical Abstract of the United States, 1986:* 255 for 1984. *Congressional Quarterly* for 1986.

House and Senate.[13] The relatively issue-free content of voting choices for Congress is summarized well by two leading scholars of American elections:

> In the congressional election . . . the country votes overwhelmingly for party symbols, but the symbols have limited meaning in terms of legislative policy. . . . The electorate sees very little altogether of what goes on in the national legislature. Few judgments of legislative performance are associated with the parties, and much of the public is unaware even of which party has control of Congress.
>
> What the public's response to the parties lacks in programmatic support is not made up by its response to local congressional candidates. Although perceptions of individual candidates account for most of the votes cast by partisans against their parties, these perceptions are almost untouched by information about the policy stands of the men contesting the House seat. The increment of strength that some candidates, especially incumbents, acquire by being known to their constituents is almost entirely free of policy content.[14]

This absence of policy content in congressional elections in the mass sense enables members to exercise relatively independent judgment in weighing personal feelings about policy issues against the perceived needs or claims of constituencies. Members do not need to feel terribly constrained to vote exactly as they think their districts would prefer, although some feel more independent than others. And there are some individual votes on issues about which sizable portions of some constituencies care a great deal. Examples in recent years include school busing, gun control, abortion, control of nuclear weapons or nuclear power, and disposal of toxic waste.

The absence of policy content in mass voting also contributes to the incumbent members' chances for re-election. Basically, members are not judged at election time on the basis of their policy stands or performance. They are well aware that a very large part of the elector-

[13]This assertion is supported by most of the literature. For dissenting views see Gerald C. Wright, Jr., "Candidates' Policy Positions and Voting in U.S. Congressional Elections," *Legislative Studies Quarterly* 3 (1978): 445–64; John C. McAdams and John R. Johannes, "The 1980 House Elections: Re-examining Some Theories in a Republican Year," *Journal of Politics* 45 (1983): 143–61; and Wright and Berkman, "Candidates and Policy in United States Senate Elections."
[14]Donald E. Stokes and Warren E. Miller, "Party Government and the Saliency of Congress," in Angus Campbell and others, *Elections and the Political Order* (New York: Wiley, 1966): 209–10.

ate in their districts does not know their policy stands and, even if it did, it would not vote solely on that basis.[15]

## THE ELECTORAL DISTRICTS

The apportionment of Senate seats and the provision of constituencies for senators present no problem: each state gets two senators and all senators represent entire states. House seats, however, are more difficult to create. First, the number of seats must be *apportioned* among the fifty states on the basis of population. Then, within each state that has more than one representative, geographic areas, called districts, must be created. This distribution of seats within a state, called *districting,* is also done on the basis of population. Apportionment is done by Congress itself (now using a virtually automatic formula based on the census figures that are collected every ten years). Districting is done by state governments. In recent years, federal courts have also become heavily involved in the redistricting process.

Apportionment can have some impact on the content of congressional decisions as regional strength changes. Districting within states is even more important, however, as skillful manipulation of district lines can alter the party and ideological complexion of both individual seats and entire state delegations. For example, in the redistricting in California that followed the 1980 census, Democrats carefully crafted a plan that increased their own seats from 22 to 27 and reduced the Republicans from 21 to 18. In addition, the Democratic seats are virtually all safe for that party.

### Reapportionment

Reapportionment takes place every tenth year immediately after the census. This practice began following the 1790 census, and has occurred regularly with the exception of 1920. Different specific methods of translating population figures into House seats have been used. The size of the House grew rapidly from 1790 until 1830 (increasing from 65 to 242 members). For the next several decades the size of the House

---

[15]See Clapp, *The Congressman,* 377, for a discussion of representatives' attitudes in 1959. See also Charles O. Jones, "The Role of the Campaign in Congressional Politics," in M. Kent Jennings and L. Harmon Zeigler (eds.), *The Electoral Process* (Englewood Cliffs, N.J.: Prentice-Hall, 1966).

was stable. Growth resumed following the 1870 census until the number of seats reached the present 435 in 1913, after the 1910 census.

The size of the House was not fixed permanently at 435 by Congress until 1929, because no agreement on an alternative number could be reached before that time. Then, as now, reapportionment touched fundamental political nerves. Prior to the 1920 census, all states had benefited from reapportionments by receiving an increased number of seats in the House. But following that census (and the population shifts following World War I) many states were faced with a loss of seats for the first time. The result was a stalemating of reapportionment efforts until 1929 when President Hoover convened a special session of Congress and insisted on apportionment legislation. By that time it was evident that population distributions were not going to return to prewar patterns, and new urban areas were clamoring for greater representation; Congress relented, fixing permanently the number of seats at 435, and requiring that these seats be distributed among the states on the basis of population after each census. With the single exception of a temporary increase to 437 from 1959 to 1963 to accommodate the inclusion of Alaska and Hawaii in the Union, there have been no changes in the size of the House since 1913. Attempts to increase its size, usually initiated by states faced with the loss of seats because of reapportionment, have met with failure. Following the 1980 census no such attempts were even made.

## Redistricting

The districting of states has even more explosive political potential than reapportionment, since the way in which district lines are drawn define constituencies and hence affect chances of election success or failure. It is not uncommon to see a state's districts redrawn after the censuses to the explicit benefit of the party in the majority in the state legislature. Gerrymandering (named after Elbridge Gerry, a governor of Massachusetts in the early nineteenth century) is the name given to the manipulation of the shape of a district to benefit a specific party or candidate. It would be too idealistic to expect state legislators to strive for impartiality and resist the political influences that bear on them as they grapple with redistricting. Parties want to maximize the number of their seats in Congress. Incumbent representatives want to be assured of re-election through the creation of "safe" districts. Potential candidates want to create districts for themselves in which they can win. Even though gerrymandering does not always produce the results desired by the majority party in the state legislature, politicians are committed to sustaining its practice.[16]

Until the 1960s state legislatures were free to manipulate district lines without regard to the distribution of population within a state, with the result that a single district could have as many as four times the number of people as another district in the same state. This practice was challenged in a 1946 court suit in Illinois.[17] When the case reached the Supreme Court, however, the majority declined to intervene, claiming that it was inappropriate for the Court to enter the "political thicket."

In a 1962 apportionment case[18] the Court reached an opposite conclusion: the majority ruled that legislative apportionment *was* a justiciable issue, and that if a violation of rights was involved then a judicial remedy was appropriate. Applying the equal protection of the laws clause of the fourteenth amendment, the Court ruled that districts for state legislatures must be equal in population. This decision led to a broader decision in 1964, *Wesberry* v. *Sanders,*[19] in which a six to three majority ruled that the Constitution required that U.S. House districts created by state legislatures must be equal in population. The Court endorsed the notion of "one man, one vote."

The *Wesberry* case did not address the question of how equal the population of districts had to be in order to satisfy the requirements of the majority opinion. Federal courts involved in various redistricting suits following the *Wesberry* decision applied a variety of standards in determining what equality of size meant in practice. In 1969 the Supreme Court gave its own meaning to equality in the case of *Kirkpatrick* v. *Preisler.*[20] By a six to three majority the Court held that equality meant absolute equality. Justice William Brennan, writing for the majority, said "Equal representation for equal numbers of people is a principle designed to prevent debasement of voting power and diminution of access to elected Representatives. Toleration of even small deviations detracts from these purposes."[21] In a 1983 case[22] the Court applied the principle of numerical equality stringently and

---

[16]Richard Born, "Partisan Intentions and Election Day Realities in the Congressional Redistricting Process," *American Political Science Review* 79 (1985): 305–33.
[17]*Colegrove* v. *Green* (328 U.S. 549).
[18]*Baker* v. *Carr* (369 U.S. 186).
[19]*Wesberry* v. *Sanders* (376 U.S. 1).
[20]*Kirkpatrick* v. *Preisler* (394 U.S. 526).
[21]*Kirkpatrick* v. *Preisler* (394 U.S. 531).
[22]*Karcher* v. *Daggett* (462 U.S. 725).

disallowed a New Jersey redistricting plan in which the variation in population between the largest district and the smallest district was less than seven-tenths of one percent.

In 1986 the Court declared gerrymandering for partisan advantage unconstitutional.[23] But the Court did not spell out clear standards for applying this decision. What is important is that the Court reversed a long-standing tradition of avoiding this particular "political question."

Court action on redistricting may make good theoretical sense in a representative democracy, but there is no evidence that all of this judicial activity has altered the nature of the membership or decisions of Congress. Members of the House still come from fairly small districts, many of which are relatively homogeneous.

## CANDIDATES AND CAMPAIGNS

People run for seats in Congress for many different reasons. In general, they are attracted by the chance to influence public policy as well as the opportunity to achieve the high personal status that public office affords. Once in Congress most of them want to stay.[24] Ambition to win is the central factor in the self-selection of potential candidates. It is tempered by calculations about the chances of winning.

### Nominations

Virtually all nominations for the House and Senate are made in primary elections held within the parties in the individual states and districts. In a few districts and states the primaries merely serve to ratify the choice of the dominant political organization, but most

[23] *Davis* v. *Bandemer* (106 S.Ct. 2797).
[24] On various aspects of the decision to run, the decision to retire, and ambition for a congressional career see Jeff Fishel, *Party and Opposition* (New York: McKay, 1973); John R. Hibbing, "Voluntary Retirement from the U.S. House of Representatives: Who Quits?" *American Journal of Political Science* 26 (1982): 467–84; Hibbing, "Voluntary Retirements from the House in the Twentieth Century," *Journal of Politics* 44 (1982): 1020–34; Hibbing, "Ambition in the House: Behavioral Consequences of Higher Office Goals among U.S. Representatives," *American Journal of Political Science* 30 (1986): 651–65; Thomas A. Kazee, "The Decision to Run for the U.S. Congress: Challenger Attitudes in the 1970s," *Legislative Studies Quarterly* 5 (1980): 79–100; Louis Sandy Maisel, *From Obscurity to Oblivion*, rev. ed. (Knoxville: University of Tennessee Press, 1986); and Donald R. Matthews, "Legislative Recruitment and Legislative Careers," in Gerhard Loewenberg, Samuel C. Patterson, and Malcolm E. Jewell (eds.), *Handbook of Legislative Research* (Cambridge, Mass.: Harvard University Press, 1985): 17–55.

primaries have at least the potential for being genuinely competitive. Likewise, in most districts and states the "party organization" is relatively unimportant in selecting nominees. As one commentator has put it, "Nominations are . . . generally on a do-it-yourself basis."[25] The primaries that actually attract competition are, understandably, in states and districts where the nominee of the party has a reasonably good chance of winning.

Incumbents have very important advantages in primaries. These advantages are not iron-clad guarantees of success, however; some incumbents are defeated each year in primaries. In the 21 elections from 1946 through 1986 two percent of all House candidates seeking re-election succumbed in a primary. During the same period of time about six percent of all Senators seeking re-election lost in a party primary.

There is some evidence that an incumbent senator who survives a competitive primary is more likely to lose the following general election than a senator who does not have such a primary. The negative effect of divisive primaries on House incumbents in the general election is quite small.[26] In some districts and states the primary is, in effect, the most important election because the general election is virtually always won by the candidate of the same party.

The primary system of nominating candidates for Congress underscores the decentralized nature of American politics. National party leaders rarely play any part in seeking or supporting candidates for House and Senate seats. The men and women who run emerge in a variety of ways, but not because of the labors of national figures.[27]

## General Election Campaigns

A candidate for Congress faces one central problem: how to make herself or himself known and preferred over the opponent. solving this

[25]H. Douglas Price, "The Electoral Arena," in David B. Truman (ed.), *The Congress and America's Future* (Englewood Cliffs, N.J.: Prentice-Hall, 1965): 41.
[26]On the Senate see Robert A. Bernstein, "Divisive Primaries Do Hurt: U.S. Senate Races, 1956–1972," *American Political Science Review* 71 (1977): 540–45. On the House see Richard Born, "The Influence of House Primary Election Divisiveness on General Election Margins, 1962–76," *Journal of Politics* 43 (1981): 640–61.
[27]For a good discussion contrasting the situation in the United States with the centralized nature of nominations for seats in the House of Commons in the United Kingdom see Mayhew, *Congress: The Electoral Connection,* 19–27. In the late 1970s and early 1980s national Republican committees did begin to play a small role in nominations. See Mann, "Elections and Change in Congress," 51.

problem is predicated on solving another major problem: the acquisition of sufficient finances to achieve the goal. Incumbents have a natural advantage in solving the first problem and this helps, to some extent, reduce the magnitude of the second problem. Those who challenge incumbents have a much more difficult time in the areas of both recognition and money.

The high rate of success among incumbents (which will be examined later in the chapter) can be explained in both personal terms and in terms of the electorate. At the personal level the incumbent is known to a much larger proportion of his or her constituents than the opponent because of media coverage received while in office. An incumbent receives a salary while campaigning, can use congressional staff to help in the campaign, can use franking (free mailing) privileges to mail materials to constituents that help establish both name recognition and a favorable image, can use that same privilege to conduct opinion polls of constituents, and has already established links to contributors and campaign workers who have helped in the past and for whom he or she has provided favors while in office.

The high rate of incumbents' electoral success can also be explained by the relatively stable party identification of the voters. Since voting for Congress tends to be largely on the basis of party labels, most districts elect members to Congress who share the most popular label. Party identification and voting stability are closely linked in the case of congressional elections. (They are much less closely tied in the case of presidential elections, in which there is room for the large-scale intervention of other factors such as personality.) Defections from party that do occur usually work to the advantage of the incumbent.

Like nominations, election campaigns are run largely on a do-it-yourself basis. Most members of the House and Senate do not receive extensive aid (financial or otherwise) from their political parties, even though those political parties have various state organizations, national committees, and congressional campaign committees that are in business partially to provide such aid.

## Campaign Finance

The cost of campaigns for House and Senate seats is, in the aggregate, enormous. In 1983–84, for example, total spending for all Senate and House races totalled over $400 million. About $177 million of this was spent in House races, a mean expenditure of over $215,000 for every individual campaign by both winners and losers. The remainder was spent in Senate campaigns, a mean expenditure of about $3 million. Some races were incredibly expensive. The Jesse Helms vs. James Hunt contest for a Senate seat from North Carolina in 1984 cost over $21 million. In 1985–86 total spending for all House and Senate races came to more than $450 million. In both parties, individual contributions accounted for over half of the money available (52 percent in the case of the Democrats and 62 percent in the case of the Republicans). Political Action Committees (PACs) accounted for about 25 to 30 percent of the funds for both parties. These committees, first created in 1943, grew rapidly in the 1970s and the 1980s, both in number and in the amount of money they raised. They are the political arms of interest groups. Their importance in campaign finance raises the question of whether members of the House and Senate become their "captives" on some specific issues.[28]

Federal statutory limits on spending are virtually non-existent. The limits that exist are on direct contributions to candidates by individuals, political parties, and PACs. However, both parties and PACs are allowed to give a great deal more for general campaign purposes: providing services such as polling, ads, or TV time to candidates in the case of parties, ("coordinated spending"), and running general ideological campaigns or campaigns without direct involvement of candidates in the case of PACs ("independent spending").

In the last several elections for House and Senate, between two-thirds and three-fourths of the funds spent in campaigns have come from individual donations, including loans from the candidate to his or her own campaign. Roughly 20 to 30 percent has come from PAC contributions, with House candidates more dependent on these than Senate candidates. Between 6 and 10 percent of total expenditures have come from party contributions, with a somewhat higher percentage in the case of Senate campaigns.

In general, incumbents get more money than challengers. Republican party committees can often raise ten times as much money as Democratic party committees. About a third of all PAC money comes from corporate PACs, another quarter comes from labor PACs, and another quarter comes from trade PACs. Because of the long period of Democratic control of the House and the advantages of incumbency

---

[28]On PACs see Larry J. Sabato, *PAC Power: Inside the World of Political Action Committees* (New York: Norton, 1984).

# THE ATTACK ON PACS: IT'S A SMOKE SCREEN THAT OBSCURES THE REAL CORRUPTION

BY LARRY SABATO

Sens. Robert Byrd and David Boren, the new champions of reform in campaign financing, are absolutely right to be concerned about rising campaign costs, about a system that is weighted heavily against challengers and about the appearance of corruption in the political system. But they are absolutely wrong about the causes of these problems and the best solutions for them. Their opposition to political action committees is wrongheaded and futile, and their obsession with PACs draws attention away from some deeply troubling aspects of political money. Far more valuable remedies than theirs are available.

The current Byrd-Boren proposal seeks to cure the ills of campaign finance by curtailing PAC contributions and attempting to place a strict lid on spending in Senate races (by offering various incentives to candidates who accept spending limits). In this, the sponsors have failed to make the vital distinction between real corruption and pseudo corruption.

The pseudo corruption is PAC money. First, the power of PACs has been greatly exaggerated. Not only are the 4,211 PACs an extremely diverse lot that work at cross-purposes and check each other, but all PACs together provide only a third of all money raised by House candidates and just a fifth of the war chests of Senate contenders. Most of the solid academic studies of the relationship between congressional decision-making and PAC contributions have reached the same basic conclusion: PAC money usually has little influence on the legislative votes cast by congressmen. The members' party affiliations, ideological orientations and, most of all, the wishes of their constituencies are far more important in determining their votes than the PAC gifts they have received.

Moreover, a strong defense of the legitimacy of PAC and interest-group campaign activity can easily be made. Vigorously competing interests of great variety, after all, are one significant indicator of a thriving democracy. And if nothing else PACs are a useful vehicle for disclosure of the interest-group money which has always reached campaigns—and which always will find a political outlet in a free society.

A limitation on what candidates can accept from PACs won't do any good: PAC largess, which is not going to just disappear, will flow into less accountable channels such as independent expenditure. And suppression of PACs will only result in the money's being given in less discernible ways, as illustrated by Boren himself. He virtuously refuses all PAC donations but accepts the very same kind of special-interest gift from individuals. According to a "Campaign Practices Reports" study, at least a quarter of the million-dollar war chest he raised in 1983 and 1984 came from executives and employees of the energy and banking industries—individuals whose interests were not always easy to identify in the Federal Election Committee records. This included women related to the executive contributors but listed only as "homemaker."

The reformers' big PAC attack," an increasingly popular campaign sport, serves as a smoke screen that obscures the real corruption, such as:

- Honoraria of millions of dollars each year that go directly into the pockets of congressmen for their *personal* use. By contrast, campaign contributions are expended for a worthy public enterprise.
- Free trips for congressmen that are often lengthy and lavish sojourns to resorts, which have sometimes included family members and are paid in full by the special interests.

- A singularly seedy loophole in election law that permits the 221 current representatives who were in office on Jan. 8, 1980, to convert all remaining campaign funds to personal use after their retirement. These often-massive supplementary pensions are obtained under false pretenses for a reelection bid that never occurs.
- Phony fund raising by many independent political groups and committees that rivals PTL's. This fraud, perpetrated mainly by direct mail, raises money by means of extravagant, never-fulfilled promises to contribute to certain causes and candidates dear to the hearts of naive donors on targeted lists.

**Source:** Larry Sabato, "The Attack on PACs: It's a Smoke Screen That Obscures the Real Corruption," *Washington Post*, August 7, 1987. © *The Washington Post*.

there is not, on average, a wide disparity in funding available for Democratic candidates and Republican candidates. In any given campaign, of course, one side or the other may have a lopsided advantage in spending.

The biggest spenders don't necessarily win. In 1986, for example, eight Republican senatorial candidates who outspent their Democratic opponents lost. On the other hand, Democratic spending in all of these cases was also substantial, often close to the Republican figure. But money clearly did not buy victory in the simple-minded sense that the person with the most automatically won. Non-incumbents necessarily have to spend a considerable sum simply to get name recognition on the part of the voters. This often generates a response of high spending on the part of the incumbent. Much of the money flows to what are perceived to be competitive contests, particularly cases in which there is no incumbent. Much of the spending may be concentrated in a minority of the formally contested elections. In many cases, especially for House seats, an incumbent receives no real contest from the challenger, in part because the challenger does not have sufficient financial resources to make a serious effort.

A good summary of the impact of spending on election results made the following points:[29]

1. Spending seems to be more productive of votes in primary elections compared to general elections.
2. Spending increases turnout.
3. Spending by challengers is more important than spending by incumbents. As the challenger's spending increases, his or her chances of victory increase, although they are far from guaranteed.
4. At some point there appears to be a "threshold effect"—that is, a challenger to an incumbent needs to spend a sizable amount to be in the race at all, but beyond that threshold amount extra spending seems to have little impact on his or her chances for winning.

The rise in the importance of PACs since the 1970s has been dramatic. Changes in campaign finance law promoted the rise.[30] By the end of 1986 there were over 4,000 PACs. In 1985–86 they gave well over $150 million to candidates for seats in the House and Senate.

A careful analysis of 1983–84 figures suggests PAC priorities. Over three-quarters of PAC spending on House races ($75 million) went to incumbents. Two-thirds of that money went to Democrats. The one-quarter of PAC House contributions that went to challengers and to candidates for seats with no incumbents ("open seats") was split about 55 percent for Republican candidates and 45 percent for Democratic candidates. Overall, over 60 percent of PAC money for House races went to Democrats.

Not surprisingly, labor PACs favored Democrats heavily regardless of whether they were incumbents, challengers, or competitors for open seats. Corporate PACs, however, gave almost evenly to incumbents of both parties (with a slight edge for Democrats) and displayed a preference for Republicans only in connection with funding for challengers and for open seats. Overall, corporate PACs made about

[29]Gary W. Copeland and Samuel C. Patterson, "Reform of Congressional Campaign Spending," *Policy Studies Journal* 5 (1977): 424–31.
[30]For a thorough analysis of congressional campaign finance see Gary C. Jacobson, *Money in Congressional Elections* (New Haven: Yale University Press, 1980). See also Michael J. Malbin (ed.), *Money and Politics in the United States* (Chatham, N.J.: Chatham House, 1984). For summaries of current figures on contributions and spending see periodic reports issued by the Federal Election Commission. For some historical data see Norman J. Ornstein and others, *Vital Statistics on Congress, 1987–1988* (Washington, D.C.: Congressional Quarterly, 1987): 67–121. Figures on spending are complicated and often difficult to interpret, however.

45 percent of their contributions to Democrats. Trade PACs followed roughly the same pattern as corporate PACs.

In 1983–84 there were twelve PACs that each contributed over $1 million to federal candidates (a lot of this money went to presidential and senatorial candidates). Realtors, doctors, home builders, educators, various unions, retired federal employees, milk producers, and automobile and truck dealers controlled these PACs.

Interest groups support members and candidates they find most congenial to their points of view, regardless of the state of the law. There is little evidence that the pattern of PAC contributions influences roll call voting in Congress in a sustained and systematic way.[31] However, even if one assumes totally honorable winners and undemanding campaign contributors, members of Congress will at the minimum unconsciously give extra weight to the interests and opinions of the largest contributors to their campaigns in reaching some of their decisions. Of course, not all large contributors are undemanding. The definition of honorable behavior by members of the House and Senate varies from individual to individual.

Before the 1970s there were only weak statutory efforts to limit campaign contributions and spending and to require full reporting. Many states have laws that supposedly limit the amount of spending in congressional campaigns, but they have had virtually no impact. In 1925 Congress passed a Corrupt Practices Act that had no impact on the financing of congressional campaigns.

In the 1970s, however, Congress began to deal seriously with questions of reporting, limits on contributions, limits on spending, and public financing of campaigns. Much of the attention was focused on presidential campaigns. Congressional elections have also received substantial attention and continue to be the subject of debate.

Congress passed acts in the area of campaign finance throughout the 1970s, with the major efforts coming in 1974 and 1976. The latter was necessitated in part because the Supreme Court invalidated part of the 1974 act.[32] As of 1988 the law had a complicated set of limits on giving and reporting requirements, no limits on total spending, no limits on candidates' use of their own money, and no provision for public funding of congressional campaigns.

---

[31]For a careful study that reaches this conclusion see John R. Wright, "PACs, Contributions, and Roll Calls: An Organizational Perspective," *American Political Science Review* 79 (1985): 400–14. See also Janet M. Grenzke, "Shopping in the Congressional Supermarket: The Currency is Complex," *American Journal of Political Science* (forthcoming).
[32]*Buckley* v. *Valeo* (424 U.S. 1).

## ELECTION RESULTS

Congressional election results can be analyzed in many different ways. This section focuses on five important aspects of congressional elections. First, because elections determine which individuals get to Congress, a profile of the characteristics of the members is presented. Second, because elections determine which party will control the House and the Senate in organizational terms, patterns of party control are summarized. Third, the question of turnover of members (or lack thereof) is examined. This leads to a fourth consideration, the relationship of turnover to policy and institutional change. Finally, the general nature of congressional elections in presidential years and non-presidential years is considered briefly.

### A Profile of the Members

The winners of seats in the House and Senate are by no means a cross section of the American population. By almost any measure they come from a social and economic elite. The same is true of the men and women they defeat.[33] The system of nominations and elections used in this country produces a certain kind of member, defined in socio-economic terms. In a narrow sense, Congress is never fully representative of the American people. This does not mean that only upper-class interests prevail in the decisions of Congress but it does suggest that some of the less well-off classes in society may have little reason to identify with the decisions reached by Congress because they do not identify with the decision-makers.

EDUCATION AND OCCUPATION. One striking characteristic of members of Congress is that they are highly educated in formal terms. The overwhelming majority have graduated from college and a sizable majority have professional or graduate education. In 1984 only 12 percent of all House members did not have at least a college degree; the same was true of only 7 percent of the members of the Senate. In the same year, over 80 percent of adult Americans had not completed four years of college.[34]

The two most dominant occupational backgrounds in Congress

---

[33]Fishel, *Party and Opposition.*
[34]For the figures on House and Senate see John H. Kessel, *Presidential Parties* (Homewood, Illinois: Dorsey, 1984): 199; the figures on the general population can be found in *Statistical Abstract of the United States,* 1986: 133.

have, for a number of years, been law and business. Education is a distant third. In the One Hundredth Congress, which convened in early 1987, 42 percent of the members of the House were lawyers, about a third had a business background, and about 9 percent were educators. In the Senate 62 percent were lawyers, 28 percent were from a business background, and 12 percent were educators.

AGE. In 1987 the average age of a House member was almost 51. The average age had fluctuated very little in the previous two decades, ranging between 46 and 52, with no trend evident. The average age of senators in 1987 was just over 54. This had also been quite stable for the previous two decades, fluctuating between 53 and 58.

GENDER. [35] By 1987 well over 100 women had served in either the House or Senate at one time or another. The first House member was Jeanette Rankin (R-Montana), elected in 1916 for one term. She was re-elected in 1940 for one more term. Fourteen had been in the Senate. Of those, eight served by appointment only, to fill unexpired terms; six won election. Only three won a Senate seat without being preceded by a husband in Congress. A woman did not sit in the Senate until 1922; the first was Rebecca Felton, a Georgia Democrat, an appointee who only held the seat for one day. The two women senators in the One Hundredth Congress are Republican Nancy Kassebaum of Kansas and Democrat Barbara Mikulski of Maryland, both elected in their own right without prior appointments or senatorial husbands.

Since 1929 there have always been at least 5 women among the 435 representatives. For most of the last three decades there has been a minimum of 15 women in the House. In the One Hundredth Congress (1987–89) 23 of the 435 representatives are women. Obviously, Congress remains overwhelmingly male.

RACE AND ETHNICITY. Congress has also been overwhelmingly populated by non-Hispanic whites. A few Asian-Americans have served as Senators and Representatives.

The Senate in 1987–88 had no black members, no Hispanic members, and two Asian-Americans (the two senators from Hawaii, both Democrats). The House had 22 blacks and 11 Hispanics among its 435 voting members. One of the Hispanic members is a Republican. The other 32 individuals are Democrats.

---

[35]See Irwin N. Gertzog, *Congressional Women: Their Recruitment, Treatment, and Behavior* (New York: Praeger, 1984).

Blacks have been the most sizable minority group in Congress. Before Reconstruction no blacks served in Congress. During Reconstruction two black senators and 20 black representatives served. All of these individuals were Republicans from the former Confederate states. Shortly after the end of Reconstruction in 1877 all of these black members disappeared from Congress. The first black member after Reconstruction was not elected until 1929. Since that time there have been over 30 different black individuals who have been elected to the House and one black individual who was elected to the Senate. All, except one member of the House and the one senator, have been Democrats. Very few have come from southern states. In 1987 only 4 of the 22 black representatives came from southern states. All 22 came from districts with a black majority in the population. Only two districts in the country with a black majority elected white representatives.

POLITICAL AND GOVERNMENTAL EXPERIENCE. The typical members of the House and Senate have considerable governmental and political experience before they come to Congress. As long ago as the decade between 1947 and 1957 only 10 percent of all senators held no public office prior to being elected to the Senate. Over 80 percent of them had held public office for more than five years before coming to the Senate and 55 percent of them had held public office for more than ten years.[36] In 1963 a sample of House members showed that three-quarters of them had held a state or local party position, almost half of them had served in a state legislature, and only 6 percent had no apparent political experience.[37]

A study of occupation and experience in 1984 showed that two-thirds of House members and three-fourths of senators had had "government" as their occupation for at least ten years. Almost 40 percent of the House members and almost 30 percent of the senators had held a responsible state and local governmental position at some point in the previous twenty years. Naturally, some of the most senior members had been in Congress for twenty years or more and had had state and local governmental experience before that.[38] In short, many members of Congress make government and politics their career, often moving from the state and local level to the national level.

[36]Donald R. Matthews, *U.S. Senators and Their World* (Chapel Hill: University of North Carolina Press, 1960): Chapter 3.
[37]Roger H. Davidson, *The Role of the Congressman* (New York: Pegasus, 1969): 50.
[38]Kessel, *Presidential Parties,* 200–1. Published material is supplemented by analysis of raw data provided by Professor Kessel.

## Elections and Party Control

Virtually every congressional election in American history has provided a single party in the House and in the Senate that had a clear majority of the seats. Before 1855 several different parties took their turn at organizing the House and Senate. Since 1855 only Republicans or Democrats have had majorities in either house.

Which party controls the House and Senate is important because of party differences on some major policy issues. Party control has implications for eventual policy decisions, even allowing for slippage between party promises and performance and for a considerable amount of diversity within a party.

The pre-1855 House was not a particularly competitive body. For three-fifths of the time between 1789 and 1855, there was a majority party that held 60 percent or more of the seats. This meant that the difference in the size of the majority and the minority parties was so large that the minority had little chance of defeating the wishes of the majority.

In the House of the post-1855 period there has been a majority party holding 60 percent or more of the seats about 35 percent of the time. Because large (60 percent or more) majorities were less frequent than in the pre-1855 period, there was more opportunity for competition between the majority and minority parties. For 65 percent of the time from 1855 to 1989 the minority party had a realistic chance of defeating the legislative wishes of the majority party because only relatively few defections from the majority party to the minority party were necessary to make the majority party lose.

In the Senate the level of party competition as measured by the percent of seats held by each party has been more constant than in the House. In the pre-1855 Senate, the majority party held 60 percent or more of the seats 45 percent of the time. That figure dropped only slightly in the post-1855 Senate.

Not only are the modern House and Senate often competitive in terms of a majority party with less than 60 percent of the seats, but the sectional ties of the parties have become more diffused. No longer is the south reliably Democratic in terms of its representation in Congress and in terms of the dominant place of southerners in the congressional Democratic party. Likewise, the Midwest, Plains, and New England have all become competitive instead of being reliably Republican. Members of the House and Senate from those areas no

**Table 3–1.** Percentage Democratic House Members, by Region, Elected in Selected Years between 1924 and 1986

| | PERCENTAGE OF SEATS HELD BY DEMOCRATS FOLLOWING ELECTION OF: | | | | | | |
| REGION | 1924 | 1936 | 1948 | 1960 | 1972 | 1980 | 1986 |
|---|---|---|---|---|---|---|---|
| South | 98 | 98 | 98 | 93 | 69 | 65 | 66 |
| Border States | 60 | 95 | 88 | 84 | 77 | 69 | 68 |
| New England | 13 | 48 | 39 | 50 | 60 | 64 | 63 |
| Mid-Atlantic | 26 | 68 | 49 | 49 | 54 | 54 | 56 |
| Midwest | 16 | 78 | 44 | 41 | 38 | 50 | 58 |
| Plains States | 13 | 45 | 16 | 19 | 36 | 36 | 46 |
| Rocky Mountain | 21 | 100 | 75 | 73 | 42 | 37 | 38 |
| Pacific Coast | 11 | 82 | 36 | 51 | 58 | 56 | 60 |
| Difference between highest and lowest Democratic percentages | 87 | 55 | 82 | 74 | 41 | 33 | 30 |

The states contained in the various regions are as follows: South (Alabama, Arkansas, Florida, Georgia, Louisiana, Mississippi, North Carolina, South Carolina, Tennessee, Texas, and Virginia), Border States (Kentucky, Maryland, Missouri, Oklahoma, and West Virginia), New England (Connecticut, Maine, Massachusetts, New Hampshire, Rhode Island, and Vermont), Mid-Atlantic (Delaware, New Jersey, New York, and Pennsylvania), Midwest (Illinois, Indiana, Michigan, Ohio, and Wisconsin), Plains States (Iowa, Kansas, Minnesota, Nebraska, North Dakota, and South Dakota), Rocky Mountain (Arizona, Colorado, Idaho, Montana, Nevada, New Mexico, Utah, and Wyoming), and Pacific Coast (Alaska, California, Hawaii, Oregon, and Washington).

Third party members are omitted; the percentages are calculated on the combined Democratic and Republican seats.

SOURCE: Data in the first three columns come from Milton C. Cummings, Jr., *Congressmen and the Electorate* (New York: Free Press, 1966): 221. Data in the other columns were calculated by the author.

longer necessarily dominate the Republican Party. Table 3–1 summarizes the changing regional mix of seats in the House of Representatives for selected years between 1924 and 1986. All regions are now competitive. The same is true in the Senate.

## Competition, Turnover, and Incumbency

There are elements of both stability and instability introduced into Congress through the electoral process. Questions about the degree of each can be broken into separate questions about competitiveness of individual seats, the rate of turnover, and the degree of advantage in an election enjoyed by the incumbent.

In general, the following sections underscore several interrelated points. First, competition for individual seats and between the parties is limited to a small proportion of those seats in any single election. Second, there is a high degree of continuity in the membership of the

House and Senate; new members come in as only a small percentage of each body every two years. Third, most incumbents are relatively safe in any specific election. Fourth, despite the first three points, when more than a single election is considered, the electoral system does, in fact, produce a considerable amount of competition and turnover. The most general point in analyzing these matters is that there are no simple generalizations about how much change elections produce. Different measures produce somewhat different impressions. More important, the length of time chosen for analysis (a single election contrasted with a series of elections) can produce substantially different conclusions.

COMPETITION. The percentage of House seats won by a large margin (defined as 60 percent or more of the two-party vote in a district) has been high over the last three or four decades, especially for incumbents. In the elections between 1956 and 1986 between about three-fifths and four-fifths of all incumbents running for re-election won by 60 percent or more. In Senate elections from 1944 through 1986 almost 45 percent of all elections involving incumbents resulted in those incumbents winning by margins of 60 percent or more—considerably lower than the case in the House. Incumbents did considerably better than that average in the three most recent elections, however: close to 60 percent of the incumbents running in 1982, 1984, and 1986 won by margins of 60 percent or more. However, the generalization still holds that statewide electorates tend to be more competitive than electorates in congressional districts. They are more diverse in their interests and more volatile, in part because of very heavy use of media advertising for state-wide senatorial campaigns.

Another way to consider competitiveness for seats is to assess change in party control of seats. The frequency of such change has been quite low since the 1940s.[39] In the 17 congressional elections from 1954 through 1986 an average of only 32 House seats and 8 Senate seats have changed parties at any single election. Those figures represent 7 percent of all House seats and 8 percent of all Senate seats, hardly dramatic in magnitude. Even in the year with the greatest change in party control of individual House seats (1964) there were only 57

[39]See Charles O. Jones, "Inter-Party Competition for Congressional Seats," *Western Political Quarterly* 17 (1964): 461–76; and Charles S. Bullock III, "Redistricting and Congressional Stability, 1962–72," *Journal of Politics* 37 (1975): 569–75. Changes in party control of House seats are more likely in special elections than in general elections. See Lee Sigelman, "Special Elections to the U.S. House: Some Descriptive Generalizations," *Legislative Studies Quarterly* 6 (1981): 577–88.

changes (13 percent of all House seats). Even though that was a very good year for Democrats, they only made a net gain of 37 seats (47 seats passed from Republican to Democratic control, but 10 seats also passed from Democratic to Republican control in the same election).

In the Senate, 1976 saw the greatest change in party control: 14 seats. But each party gained 7 at the expense of the other and there was no net change in the partisan composition of the Senate.

At the other end of the range of party change, only 11 House seats changed parties in 1968 (7 went to the Republicans but 4 went to the Democrats). In 1960 only 2 Senate seats changed parties.

In the Senate there is no difference in partisan change between presidential election years and non-presidential election years. An average of 8 senate seats changed hands in the 9 non-presidential elections from 1954 through 1986 and an average of 8 seats also changed hands in the 8 presidential election years from 1956 through 1984. In the House there is little difference between presidential and non-presidential years. An average of 34 seats changed partisan affiliation in the non-presidential years and an average of 29 seats changed in presidential years.

TURNOVER. Turnover in any given Congress is a function of the number of members who choose to retire to run for another office, the number of members who choose to retire from public life altogether, the number of incumbent members defeated for renomination in primary elections, and the number of incumbent members defeated in the general election. The net impact of retirements and defeats produces the total number of new members entering each new House and Senate. Table 3–2 summarizes data for both houses on the 21 general elections conducted from 1946 through 1986 on number of retirements, incumbents seeking re-election, primary defeats, general election defeats and successes, and the percentage of those running who were successfully re-elected.

The degree of fluctuation among the 21 different elections has been quite low in the case of the House. Even in those years in which the elections produced a significant political change in the general complexion of the House, only about 40 incumbents were defeated. Only twice did the number of incumbents defeated rise above 50. Only once in the 21 times did fewer than 80 percent of the incumbents seeking re-election actually wind up in the next House—and that case (1948) was just a whisker below 80 percent. Perhaps the single most significant figure in the House column is the mean percentage of incumbents seeking re-election who won: 91. In 16 of the 21 elections 90 percent

**Table 3–2.** Incumbent Retirement and Electoral Fate in 21 Elections, 1946–1986

| NUMBER OF INCUMBENTS WHO: | | HOUSE | SENATE |
|---|---|---|---|
| Retired | Range: | 21–49 | 2–10 |
| | Mean: | 33 | 6 |
| Ran for re-election | Range: | 382–411 | 25–35 |
| | Mean: | 399 | 29 |
| Were defeated in a primary | Range: | 3–18 | 0–6 |
| | Mean: | 8 | 2 |
| Were defeated in a general election | Range: | 6–68 | 1–10 |
| | Mean: | 27 | 5 |
| Were re-elected | Range: | 317–396 | 15–29 |
| | Mean: | 364 | 22 |
| *Percentage of Successful* | Range: | 79–98 | 55–97 |
| *Incumbent Candidates* | Mean: | 91 | 75 |

*Range* represents the highs and lows for the 21 cases. *Mean* is simply the arithmetic average of the 21 cases. This table does not include seats vacated by death or resignation before the general election. Special elections for open seats between regular biennial elections are not included.
SOURCE: Based on raw data in Norman J. Ornstein and others, *Vital Statistics on Congress, 1984–1985* (Washington, D.C.: American Enterprise Institute, 1984): 49–51. Updated by author for 1984 and 1986.

or more of the incumbents seeking re-election were successful. The last time that percentage fell below 90 was in 1974. In 1986 the incumbents had the most success of all: 394 sought re-election and only 9 failed (3 were defeated in primaries and only 6 were defeated in general elections). An astounding 98 percent succeeded in returning. In short, elections to the House alter the membership of that body only incrementally. A familiar cast of characters returns in January following an election.

The Senate column in Table 3–2 shows more fluctuation. However, three-quarters of all incumbents seeking re-election in these 21 elections were successful. The range is considerably broader than in the House. In 1980 only 16 of 29 incumbents seeking re-election made it back to the Senate. At the other end of the scale, in 1960, only 1 of 29 incumbents seeking re-election lost. The 1986 election was quite typical in that 21 of 28 (75 percent) incumbents seeking to return did so.

In Chapter 2 we explored turnover of membership for the whole sweep of congressional history. Here we want to look in more detail at the period following World War II. Figure 3–2 shows the percent of experienced members (non-freshmen) entering both the new House and new Senate convening every January in odd-numbered years from 1947 through 1987.

In the House, the figure for experienced members has fluctuated between 73 percent and 91 percent. Put differently, between 9 percent

**Figure 3–2.** Percent of Experienced House and Senate Members, 1947–1987

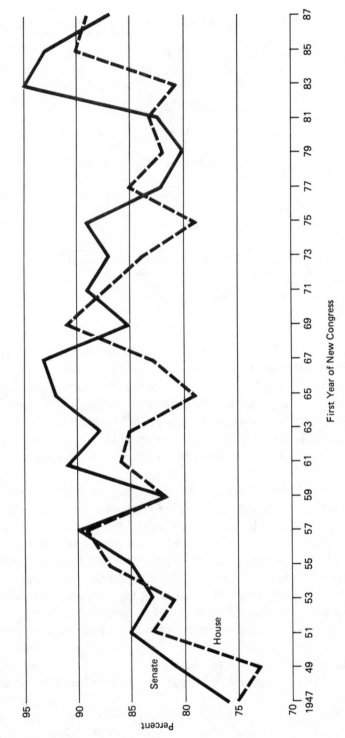

First Year of New Congress

SOURCE: Based on raw data for the House contained in Norman J. Ornstein and others, *Vital Statistics on Congress, 1984–1985 Edition* (Washington, D.C.: American Enterprise Institute, 1984): 49–50; and raw data for the Senate contained in *Congressional Quarterly Weekly Report* (November 8, 1986): 2815. House data for 1984 and 1986 calculated by author.

and 27 percent of the members of these 21 Houses have been freshmen. On average, experienced members have represented almost 84 percent of a new House and just over 16 percent have been freshmen. The fluctuations over these four decades show no particular pattern.

In the Senate, the figure for experienced members has fluctuated between 76 percent and 95 percent; between 5 percent and 24 percent of each new Senate has been composed of new members. The average Senate after these 21 elections had over 86 percent experienced members and under 14 percent new members. It is worth noting that, despite the stability in the Senate, guaranteed because only one-third of the seats are up for election every two years, the Senate figures for experienced members are very close to the House figures. In six cases there was even a higher percentage of freshmen in the Senate than in the House. This comparison underscores the low electoral turnover in House elections and the somewhat higher turnover in Senate elections, although incumbents still tend to win. Like the House line in Figure 3–2, the Senate line shows no particular trends.

The conclusion about both houses is the same: these are bodies in which there is a great continuity of membership. The advantages of incumbents, the proclivity of voters to prefer incumbents to relatively unknown challengers much of the time, and the tendency of state legislatures to draw many House districts so that they are quite safe for one party or the other all help explain this result. And even though Senate seats are generally less safe, only one-third of them are subject to election at any one time, which mutes the effect of turnover stemming from a single election.

INCUMBENCY. There has been a lengthy debate in political science journal articles in the 1970s and 1980s about the supposed growing advantages of incumbency in elections for House seats that, presumably, began in the 1960s. In fact, an analysis of these elections shows that there has been a growing trend toward safety of House seats since at least 1932 and perhaps since 1894. For a long time, then, House members have been safer from challenge than they were in earlier times. At the same time, there have been fewer "marginal" seats— those won in close elections.[40] And it is not just incumbents that have increased their winning margins; non-incumbent winners have done the same thing.

[40]James C. Garand and Donald A. Gross, "Changes in the Vote Margins for Congressional Candidates: A Specification of Historical Trends," *American Political Science Review* 78 (1984): 17–30. See also Gross and Garand, "The Vanishing Marginals, 1824–1980," *Journal of Politics* 46 (1984): 224–37.

Figure 3–3 shows the percentage of incumbents who were candidates for re-election and won from 1946 through 1986 for both houses. The line for the House shows that the first two elections in this series (1946 and 1948) had unusually low success rates for incumbent House members seeking re-election, although those success rates were still 82 percent and 79 percent, respectively. The rest of the period beginning with 1950 shows a high and quite stable success rate for incumbents, one that rarely dips below 90 percent, and then only barely.

The line for the Senate shows more instability and also, in all cases but two, a lower success rate for incumbents. Six year terms, the greater age of most Senate incumbents seeking re-election compared to most House incumbents, the very low success rate of incumbents appointed to replace members who die or resign mid-term, and the greater visibility of Senate campaigns compared to House campaigns all help explain this difference.[41]

PERSPECTIVES ON ELECTORAL STABILITY AND INSTABILITY. All of the discussion above leads to the conclusion that there is considerable stability in the membership of the House and Senate. Such is the case at any single point in time. On the other hand, it is easy to overlook the fact that incumbents—including some very senior incumbents—are defeated and that, over a series of elections, there is substantial change in the membership of Congress specifically because of electoral defeat. If Congress is looked at over a series of years rather than election-by-election, a somewhat different picture emerges. One study that took this perspective reached the following conclusion:

> Many a congressional district will send one congressman to Washington for a number of terms and be stereotyped as "safe" for his party. Then, its veteran representative is defeated in an "upset" win by a new challenger, who goes on to win a series of elections, perhaps only to be unseated himself in another "upset." . . . A sizable proportion of congressmen get to Washington by defeating the previous incumbent. Many are themselves forced out of office by a defeat at the polls.[42]

To support his point, the author examined the circumstances of victory for 322 members of the House elected or re-elected in 1972 (he

[41]On the high degree of vulnerability of appointed senators seeking re-election see William D. Morris and Roger H. Marz, "Treadmill to Oblivion: The Fate of Appointed Senators," *Publius* 11 (1981): 65–80. Vacant House seats can be filled only by special elections. Governors fill vacant Senate seats by appointment.

[42]Robert S. Erikson, "Is There Such a Thing as a Safe Seat?," *Polity* 8 (1976): 623–32.

**Figure 3-3.** Percent of House and Senate Incumbents Seeking Re-election Who Won, 1946–1986

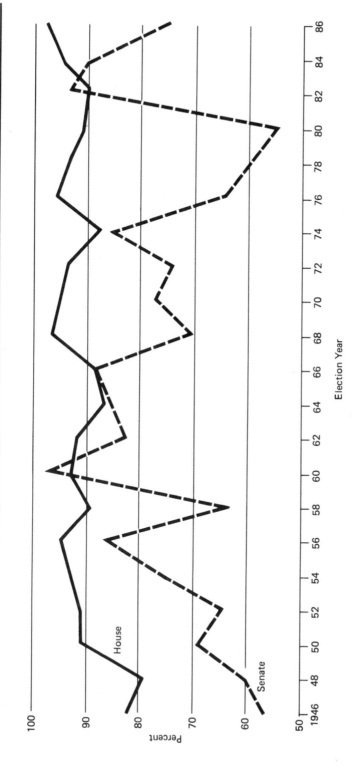

SOURCE: Based on data in Norman J. Ornstein and others, *Vital Statistics on Congress,*
*1984–1985 Edition* (Washington, D.C.: American Enterprise Institute, 1984): 49–51 for 1946 through
1982; updated by author for 1984 and 1986.

excluded members first elected prior to 1954 and those elected from districts drastically altered by redistricting.) Of these 322 individuals, 28 percent first came to Congress by defeating an incumbent in a general election. Another 8 percent defeated an incumbent in a primary election.

When the circumstances surrounding leaving the House are examined, the same kind of picture emerges. After the 1972 election 378 of the 435 members of the House who had won election or re-election in 1952 had left. Of those individuals, 25 percent had left because of defeat in a general election. Another 10 percent had left because of defeat in a primary.

It also needs to be noted that few members *always* win seats by large margins. A member may have a safe seat most of the time, but he or she is likely to have at least one electoral scare during a congressional career. In the Ninety-eighth Congress (1983–85), for example, almost three-quarters of all House members had won at least one of their elections by less than 60 percent of the two-party vote and seven-eighths of all senators fell into the same category. Almost half of all House members had won at least one election with less than 55 percent of the two-party vote; 64 of the 100 senators had had a similar experience.[43]

The cumulative impact of electoral turnover plus retirements provides new blood in the House and Senate. The rate of infusion of that new blood varies. In the 1960s the process was quite slow. In the 1970s and 1980s it accelerated. One study shows that House incumbents are no safer in the 1980s than they were in the 1950s.[44]

Various features of incumbency, however, usually produce advantages for incumbents at any specific election.[45] That situation can be explained in several ways. First, party voting has steadily declined for House seats in the last several decades and incumbency has become an increasingly important cue for voters. Incumbency is important both because an incumbent is likely to be known to a fair number of voters and may be genuinely popular or well-regarded by some of them. Challengers have an uphill battle simply to overcome invisibility and, in many cases, inexperience. Raising a substantial amount of

[43]Ornstein and others, *Vital Statistics,* 54. For an elaboration of this argument see Mann, *Unsafe at Any Margin.*
[44]Gary C. Jacobson, "The Marginals Never Vanished: Incumbency and Competition in Elections to the U.S. House of Representatives, 1952–82," *American Journal of Political Science* 31 (1987): 126–41.
[45]For a summary discussion of this general point see Jacobson, *The Politics of Congressional Elections:* Chapter 3.

money is, of course, a first major obstacle to becoming visible. Viable and visible challengers have a decent chance of doing well in the election, but the first hurdle is a very large one.

Second, incumbent members have a large number of resources and opportunities denied challengers. No single resource or opportunity is likely to guarantee a free ticket to re-election. But a skillful use of the full range of resources and opportunities gives incumbent Representatives an enormous advantage in seeking re-election. These resources and opportunities include free mailing privileges, a large staff to work on constituency problems, and considerable subsidized travel. Members focus much of their total activity and energy on constituency-oriented matters such as bringing federal largesse into their districts or dealing with individual constituents' problems through casework activities. The resources allow visibility; the focus on constituency matters helps move voter opinion in a positive direction.

Two major consequences supportive of fragmentation in the House stem from the situation described above, especially when that situation is coupled with the fact that elections are very much local events and winners typically owe very little to their party when they assess why they won. The first consequence is that fragmentation of policy will be promoted because members will continue to pay most of their attention to constituency-oriented matters or casework rather than to broad national policy. Second, incumbents can feel independent of their party leaders in the House because those leaders have little to do with electoral success. This reduces the chances of party cohesion in support of integrated policy, particularly if the President is not adroit at rallying his own party members on occasion for at least temporary shows of such cohesion.

The Senate presents a different situation. Incumbents are not particularly safe. The problem of invisibility for a senatorial challenger is not nearly as serious as it is for a House challenger, even though, paradoxically, such a challenge costs a great deal more in dollars. States are large and diverse and some interests and individuals with money are almost surely going to be willing to help finance a serious challenge in most cases. States also lend themselves to television campaigns, whereas heavy use of television is impractical because of cost and geography in most House districts. A relatively unknown challenger for a Senate seat can become quite well known through television exposure in a fairly short period of time.

Incumbent senators, however, also spend a good deal of personal and staff time and energy on constituency-oriented activities. They, too, typically owe little of their electoral success to any central party organs. As in the House, the Senate party leaders have almost nothing to do with an individual's electoral success with his or her constituents.

## Turnover of Members Related to Policy and Institutional Change

Although turnover in Congress is gradual and new members enter in small groups, Congress is a dynamic institution, capable of changing its collective mind both about the substance of policy and about the procedures by which it arrives at decisions. This dynamism is enhanced because the electoral system in the United States allows turnover, because elections are automatically held every two years, because even slow turnover aggregates fairly quickly, and because there are occasional elections in which there are unusually large numbers of newcomers who win.

The fact of turnover and the constant replacement of old members by new members help keep Congress dynamic in at least three specific ways.

First, new cohorts of members stemming from a single election or several elections in a row can help alter the general liberal-conservative balance in Congress.[46] National trends in ideologically oriented voting can be reflected fairly quickly in the membership of Congress.

Second, changed policy outcomes can be generated by Congress specifically because of new members who bring altered perspectives, values, and commitments to Congress. For example, the large group of new members who won in the 1964 election helped produce the mass of domestic legislation collectively labeled as "The Great Society" by President Johnson.[47] New members elected in 1980 helped President

[46]Alan L. Clem, "Do Representatives Increase in Conservatism as They Increase in Seniority?," *Journal of Politics* 39 (1977): 193–200.

[47]David W. Brady and Naomi B. Lynn, "Switched-Seat Congressional Districts: Their Effect on Party Voting and Public Policy," *American Journal of Political Science* 17 (1973): 528–43. See also Thomas P. Murphy, *The New Politics Congress* (Lexington, Mass.: Lexington Books, 1974); and Michael J. Malbin, "Times Change, but Congressmen Still Vote the Way They Used to," *National Journal* (20 March 1976): 370–74.

For an argument about change that encompasses the first two items mentioned in the text (including the phenomenon of partisan turnover) and also adds the factor of evolution in the issues themselves see Herbert B. Asher and Herbert F. Weisberg, "Voting Change in Congress: Some Dynamic Perspectives on an Evolutionary Process," *American Journal of Political Science* 22 (1978): 391–425.

Reagan dismantle some of that legislation and reverse Democratic policies of the 1970s.

Third, new members are often important in efforts to revise the procedures by which Congress conducts business.[48] It seems very unlikely, for example, that the House Democratic party would have instituted such major changes in its way of proceeding in 1975 (changes to be discussed in subsequent chapters) without the presence of seventy-five new Democrats from the 1974 election.

There is also evidence that "marginal" congressmen—that is, those who win by small margins or think that their next election will be decided by a small margin—are particularly important as policy innovators in Congress. They use policy innovation as a way of distinguishing themselves to their constituents and as a way (they hope) of creating or reviving a winning electoral coalition at home.[49]

## The General Context of Congressional Elections in Presidential and Non-Presidential Years

PRESIDENTIAL YEAR CONGRESSIONAL ELECTIONS. Until the election of 1960 there was a reasonably high correlation between voting for members of Congress and voting for president on a district-by-district basis. But since that time the correlation has gone down dramatically, indicating that voters are engaging in more ticket-splitting. Therefore, close articulation between presidential and congressional voting no longer exists.[50]

There are "coattail" effects in presidential year voting, but they can run in both directions. That is, a heavy vote for a popular presidential candidate in a state or district can help candidates of his party for the Senate and House win. But popular candidates for Congress can also help pull a weaker presidential candidate to victory in a state or district. Even before the period of reduced articulation of party voting (specifically, in the period between 1924 and 1964) the coattails ran

---

[48]See Murphy, *The New Politics Congress.*

[49]David J. Vogler, *The Politics of Congress,* 4th ed. (Boston: Allyn and Bacon, 1983): 86–88. See also Morris P. Fiorina, *Representatives, Roll Calls, and Constituencies* (Lexington, Mass.: Lexington Books, 1974).

[50]For treatments of articulation see Key, *Politics, Parties, and Pressure Groups,* Chapter 20; and Milton C. Cummings, Jr., *Congressmen and the Electorate* (New York: Free Press, 1966). On the decay of the correlation between presidential voting and voting for congressional candidates see Walter Dean Burnham, "Insulation and Responsiveness in Congressional Elections," *Political Science Quarterly* 90 (1975): 411–35.

from presidential candidate to House candidate about 60 percent of the time and in the other direction about 40 percent of the time.[51] The basic strength of the Democratic party in congressional elections helped carry Presidents Truman, Kennedy, and Carter to their victories in 1948, 1960, and 1976, respectively. In 1964 Lyndon Johnson's strong showing pulled some Democratic congressional candidates to victory. In 1980 and 1984 Ronald Reagan's appeal to the electorate helped some GOP congressional candidates. But Richard Nixon in 1968 and 1972 and Jimmy Carter in 1976 did not exhibit electoral appeal that helped congressional candidates of their parties win.

One factor that seems to have a predictable impact on voting for House and Senate candidates in both presidential and non-presidential years is the state of the economy. In general, the candidates of the party of the incumbent president suffer if there is an economic downturn in the year prior to the election, although an upturn does not reliably produce extra votes for the same candidates. The party with the White House gets blame, but not credit, for national economic performance.[52]

MIDTERM CONGRESSIONAL ELECTIONS. Until very recently, it was thought that midterm congressional elections represented the "decline" phase of a "surge and decline" phenomenon characterizing the relationship between presidential year and non-presidential year congressional elections.[53] Presidential year congressional elections were thought to produce an abnormally large congressional majority, and the almost inevitable loss of seats two years later by the president's party was thought to reflect primarily a return to the "normal" party balance rather than a negative judgment about the president's per-

---

[51]Cummings, *Congressmen and the Electorate.*

[52]See Howard S. Bloom and H. Douglas Price, "Voter Response to Short-Run Economic Conditions: the Asymmetric Effect of Prosperity and Recession," *American Political Science Review* 69 (1975): 1240–54; Saul Goodman and Gerald H. Kramer, "Comment on Arcelus and Meltzer, The Effect of Aggregate Economic Conditions on Congressional Elections," *American Political Science Review* 69 (1975): 1255–65; and Gerald H. Kramer, "Short-Term Fluctuations in U.S. Voting Behavior, 1896–1964," *American Political Science Review* 65 (1971): 131–43. For a contrary view see Francisco Arcelus and Allan H. Meltzer, "The Effect of Aggregate Economic Variables on Congressional Elections," *American Political Science Review* 69 (1975): 1232–39; and Arcelus and Meltzer, "Aggregate Economic Variables and Votes for Congress: A Rejoinder," *American Political Science Review* 69 (1975): 1266–69.

[53]For presentations of variations of this general view see Key, *Politics, Parties, and Pressure Groups,* Chapter 20; Angus Campbell, "Surge and Decline: A Study of Electoral Change," in Campbell and others, *Elections and the Political Order,* Chapter 3; and Barbara Hinckley, "Interpreting House Midterm Elections: Toward a Measurement of the In-Party's 'Expected' Loss of Seats," *American Political Science Review* 61 (1967): 694–700.

formance. This view had considerable plausibility when there was high correlation between presidential and congressional vote in presidential years. But, given the collapse of that correlation and the increased value of incumbency, some alternative explanations seem necessary.

Three factors have emerged as particularly important in explaining midterm results as other than a return to a "normal" party balance: presidential popularity, the state of the economy, and short-term party evaluations (that is, a temporary trend in public opinion particularly favorable to one party and/or particularly unfavorable to the other).[54] Midterm results can be interpreted at least in part as a referendum on presidential performance for the preceding two years, especially performance in terms of how the economy is thought to be doing. It is still "natural" for the in-party to lose seats, but those losses are cut substantially if the president is popular and/or if the economy is doing well. Part of the reason for this impact is that when the economy is doing badly and when the president's popularity is low it is difficult for his party to attract good candidates for congressional seats and to attract the money to finance viable campaigns.[55]

## THE IMPLICATIONS OF ELECTIONS FOR CONGRESSIONAL POLICY BEHAVIOR

The continuous presence of frequent elections has a profound influence on the ways in which Congress works. In general, the almost universal desire for re-election on the part of incumbents has led Congress to structure itself internally to maximize re-election chances and also leads Congress to handle policy questions in ways supportive

[54]On presidential popularity and the state of the economy see Samuel Kernell, "Presidential Popularity and Negative Voting: An Alternative Explanation of the Midterm Congressional Decline of the President's Party," *American Political Science Review* 71 (1977): 44–66; Donald R. Kinder and D. Roderick Kiewiet, "Economic Discontent and Political Behavior: The Role of Personal Grievances and Collective Economic Judgments in Congressional Voting," *American Journal of Political Science* 23 (1979): 495–527; James E. Piereson, "Presidential Popularity and Midterm Voting at Different Electoral Levels," *American Journal of Political Science* 19 (1975): 683–94; Edward R. Tufte, "Determinants of the Outcomes of Midterm Congressional Elections," *American Political Science Review* 69 (1975): 812–26; and the articles cited in footnote 52, above.

On short-term party evaluations see Alan I. Abramowitz, Albert D. Cover, and Helmut Norpoth, "The President's Party in Midterm Elections: Going from Bad to Worse," *American Journal of Political Science* 30 (1986): 562–76.

[55]Gary C. Jacobson and Samuel Kernell, *Strategy and Choice in Congressional Elections* (New Haven: Yale University Press, 1981).

of the same end. The frequency of elections and the desire for re-election lead to both institutional and policy fragmentation most of the time.

In many ways the electoral system pushes in the direction of policy conservatism in the sense that members normally have a stake in avoiding highly controversial issues, keeping the substantive agenda static, and not exploring fresh solutions to problems, many of which may have been present for years. Six different aspects of congressional elections push in the direction of policy conservatism.

First, only certain kinds of individuals tend to be viable candidates—generally white, upper-middle-class males. This tendency toward socioeconomic homogeneity in Congress probably helps limit the perspective and imagination of members, although it is certainly does not create rigid limits on what Congress can achieve if it wants to.

Second, the low turnout for congressional elections helps result in at least a partially stagnant congressional agenda. Rarely are new voices in the electorate loud enough or numerous enough to add items to the congressional agenda.

Third, the high rate of electoral success on the part of incumbents also promotes stability of agenda and solutions.

Fourth, the low degree of competition for most seats—especially in the House—also tends to reduce the innovative potential within Congress. Knowledge is limited on the question of the link between election margins and policy behavior by members, but the most persuasive evidence suggests that those elected by relatively narrow margins tend to be the most "innovative" or "extreme" in their policy positions rather than instinctively always seeking a presumably safe middle of the road.[56] Their "innovation" may stem from a need to gain higher visibility in their constituencies.

Fifth, the high cost of campaigns helps reinforce the attractiveness of "playing it safe" in Congress. If members do not offend important constituents, serious threats in either the primary or general election may be avoided. Since incumbents of both parties share this interest, they may seek to protect each other from controversial issues. They may not share either party labels or beliefs but all have a common stake in returning to Washington.

[56]Morris P. Fiorina, "Electoral Margins, Constituency Influence, and Policy Moderation: A Critical Assessment," *American Politics Quarterly* 1 (1973): 479–98; Fiorina, *Representatives, Roll Calls, and Constituencies;* Barbara Sinclair Deckard, "Electoral Marginality and Party Loyalty in House Roll Call Voting," *American Journal of Political Science* 20 (1976): 469–81; and Vogler, *The Politics of Congress,* 86–88.

Sixth, for much significant policy change to occur, a change in the partisan control of Congress is often necessary. Yet the great advantage of incumbents, coupled with the predominantly Democratic sympathies of the electorate, have made such party turnover rare for the last five and a half decades. Even when voters do alter the percentage of the vote they give the Democrats on a national basis, that drop is not reflected in a corresponding drop in the percentage of the seats controlled by the Democrats. Increased competitiveness in the vote in all districts aggregated is usually not reflected very well in increased competitiveness inside Congress.[57] The importance of party turnover in promoting real policy change is well illustrated by the critical role of the newly Republican Senate in 1981 in helping President Reagan begin to make some changes in policy direction.

The electoral system, however, also has two major features that can promote responsiveness to changing views in the electorate, a broadened policy agenda, and innovativeness in seeking solutions: the existence of a two-party system and single-member districts. This means that every Congress meets with a single majority party in at least nominal control of the House and Senate. Usually the same party controls both houses (1981–86 was an exceptional period when a different party controlled each house). When the nominal majority is also a new majority—that is, when the electorate has put a different party in control—a situation is created in which the likelihood of aggressiveness on the part of that majority is relatively high *because* it is likely to have come into majority status after a number of frustrating years in minority status.

Apathy and ignorance on the part of the electorate are features of the electoral scene that can cut two ways. They may allow members to be lethargic, uninnovative, and responsive to only a few selected interests. But they also allow members the freedom to be creative, innovative, and responsive to some larger vision of pressing public needs.

Finally, it needs to be repeated that the electoral system does allow turnover of members, even if it does not encourage it. New members are critical in terms of helping produce policy change over time in Congress. New perspectives and commitments, based on new electoral coalitions, are not guaranteed by new members. But electing new members is the most reliable way of infusing substantive change into the congressional agenda and the congressional policy product.

[57]For a discussion of this phenomenon see Edward R. Tufte, "The Relationship between Seats and Votes in Two-Party Systems," *American Political Science Review* 67 (1973): 540–54.

# II

## The Internal Environment for Congressional Policy-Making

# 4

# Congressional Decision-Making

On August 11, 1986, the chaplain of the Senate offered the following prayer in that body:[1]

God of truth and order, we are grateful for passage of the defense authorization bill—but we regret the cost in time and energy, emotional strain and frustration. Dear God, the Senate faces a week with an impossible load of work—spare the senators another week of inordinate hours and stress which threatens dignity, civility, health and sanity.

Father, I honor the Senate and count it a great privilege to serve here. I love the senators and respect them, but feel profound concern that it not neutralize its effectiveness by the weight of its own practices. Save it Lord, from becoming like a powerful engine frozen because of the friction of its parts—powerless to maintain its own schedule or meet its own deadlines. Preserve it gracious God, from becoming a musclebound giant, victim of its own rules, procedures and precedents.

Prove that you are real, alive and relevant to the political process. Grant to the Senate and its members a special dispensation of grace, wisdom, love and peace. Make this a profitable, productive week of satisfaction and fulfillment. In the name of Him who is incarnate love.

Amen

[1]This appeared in the *Washington Post,* August 12, 1986.

Congress is sometimes a tense place. Interests and values clash. Yet, somehow, decisions must be made. The people making the decisions, despite disagreements that are sometimes profound, must continue to work together.

In addition, decision processes are shaped by three central facts about Congress: 1) the members are elected representatives; 2) they are confronted by a powerful presidency, and 3) they are simultaneously confronted by a vast professional bureaucracy.

This chapter deals with the congressional response to the twin necessities of making decisions and, simultaneously, continuing to live together. It also treats the impact of the major institutional environment in which Congress is set on these responses. The first major section presents a sketch of that institutional environment. Subsequent sections examine aspects of the major processes, both formal and informal, by which Congress makes decisions: the inculcation of norms, the giving and receiving of behavioral cues, and the formal rules and procedures of the two chambers. The overriding theme of the chapter is one of continuity and stability. Decision-making routines are influenced by changes in personnel and priorities in both Congress and the executive branch, including the presidency. But the aspects of decision-making that change very slowly and relatively little far outweigh short-term changes induced by new people and new programmatic priorities. The "Roosevelt revolution" or the "Reagan revolution" or any other alleged "revolution" in American politics does relatively little with any rapidity to alter the basic nature of congressional decision-making.

## THE BROAD CONGRESSIONAL RESPONSE TO INSTITUTIONAL ENVIRONMENT

All members of the House and Senate are elected from individual constituencies (with the relatively insignificant exception of a few senators who may hold short-term appointments from governors to fill vacant seats). Virtually all members are genuinely concerned with the way they "represent" their constituents. Virtually all of them bear one of two party labels both in the electoral process and in Congress. These labels, however, are associated with a national party system that is weak and somewhat mythical, with district parties that are often unimportant, and with congressional parties that are only sporadically cohesive and demanding. This combination of circumstances allows individual members a great deal of freedom as they make up their minds on substantive questions. They can easily rationalize whatever behavior they decide on in terms of representation of constituents despite the competing demands of the president, party leaders, committees, interest groups, or bureaucrats.

A major congressional norm legitimizes this independence in the name of representation. At the same time, the norm does not demand rigorous attention to ferreting out "real" constituency opinion, so that members are free to provide their own definition of the interests and opinions that deserve attention. Members can maximize their freedom of action in Congress by playing off presumed constituency pressure against pressures brought by congressional party leaders, the executive branch, or committees. If, for example, the president and party leaders actively advocate a gun control bill, a member opposed to the bill can claim in talking with a leader urging him to vote for it that he would like to but that constituency opinion prohibits a "yes" vote. The leader will neither check (because he has no way) nor even challenge the member's assertion about the views of his constituents. This freedom is not granted members simply for its own sake; the main point of allowing members such latitude is to maximize their chances of re-election—a goal virtually all members have in common.

Congress must also confront a president endowed by the Constitution with great powers that have been expanded in practice through the aggressiveness of a number of specific presidents and the attentions of the media and the public. On selected issues the president can appeal directly to the electorate for support, thus pressuring Congress for a favorable response. John Kennedy made such an appeal on tax reform, Lyndon Johnson did the same on civil rights, Richard Nixon took a similar route in promoting revenue sharing, Jimmy Carter followed suit on energy policy, and Ronald Reagan kept the essentials of his economic program constantly before the public in 1981 and incessantly touted the virtue of aiding the anti-governmental forces in Nicaragua throughout his presidency. The institutionalization of the presidency has also enhanced its potential for influence.

The existence of a powerful chief executive has stimulated the development of elaborate Congressional leadership structures and apparatus, the function of which is not only to centralize congressional response to presidential proposals but also, importantly, to mediate between the rank-and-file members (and sometimes committee and subcommittee chairmen and senior members) and the president. The leaders are channels for information and presumed influence flowing both ways. If the members have a grievance or a strongly felt position, the leaders are expected to inform the president. If the president has a strongly held position, the leaders of his party are expected to communicate that position to the members. There is a natural tension surrounding the positions of leadership: the president tends to view the leaders of his party as his lieutenants; members often prefer to think of the leaders as being responsible for defending congressional autonomy against the encroachments of the president and executive branch.

The professional bureaucracy that Congress must face is nominally under the control of the president but is, in practice, a set of independent forces. The presence of such a bureaucracy, which administers the programs Congress legislates, has contributed to the growth and entrenchment of a well-developed structure of relatively autonomous committees and subcommittees with fixed jurisdictions and fairly stable memberships. In addition, the presence of the bureaucracy helps determine the functions that the committees will perform: oversight (review of bureaucratic activities), authorization of new programs or renewals of existing programs, and appropriation of funds are all carried on with specific reference to parts of the bureaucracy. To facilitate oversight of existing programs and consideration of new legislation, the subject-matter division of labor among the committees roughly parallels that in the bureaucracy. Within the committees the workload is further divided among subcommittees with jurisdictions that often parallel the responsibilities of specific units in the bureaucracy.

The advantage of this method of division of labor is that it encourages members to become knowledgeable and expert in particular issue areas and enables them to compete with the experience and expertise of the bureaucrats with whom they interact. The disadvantage of this same division of work, particularly when coupled with the fact that committee memberships are stable, is that it encourages the formation of cozy relationships between a small number of bureaucrats and legislators who come to see eye-to-eye on matters in their particular policy sphere. This results in policy that does not change much.

An additional effect of the large bureaucracy has been that Congress has turned to the use of professional staff in an effort to compete with the bureaucrats' generally superior command of information about programs. Individual members simply have too many responsibilities to delve deeply into all of them, and they need assistance to match the advantage that size alone gives the bureaucracy. Thus they have created a sizable group of knowledgeable staff members who possess considerable technical competence in a variety of legislative fields. Many of these individuals become permanently tied to a committee regardless of personnel or even party turnover.

# NORMS AND SOCIALIZATION

Norms are standards that prescribe acceptable and unacceptable behavior in an organization. They are "informal rules, frequently unspoken because they need not be spoken, which may govern conduct more effectively than any written rule. They prescribe 'how things are done around here.' "[2]

Norms do not appear in Congress by magic. Rather, they stem from institutional process and interaction. By the same token, they are not immutable. They change as personnel and the issues confronting Congress change. The single most important source of change in norms is turnover in personnel.

New people are rarely socialized perfectly into an institution in the sense that they both understand and accept its norms totally. The greater the number of newcomers to an institution the more likely that the norms will change. Newcomers bring their own views to an institution. These views are the result of differing ideologies, ages, and societal norms acquired during childhood and young adulthood. New members may affect the views of more senior members toward congressional norms, particularly if the senior members sense a widespread feeling in support of some changed views.

A classic example of changing norms and the differences those changes make is provided by the Senate between the 1950s and 1970s. Observers of the Senate during the late 1940s and 1950s concluded that that body was in the grip of norms that produced an ideologically conservative bias in the decisions it made.[3] It was implied that these specific norms—that junior members should act as apprentices, work hard mainly on legislative details, defer to the wisdom of senior members (who also happened to be the most conservative senators), and that all senators should approach the task of legislating in a sober spirit that would produce only minor changes from a status quo— were permanent features of Senate life.

Subsequent studies of the Senate, however, have pointed out that the norms of the Senate differed both before and after the particular period of the 1950s.[4] In the 1960s and 1970s it became clear that junior

---

[2] Barbara Hinckley, *Stability and Change in Congress* (New York: Harper and Row, 1971): 59.
[3] See William S. White, *Citadel* (New York: Harper and Brothers, 1956); and Donald R. Matthews, *U.S. Senators and Their World* (Chapel Hill: University of North Carolina Press, 1960).
[4] See Ralph K. Huitt, "The Outsider in the Senate: An Alternative Role," *American Political Science Review* 55 (1961): 566–75; Norman J. Ornstein, Robert L. Peabody, and David W. Rohde, "The Changing Senate: From the 1950's to the 1970's," in Lawrence C. Dodd and Bruce I. Oppenheimer (eds.), *Congress Reconsidered* (New York: Praeger, 1977): 6–9; Nelson W. Polsby,

members, often of an aggressively liberal persuasion, could also wield substantial legislative influence and produce important changes from the status quo that were not to the liking of the senior, conservative members. The norms changed to become less restrictive.

A summary of the status of Senate norms in the mid-1970s compared to the mid-1950s[5] concluded that only three of the six norms observed two decades earlier still continued in force without much change: courtesy, reciprocity, and institutional patriotism. Two more—legislative work and specialization—had diminished considerably. And one—apprenticeship—had been altered so substantially as to be almost unrecognizable.

Norms also changed substantially in the House in the 1970s.[6] The norm of apprenticeship was particularly weakened. Full and important participation of junior members became both commonplace and accepted.

## Predominant Norms in the Contemporary House and Senate[7]

Four norms or clusters of norms are most significant in the contemporary House and Senate: institutional loyalty, reciprocity and accommodation, specialization, and seniority and apprenticeship. None are

"Goodbye to the Inner Club," *Washington Monthly* (August 1969): 30–34; Randall B. Ripley, *Power in the Senate* (New York: St. Martin's, 1969); and Michael Foley, *The New Senate: Liberal Influence on a Conservative Institution, 1959–1972* (New Haven: Yale University Press, 1980): Chapter 4.

[5]Ornstein, Peabody, and Rohde, "The Changing Senate: From the 1950's to the 1970's," 6–9. See also Barbara Sinclair, "Senate Styles and Senate Decision Making, 1955–1980," *Journal of Politics* 48 (1986): 877–908. Sinclair also argues that the *intercommittee* aspects of reciprocity disappeared. That is true, but is not inconsistent with the survival of a more general norm of reciprocity.

[6]See Lawrence C. Dodd and Bruce I. Oppenheimer, "The House in Transition," in Dodd and Oppenheimer (eds.), *Congress Reconsidered,* 21–53; and Burdett A. Loomis, "The 'Me' Decade and the Changing Context of House Leadership," in Frank Mackaman (ed.), *Understanding Congressional Leadership* (Washington, D.C.: Congressional Quarterly Press, 1981).

[7]For the fullest discussion of Senate norms, see Matthews, *U.S. Senators and Their World,* Chapter 5; Matthews, "The Folkways of the United States Senate: Conformity to Group Norms and Legislative Effectiveness," *American Political Science Review* 53 (1959): 1064–89; and David W. Rohde, Norman J. Ornstein, and Robert L. Peabody, "Political Change and Legislative Norms in the United States Senate," (paper prepared for delivery at the 1974 annual meeting of the American Political Science Association). On the House see Richard F. Fenno, Jr., "The Internal Distribution of Influence: The House," in David B. Truman (ed.), *The Congress and America's Future,* 2nd ed. (Englewood Cliffs, N.J.: Prentice-Hall, 1973): 83–90. For another useful discussion of norms, see Hinckley, *Stability and Change in Congress,* 59–69.

Note that there is no standard "listing" of congressional norms. Different observers use different language to label and describe the same phenomena.

universally obeyed; all have undergone recent change, although some are more stable than others. The House and Senate differ in some important respects.

INSTITUTIONAL LOYALTY. Both houses have strong norms demanding the loyalty of the members to their respective institution, although the norm is stronger in the Senate than in the House. It means that members should not, by and large, make public criticisms of their fellow members or of the functioning of their institution, although considerable deviation from this norm is tolerated during election campaigns. Members should take the place of the House or Senate in the governmental scheme seriously and make this seriousness evident. For the most part, members are expected to anticipate a career in the House or Senate, although many House members are eager to obtain Senate seats. Members are expected to defend the institution against the encroachment of the president or the bureaucracy and are expected to defend the prerogatives of their own chamber against perceived imperialistic behavior of the other chamber.

Most of the few senators and representatives who have been disciplined by the House and Senate by removal or by loss of seniority or committee assignments were guilty mainly of bringing discredit to their chamber. In two of the most celebrated recent cases—the censure of Senator Joseph McCarthy in 1954 and the refusal to seat Representative Adam Clayton Powell in 1967—it seems clear that one of the prime offenses of both was that they brought the "good name" of the Senate and House, respectively, into public question. McCarthy was censured because of excesses connected with his chairmanship of the Permanent Investigations Subcommittee and his refusal to testify before the Senate Rules Committee in connection with accusations he and another Senator, William Benton of Connecticut, had made against each other. Powell was excluded from his House seat because of misuse of funds of the committee he chaired, refusal to pay a New York libel judgment, and noncooperation with House committees investigating his behavior.

In 1980 and 1981 juries convicted six Representatives and one Senator for accepting bribes during a Federal Bureau of Investigation undercover operation that became known as "Abscam." The operation involved phony Arab sheiks, bribes, wiretapping, videotaping, and other questionable practices. Two of the House members resigned and three were defeated for re-election. The House expelled the sixth member. This expulsion was only the fourth in the history of the House (the previous three had all been of border-state representatives in 1861 for support of the Confederate cause—in effect, treason). The Senate proceeded very deliberately against its one convict: Harrison Williams (D-N.J.). Floor action was postponed several times after the Select Committee on Ethics had voted in favor of expelling the senator. Finally, faced with almost certain expulsion by the full Senate, Williams resigned, blasting the tactics of the Abscam investigation in his final address.

A number of senators and representatives have felt free to criticize the decline of congressional power. Included in this general criticism are specific allegations that outmoded procedures may help relegate Congress to a subordinate position. This criticism is tolerated because the motivation behind it is the desire to restore Congress to its "rightful" place in the governmental scheme—a place in which it cannot be dominated by the president and bureaucracy.

RECIPROCITY AND ACCOMMODATION. The House and Senate process a vast number of bills each year. Each bill must go through a large number of stages. It is imperative that senators and representatives help each other or very little would be accomplished. It is expected of all members that they will learn to be mutually helpful, to accommodate themselves to each other's needs, and to bargain in a way that always leaves room for compromise. This norm necessarily requires an extensive amount of mutual courtesy and deference, particularly on matters in which one individual is reputed to be expert. This norm also tends to reduce extreme partisanship, which makes bargaining and accommodation more difficult.

In impact, the norm underscores the virtues for members of bargaining, compromise, and logrolling (that is, trading support for a variety of matters each important to only a few members). The tie between reciprocity (which sounds fancy) and logrolling (which sounds earthy) is well illustrated by a comment by former Senator Sam Ervin, a Democrat from North Carolina, on his relations with Senator Milton Young, a Republican from North Dakota (to a North Dakota audience): "I got to know Milt Young very well. And I told Milt, 'Milt, I would just like you to tell me how to vote about wheat and sugar beets and things like that, if you just help me out on tobacco and things like that.' "[8]

In 1979 a conservative freshman Senator, Gordon J. Humphrey (R-N.H.), violated an unwritten norm of Senate behavior by directly

[8]Quoted in *Minot (N.D.) Daily News,* June 17, 1976.

urging the defeat of five Democratic colleagues through signing a letter targeting them for defeat. The letter was written and sent by the National Conservative Political Action Committee. Humphrey removed his name from the letter after it was pointed out to him (in part by editorials in New Hampshire newspapers) that he would jeopardize legislation needed for New Hampshire projects because he would inevitably need at least the neutrality of some of these targeted members some of the time.

SPECIALIZATION. In the House, members are expected to specialize in one or, at most, a small number legislative areas. Each member has only a few subcommittee assignments, and the specialization is supposed to coincide with these assignments. Many House members choose their specialties to coincide with important interests in their districts.

In recent years in the Senate specialization has largely disappeared as a norm. Because the Senate has fewer members than the House, each senator has a large number of committee and subcommittee assignments. Furthermore, there is no expectation that senators will speak and develop their ideas primarily in committee or only on topics under the jurisdiction of their committees and subcommittees. In part, they are expected to help develop a national policy agenda rather than proceeding primarily as craftsmen in relatively small and technical areas. Also, given the relatively large numbers of senators who explore the possibility of running for president, their tendency to make statements on a wide range of topics is reinforced.[9]

SENIORITY AND APPRENTICESHIP. Until recent years, the grip of the seniority and apprenticeship norms was very strong in both the House and Senate. Senior members had most of the good positions and made most of the important decisions while junior members mainly kept quiet and worked hard on less important matters while waiting to become senior.

This situation has changed in both houses. It began changing slowly in the Senate in the 1950s and slowly in the House in the 1960s. The

[9]On the Senate as "a hot-house for significant policy innovation" see Nelson W. Polsby, "Strengthening Congress in National Policymaking," in Polsby (ed.), *Congressional Behavior* (New York: Random House, 1971): 3–13. On the Senate as "a presidential incubator" see Robert L. Peabody, Norman J. Ornstein, and David W. Rohde, "The United States Senate as a Presidential Incubator: Many Are Called but Few Are Chosen," *Political Science Quarterly* 91 (1976): 237–58.

# DECISION-MAKING ON IMMIGRATION, 1986

The immigration law signed by President Reagan on November 6, 1986 was notable not only for its substance—it overhauled the nation's policy on illegal immigration and employment of illegal aliens—but also for the tenacity and political skill of its supporters, who persisted for five years to achieve final passage.

The legislation's purpose was to stem the flood of illegal immigration to the U.S. by prohibiting employers from hiring such individuals. Fines and jails terms were specified to deter employers. The bill also gave amnesty (i.e., legal status) to illegal aliens already in the U.S. who could document their residence. Finally, the bill permitted use of foreign "guest" workers in agricultural employment and gave them temporary legal residency. These elements embodied conflicting features and generated intense pressure from a raft of interest groups:

- Western agricultural growers insisted that immigration reform would deprive them of their source of workers and that an alternate source would have to be provided in order for them to withdraw opposition to the bill.
- Hispanic groups opposed the employer sanctions because they feared discrimination in hiring would be directed against persons with an accent or a dark skin or foreign sounding names.
- Employer groups also opposed the sanctions and the requirements for checking applicants' residency documentation.
- Labor unions wanted to ensure that any farm-worker program would guarantee those workers minimum employment benefits and access to social services. They also wanted to insure that domestic workers were not undercut.
- Border states opposed the amnesty provisions because they feared the costs of absorbing the newly legalized residents would overwhelm their strained social services budgets. They wanted the federal government to pick up the costs.
- Civil rights groups were concerned that the rights of guest workers be preserved and that the legalization program did not undercut the rights of resident aliens who were applying for permanent status through official means.

Credit for forging an acceptable compromise among the competing claims goes to a trio of House Democrats: Charles E. Schumer (N.Y.), Howard L. Berman (Cal.), and Leon E. Panetta (Cal.), none of whom were sponsors of the bill. Led by Schumer, who had actively tried to save the 1984 immigration bill during last minute conference negotiations, and with the consent of Judiciary Chairman Peter Rodino (D-N.J.) who himself opposed the large guest worker program contained in the Senate bill, the trio met privately over the course of seven months with interest groups and Senate members to find common ground. The Senate had already passed—for the third time in five years—a bill very responsive to western and southern agricultural interests. Berman, 45, and Schumer, 35, were both Judiciary Committee members, but had no agricultural interests in their districts. Panetta, 47, represented a California agricultural district and sat on the Agriculture Committee, which had impeded passage of an immigration bill in previous years. They were only moderately senior in the House: in 1986 Schumer was finishing his third term, Berman his second term, and Panetta his fifth term.

The farm-worker program proved to be the most contentious issue. The powerful western growers were adamant in their insistence that a labor supply be provided to replace the illegal aliens on which they had traditionally relied for harvesting perishable crops. Labor unions were insistent that any such alternate program would have to guarantee protections to the workers. Schumer succeeded in getting both groups to support a compromise. Their failure to unite behind the 1984 bill had been a major factor in its defeat.

Chairman Rodino delayed consideration by the Judiciary Committee until late June so that Schumer's group could get the necessary consensus. Committee support was lukewarm, despite a sizable majority vote to report the bill. Several Republicans wanted another shot at changing the bill on the floor and so voted "aye" in committee to get it there. The debate over the rule for floor consideration temporarily killed the bill. Supporters wanted to protect it from floor amendments, but opponents of the farm worker program led by Dan Lungren (R-Cal.) prevailed and rejected the rule on September 26. Schumer immediately consulted with Lungren to try to draft an amended farm-worker program. By early October, Lungren, Schumer, and other key players had reached agreement on a farm-worker program that was more generous to agricultural interests than Schumer's previous version but still less liberal than the Senate version. The full House voted to approve the compromise 230 to 166.

The conference committee began meeting immediately. The principal Senate sponsor, Alan K. Simpson (R-Wyo), had already been consulted by Schumer's group and differences between his bill and the House bill were resolved in private sessions of the conference committee. The conference report was adopted in mid-October by the House 238 to 173 and by the Senate 63 to 24. The historic revision was finally achieved.

Conferees agreed that the urge to complete action was a strong motivation and that the overall spirit was more conciliatory than in 1984. Members were reaching a fatigue threshold, and as the issue had become more publicized, there was a growing desire to get a bill out. Compromise was more easily achieved in such an atmosphere. In the words of Sen. Simpson, "Everyone of us gave up something painful as hell, but we stayed at the table." For legislators like Representatives Schumer and Berman, the satisfaction of getting a bill out was an important reward, but the zest of the process was just as important. Schumer admitted: "I like the idea . . . of putting ideas into real action. In this kind of body that means working out compromises." And Berman concluded that negotiating "is the excitement of the legislative process . . . that kind of work has more of an effect than all the speeches you could give on the House floor."

1970s saw a great acceleration of change in both houses so that, at present, the hold of seniority in both a formal and informal sense has been weakened and only a few vestiges of apprenticeship remain.

By far the most important use of seniority was in making committee assignments and in the advancement of committee members toward chairmanships (these topics will be considered in more detail in Chapter 5). Changes began in the Senate when Minority Leader Lyndon Johnson instituted the "Johnson rule" in 1953 that all Democratic senators would have a seat on one major committee before senior Democrats would be able to go on a second major committee. The Republicans adopted a similar practice informally in 1959 and made it formal in 1965, along with the provision that no Republican could serve on more than one of the four most important Senate committees (Appropriations, Armed Services, Finance, and Foreign Relations).

Then, in the 1970s, changes were adopted by both parties in both houses that involved the choosing of committee leaders—chairpersons in the case of the majority party and ranking minority members in the case of the minority party. The practices adopted in the 1970s remain in place in the late 1980s.

In 1973 the Senate Republicans agreed to an arrangement whereby the Republican members of each standing committee elect the ranking member and that choice is then subject to approval by all Republican senators through a vote in the Republican conference (the meeting of all Republicans).

In 1975 the Senate Democrats agreed to hold a secret ballot on any ranking committee member when such a ballot was requested by one-fifth of the membership of the Democratic caucus (all Democrats). Nominations come from the Steering Committee.

In 1971 the House Republicans agreed to vote in conference on the nominations for ranking members coming from the Republican Committee on Committees.

The House Democrats made changes in their procedures in 1971, 1973, and 1975, each with more potential for limiting strict seniority appointments than the previous change. In 1971 the House Democrats agreed that the caucus should vote on any nomination for a chairmanship coming from the Committee on Committees (at that time the Democratic members of the Ways and Means Committee) if as many as ten members requested such a vote. In 1973 the procedure was changed virtually to guarantee secret ballot votes on each chairmanship nomination in the Democratic caucus. Three party leaders were also added to the Committee on Committees. In 1975 the power of making assignments was transferred to the Steering and Policy Committee and all chairpersons of full committees plus the chairpersons of the Appropriations Committee subcommittees were made subject to secret ballot votes in the caucus, with additional provisions for nominations from the floor.

Except for the House Democrats, the procedures have not resulted in non-seniority appointments to the top spots on committees. In the case of the House Democrats one chairman almost lost his position in a hard 1971 fight and in 1975 three senior southerners lost their chairmanships and a fourth chairman almost lost. In 1977 one Appropriations Subcommittee chairman was replaced. In 1985 the seventh-ranking Democrat on the Armed Services Committee, Les Aspin (D–Wisc.), became chairman of the committee. The Democratic caucus first ousted the sitting chairman by a vote of 121 to 118. Then the seventh-ranking individual defeated the second-ranking individual by a vote of 125 to 103. This "usurper" himself barely avoided defeat in 1987.

The specific change in personnel resulting from these procedures adopted in the 1970s has been relatively small. But the spirit of the changes has made senior members more aware of and responsive to procedural equity for less senior members and, in some cases, to differing substantive commitments on the part of large numbers of members of their committees or parties.

With these formal supports for awarding the most powerful institutional positions to the most senior members weakened, attitudes toward the relative place of junior and senior members have also changed. It is no doubt true—and is probably usually true in any human group—that those individuals with more experience are likely to have more influence. But those with less experience can also have considerable influence.

The norm of apprenticeship—the belief that junior members should serve for a period of time as apprentices before beginning to speak out and take an active role in legislative matters—has vanished in the Senate and has been substantially weakened in the House. This norm applied both on the floor and in committees. On the floor it meant that junior members should be restrained in speaking, offering bills, and offering amendments. In committee it meant little participation in the questioning of witnesses in hearings and deference to the judgment of more senior members on substantive matters.

More senior members may continue to be the most potent in floor actions simply because they can, in many instances, generate respect and support by their mastery of certain subject matters. But junior members have become much more active. By the mid-1960s apprenticeship for senators on the floor was rarely evident. Likewise, good committee assignments were so widespread that having less seniority was not terribly limiting even within the committee structure. Freshmen senators became known as experts on specific topics almost immediately both on individual committees and in the chamber as a whole. Relatively junior senators—Bill Bradley (D-N.J.) on taxes and Phil Gramm (R-Texas) on budget matters serve as good examples in the late 1980s—became the experts to whom most other members turn.

A study of the Senate as it had become in the mid- and late-1960s reached a conclusion that remains accurate:

> Virtually all senators can acquire substantial legislative influence. Those who do not have it usually have disqualified themselves by violating the Senate's code of acceptable conduct that is understood by most members. The code is not highly restrictive, and only repeated violations bring sanctions. . . .
>
> The Senate is not composed of a few omnipotent and happy senior senators and a great many impotent and unhappy junior senators. Most senators are content with their lot. Most of them feel that they have a considerable amount of legislative potency, at least in selected fields.[10]

The norm of apprenticeship has also been diluted in the House: "The need for a lengthy inactive apprenticeship no longer seems to be accepted; freshmen appear to be participating more frequently and earlier in their careers than the traditional description of the newcomer would lead one to expect."[11]

In both houses it remains true that, despite improvements in the committee assignments of junior members, some seniority is generally still helpful in obtaining the best assignments.

Within Senate committees there seems to be little concern for maintaining apprenticeship. The status of junior members varies more from committee to committee in the House. Given the general "legislative craftsman" self-image of most House members and committees and subcommittees, seniority continues to play a large role in some committees in terms of allocating influence over substantive outcomes.

A picture of Congress slavishly devoted to elevating senior mem-

[10]Ripley, *Power in the Senate,* 185.
[11]Herbert B. Asher, "The Changing Status of the Freshman Representative," in Norman J. Ornstein (ed.), *Congress in Change* (New York: Praeger, 1975): 233. See also Asher, "The Learning of Legislative Norms," *American Political Science Review* 67 (1973): 499–513.

bers to positions of power and suppressing junior members is inaccurate. That picture is based on the practices and performance of Congress for the first half of the twentieth century. The picture has changed substantially.

SUMMARY OF OPERATIVE NORMS IN THE LATE 1980S. The omnipresent norm in both the House and Senate is to take representation of constituents seriously. Additional major normative mandates are also present, although not universally observed by all members on all occasions:

1. Speak well of Congress and particularly of your own chamber. If you criticize, do it constructively and in a way designed to make clear that your goal is to strengthen the institution.
2. Respect your fellow members—both as individuals and as experts in specific substantive areas. Deal with them openly and courteously in ways that will lead to the maximum achievement of their goals and your own. Do not let party or ideological stances get in the way of making mutually agreeable and profitable bargains.
3. If you are a House member, specialize in a few substantive areas and work hard in those areas. If you are a senator, be active in the legislative arena but do not necessarily restrict your activity to any particular subject matter areas.
4. If you are a House member, be sure you have something to say before saying it, but do not let the fact of relatively junior status inhibit you from contributing to the legislative process.

## The Process of Transmitting Norms: The Socialization of Freshmen

Freshmen members of Congress seem to know the general norms of the House or Senate before they even arrive in Washington. One study observed that freshman representatives are conversant with congressional norms because these norms parallel the codes of behavior common to many institutions.[12]

This is not to argue, however, that freshmen have nothing to learn. They need to learn how the system actually operates: which committees do what, which individuals have what kinds of influence, what specialization means in practice, and so on. This kind of information

[12]Asher, "The Learning of Legislative Norms," 512.

often fleshes out the bare bones of norms, and to acquire it, new freshmen observe and talk to knowledgeable people such as senior colleagues, staff members, and the press when they come to Washington.[13] Freshmen also spend a considerable amount of time with each other, sharing experiences, observations, and the information they have picked up. Likewise, they tend to hire at least some experienced staff members who are able to pass on relevant information to them.[14]

Freshmen members also begin to learn where to look for cues on how to vote on the floor. It has been found that, in the House, they initially look to their state delegations. As the session wears on they broaden their search for cues to members of relevant committees.[15]

Freshmen in both the House and Senate are now incorporated into the life of those two bodies very quickly. The new members come to Washington already aware of the norms of the chamber in which they will sit. They learn additional details quickly. Their voting does not distinguish them from others, nor do their committee assignments, except for scarce representation on the most prestigious committees.[16]

There are a number of formal orientation programs for newly elected members. Some are partisan; some are bipartisan. Some deal with nuts-and-bolts questions such as how to organize and staff an office; others deal with national and international issues. Some are sponsored by units of Congress itself such as the party leadership or a committee; others are sponsored in whole or in part by organizations such as the Kennedy School at Harvard University, the Brookings Institution, and the American Enterprise Institute.

The first lesson learned by members of both houses, especially the House, is that their "bosses" are the voters back home. Therefore, if they are wise, from day one they orient their behavior to their district or state and assess it in terms of potential impact on and perceptions

[13]See Richard F. Fenno, Jr., "The Freshman Congressman: His View of the House," in Nelson W. Polsby (ed.), *Congressional Behavior* (New York: Random House, 1971): 125–35.

[14]On these two sources of information see Irwin N. Gertzog, "The Socialization of Freshmen Congressmen: Some Agents of Organizational Continuity" (paper prepared for delivery at the meeting of the American Political Science Association, September 1970).

[15]Herbert B. Asher, *Freshmen Representatives and the Learning of Voting Cues,* Sage Professional Paper in American Politics 04-003 (Beverly Hills: Sage, 1973).

[16]On voting see Theodore Urich, "The Voting Behavior of Freshmen Congressmen," *The Southwestern Social Science Quarterly* 39 (1959): 337–41; William Mishler, James Lee, and Alan Tharpe, "Determinants of Institutional Continuity: Freshmen Cue-taking in the U.S. House of Representatives" (unpublished paper); and J. Richard Emmert, "Freshmen Congressmen and the Apprenticeship Norms," *Capitol Studies* 2 (1973): 49–64. On assignments of freshmen to committees see Charles S. Bullock III, "Freshmen Committee Assignments and Re-Election in the United States House of Representatives," *American Political Science Review* 66 (1972): 996–1007.

by constituents. Freshmen members are not tightly restrained from having input into the legislative process but most try to use that freedom to enhance their standing with their voters.

## The Impact of Norms on Congressional Behavior

The most effective members of Congress are those who observe the norms of institutional loyalty and reciprocity and accommodation. In the House the most effective members also observe the norm of specialization. But in both houses there is great tolerance of deviant behavior. Short of actions so outrageous as to call into question the good name of the House or Senate, there is little or no "punishment" for any kind of behavior. The psychological pressure to conform to the norms is probably stronger in the House than in the Senate.[17] The Senate is now a very tolerant body. The "Club" dominated by conservative southerners that seemed to rule the Senate in the 1940s and 1950s has long since closed its doors.[18]

The most prominent of the Senate mavericks to emerge in the spotlight with the apparent national conservative shift in the electorate in the 1980 elections was Jesse Helms, a North Carolina Republican first elected to the Senate in 1972. Helms exemplifies both the influence a maverick can develop *and* the limits on his ability to be effective inside the Senate.[19] Helms is an unwavering right-wing ideologue who focuses on so-called "social issues," such as prayer in public schools, abortion, and school busing to achieve integration, much of

[17]On the use of psychological pressure on House members who consistently oppose their party see Randall B. Ripley, *Party Leaders in the House of Representatives* (Washington: Brookings, 1967): 158–59.

[18]For highlights of the debate over whether there was or was not a club in the Senate and its alleged impact see White, *Citadel;* Matthews, *U.S. Senators and Their World;* Joseph S. Clark and other senators, *The Senate Establishment* (New York: Hill and Wang, 1963); Wayne R. Swanson, "Committee Assignments and the Non-Conformist Legislator: Democrats in the U.S. Senate," *Midwest Journal of Political Science* 13 (1969): 84–94; Huitt, "The Outsider in the Senate"; Ralph K. Huitt, "The Morse Committee Assignment Controversy: A Study in Senate Norms," *American Political Science Review* 51 (1957): 313–29; Polsby, "Goodbye to the Inner Club"; and Ripley, *Power in the Senate.* See also Foley, *The New Senate.*

[19]On Helms see Dom Bonafede, "Though He's Riding a Conservative Tide, Jesse Helms Remains the Lonely Maverick," *National Journal* (July 18, 1981): 1284–88; Elizabeth Drew, "Jesse Helms," *New Yorker* (July 20, 1981): 78–95; and Albert R. Hunt and James M. Perry, "Despite Courtly Ways, Sen. Jesse Helms Is One Shrewd Operator," *Wall Street Journal,* July 16, 1981. The quotation from the White House aide in the text comes from Bonafede, 1285. The quotation from Helms after his defeats on abortion and school prayer in September 1982 comes from Steven V. Roberts, "Senate Makeup on Social Issues: 'Conservative It Ain't'," *New York Times,* September 25, 1982.

the time. He also focuses on developing a national following and national allies. This stance—both the ideological rigidity and the play for a national audience rather than an internal Senate audience—makes him an influential figure in general but means that he does not get all he wants out of the Senate. His work on the committees on which he serves receives mixed reviews. A White House aide made perhaps the best summation of Helms' standing by putting it in the context of the nature of the present Senate: "The Senate is basically made up of independent people. Helms has no big following—but who has? It's damn hard being a leader in the Senate these days." Helms makes his own Senate path more rocky by his maverick, nationally oriented strategy—but even the smoothest paths in the case of other senators do not lead to the "power" to control very much of what goes on in a highly fragmented institution.

In September 1982 the limits on Helms' influence inside the Senate were clearly demonstrated when he lost on two of his pet social issues. On September 15 the Senate voted 47 to 46 to table a Helms amendment that would have severely curtailed the right of women to obtain abortions. This vote came after three attempts to stop a liberal filibuster had failed. On September 23 Helms again lost, this time on the issue of prayer in the public schools. He had proposed altering federal court jurisdiction so as to remove the prayer issue. The Senate again refused to stop a liberal filibuster several times, finally by a vote of 53 to 45 for cloture on September 23 (60 votes were needed for cloture). Then, in the death blow, the Senate voted 51 to 48 to table Helms' motion to send the issue back to committee with instructions to send it again to the floor. The Senate ran true to form in that it voted against the two social-agenda items on procedural motions rather than on the issues themselves. It also denied victories to a leading Senate maverick. Helms himself, surveying the scene after his defeats, also reached a conclusion about the Senate: "Conservative it ain't, Republican it is." Since 1982 these issues have not been up for decision in the Senate. The Helms' high-water mark came in that year and he lost. The 1986 elections that returned the Senate to Democratic control and defeated some key Helms' allies further reduced the chances of Senate action on these issues.

In both houses the norms of specialization and reciprocity and accommodation give added support to the dominance of substantive decisions by the standing committees and particularly by subcommittees. This, in turn, underscores the fragmented nature of policy emerging from Congress. This effect of these two norms may not have a conservative effect in terms of substance in all cases, but it has a conservative effect in the sense that it helps make centralized leadership difficult except for short periods of time. Coordinated programs of legislation are less likely to emerge from a number of committees simultaneously in response to leadership requests. Scattered bills are reported on a sporadic basis; central direction of a range of measures is rare.

Many of the operating norms of the House and Senate acknowledge the members' concern with representation and re-election, and allow them considerable freedom in balancing perceived constituency pressure against pressure from party leaders. The consequence of these norms is that the power of the party system in Congress to command and receive cooperation from party members in policy matters is limited. There are other factors contributing to a relatively weak and decentralized party system; none, however, is more critical than the recognition of each member's need to vote in accord with the presumed interests of his constituency.

Because many of the governing norms are oriented toward promoting a stable membership, the norms operate against handling controversial matters openly because they are potentially damaging politically to at least some incumbents. If they are handled at all, an effort is made to arrive at compromises that either defuse explosive issues or at least minimize the political costs of the detonation.

## CUES FOR INDIVIDUAL BEHAVIOR

Members of the House and Senate are called on to make a very large number of decisions each year. They must vote publicly hundreds of times on the floor. They must vote many more times on the floor by voice vote or in other less visible ways. They must vote in committee and subcommittee. They must make a raft of other decisions in committee and subcommittee on which no formal vote is taken. They are asked to be familiar enough with everything the government does to make intelligent choices.

Obviously, no single individual can become even semi-expert in everything on the governmental agenda. Therefore, members seek shortcuts as they try to make up their minds. They seek cues for how to behave and how to vote on a great variety of policy matters. They want sources for those cues whose judgment they trust and who will lead them to "proper" decisions—that is, decisions that will help the senator or representative reach his own goals: whether they be reelection, ideological consistency, the "public good," personal status, or a combination of these goals.

Some observers have argued that if only Congress had more "information" on the substance of policy available to it, it could make "better" decisions. In fact, however, there are at least three limits to this view. First, good information is very difficult to come by in many areas. Second, even if it were available, it would be so vast in quantity that no member could absorb it, even for part of the policy areas with which each member must deal. Third, the norms of Congress that support fragmentation also support a limited search for information and a limited responsiveness to what has come to be called "policy analysis."[20] The shortcuts that members seek include a deliberate decision to limit the amount of information they want and to which they will pay any attention. The specific contexts in which decisions are made, which vary, influence the decision rules members use in making up their minds.[21]

Figure 4–1 portrays, in highly simplified fashion, the pressures (or cues) involved in the decision process by which an individual senator or representative makes up his or her mind on what position to take on any specific policy.

Pressures from outside Congress include those stemming from the public (mass opinion, the opinion of various specialized publics, and the opinion of voters as registered in their electoral decisions), interest groups, the various parts of the executive branch (the presidency and bureaucracy), and state and local officials. These pressures have an impact on the institutional clusters within Congress (relationship A in the figure) and also have an impact on the individual member directly (relationship B).

Pressures from inside Congress include those generated by party

[20]On some of the issues on the relations between Congress, information, and policy analysis see Charles O. Jones, "Why Congress Can't Do Policy Analysis (or words to that effect)," *Policy Analysis* 2 (1976): 251–64; and Allen Schick, "The Supply and Demand for Analysis on Capitol Hill," *Policy Analysis* 2 (1976): 215–34.

[21]See John W. Kingdon, *Congressmen's Voting Decisions*, 2nd ed. (New York: Harper and Row, 1981): Chapter 9. See also the discussion of Kingdon's findings, below. There is also evidence that members of the House not on a subcommittee reporting a bill routinely limit their search for information in many cases to colleagues on the subcommittee (the presumed experts) and to constituency opinion. See Robert Zwier, "The Search for Information: Specialists and Nonspecialists in the U.S. House of Representatives," *Legislative Studies Quarterly* 4 (1979): 31–42. On the impact of different "decision settings" see David C. Kozak, "Decision Settings in Congress," in David C. Kozak and John D. Macartney (eds.), *Congress and Public Policy,* 2nd ed. (Chicago: Dorsey Press, 1987): 303–21; and Kozak, "Decision-Making on Roll Call Votes in the House of Representatives," *Congress and the Presidency* 9 (Autumn 1982): 51–78.

**Figure 4–1.** The Making of Policy Decisions at the Individual Level in Congress

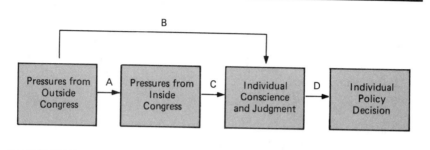

leaders, committee delegations, state delegations, informal clubs and groups, and staff members. These pressures impinge on the individual senator and representative (relationship C). These sources of outside and inside pressure also interact with each other.

Once the individual legislator has received the various outside and inside pressures he views them through the filters of his conscience and judgment and reaches his decision on his position (relationship D).

A number of studies have attempted to determine the cues to which members respond. Many of these studies examine the relationship between potential cues and roll call voting on the floor. They do not prove causality in the sense that a member consciously searches for a cue, receives it, and behaves accordingly; instead they infer that patterns of behavior reflect patterns of cue-giving and cue-taking.[22] Such studies of the House have outnumbered those of the Senate, but it is reasonable to assume that senators and representatives share similar thought processes.[23] They are also confronted with approximately the same workload. There is evidence that "Senators are less subject to constituency pressures and more independent of partisan constraints,"[24] because most states have more diverse constituencies than most House districts and because Senate party leaders are usually less demanding than House party leaders. But these differences are not

[22]For discussions relying specifically on an analysis of decision-making, cue-giving, and cue-taking see Kingdon, *Congressmen's Voting Decisions;* Donald R. Matthews and James A. Stimson, *Yeas and Nays: Normal Decision-Making in the U.S. House of Representatives* (New York: Wiley, 1975); Matthews and Stimson, "Decision-Making by U.S. Representatives: A Preliminary Model," in S. Sidney Ulmer (ed.), *Political Decision-Making* (Cincinnati: Van Nostrand Reinhold, 1970); and Aage R. Clausen, *How Congressmen Decide* (New York: St. Martin's, 1973).
[23]Clausen, *How Congressmen Decide.*
[24]Aage R. Clausen and Richard B. Cheney, "A Comparative Analysis of Senate-House Voting on Economic and Welfare Policy: 1953–1964," *American Political Science Review* 64 (1970): 151.

so great as to suggest that completely different decision-making processes exist in the two houses.

A number of studies have tried to assess the impact of constituency on individual decision making. The patterns that emerge from these studies are less than crystal clear. The safest conclusion seems to be that in terms of socio-economic characteristics, certain kinds of districts (for example, poorer urban districts) are more likely to elect Democrats, other kinds of districts (for example, relatively well-off suburban districts) are apt to elect Republicans, and that some ideological and programmatic differences are built into the basic difference between "Democratic districts" and "Republican districts."[25] The effect of typical constituency characteristics on the voting habits of members is not at all clear.[26]

Occasionally, constituency interests (as opposed to constituency characteristics) will account for changed voting patterns. Southern Democratic attitudes about foreign trade, for example, changed markedly from free trade to protectionism as the southern states industrialized and brought in industries concerned with protection—particularly the textile industry. At a more general level it can be argued that constituency characteristics (for example, percent blue-collar workers, percent Catholic) reflect constituency interests (higher minimum wages, urban renewal, aid to parochial schools).[27]

A number of cue-givers inside the House have also been identified. Usually they have been studied in isolation—the impact of state delegations as a separate topic, the impact of committee delegations as a separate topic, the impact of party leaders as a separate topic, and so on. But several studies have looked at these influences simultaneously in order to compare them. One of the most interesting studies was done by Matthews and Stimson on the period between 1957 and 1964.[28] They investigated the relative potency of state party delegations, the president, party leaders, party majority, majority of the House, committee chairpersons and ranking committee members, and the Democratic Study Group as cue-givers.

Matthews and Stimson summarize their principal findings succinctly:

[25]See Lewis A. Froman, Jr., *Congressmen and Their Constituencies* (Chicago: Rand McNally 1963): 95; and W. Wayne Shannon, *Party, Constituency and Congressional Voting* (Baton Rouge: Louisiana State University Press, 1968): Chapter 9.
[26]See Shannon, *Party, Constituency, and Congressional Voting,* 178.
[27]Thomas A. Flinn and Harold L. Wolman, "Constituency and Roll Call Voting: The Case of Southern Democratic Congressmen," *Midwest Journal of Political Science* 10 (1966): 192–99.
[28]Matthews and Stimson, "Decision-Making by U.S. Representatives."

**Table 4–1.** Cue Sources for Congresspersons, 1957–1964

| | AVERAGE CUE SCORES | | | |
| | DEMOCRATS | | REPUBLICANS | |
| CUE SOURCE | 1957–60 | 1961–64 | 1957–60 | 1961–64 |
| --- | --- | --- | --- | --- |
| State Party Delegation | .42 | .43 | .37 | .38 |
| President | .04 | .32 | .13 | −.16 |
| Party Leaders | .27 | .34 | .26 | .28 |
| Party Majority | .34 | .37 | .35 | .37 |
| House Majority | .31 | .39 | .20 | .23 |
| Committee Chairmen | .19 | .31 | −.05 | −.09 |
| Ranking Members | −.05 | −.01 | .08 | .19 |
| Democratic Study Group | .29 | .35 | −.09 | −.09 |

SOURCE: *Adapted from Donald R. Matthews and James A. Stimson, "Decision-Making by U.S. Representatives: A Preliminary Model," in S. Sidney Ulmer (ed.)* Political Decision-Making *(Cincinnati: Van Nostrand Reinhold, 1970): 31.*

The consistently most important single cue-giver in both parties is the member's state party delegation. . . . Two additional collective cues—the party majority and the House majority—are also potent, especially among the Democrats (who were in the majority all eight years). The President as a *direct* cue-giver is seemingly less significant, although Kennedy and Johnson did considerably better among Democrats than Eisenhower did among Republicans as a direct source of cues.[29]

Table 4–1 summarizes the Matthews-Stimson findings. The possible variation in the figures reported ranges from .50 (perfect agreement between the average Democratic or Republican congressman and a cue-giver) to −.50 (perfect disagreement). Figures greater than .30 are quite high. The table reports two periods: 1957–60, when a Republican was president, and 1961–64, when a Democrat was president.

State party delegations were the most important cue-givers in both parties, although they were more important for the Democrats than for the Republicans. The president was an important positive cue-giver for the Democrats when he was a Democrat and a relatively important negative cue-giver for the Republicans. The Republican president was only moderately important as a cue-giver for the Republicans and was about neutral as far as the Democrats were concerned. No doubt the personal style of individual presidents is important in his effectiveness as a cue-giver. Unfortunately, the model developed in the study of 1957–64 has not been used for subsequent periods of time.

[29]Ibid., 31–32.

Party leaders, particularly for the Democrats under a Democratic president, were important cue-givers. The party majority was consistently and about evenly important for members of both parties. The House majority was, predictably, a more important cue-giver for the members of the majority party throughout the period.

Committee chairmen were important as cue-givers for the members of their party and provided some negative cues for the members of the other party. Like the party leaders, they were most important when a member of their party was also president. This underscores the point that the party becomes most important when the president and congressional majority are of the same party.

Ranking minority members are not quite the mirror image of committee chairmen. They provided mildly negative cues for the members of the majority party, but were only moderately important in providing positive cues for the members of their own party. They were also more important in this regard when a Democrat was president, lending support to the image that the Kennedy-Johnson term was much more partisan in Congress than the second Eisenhower term.

The Democratic Study Group (DSG) did about as well providing cues to the Democrats as the party leaders and party majority, largely because the views of the DSG were similar to the views of most Democrats except the southern conservatives. The DSG also provided mildly negative cues for the Republicans.

There is valid evidence that members of the House and Senate take stable positions over time on general classes of policy issues. Voting change on the floor is evolutionary, not rapid.[30] Clausen has identified five predominant policy dimensions: government management, social welfare, international involvement, civil liberties, and agricultural assistance.[31] He found that in the 1950s and 1960s members' positions on these issues exhibited great stability. The influential factors on the five dimensions also remained quite stable: party influence dominated the government management dimension, a combination of party and constituency influence dominated the social welfare and agricultural assistance dimensions, constituency influence dominated the civil liberties dimension, and a combination of constituency and presidential influence dominated the international involvement dimension. These findings suggest that the Matthews-Stimson analysis would be even

[30]See Herbert B. Asher and Herbert F. Weisberg, "Voting Change in Congress: Some Dynamic Perspectives on an Evolutionary Process," *American Journal of Political Science* 22 (1978): 391–425.
[31]See Clausen, *How Congressmen Decide.*

more potent if it were done separately for the different policy dimensions. In any event, the work of Matthews-Stimson and Clausen suggest that cue-giving and cue-taking is not a random matter in Congress but that patterns of regularity and predictability do exist. The varying sources of influence will be examined in detail in subsequent chapters.

One of the most convincing summaries of how individual members of Congress make up their minds is provided by Kingdon, based on his close first-hand observation and interviewing in the House of Representatives in 1969.[32] Kingdon's basic argument can be summarized as follows:

1. Members search for information about a decision they must make only if they define that decision as having some kind of "problem" associated with it.
2. There are no problems with, or difficulty in making, many decisions. This is true when: (a) all of the forces that normally affect the member's decisions (interest groups, constituency, staff, administration, party leadership, fellow congressmen, and own attitude) agree that a given decision is proper; or (b) he or she feels very strongly about the matter at hand in a personal sense; or (c) the member has a well-established voting record on the same or similar issues.
3. Members make up their minds in a "consensus mode of decision" most of the time. This means that they first determine if a vote is controversial. If the answer to that is no, then any decision is relatively cost-free. When controversy is perceived then the member will check his or her "field of forces" to see how much conflict is present. If the actors in the field of forces all agree on the proper decision, the member will go along with them. If only one actor is out of line, most of the time the member will vote against the actor (93 percent of the time in Kingdon's data). If two actors are out of line, then the chances of going with the minority of forces rise (17 percent of the time in Kingdon's data). It is worth noting that the force called "own attitude" is by far the most potent in explaining defections by the member from the majority of a field of forces in agreement against his or her own attitude. Members use a calculus—which varies in detail from person to person—in arriving at decisions. The calculus allocates weight both to outside forces and to the member's own judgment.

[32]Kingdon, *Congressmen's Voting Decisions,* Chapters 9 and 10.

# THE SUBSTANTIVE IMPACT OF RULES AND PROCEDURES[33]

The general impact of the rules in both the House and the Senate is the same: the rules create a situation that promotes both legislative and organizational fragmentation, especially through protecting the power and prerogatives of the standing committees and subcommittees. The rules in both houses make it difficult for a bill that does not have committee approval to come to the floor. The fragmenting impact of stable standing committees and particularly subcommittees is enhanced and perpetuated. Floor amendment of committee products has become more common in recent years, but is used to pursue special concerns rather than in pursuit of a coordinated legislative package.

The rules create a situation in which there are multiple "veto points" through which every piece of legislation must pass. Every item that finally becomes a statute must usually be acted on affirmatively by two subcommittees (one in each house), two committees (one in each house), the House Rules Committee, the entire House, the entire Senate, a conference committee, both houses again if a conference committee was necessary, and the president. At each step in the congressional process there are opportunities for delay or defeat. There are also opportunities for amendment that may render the final product unrecognizable to the original sponsors. Ultimately, a statute may also face review by federal courts on constitutional questions. Some statutes and portions of statutes are declared unconstitutional and, therefore, void.

The rules of the House and Senate underscore the necessity of bargaining if anything is to be accomplished in Congress. The rules are structured to prevent domination of the process by any one person or small group. An unavoidable result of the rules is that coalitions must be built for positive action to be taken. Bargaining and fragmentation are closely linked.

## The Privileged Status of Committee Decisions

THE HOUSE. Ordinarily no legislation can come to the floor of the House unless it has been considered and reported by a standing com-

---

[33]For a particularly good discussion of the rules and their impact see Walter J. Oleszek, *Congressional Procedures and the Policy Process,* 2d ed. (Washington, D.C.: Congressional Quarterly Press, 1984). The general protection afforded the power and prerogatives of committees and subcommittees is reduced in cases in which statutes require expedited committee procedures.

mittee. There are ways around the committee system, but they are cumbersome and rarely successful. For example, a discharge petition to remove a bill from a committee and bring it to the floor requires the signatures of an absolute majority of the House (218 individuals). From 1937 through 1982 only 19 petitions of 371 filed received the necessary signatures. The House passed 15 of the bills, but only two became law, one in 1938 and one in 1960.

A procedure called suspension of the rules can also be used to circumvent House committees, but this procedure requires a two-thirds vote. Controversial bills have a difficult time passing under it. The Rules Committee can also bring any bill to the floor regardless of committee action. It rarely does so, because its members properly perceive that they too have a stake in preserving the sanctity of the committee process.

When bills come to the House floor through the regular committee process they may have special safeguards to insure their prompt consideration and perhaps their passage. Appropriations and tax bills, for example, may come to the floor as privileged business at any time, although the Appropriations Committee and Ways and Means Committee may prefer to go through the Rules Committee in order to obtain conditions they deem favorable placed on the debate.

The rules of the House plus the actions of the Rules Committee make it difficult for committee bills to be amended. Debate on amendments is strictly limited. Amendments rejected in the Committee of the Whole (a procedure used to facilitate floor debate by the whole House) cannot be made subject to a formal roll call after the Committee has risen; but amendments that are passed in the Committee of the Whole can be retested on a roll call. On most bills the minority party is, in effect, limited to one major effort to amend or kill the bill—the recommittal motion that immediately precedes the vote on final passage. If the majority party members of the committee are in agreement with a large part of the majority party in the House the committee version of a bill is likely to pass unchanged.

THE SENATE. The Senate rules have a discharge provision that is very difficult to use. But there are other provisions, easier to use, that can bypass a committee stage and produce floor action. The Senate suspension of the rules procedure is easier to use than the House procedure and requires only a majority vote; it is used mainly for appropriations bills. Non-germane amendments (also called "riders") can also be added to Senate bills through the normal amending procedure in committee or on the floor, again unlike the House, which has a strict rule of germaneness. With some frequency, important measures reach the Senate floor as riders to trivial bills. Finally, bills passed in the House can be brought directly to the Senate floor without consideration by a Senate committee.

All of these measures are unusual; but their greater availability suggests that the Senate is less dedicated to protecting the sanctity of the committee stage than is the House. Similarly, on the floor even those bills coming through the normal committee procedure (the vast majority of bills) are less protected against amendment than in the House. Senators have a number of committee assignments; this helps lead them to attach less negative symbolism to the amendment of committee products.

## Multiple Vetoes

In both houses there are a number of points at which a few determined members (or perhaps even a single determined member) can stop or at least significantly delay the passage of a piece of legislation. Committee procedure and floor procedure are both very complex. As a bill travels between houses and from the committee to the floor in either house (particularly the House) there are other dangers. Table 4–2 summarizes the points at which delay or defeat may occur in the House alone. The same table would apply to the Senate with the deletion of the references to the Rules Committee, some minor changes in the details of stalling action on the floor, and the significant addition of the filibuster as a weapon for either delay or defeat.

## The Special Case of the Senate Filibuster

Throughout the history of the Senate, a small number of senators, even as few as one, have been able to prevent action on specific measures by filibustering—that is, by engaging in "unlimited debate" that prevents a vote on the matter under discussion from being taken. Since 1917 the Senate has provided various mechanisms for invoking cloture—that is, ending the filibuster and allowing the Senate to vote on the matter under discussion. The filibuster has been used by minorities that, knowing they were in the minority were nonetheless so intense in their opposition to some issue that they were willing to disrupt the normal proceedings of the Senate in an effort to prevent the action they found abhorrent. For several decades before the 1960s a variety of civil-rights initiatives died because of southern filibusters.

**Table 4–2.** Points at which Delay or Defeat May Occur in the House

| DELAY | DEFEAT |
|---|---|
| Committee inaction in referring to a subcommittee | Committee inaction |
| Subcommittee inaction (prolonged hearings; refusal to report) | Negative vote in committee |
|  | Subcommittee inaction |
| Committee inaction (prolonged hearings; refusal to report) | Negative vote in subcommittee |
|  | Rules Committee inaction |
| Rules Committee inaction (refusal to schedule hearings; prolonged hearings; refusal to report) | Negative vote in Rules Committee |
| Slowness in scheduling the bill | Defeat of rule on the floor |
| Floor action (demanding full requirements of the rules) reading of the journal | Motion to strike enacting clause |
| repeated quorum calls | Motion to recommit |
| refusing unanimous consent to dispense with further proceedings under the call of the roll | Final passage |
| prolonging debate |  |
| various points of order |  |

SOURCE: *Lewis A. Froman, Jr.,* The Congressional Process *(Little, Brown, 1967): 18.*

On many issues filibusterers have forced compromises on specific provisions they find particularly objectionable.

Filibusters will sometimes go unchallenged and thus succeed. This is most true at the end of a session, particularly at the end of a Congress, when time simply has run out. Since 1917 the Senate has provided a cloture mechanism by which filibusters can be ended. From 1917 to 1949 and again from 1959 to early 1975 this rule provided for cloture by two-thirds of those senators present and voting. Between 1949 and 1959 the rule was interpreted to mean that two-thirds of the entire Senate had to vote for cloture before it could be imposed. Since March 7, 1975, the rule is that three-fifths of the entire membership (sixty senators out of the hundred members) must agree to cloture. In 1979 the Senate tightened its rules so that, after cloture is voted, time used in various procedural maneuvers to stall further would be counted against the post-cloture limit of 100 hours of debate.

From 1917 through 1985 215 cloture votes were taken, of which 71 (one-third) were successful.[34] The pattern of usage has varied over time. In the early years in which the rule was in effect (1917–1929) the

[34]For a listing of all cloture votes from 1917 through 1985 see the *Congressional Quarterly Almanacs* for 1977 (p. 813) and for 1985 (p. 27). For a discussion of the relation of the filibuster to time constraints on the modern Congress see Bruce I. Oppenheimer, "Changing Time Constraints on Congress: Historical Perspectives on the Use of Cloture," in Lawrence C. Dodd and Bruce I. Oppenheimer (eds.), *Congress Reconsidered,* 3rd ed. (Washington, D.C.: Congressional Quarterly Press, 1985): 393–413. For a good interpretation of the present state of the filibuster see Jacqueline Calmes, " 'Trivialized' Filibuster Is Still a Potent Tool," *Congressional Quarterly Weekly Report* (September 5, 1987): 2115–20.

procedure was used ten times and was successful four times. None of these votes involved civil-rights questions. However, in the next three decades (1930–1959) the procedure was used only twelve times; eight of those occasions involved civil-rights questions, and none of the cloture motions were successful. It was during this period that the reputation of the filibuster as the unbeatable southern weapon against civil rights legislation was established.

During the 1960s cloture was attempted 23 times, 11 of which attempts involved civil rights matters. Four of the 23 motions were successful, and three of those successes were on civil-rights bills. From 1970 through 1985 cloture motions were voted on 170 times. Sixty-three of the votes imposed cloture. No filibuster prevented civil-rights legislation from being enacted.

Cloture has become routine in the Senate. The filibuster is not a reliable weapon in the hands of a minority. One study of the filibuster in the 1940s and 1950s concludes it was overrated even then:

> (1) Filibusters have been so unthreatening to various presidents' legislative programs that the actual postwar occupants of the White House either have remained aloof from attempts to curb this presumed impediment to their power or have even covertly helped defeat and distract such efforts. (2) With one possible exception, in no case between the war and 1966 was the filibuster responsible for the death of a civil rights bill supported by majorities in Congress.[35]

Perhaps the most important impact of the filibuster is to gain concessions by threatening to use it, particularly when time is short at the end of a session, especially the second session. Those who threaten a filibuster may achieve some of their legislative aims even if they don't filibuster or even if cloture is voted, since some changes in the bill under discussion may be made in order to get the special majority needed to vote cloture.

## SUMMARY: AN OVERVIEW OF CONGRESSIONAL DECISION-MAKING

This chapter has outlined the setting in which both Congress as an institution and senators and representatives as individuals operate. In

[35]Raymond E. Wolfinger, "Filibusters: Majority Rule, Presidential Leadership, and Senate Norms," in Wolfinger (ed.), *Readings on Congress* (Englewood Cliffs, N.J.: Prentice-Hall, 1971): 305.

general, a number of regularities in congressional behavior, both individual and collective, are visible. These regularities have been explained primarily in terms of major environmental features—the electoral and representational system, the nature of the executive branch, and the nature of the workload. These features impinge on individual members directly and are also transmitted through the norms of behavior in the two houses, the cue-taking patterns used by the members, and the nature and impact of the rules and procedures of both houses.

The norm of specialization is a reaction to the existence of a specialized bureaucracy and a large and demanding workload. It also serves to promote narrow constituency interests. The norm of reciprocity and accommodation also facilitates the representation of those interests as well as making feasible the processing of an extensive agenda.

Among the cue-givers that have the most impact on patterns of congressional decisions, the constituency (including state delegations) and the president stand out, in addition to political parties and party leaders in the House and Senate. This fact highlights both the importance of the constituencies and president in the congressional environment and the complex role of the congressional parties as entities that in some ways serve the interests of the constituencies and president but in other ways are the main potential rallying points for a genuinely *congressional* point of view on policy.

The rules also afford members the opportunity to respond to perceived constituency interests (often by delaying or preventing action) if they so desire. At the same time, skillful parliamentarians can also maximize their responsiveness to the president or to some party position on policy. These activities are allowed by the rules, even though in general the rules also promote the relatively orderly disposition of the large workload. At times, however, orderliness takes second place to serving constituency, president, or party.

# 5

Committees
and Subcommittees

Committees and subcommittees are the basic units of Congress dealing with substantive matters. They have a great deal of independence, but they are not autonomous. In their deliberations the details of the congressional agenda are developed, the basic alternatives are posed, and legislation is cleared for final floor action. The details of the relationships of committees with subcommittees and of both with central party leaders and the total membership of the House or Senate have varied throughout congressional history. But, as a recent overview of committees concludes, "most members' legislative activity remains structured by their committee and subcommittee assignments."[1] This has been true for many decades.

Congress has conducted its business through committees since early in its development. The modern Congress is characterized by a

[1]Steven S. Smith and Christopher J. Deering, *Committees in Congress* (Washington, D.C.: Congressional Quarterly Press, 1984): 271.

stable system of standing committees with fixed jurisdictions and relatively unchanging memberships. This committee structure is at the heart of all congressional activities; it embodies the principal congressional response to the subject specialists in the bureaucracy and to its own heavy workload. Without resorting to this labor-saving device, a body of 535 members in two chambers would be incapable of processing the extensive amount of legislation necessary to govern. Yet the very device that permits the legislature to legislate contains the potential for dilution of congressional impact: individual committees and subcommittees can become highly responsive principally to selected interests. The committee structure is a fragmenting force. Numerous specialized clusters of individuals each proceed on their separate courses never united by any common vision of national policy goals. However, the presence of party leaders, and the types of interaction that must occur between the leaders and the committees can help curb the fragmenting tendency of committees.

The congressional committee system has been in flux in the last few decades. But its central importance in determining what policies emerge from Congress remains unchanged. The changes involve committee assignment processes, sizable dents in the "rule" of seniority for determining chairmanships, open meetings, restrictions on chairpersons, and the devolution of power to subcommittees.

In broad terms—with significant differences between the two houses and among committees in each house—full committees and their chairs dominated in the 1950s and the first part of the 1960s. Throughout the remainder of the 1960s and most of the 1970s subcommittees proliferated in number and gained in power. With the shrinkage of the federal domestic agenda and the increased fixation on spending and taxing in the Reagan era the growth of subcommittee power ceased and there was even some reconsolidation of power, particularly in the committees dealing with budget, taxing, and appropriations. However, the formal safeguards for subcommittee power that emerged in the 1970s remained. By the late 1980s the fragmenting potential of the committee and subcommittee system persists, although the major domestic policies on the governmental agenda limits the amount of work for committees other than those dealing with money matters.[2]

---

[2]For a lengthier argument about the changing nature of committees and subcommittees during the years since World War II see Roger H. Davidson, "Congressional Committees as Moving Targets," *Legislative Studies Quarterly* 11 (1986): 19–33.

# AN OVERVIEW OF THE PRESENT COMMITTEE SYSTEM

## A Description of the Committee System

There are several different kinds of committees in Congress. By far the most important are the *standing committees* and their *subcommittees*. These are committees that exist from Congress to Congress, with relatively stable memberships and jurisdictions. The entire range of legislation that Congress considers is parceled out to the standing committees. In 1987–88 there were twenty-two standing committees in the House and sixteen in the Senate. The jurisdictions are relatively well denoted by the names of the committees. In general, the two houses have parallel committee structures, although they use different titles for some committees (for example, Ways and Means in the House and Finance in the Senate have roughly the same jurisdiction; Education and Labor in the House and Labor and Human Resources in the Senate have about the same jurisdiction).

The House has six committees that the Senate does not have: District of Columbia, and Post Office and Civil Service (these matters are handled by the Governmental Affairs Committee in the Senate); Merchant Marine and Fisheries, and Science and Technology (these matters are handled by the Commerce, Science, and Transportation Committee in the Senate); Standards of Official Conduct (these matters are handled by the Select Committee on Ethics in the Senate); and Rules (this is a committee unique to the House because of its rules of procedure). Table 5–1 lists the committees of the House and Senate along with the number of members on each and the number of subcommittees established by each for the One Hundredth Congress (1987–88).

As Table 5–1 shows, there is a wide range in the size of committees. House committees are uniformly larger than Senate committees. There is also a wide range in the number of subcommittees established by any given committee. A few have no subcommittees and conduct all of their business in full committee. Most have a number of subcommittees. Many conduct virtually all of their business through subcommittees; the full committee becomes a holding company for the subcommittees.

Both houses also make use of *select* and *special* committees. The importance of these committees varies. In both houses, for example, the standing Small Business Committees started life as select committees. In 1987–88 the Senate had several select or special committees

**Table 5–1.** Standing Committees of Congress, 1987–1988

| COMMITTEE IN HOUSE OF REPRESENTATIVES | NO. OF MEMBERS[a] | NO. OF SUBCOMMITTEES[b] | PARALLEL COMMITTEE IN SENATE | NO. OF MEMBERS | NO. OF SUBCOMMITTEES |
|---|---|---|---|---|---|
| Agriculture | 43 | 8 | Agriculture, Nutrition, and Forestry | 19 | 7 |
| Appropriations | 57 | 13 | Appropriations | 29 | 13 |
| Armed Services | 51 | 9 | Armed Services | 20 | 6 |
| Banking, Finance, and Urban Affairs | 49 | 8 | Banking, Housing, and Urban Affairs | 19 | 4 |
| Budget | 35 | 8 | Budget | 24 | 0 |
| District of Columbia | 10 | 3 | — | — | — |
| Education and Labor | 34 | 8 | Labor and Human Resources | 16 | 6 |
| Energy and Commerce | 42 | 6 | Commerce, Science, and Transportation | 20 | 8 |
| Foreign Affairs | 42 | 8 | Foreign Relations | 20 | 7 |
| Government Operations | 39 | 7 | Governmental Affairs | 14 | 5 |
| House Administration | 19 | 7 | Rules and Administration | 16 | 0 |
| Interior and Insular Affairs | 37 | 6 | Energy and Natural Resources | 19 | 5 |
| Judiciary | 35 | 7 | Judiciary | 14 | 6 |
| Merchant Marine and Fisheries | 42 | 6 | — | — | — |
| Post Office and Civil Service | 21 | 7 | — | — | — |
| Public Works and Transportation | 50 | 6 | Environment and Public Works | 16 | 5 |
| Rules | 13 | 2 | — | — | — |
| Science and Technology | 45 | 7 | — | — | — |
| Small Business | 43 | 6 | Small Business | 19 | 6 |
| Standards of Official Conduct | 12 | 0 | — | — | — |
| Veterans' Affairs | 34 | 5 | Veterans' Affairs | 11 | 0 |
| Ways and Means | 36 | 6 | Finance | 20 | 7 |

[a]This figure does not include delegates, only full voting members of the House.
[b]In a few instances a title other than subcommittee is used.
SOURCE: *Congressional Directory, 1987–1988.*

that had some importance: the Select Committee on Ethics, the Select Committee on Intelligence, the Special Committee on Aging, and—above all—the Select Committee on Secret Military Assistance to Iran and the Nicaraguan Opposition. The last-named committee met jointly with its House counterpart to investigate the secret sale of arms to Iran and the subsequent diversion of the proceeds to aiding the Nicaraguan contras despite a congressional ban on such aid. In addition to its Select Committee to Investigate Covert Arms Transactions with Iran, the House also had two other important select committees: the Permanent Select Committee on Intelligence and the Select Committee on Aging.

Congress also has *joint committees* made up of equal numbers of senators and representatives. In 1987–88 Congress had five such committees, two of which had considerable policy importance: the Joint Committee on Taxation and the Joint Economic Committee. The former has a respected staff in the field of taxation.[3] The latter helps shape national thinking about economic policy by producing reports and holding hearings on broad questions involving the economy.

When standing committees, select and special committees, and joint committees are viewed together, two impressions emerge. First, the division of a vast jurisdiction into a finite number of units inevitably helps promote some fragmentation of matters that should logically be considered together rather than separately. On the other hand, the impression also emerges that Congress can and does change the committee units with which it conducts its primary substantive business. Committees are created and committees die. New developments in the realm of policy and in the organization of the executive branch are reflected in changes made by Congress itself in its own organizational structure. Some of these changes are slow. A good example is the death of the House Internal Security Committee (formerly the House Un-American Activities Committee), which did not come until 1975, despite the fact that it had never been important legislatively and had even ceased being important politically many years before. On the other hand, more speed is sometimes shown. For example, after a variety of investigations stemming from Watergate had revealed substantial abuses by American intelligence agencies in terms of violating rights of Americans, the Senate created a select committee in 1976 and the House followed suit in 1977. Even more speed was demonstrated

---

[3]See John F. Manley, "Congressional Staff and Public Policy-Making: The Joint Committee on Internal Revenue Taxation," *Journal of Politics* 30 (1968): 1046–67.

in late 1986, when each house created its own select committee to investigate the sale of arms to Iran and the linkage between those sales to the release of American hostages in Lebanon and the diversion of some profits from the sales to the forces fighting the government in Nicaragua. The establishment of these committees prevented numerous, fragmented investigations by a variety of standing committees.

After a rules change in 1975 the House also began to refer a number of bills to more than one committee. This represented an attempt to overcome some of the problems of fragmentation caused by the structure of the committee system.[4]

Congress uses *conference* committees to resolve differences between the House and Senate versions of bills. These committees are appointed only for the duration of the discussion of a single bill; they disband once their report has been accepted by both houses and the bill is forwarded to the president for his signature. The same members may serve on a large number of conference committees in any given session. Typically, senior members are assigned to many more conference committees than are junior members because they are expected to have more knowledge and influence that will help the two chambers reach final agreement.

In general, the ratio of Democrats to Republicans on committees is determined by approximating the ratio of Democrats to Republicans in the whole House or Senate. Details are negotiated between the leaders of the two parties. The majority party has a majority on each committee (with one exception noted below) no matter how small its majority is in the whole chamber. In the House the majority party has for a number of decades routinely allocated itself larger majorities on three critical committees (Appropriations, Rules, and Ways and Means) than the use of the overall party ratio would provide. The Budget Committee has also been treated this way since its creation. In 1987, for example, the Democrats represented about 59 percent of the members of the House, but they held 61 percent of the seats on the Appropriations Committee, 64 percent of the seats on Ways and Means, two-thirds of the seats on the Budget Committee, and 70 percent of the seats on Rules. (An exception in the other direction is that the Committee on the Standards of Official Conduct is evenly divided between the parties to prevent partisan decisions; the Senate Select Committee on Ethics follows the same practice.)

[4]Roger H. Davidson, Walter J. Oleszek, and Thomas Kephart, "One Bill, Many Committees: Multiple Referrals in the House of Representatives," unpublished paper, 1986.

There are constant pressures to expand the size of the most sought after committees in order to increase the number of choice seats. Table 5-2 summarizes the growth of committees in both houses between 1947 and 1987 for committees that existed continuously during those years.

As the table shows, only three minor House committees and no Senate committees shrank in size during these 40 years. Every other committee increased in size, with the most important committees tending to increase the most. Between 1947 and 1987 the total number of seats on all standing committees grew from 203 to 296 in the Senate and from 484 to 789 in the House, even though the Senate increased in size by only four members (those added when Alaska and Hawaii became states in 1959) and the House was stable in size.

## The Politics of Major Change in the Committee System

Any change in the committee structure of either house inevitably involves a variety of political and substantive considerations. These considerations are more numerous when the House or Senate is looking at its total committee structure and pondering changes. Each house has undertaken a major investigation and decision process in recent years. In general, the same pattern was followed in the two instances: fairly substantial changes were proposed by the panel that had studied the situation most closely and the full chamber finally made some changes, but only after those most threatening to the entrenched interests of incumbent members had been removed.

In 1973 the House created a Select Committee on Committees to study the House committee structure and to make recommendations. The committee made numerous studies and held extensive hearings. Members of the House, lobbyists, academics, and a capable staff were all involved. The report of the committee proposed some substantial changes. Members whose own personal position or preferred policies seemed threatened mobilized to oppose a number of specifics in the plan. Lobbyists for various organizations and interests that felt change would jeopardize their close and productive relationships with existing committees also began to push against specific parts of the bill. Consequently, a much milder version of change was adopted by the House in October, 1974.[5]

[5]For a summary of House action see "Hansen Reorganization Plan Adopted," *Congressional Quarterly Weekly Report* (October 12, 1974): 2896–98. For a thorough description and analysis of the whole process see Roger H. Davidson and Walter J. Oleszek, *Congress Against Itself* (Bloomington: Indiana University Press, 1977).

**Table 5–2.** Growth of Committee Size, 1947–1987[a]

| | NUMBER OF MEMBERS | | |
| --- | --- | --- | --- |
| | 1947 | 1987 | NET CHANGE |
| *House Committees* | | | |
| Agriculture | 27 | 43 | 16 |
| Appropriations | 43 | 57 | 14 |
| Armed Services | 33 | 51 | 18 |
| Banking, Finance, and Urban Affairs | 27 | 49 | 22 |
| District of Columbia | 25 | 10 | −15 |
| Education and Labor | 25 | 34 | 9 |
| Energy and Commerce | 27 | 42 | 15 |
| Foreign Affairs | 25 | 42 | 17 |
| Government Operations | 25 | 39 | 14 |
| House Administration | 25 | 19 | −6 |
| Interior and Insular Affairs | 25 | 37 | 12 |
| Judiciary | 27 | 35 | 8 |
| Merchant Marine and Fisheries | 25 | 42 | 17 |
| Post Office and Civil Service | 25 | 21 | −4 |
| Public Works and Transportation | 27 | 50 | 23 |
| Rules | 12 | 13 | 1 |
| Veterans' Affairs | 27 | 34 | 7 |
| Ways and Means | 25 | 36 | 11 |
| *Senate Committees* | | | |
| Agriculture, Nutrition, and Forestry | 13 | 19 | 6 |
| Appropriations | 21 | 29 | 8 |
| Armed Services | 13 | 20 | 7 |
| Banking, Housing, and Urban Affairs | 13 | 19 | 6 |
| Commerce, Science, and Transportation | 13 | 20 | 7 |
| Energy and Natural Resources | 13 | 19 | 6 |
| Environment and Public Works | 13 | 16 | 3 |
| Finance | 13 | 20 | 7 |
| Foreign Relations | 13 | 20 | 7 |
| Governmental Affairs | 13 | 14 | 1 |
| Judiciary | 13 | 14 | 1 |
| Labor and Human Resources | 13 | 16 | 3 |
| Rules and Administration | 13 | 16 | 3 |

[a]Some committees had different names in 1947. Committees created after 1947 are not included.
SOURCE: Congressional Directory, 1947 and 1987.

The House experience was repeated in the Senate in 1976–77. A Select Committee to Study the Senate Committee System was created in 1976. It reported an ambitious plan of reorganization, although not as ambitious as the one proposed in the House. But both in the Rules Committee and on the Senate floor the changes were moderated, largely because of the opposition of senators who would lose important positions and jurisdiction (including chairpersons) and because of the opposition of lobbyists who felt threatened. Some shifts of jurisdictions and organizations were made. Limits were also placed on the number of assignments any individual could receive—memberships on three committees and eight subcommittees and chairmanships of no more than three committees and subcommittees beginning in 1979. Overall, the change achieved in the Senate was greater than that in the House.[6]

The general lesson from these experiences is that reorganization is difficult to accomplish because, by definition, members of the House and Senate as well as important outside interest groups have a stake in maintaining existing arrangements. They are comfortable with those arrangements and are afraid of the unknown. It should also be observed, however, that the outside interests are likely to reassert and reestablish themselves in alliance with key members of Congress almost no matter what jurisdictional and organizational structure is adopted.

## COMMITTEE ASSIGNMENTS

Each of the four parties in Congress (House Democrats, House Republicans, Senate Democrats, and Senate Republicans) uses different methods for assigning members to vacancies on standing committees.[7]

The House Democrats used the Democratic members of the Ways

[6]For a good summary of the Senate experience see Thomas P. Southwick, "Senate Approves Committee Changes," *Congressional Quarterly Weekly Report* (February 12, 1977): 279–84. For an insightful comparison of the House and Senate reorganization experiences in the 1970s see Roger H. Davidson, "Two Avenues of Change: House and Senate Committee Reorganization," in Lawrence C. Dodd and Bruce I. Oppenheimer (eds.), *Congress Reconsidered,* 2nd ed. (Washington, D.C.: Congressional Quarterly Press, 1981): 107–33.

[7]For a fine review of the literature on committee assignments from 1950 to 1984 see Heinz Eulau, "Legislative Committee Assignments," *Legislative Studies Quarterly* 9 (1984): 587–633. This is also included in Gerhard Loewenberg, Samuel C. Patterson, and Malcolm E. Jewell (eds.), *Handbook of Legislative Research* (Cambridge, Mass.: Harvard University Press, 1985): Chapter 5.

and Means Committee to recommend assignments to the Democratic caucus (all Democrats in the House) from 1911 through 1974. Beginning in 1975 this power was transferred to the Steering and Policy Committee, which is chaired by the Speaker, contains the other principal party leaders, and reflects the range of policy views in the party membership. In 1987 this committee had 31 members. The caucus possesses the final authority to accept or reject the recommendations of the Steering and Policy Committee. The caucus gives virtually automatic acceptance to the full slate of assignments, with the possible exception of a few nominations to chairmanships. The Speaker appoints all Democratic members of the Rules Committee over which the caucus also has a formal right of review and approval. The change in 1975 in who constituted the Committee on Committees did not result in dramatic differences in assignments, although it allowed party leaders to be more explicit in rewarding loyalty on the part of non-freshmen.[8]

The House Republicans have a special Committee on Committees comprised of one member from every state having at least one Republican in the House. The Republican floor leader chairs the committee. Since the committee is so large the actual work of making assignments is done by an executive committee that always includes representatives of the states with the largest Republican delegations and is chaired by the floor leader. Since voting is on the basis of the number of Republicans from a state, the states with the most Republicans dominate the process. In 1987, however, small state members coalesced and defeated large state members for many of the most desirable openings. The full House Republican Policy Committee approves the nominations. The Republican Conference approves only the ranking minority members.

The Senate Democrats have a steering committee appointed by the floor leader that makes the Democratic appointments. The floor leader also serves as chair. The steering committee is comprised of the senior members of the party (many of them committee chairs); once on the committee they are automatically reappointed. It has about 25 members. The decisions of this committee are limited by the unwritten rule that all Democrats should have one choice assignment before any Democrat is given two (this is called the "Johnson rule" because it was first implemented in the early 1950s when Lyndon Johnson was the Democratic floor leader). The Democratic Conference must approve the Steering Committee nominations.

[8]Steven S. Smith and Bruce A. Ray, "The Impact of Congressional Reform: House Democratic Committee Assignments," *Congress and the Presidency* 10 (1983): 219–40.

The Senate Republicans have a committee on committees that makes initial assignments on the basis of seniority. The chair of the party conference appoints the committee, which has about 15 members, and also chairs the committee. The committee is limited, however, by a rule adopted by the Republicans in 1965 that no Republican can hold seats on more than one of the four most important committees (Appropriations, Armed Services, Finance, and Foreign Relations) before every Republican senator at least has a chance to refuse such a seat. The Republican Conference does not approve nominations.

Many criteria are used in making initial assignments to committees. These include seniority, region, ideology, preferences of the individual members, and—at least in some cases—religion and race. In general, all of the parties use the same mix of criteria. Additional factors that affect committee assignments include the expressed preferences of individuals such as party leaders, senior committee members, and, occasionally, representatives of interest groups. In general, the assigning authorities are amenable to the argument that a particular assignment will help a member retain his or her seat in forthcoming elections. This is the most commonly used criterion and the most persuasive argument a member can make.

The precise mix of criteria for assignment change from year to year, from committee to committee, and from member to member. A veteran member of the House who became Speaker in 1987, Jim Wright (D-Tex.), provides a nice summary:

> Being appointed to the committee of one's choice is a matter of application and luck. The freshman member should certainly make his wishes known to the Speaker (if he is of the same political faith) and the leaders of his party in the House in either event. He also should try to line up as much support as he can muster among the colleagues of his own state delegation.
>
> Sometimes, however, even the most careful plans will not avail an aspirant. Naturally, if a freshman is to be successful in his quest there must be a vacancy on the desired committee, and generally there must be no one with seniority from his own geographic zone and in his own political party who wants this particular assignment. . . .
>
> But other considerations might prevail. During President Eisenhower's Administration, for instance, the conservative bloc of the Republican Party in the House controlled the party leadership. They would not permit any Republican member to be appointed to the powerful Ways and Means Committee unless he *opposed* Eisenhower's liberal position on reciprocal trade. On the other hand, while Sam Rayburn held sway as Speaker, no

Democrat was chosen to this committee unless he agreed to *support* the reciprocal trade program.[9]

Members seek to achieve one or more of three general goals as they seek committee assignments: to increase their influence on some policy area that interests them, to increase their chances of re-election, or to increase their influence in the House or Senate.[10] Interviews with freshmen in the Ninety-second Congress (1971–72) showed most of them interested either in re-election or in policy (or in both) as they sought their first assignments.[11] A study of large number of Senate Democratic requests from 1953 to 1971 showed the same pattern.[12]

At different periods in congressional history, policy preferences and ideological biases get built into assignment patterns, although the biases are likely to change over time. For example, for many years both parties in the Senate assigned their more conservative members to the Finance Committee. Senate Democrats also used to put an unusually large proportion of conservatives on the Appropriations, Armed Services, and Judiciary Committees.[13] A systematic study of the progress of senators through shifting committee assignments supports the claim that for the period from 1947 through 1963, Senate Democrats regularly discriminated against liberal senators who were eager to change the rules of the Senate.[14] In the House a study of assignments in the early 1960s suggested that the more liberal Democrats were more likely to get their preferences.[15] In the House Republican party the more conservative members generally do better.

Since both the House and Senate have equally elaborate committee and subcommittee structures it is inevitable that senators will have more assignments than representatives. Table 5–3 summarizes the average number of committee and subcommittee assignments for individual senators and representatives in six different congresses. This table shows that senators have many more assignments than representatives. It also shows roughly a doubling of the number of assignments

[9]Jim Wright, *You and Your Congressman* (New York: Coward-McCann, 1965): 131.
[10]Richard F. Fenno, Jr., *Congressmen in Committees* (Boston: Little, Brown, 1973).
[11]Charles S. Bullock, III, "Motivations for U.S. Congressional Committee Preferences: Freshmen of the 92nd Congress," *Legislative Studies Quarterly* 1 (1976): 201–12.
[12]Charles S. Bullock, III, "U.S. Senate Committee Assignments: Preferences, Motivations, and Success," *American Journal of Political Science* 29 (1985): 789–808.
[13]See Randall B. Ripley, *Power in the Senate* (New York: St. Martin's 1969): Chapter 3.
[14]Wayne R. Swanson, "Committee Assignments and the Nonconformist Legislator: Democrats in the U.S. Senate," *Midwest Journal of Politics* 13 (1969): 84–94.
[15]See Randall B. Ripley, *Party Leaders in the House of Representatives* (Washington, D.C.: Brookings, 1967): 60. For a dissenting study see Timothy E. Cook, "The Policy Impact of the Committee Assignment Process in the House," *Journal of Politics* 45 (1983): 1027–36.

**Table 5–3.** Number of Committee and Subcommittee Assignments for Senators and Representatives, Selected Congresses, 1955–1988

| CONGRESS (YEARS) | MEAN NO. OF STANDING COMMITTEE ASSIGNMENTS | MEAN NO. OF SUBCOMMITTEES OF STANDING COMMITTEE ASSIGNMENTS | MEAN NO. OF OTHER COMMITTEE ASSIGNMENTS[a] | TOTAL |
|---|---|---|---|---|
| *Senators* | | | | |
| 84th (1955–56) | 2.2 | 4.8 | 0.9 | 7.9 |
| 92nd (1971–72) | 2.5 | 9.5 | 3.3 | 15.3 |
| 94th (1975–76) | 2.5 | 11.0 | 4.1 | 17.6 |
| 96th (1979–80) | 2.3 | 6.6 | 1.5 | 10.4 |
| 98th (1983–84) | 2.9 | 7.5 | 1.2 | 11.6 |
| 100th (1987–88) | 2.9 | 7.0 | 1.2 | 11.1 |
| *Representatives* | | | | |
| 84th (1955–56) | 1.2 | 1.6 | 0.2 | 3.0 |
| 92nd (1971–72) | 1.5 | 3.2 | 0.4 | 5.1 |
| 94th (1975–76) | 1.8 | 4.0 | 0.4 | 6.2 |
| 96th (1979–80) | 1.7 | 3.6 | 0.5 | 5.8 |
| 98th (1983–84) | 1.7 | 3.6 | 0.5 | 5.8 |
| 100th (1987–88) | 1.7 | 3.8 | 1.0 | 6.6 |

[a]"Other" committees include: select and special committees; subcommittees of select and special committees; joint committees; and subcommittees of joint committees.
SOURCE: Norman J. Ornstein and others, *Vital Statistics on Congress, 1987–1988* (Washington, D.C.: Congressional Quarterly, 1987): 130.

for representatives between the mid-1950s and the mid-1980s. In the Senate, however, after the committee reorganization discussed above was adopted in the late 1970s, the number of assignments was cut significantly, although not back to the levels of the mid-1950s.

## The Impact of Seniority

No assignment system is likely to be neutral or unbiased. Seniority (longevity of service) as a primary consideration in committee assignments in the United States Congress is no exception. For many years it was argued that seniority promoted the interests of conservatives, especially southern Democrats. That claim was exaggerated, although there was some truth to it.[16]

[16]See Barbara Hinckley, *The Seniority System in Congress* (Bloomington: Indiana University Press, 1971).

Even during the period in which southerners, mostly conservatives, did seem to be unusually important in Congress—especially the Senate—seniority was only one factor that promoted and sustained their importance. By the late 1970s southern power in both houses had declined substantially. And, of course, not all southern Democrats are conservatives.

The use of seniority as a criterion for making assignments (this involves length of service in the chamber) and designating chairpersons (this involves length of service on a specific committee) does not automatically favor either liberals or conservatives. Electoral results and career patterns in the House and Senate play independent roles in determining the nature of the bias that appears in committee assignments, although the bias is often mistakenly attributed to the use of seniority alone. The main impact of using seniority for choosing chairpersons is that they are older than the rest of the members, but there is no evidence that age is related systematically to ideological views.

The impact of seniority means even less when it is realized that most of the policy action is now in subcommittees rather than in full committees. Seniority has come to mean less in choosing subcommittee chairs in both houses. In the Senate virtually every member of the majority party can count on being chairperson of at least one subcommittee and virtually every member of the minority party can count on being ranking minority member on at least one subcommittee. This has been the case since the 1960s. The more senior members still have the more important posts but everyone has something he or she considers important.

As already indicated, the House Democrats in 1975 made less automatic the nature of succession to chairmanships. In that year three full committee chairs were deposed. The next successful challenge to a full committee chair did not occur until 1985, when seventh-ranking Les Aspin (D-Wisc.) replaced the sitting chairman, Melvin Price (D-Ill.) on the Armed Services Committee and also defeated the second-ranking Democrat in doing so. Aspin had established a reputation for knowledge and hard work and Price was in failing health and not in full control of what was going on in the committee. In early 1987 Aspin himself was briefly deposed as chairman because he had lost touch with enough Democrats on the committee that they no longer thought he was the best chair. In early January the Democratic caucus voted to replace Aspin by 130 to 124, but did not name a successor. The Democratic party leadership endorsed the most senior member of the committee after Price (who still sat on the committee after his deposition in 1985), Charles Bennett of Florida. Two other members of the committee also challenged Aspin. Both were well down the seniority list (11th and 14th) and represented different policy positions. When the caucus reconvened two weeks after deposing Aspin, he had successfully wooed back enough support to win after three ballots, defeating the last challenger 133 to 116 on the final ballot. Aspin had the most votes on the first and second ballot (the lowest challenger was dropped after each ballot) but did not get his needed majority until he had only one challenger left. Aspin made it clear after his narrow squeak that he had learned a lesson: "There are lots of things I need to do differently in dealing with people. It has to do with the way I deal with my colleagues on a one-to-one basis. A need to be more open, more up front. The message is not that you have to toe the party line on issues. What it does say is . . . you can't surprise people. You've got to be frank about what you're doing. And if you're not with them be clear about it very early."[17]

The Senate Republicans also confronted the meaning of seniority in early 1987 and came down on the side of not violating seniority in relation to who should serve as a ranking minority member of an important committee. In 1985 Senator Jesse Helms of North Carolina was the senior Republican on both the Agriculture and Foreign Relations Committees. He had pledged to his constituency that he would choose Agriculture, which is important to North Carolina. Since no senator could be chairperson of more than one committee, the Foreign Relations chair went to Richard Lugar of Indiana, who was next in seniority. In 1987, after the 1986 election had returned the Republicans to minority status, Helms decided he would choose to be the ranking minority member on Foreign Relations rather than on Agriculture. Lugar, who had been an effective chairman, and his supporters argued that Lugar should remain ranking. The Foreign Relations Committee Republicans voted 7 to 0 to retain Lugar in the ranking position (Lugar and Helms did not vote). However, the Republican caucus (all Republican senators) voted 24 to 17 to give the ranking position to Helms, explicitly "in order to preserve the vital principles of party unity and Senate seniority."

Challenges by less senior members to the most senior members for the chairmanships of House subcommittees have also occurred and been successful in a number of cases. This rule change seems to have

---

[17]The quotation from Aspin comes from *Congressional Quarterly Weekly Report*, (Jan. 24, 1987): 139.

produced greater loyalty to party positions in the behavior of Democratic chairpersons in the House.[18]

## The Attractiveness of Committees

Committees vary in their attractiveness to the members of the House and Senate. Some committees—such as Appropriations, Ways and Means, or Finance—offer their members increased visibility as legislators. Some committees—such as Public Works and Transportation or Agriculture—enable the members to do things for their constituents that they might not otherwise be in a position to do; this enhances the standing of the member at home and may well increase the safety of his or her seat at election time. Some committees—such as Foreign Affairs, Foreign Relations, Education and Labor, or Labor and Human Resources—allow the members to maximize their ability to influence national policy in an area of special interest to them. The relative attractiveness of committees also changes as a fluctuating policy agenda changes the relative importance of committees.

Compilations are done from time to time of patterns of transfers between committees. These patterns give a good guide to the attractiveness of the various committees because members are not likely to seek a transfer except when they value a different committee more highly. The patterns of "prestige" or attractiveness are quite stable. In the House the most attractive committees are Rules, Ways and Means, Appropriations, and Armed Services. In the Senate the most attractive committees are Foreign Relations, Finance, Appropriations, Judiciary, and Armed Services.[19]

In large part the most attractive committees are the most important committees in terms of policy. This suggests that individual members

[18]Sara Brandes Crook and John R. Hibbing, "Congressional Reform and Party Discipline: The Effects of Changes in the Seniority System on Party Loyalty in the US House of Representatives," *British Journal of Political Science* 15 (1985): 207–26.

[19]For rankings in both houses from 1949 through 1968 see George Goodwin, Jr., *The Little Legislatures* (Amherst: University of Massachusetts Press, 1970). For additional material on the House see Charles S. Bullock, III, "Committee Transfers in the United States House of Representatives," *Journal of Politics* 35 (1973): 85–120; Malcolm E. Jewell and Chu Chi-hung, "Membership Movement and Committee Attractiveness in the U.S. House of Representatives, 1963–1971," *American Journal of Political Science* 18 (1974): 433–41; and Bruce A. Ray, "Committee Attractiveness in the U.S. House, 1963–1981," *American Journal of Political Science* 26 (1982): 609–13. The reduced rigidity of the seniority rule in the House has made members more willing to seek transfers. See Gary W. Copeland, "Seniority and Committee Transfers: Career Planning in the Contemporary House of Representatives," *Journal of Politics* 49 (1987): 553–64.

take seriously their desire to influence policy. Finance, Ways and Means, Armed Services, and Appropriations also offer a number of opportunities to perform major services for constituents and for fellow members in terms of such items as special tax provisions, protection of defense installations against closing, and appropriation of funds for pet projects.

Committees can also become unattractive. Since the early 1970s, for example, the House Judiciary Committee has had trouble getting enough applicants to fill its open seats.[20] A mix of reasons explain this case (and others like it): the committee handles controversial issues such as abortion, gun control, and school prayer proposals that make members vulnerable to the attacks of potent interest groups in their districts; much of the jurisdiction of the committee covers matters that have no interest to voters (for example, copyright laws); and there are no "goodies" at the disposal of the committee to be targeted for the districts of members who serve on the committee. The committee is not in a position to enhance the chances of members for either re-election or for running for the Senate or other statewide office. And the subject matter dealt with by the committee for those members with policy commitments does not seem intrinsically interesting or important.

## THE INTERNAL OPERATIONS OF COMMITTEES

The standing committees of the House and Senate vary in the way they work. Both houses have delegated considerable substantive decision-making power to subcommittees, although there are variations among individual committees. Both houses have limits on the power of chairpersons, although those limits are different on different committees and some chairpersons are still extremely powerful. Some committees seek internal integration that presumably enhances their autonomy and the chances that their policy decisions will go unchanged in the full House and Senate and in conference committees. Others are much more oblivious to any necessity for a high degree of integration. Some virtually eschew partisanship as they pursue agreement on policy statements and actions. Others not only carry general party disagreements into committee deliberations but also magnify and intensify them. Some, in effect, prescribe a period of apprenticeship for

[20]Lynette P. Perkins, "Member Recruitment to a Mixed Goal Committee: the House Judiciary Committee," *Journal of Politics* 43 (1981): 348–64.

junior members. Others admit junior members to full participation immediately.

## Subcommittees[21]

Most congressional committees use subcommittees to process their work. The natural tendency is for the subcommittees to move toward autonomy and for the full committees to ratify the work of the subcommittees almost automatically.

In general, the substantive work of Congress gets done largely in subcommittees. This fact maximizes the impact of individual members (particularly the senior members of the subcommittees) on policy but it also opens the committee system to the special representations of the bureaucracy and interest groups. Every bureau and every interest group can seek out "its subcommittee," and if they can befriend the chairperson and perhaps the ranking minority member they can help control federal policy in areas that interest them. In such a situation it is hard to say which persons in a triangular arrangement have the most influence: the senator or representative or the bureau chief or the lobbyist (or even, particularly in the Senate, a staff person for the subcommittee).

Power devolved to subcommittees in the 1960s in the Senate in most cases. This created a situation in which virtually all Senators were either the chairperson or ranking minority member of at least one subcommittee. Many served in those capacities on several subcommittees. Although the committee reorganization in the Senate in 1977 reduced the number of subcommittees, more than enough remained for every senator to be the most important person in his or her party in one or more substantive areas. Given the relatively small number of senators, this situation also left staff members very important in the

[21]On various aspects of subcommittee functioning in the last few decades see Roger H. Davidson, "Subcommittee Government: New Channels for Policy Making," in Thomas E. Mann and Norman J. Ornstein (eds.), *The New Congress* (Washington, D.C.: American Enterprise Institute, 1981): Chapter 4; Lawrence C. Dodd and Richard L. Schott, *Congress and the Administrative State* (New York: Wiley, 1979); Goodwin, *The Little Legislatures:* 45–63; Steven H. Haeberle, "The Institutionalization of the Subcommittee in the United States House of Representatives," *Journal of Politics* 40 (1978): 1054–65; Charles O. Jones, "The Role of the Congressional Subcommittee," *Midwest Journal of Political Science* 6 (1962): 327–44; Norman J. Ornstein, "Causes and Consequences of Congressional Change: Subcommittee Reforms in the House of Representatives, 1970–73," in Ornstein (ed.), *Congress in Change* (New York: Praeger, 1975): 88–114; Ripley, *Power in the Senate:* Chapters 3, 6, and 7; and Steven S. Smith and Christopher J. Deering, *Committees in Congress.*

# REPUBLICAN FEUD ON THE HOUSE APPROPRIATIONS COMMITTEE

BY LAWRENCE J. HAAS

It wasn't your everyday event. On the House floor, a California Republican barely six months into his first term was taking on the ranking Republican on the House Appropriations Committee as well as his party's leaders on the 13 Appropriations subcommittees.

After recalling a few occasions when the ranking members openly opposed spending cuts proposed by other Republicans, Rep. Ernest L. Konnyu told the chamber: "Yet, I do not see those same ranking members sponsoring floor amendments to reduce the spending contained in the Democrat-authored appropriations bills. I am very concerned about that because why should freshmen Republicans be offering spending cuts when it is the ranking Republican members' job to do that? . . . If they do not know their job, they ought to. I and other freshmen just met with the [Republican] leader [Rep. Robert H. Michel of Illinois] this morning and complained about this very same thing, and I hope as a result of that effort plus this speech, something is going to be done about it."

Moments later, Rep. Silvio O. Conte of Massachusetts, the ranking member on Appropriations, shot back: "In view of the fact that the gentleman referred to me, taking me to task, I have been here 29 years, and he is the first Member who has ever done that, and I resent it."

This fracas, which took place during the June 25 debate on next year's appropriations bill for the Interior Department and related agencies, was smoothed over in subsequent conversations. But it reflected a simmering dispute among House Republicans that pits leading members of a powerful committee—who have traditionally worked with Democrats to help shape appropriations bills—against newer, more conservative Members pushing for confrontation to highlight party differences.

The committee's chairman, Jamie L. Whitten, D-Miss., who has benefited from the bipartisanship, brushed aside any concern, saying, "You've got so much to do, you don't have time to worry about the future." Perhaps. But if the GOP upstarts achieve their goals, life on Appropriations could get a lot less appealing for members of both parties.

"I think there's an important element," said Ralph Regula of Ohio, the ranking Republican on Appropriations' Interior Subcommittee. "We do need to make everyone aware of the appropriations process. If I'm to be confrontational, I have to know that. But I will not be able to participate in the process. I think the country is better served if we have a collegial atmosphere."

Committee Republicans have already taken some steps to educate their colleagues about the appropriations process. Regula met with Konnyu after his exchange with Conte, and Konnyu told him afterward that he wished the two had had the conversation earlier. And Conte has proposed that at the start of each two-year congressional term, he should meet with new Members to explain the process.

What Conte and other longtime Appropriations Republicans want other Republicans to understand is that bipartisanship brings tangible rewards. "You should see the list of requests I get" from Republicans asking for federal funds to be directed to their districts, Conte said. "And we help most of them. In the course of a year, I do a lot." Regula said the Interior Subcommittee provided in the fiscal 1988 appropriation about 146 projects in Republican districts, and perhaps 10 more in Democratic districts.

Educational efforts, however, may not suffice. The intra-party dispute has bubbled over in recent months because on several occasions, the most senior GOP committee members cast deciding votes against initiatives to cut appropriations measures.

On July 15, the House voted, 218-203, to cut 4.74 per cent from the Treasury and Postal Service spending bill, saving $420.7 million. Democratic leaders, however, persuaded enough Members to change their minds and the cut was overturned on a 210-207 vote. In both cases, the cuts were opposed by Conte, the next four most senior Republican committee members and seven other GOP members.

Two days earlier, Conte and 12 other GOP committee members voted against an amendment, which was defeated 189-198, to cut 3.3 per cent from the Transportation appropriations bill and save $361 million. And on June 25, the top five Republican committee members and six others helped turn back an amendment to chop off 2 per cent from the Interior spending measure, a move that would have saved $188.8 million.

Critics of the senior committee

Republicans concede their points about the rewards of bipartisanship. But they say that the overriding GOP concern must be deficit reduction, especially because many new Members pledged during their campaigns to reduce federal spending. Michel, a former Appropriations Committee member, has expressed sympathy for that view and has asked committee Republicans to suggest how to cut the bills.

In a sense, House Republicans addressed this issue earlier in the year. With three openings on the Appropriations Committee, they chose three conservatives: Thomas D. (Tom) DeLay of Texas, Jim Kolbe of Arizona and Vin Weber of Minnesota. Asked about the appointments, DeLay said, "One main reason, and I was in the room when the discussion was being held, was to make sure that people on these major committees reflected a majority of opinion in the [House Republican] Conference."

Rep. Thomas J. Tauke, R-Iowa, who co-chairs a bipartisan group trying to trim $7 billion from the fiscal 1988 spending measures, characterized the intra-party dispute this way: "If there is no difference between Democrats and Republicans in this Congress, then I'm missing something. What's interesting about Appropriations is that we never take a different approach than the Democrats. And the public perception is that we are pleased with the level of spending. I don't feel we are challenging the Appropriations Committee members. But I think there is a need for the [Republicans] as a whole to adopt a policy for the Appropriations Committee members to follow."

That effort is under way. Rep. Lynn Martin of Illinois, vice chairman of the Republican Conference, and Rep. Mickey Edwards of Oklahoma, a committee member and the new chairman of the Republican Conference's research committee, have proposed ideas before the party's policy committee in the hope of drafting a policy.

"The problem we ran into this year is that the budget that was passed is a budget we don't believe is at all acceptable," Edwards said. As a result, the Republicans' traditional position, that spending bills must stay within the budget resolution, no longer appeared to go far enough. "It was no longer adequate," he said, "to say this appropriation is within the budget."

To maintain a bipartisan spirit but still meet GOP concerns, Edwards suggested that perhaps Republican Appropriations members could support bills that emanate from their particular subcommittee, but sign on to deficit-cutting amendments to other bills: "I don't think the [Republican] Conference would be critical if the four of us who had been on a subcommittee stuck by the agreement. I think they would look at it as a bit strange if the 18 others felt the same need to defend the package."

Even if Republicans adopt a policy, holding Members to it may be another matter. On appropriations bills, the general goal of deficit reduction often conflicts with the need to "bring home the bacon." As DeLay put it: "I'm going to do everything I can to cut spending, not only in Appropriations but in the authorizing committees. But then, when it's all said and done, and money is taken from my constituents, I think it's my responsibility to get some of that money back for my constituents."

decision making on many subcommittees. Even the most junior senators are able to develop legislative influence quickly.

Subcommittees became much more important in the House in the 1970s. Before then they were consistently dominant only on the Appropriations Committee. Now they have become the central fact of legislative life in the House on virtually all committees. Between 1955 and 1987 the number of subcommittees has grown from 83 to 143. Because of the new rules requiring the key positions (chairs and ranking minority member positions) to be spread among different members, close to half of the Democrats and most of the Republicans held such a position.

A number of developments in the 1970s produced the present situation in the House. First, in 1971 the House Democrats adopted the rule that no member can be chairperson of more than one subcommittee. Prior to that time a number of senior members had dominated the subcommittee chairs.

Second, the Democratic caucus adopted a subcommittee "bill of rights" in 1973. This bill of rights protected subcommittees from domination by the chairperson of the full committee. Specifically, the Democratic membership on each full committee (a mini-caucus) was given power to select the chairpersons of subcommittees by vote. In the last few years, several sitting subcommittee chairpersons have been replaced by these mini-caucus votes, although seniority on the full committee continues to be the most important criterion for selection as a chairperson.[22] The bill of rights also provided that subcommittees had to have fixed jurisdictions; that they were authorized to meet without approval of the chairperson of the full committee; that they would have adequate budgets under their own control; that they would have staff directly responsible to the subcommittee chairperson and ranking minority member; and that all members of the full committee would have a right to at least one "choice" subcommittee assignment. By these moves, chairpersons of the full committees were deprived of a number of powers some of them had been able to use in past years to keep subcommittees tightly under their own control.

Third, all full committees with more than twenty members except the Budget Committee must establish at least four subcommittees. Only four committees had fewer than twenty members in 1987. But two of those had subcommittees, and the Budget Committee established task forces that functioned like subcommittees. Only one House Committee—Standards of Official Conduct—had no subcommittees at all.

Fourth, all House committees are now required to have written rules of procedure. These offer additional guarantees for individual members and for subcommittees that decisions will not be made in such a way as to thwart the will of the majority.

Fifth, in December, 1974, the Democratic caucus specified that no member of a committee could hold more than two subcommittee memberships. This was aimed particularly at dispersing power on the Appropriations Committee.

Sixth, beginning in 1975 all subcommittee chairpersons on the Appropriations Committee had to win approval of the full Democratic caucus. This resulted in the deposing of one chairperson in 1977.

Since these landmark changes the Democratic caucus has also made a variety of additional changes designed to open more desirable

[22]See Thomas R. Wolanin, "Committee Seniority and the Choice of House Subcommittee Chairmen: 80th–91st Congresses," *Journal of Politics* 36 (1974): 687–702; and Jack A. Goldstone, "Subcommittee Chairmanships in the House of Representatives," *American Political Science Review* 69 (1975): 970–71.

subcommittee seats to junior members. There are more subcommittees with more autonomy with more junior members having more influence than ever before. Full committees provide only minimal direction for the efforts of their subcommittees. Party leaders attempt almost no integration of their activities.

## Committee Chairpersons

The powers of full committee chairpersons have been substantially reduced in recent years. In many cases, however, the chairpersons remain important individuals in shaping the substantive impact of Congress on legislation. In general, the chairperson of a committee still has more influence than anyone else on the committee in terms of shaping its policy decisions. They command this kind of influence either because they successfully exert independent judgment supported by the use of the resources they possess or because they are faithfully reflecting the policy preferences of a number of committee members.

For well over a century in the Senate, committee chairpersons have almost all been chosen on the basis of their seniority in a given committee, as distinguished from their seniority in the Senate as a whole. The person in the majority party who has longest service on a committee at the beginning of any given Congress is designated as chairperson; everyone below him in committee seniority is ranked accordingly for purposes of succession and, in some committees, for purposes of receiving subcommittee chairs. The minority party adopted the same pattern for choosing ranking minority members. The Civil War created some delay in the final consolidation of the seniority system, but by the mid-1870s it was well established. Violations of seniority have occurred since but they have been rare.

In 1973 the Senate Republicans decided to make their ranking minority positions elective within the Republican delegation on each committee. This policy has not yet resulted in any violations of seniority. The most senior members are likely to continue to hold the ranking positions, even if formal "elections" are held. But at least the change gives the Republican senators on individual committees a weapon to use if they are actually confronted with an incompetent, senile, gravely ill, or tyrannical ranking member.

In 1975 the Senate Democrats adopted a rule that makes committee chairpersons subject to a secret ballot vote in the conference if one-fifth of the membership requests it. This has not yet resulted in any violations of seniority but is a check on arbitrary behavior by chairpersons.

The principle of seniority was used in the House by both parties for selection of committee chairpersons with only a few exceptions from about the time of World War I until the mid-1970s. Then in the mid-1970s the Democrats made chairmanships elective within the Democratic caucus. This procedure has resulted in only a few violations of seniority. Seniority is still the single most important criterion used in the House in selecting chairpersons. But chairs are more responsive to their members than before the new procedure.

Despite limits on the power of chairpersons—limits that have been particularly well developed in the House in recent years in connection with the promotion of subcommittee influence—a skillful chairperson can parlay both his remaining powers and his knowledge of procedures and substantive matters into considerable influence. There is still considerable respect for the powers of chairpersons in both houses, in part because other members hope to rise to chairmanships themselves and do not want to inherit empty shells. Deference to a chairperson is often based on his or her genuine expert knowledge in the areas within the jurisdiction of a committee. Knowledgeable chairpersons can usually make a strong case for the positions they favor on legislation and can persuade a large proportion of the members to follow their lead.

Even before the formal rules changes adopted in the House in the last few years, committees faced with chairpersons they felt were unfair had ways of limiting their power and influence. Chairpersons who consistently antagonized committee members with tyrannical or erratic behavior sometimes found themselves severely hemmed in by unwelcome new rules.

A good example of major changes within a committee affecting the power of the chairperson is provided by the Ways and Means Committee in the House in 1973 and 1974. Even before the departure of Wilbur Mills from the chair he had held for seventeen years, these changes had begun. Mills' dominance of the committee in favor of moderate policy positions was threatened. The House rejected a major Ways and Means compromise engineered by Mills involving cost-of-living increases in social security payments. A reform adopted by the Democratic caucus left room for opening committee bills to floor amendment, whereas previously most Ways and Means bills had been granted a "closed rule" (one that allowed no amendments on the floor of the House). The Republicans became less willing to cooperate with Mills, and liberal Democrats seemed more demanding on issues such as tax reform and health insurance.

Then in October 1974, the House required Ways and Means to

establish subcommittees in the next Congress after defeating an effort to remove considerable jurisdiction from the committee. And in December 1974, the Democratic caucus removed committee assignment powers from the Democratic members of Ways and Means and increased the size of the committee from twenty-five to thirty-seven as a prelude to adding a number of new liberal Democrats in early 1975 when the Ninety-fourth Congress convened.

Although Mills' successor to the chair, Al Ullman, Democrat of Oregon, had some problems establishing himself as a genuine leader on the committee, he was still the focus of committee activity. Ullman's successor, Dan Rostenkowski, (D-Ill.), became even more visible as the central figure on the committee. Rostenkowski seemed particularly skillful in building a winning coalition for a major revision of the tax code in 1986.

The drive for subcommittee autonomy in the House has limited the powers and influence of many chairpersons more severely than in the Senate. In the Senate some of the committees are still dominated by powerful chairpersons. However, a chairperson who moves to limit subcommittee rights and powers already established is likely to cause tensions within the committee and problems for himself.

The powers of Senate committee chairpersons and ranking minority members were succinctly summarized by Walter Oleszek, a Congressional Research Service staff member:

Committee chairmen are important figures because they can call meetings and establish agendas, appoint staff members, refer bills to one rather than another subcommittee, retain bills or oversight hearings in full committee rather than refer them to a subcommittee, designate conferees, act as floor managers, control committee funds, control committee rooms, chair hearings and executive sessions, and, depending on committee rules, create subcommittees and establish their party ratios.

Ranking minority members are also important and influential figures on committees. Among their powers are nominating conferees; hiring and discharging minority staff; fixing minority staff salary rates; assisting in scheduling hearings both in Washington, D.C. and outside; authorizing the interrogation of witnesses by professional staff; sitting ex officio on all subcommittees; appointing minority members to subcommittees; and influencing the appointment of special or ad hoc subcommittees.[23]

---

[23]Walter Oleszek, "Overview of the Senate Committee System," in Commission on the Operation of the Senate, *Committees and Senate Procedures* (Washington: U.S. Government Printing Office, 1977): 15.

House chairpersons have lost many of the powers still residing in the hands of Senate chairpersons. They still have some formal powers, however, including control over the staff of the full committee and considerable control over agendas and the scheduling of meetings. Above all, if they have knowledge of their subject matter, they can be especially important figures in committee deliberations.

The symbolism of either ousting or severely restricting the power of a chairperson is important. And, no doubt, there are values to be served by "democratizing" committee procedure. But simply changing or restricting chairpersons is not likely to change the substantive output of a committee by itself. Other changes are necessary. For example, one study of the three House committees whose chairmen were deposed in 1975—Armed Services, Agriculture, and Banking and Currency—shows that the committees proceeded about the same substantively in the following year.[24]

A classic example of a powerful chairman was Senator Russell B. Long (D-La.) of the Senate Finance Committee. Long dominated his committee, which also happened to be a committee with a vast and important jurisdiction, including taxes, welfare, social security, medicare, health insurance, and foreign trade.

Long retained all important business for the full committee; there was no subcommittee autonomy on Senate Finance. The members of the committee supported him in his desire to keep a centralized committee, apparently feeling that such a procedure enhanced their own influence too.

In the years of his chairmanship (from 1966 through the Democratic loss of the Senate after the 1980 election; he served as ranking minority member for six more years and retired from the Senate when his term expired in 1986) he used his powers to consolidate his influence. He was particularly adept at expanding the staff of the committee in such a way as to buttress positions he favored. He knew the substantive business of the committee very well and was a tireless exponent of his positions in debate and conversation. But he also knew when to compromise and was not given to hopeless crusades. Above all, he also knew how to trade important favors, particularly amendments to the tax code, for support for his positions.

In the trading process Long was usually quite open about what he was doing. The committee held all of its meetings in the open

---

[24]John Berg, "Reforming Seniority in the House of Representatives: Did It Make Any Difference?," *Policy Studies Journal* 5 (1977): 437–43.

and kept transcripts of the proceedings, but that did not affect the bargains that were struck. An exchange in a 1975 committee meeting typifies the kind of openness about bargaining that characterized Long's style. Another member of the committee, Gaylord Nelson (D-Wis.) said during a session at which a bill was undergoing final specific changes in language, "I understand that in my absence, we passed the tax breaks for railroads, but omitted railroad-over-water ferries—such as the one in Wisconsin." Long replied, "I'll be happy to give you that one without need of further discussion, but I expect you in exchange to vote for this next tax credit we're about to discuss."

A good example of the powers of Senate chairmen is provided by the actions of Strom Thurmond (R-S.C.) when he became chairman of the Senate Judiciary Committee following the elections of 1980. He immediately reshuffled subcommittee organization and assignments so as to provide a solid conservative dominance on all important issues coming before the committee. One liberal Republican, Charles Mathias of Maryland, who could be expected to oppose Thurmond on some issues, was left without an important chair or membership.

In 1985–86 two Republican chairmen of key committees in the Senate stood out as particularly adept. One was Richard Lugar (R-Ind.), who became chairman of the Foreign Relations Committee in 1985. He worked hard to energize a committee that had slipped in visibility in recent years. He successfully maneuvered the first foreign aid bill in four years through the committee in 1985. He put the committee in a position of considerable influence in overseeing the administration's policies with regard to the Middle East and South Africa. He also held broad-gauged hearings on the shape of U.S. foreign policy in general. These hearings got considerable media coverage. The other Senate chairman who stood out in 1985–86 was Robert Packwood (R-Ore.) of the Finance Committee. Like Rostenkowski, he was assiduous in making substantive agreements that allowed a winning coalition to be put together behind a major tax bill that few believed could be passed when the process began.

## Integration

Integration refers to how well the parts of a committee (that is, the individuals and, to a lesser extent, the subcommittees) mesh as the committee operates from day to day. The classic example of a highly integrated committee is the House Appropriations Committee.[25] Individuals who are recruited for this committee are not passionate partisans and must maintain an aura of "responsibility." These qualities are sought to perpetuate the dominant norms about the job of the committee: to cut the federal budget and guard the treasury. In general, committee members believe—regardless of party—that the proposals coming from the executive branch almost always contain some fat. Their job is to trim that fat while providing enough money to maintain federal programs, particularly those vital to constituents, at adequate levels. Agencies that receive the largest percentage of their requests from the committee are likely to be those with noncontroversial tasks, stable workloads, and leaders held in high esteem by the committee. Agencies involved in controversy, with shifting workloads, and leaders held in low esteem by committee members are unlikely to fare very well. Agencies with strong support from external clientele groups are likely to grow more rapidly from year to year than agencies without clientele groups or with weak, apathetic, or hostile groups. Bureaus such as the Forest Service, Office of Education, and Soil Conservation Service are in a particularly strong situation because they have strong support from within and without the committee simultaneously. At the other extreme, agencies such as the Bureau of Mines, the Bureau of Reclamation, and the Census Bureau, have had neither external nor committee support.

Virtually all of the work of the committee is conducted in the appropriations subcommittees, and the full committee routinely accepts nearly all of their budget decisions. This means that individual members specialize in one or two specific areas and are expected to become experts on whom the rest of the committee (and the House) can rely for sound judgments. The prime integrating factors in this committee seem to be the mutual deference paid to one another by the various subcommittees and the widely shared vision of the central purpose of the committee.

Another example of a highly integrated committee was the House Committee on Ways and Means until 1975.[26] The integrating mechanisms of this committee were different from those of the Appropria-

[25]Richard F. Fenno, Jr., "The House Appropriations Committee as a Political System: The Problem of Integration," *American Political Science Review* 56 (1962): 310–24; and Fenno, *The Power of the Purse* (Boston: Little, Brown, 1966).
[26]John F. Manley, "The House Committee on Ways and Means: Conflict Management in a Congressional Committee," *American Political Science Review* 59 (1965): 927–39. See also, Manley, *The Politics of Finance* (Boston, Little, Brown, 1970).

tions Committee. The committee was not united substantively: the tax matters (the tax code, social security and medicare, welfare, the tariff) that the committee handles have long had major partisan aspects that divide members both of the committee and of the House. On the other hand, the committee members were agreed that their task was to legislate so well and so thoroughly that their work would be accepted virtually without question by the House and, hopefully, by the Senate Finance Committee and the whole Senate, too. The chairman of the committee from 1958 through 1974, Wilbur Mills of Arkansas, was adept at managing the substantive policy tensions that are part of his committee's province. He showed great skill in emphasizing points of agreement and minimizing points of disagreement while treating all participants fairly.[27]

A classic example of Mills at work occurred in 1965 on the question of establishing a federal program supporting medical care for the aged (medicare). The administration was supporting a bill that was funded through a payroll tax but that provided mainly hospitalization costs and left other medical expenses largely uncovered. The ranking Republican on the committee had introduced a bill with a more generous benefits package but funded on the basis of voluntary enrollment supplemented by money from general federal revenues. After listening and helping guide the debate between the contending forces, Mills cleverly proposed a compromise that adopted the more generous benefits package of the Republican bill but retained the compulsory membership-payroll tax feature of the Democratic bill. He gave virtually all members of the committee some reason for satisfaction and yet was instrumental in creating a program that was more far-reaching than anyone thought could come out of the Ways and Means Committee.

Yet another pattern of integration is evident in the House Committee on Agriculture.[28] The main work of the committee is conducted by subcommittees dealing with specific crops; the principal integrating factor is the mutual deference of these subcommittees to one another. The growers of all crops—particularly those important to the southern Democrats who have dominated the committee's majority party contingent for a number of years (for example, cotton and tobacco)—receive good treatment in the subcommittees; the full committee ratifies subcommittee decisions. When there are partisan issues before the committee that are not tied to specific crops, however, integration is

[27]See Manley, "Wilbur D. Mills: A Study in Congressional Influence," *American Political Science Review* 63 (1969): 442–64.
[28]Charles O. Jones, "Representation in Congress: The Case of the House Agriculture Committee," *American Political Science Review* 55 (1961): 358–67.

likely to be diminished as the demands of partisanship take over. The basic question of level of parity (the percent of a "fair market price" supported by governmental subsidy) has often been such a partisan issue.

The House Committee on Education and Labor provides an example of a committee not preoccupied with integration, probably because it would be virtually impossible to achieve.[29] The committee handles issues that not only provoke partisan differences (labor-management relations and federal aid to education, for example) but that also raise thorny racial and religious questions (federal aid to parochial schools, federal programs to force unions to open their ranks to black members). There is no agreement on the substance of what the committee should do (as in the case of Appropriations). Subcommittees are used, but without mutual deference among them (as in the case of Appropriations and Agriculture). There have been no chairpersons particularly skillful in muting conflict on partisan issues (as in the case of Ways and Means). And there has not even been agreement that the committee should aim for a product that will be accepted almost automatically by the House. Instead, the expectation seems to be that the debate over the divisive aspects of the committee's work will continue on the floor and in the Senate and in conference committees.

Committee integration in the Senate presents a different picture from the House. The average size of Senate committees is smaller and the average senator has many more committee assignments. Whereas a House member becomes expert in a particular field and develops a personal stake in the most minute of outcomes, the individual senator develops a personal stake in only a few scattered items. He or she is much more reliant on staff than is the House member. Mutual deference to subcommittee decisions is widely accepted in the Senate as a norm, and is not a question that each individual committee must decide.

One study of Senate committee integration found that integration (measured by agreement of committee members in roll-call voting on the floor) was related to similarity of members' constituencies (measured by income inequality) and to members' seniority in the Senate.[30]

---

[29]Frank J. Munger and Richard F. Fenno, Jr., *National Politics and Federal Aid to Education* (Syracuse: Syracuse University Press, 1962).

[30]Lawrence C. Dodd, "Committee Integration in the Senate: A Comparative Analysis," *Journal of Politics* 34 (1972): 1135–71. It should also be noted that there is no universal agreement on how to measure integration. And different measures may produce different results in terms of the presumed consequences of integration. See Lawrence C. Dodd and John C. Pierce, "Roll Call Measurement of Committee Integration: The Impact of Alternative Methods," *Polity* 7 (1975): 386–401.

Committees whose members were relatively junior and who represented similar states were more highly integrated than committees whose members were more senior and represented states that differed. When integration was related to the members' success in getting their own bills reported from their committees, it was found that members on more-integrated committees had greater success than members on less-integrated committees. Pork-barrel committees (those dealing primarily with tangible physical benefits—"pork"—for constituencies) were an exceptiontothisfinding.

What are the results of committee integration? Well-integrated committees are more likely to be able to offer inducements to members of the House and Senate that will lead them to seek membership on such committees (for example, members may receive important psychological gratification from seeing their efforts in committee result in successful legislation). Well-integrated committees (Ways and Means, Appropriations) are more desired than a partially integrated committee (Agriculture,) which is, in turn, more desired than a relatively unintegrated committee (Education and Labor). There seems to be no convincing evidence, however, that better-integrated committees "succeed" more on the floor.

## Partisanship

It has already been suggested that committees vary in terms of their partisanship.[31] Some, like House Education and Labor and Public Works, are unabashedly partisan. Others, like Ways and Means, exhibit a restrained form of partisanship. Still others, like Appropriations, are often nonpartisan. In general, in the House, reduced partisanship makes integration more likely. House committee chairpersons who are in a position to be bipartisan—whether because they deliberately seek to be or because the issues they face either force or at least allow it—tend to be with the majority in the committee when decisions are made more frequently than chairpersons who are more

[31]On Education and Labor, Ways and Means, and Appropriations see the material cited in footnotes 25, 26, and 29 above. On Public Works see James T. Murphy, "Political Parties and the Porkbarrel: Party Conflict and Cooperation in House Public Works Committee Decision Making," *American Political Science Review* 68 (1974): 169–85. There is some evidence that in the mid-1970s partisanship—and also ideology—became more prevalent in the behavior of a number of House committees. See Glenn R. Parker and Suzanne L. Parker, *Factions in House Committees* (Knoxville, Tenn.: University of Tennessee Press, 1985).

partisan. Committees with the bipartisan mode of leadership also are more likely to get stronger support on the House floor than committees led in a more partisan fashion.[32]

In the Senate there is less evidence about the extent and impact of partisanship within committees. There is, however, a range of behavior. The Senate Appropriations Committee, for example, generally operates on a nonpartisan basis.[33] In general, most Senate committees have a tradition of minimizing partisan considerations whenever possible. No committees always split along party lines, but there are occasions—predictable on the basis of the issues at stake and personalities of the most important committee members—in which committees will proceed on a highly partisan basis. The attitude of the chairperson toward partisan questions is an important factor explaining the relative presence or absence of partisanship. Only a few Senate chairpersons act as aggressive partisans. Most seek accommodation with the minority party committee members.

## Apprenticeship

All of the committees in both houses rely on division of labor and specialization on the part of members, in virtually all cases by relying on subcommittees. Specialization is necessary for committees to process their generally heavy workloads and to compete with the level of information that bureaucrats possess.

In some committees, specialization involves a differentiation between senior and junior members of the committee or subcommittees. The senior members are viewed as the genuine specialists and are given both formal and informal recognition (for example, more time for questioning during hearings) within the committee and on the floor of the chamber of which the committee is a part. On other committees junior members are accorded full rights virtually from the day they join the committee and they may, in fact, develop subject matter expertise that leads to deference very quickly. The apprenticeship norm is more prevalent in the House than in the Senate, although it has waned in many House committees in recent years.

[32]Joseph K. Unekis and Leroy N. Rieselbach, "Congressional Committee Leadership: Continuity and Change, 1971–1978," *Legislative Studies Quarterly* 8 (1983): 251–70. See Unekis and Rieselbach, *Congressional Committee Politics: Continuity and Change* (New York: Praeger, 1984).

[33]See Stephen Horn, *Unused Power* (Washington, D.C.: Brookings, 1970).

## The Special Case of the House Rules Committee[34]

The House of Representatives operates under a much tighter set of rules on the floor than does the Senate. In large part this difference is dictated by the differing sizes of the two bodies. The much larger House must have a more orderly and restricted floor procedure in order to work effectively. To help govern the conditions under which specific measures are discussed on the House floor, the House has long used a Committee on Rules.

The Rules Committee plays a role both before and after House passage of legislation and also has some general powers. Before House passage its central role is to decide whether a bill can come to the House floor and, if so, the conditions under which it will be debated. In deciding whether it is ready for floor action at all, the committee has the option of reviewing the work of the standing committee reporting the bill. If it decides to grant a "rule" (specifying the conditions under which floor debate takes place) then it decides whether to leave the bill open to amendments, whether to restrict the number of amendments, or whether to eliminate the possibility of floor amendments altogether. It also sets the time limit for the debate, always splitting the time evenly between those in favor of the bill and those opposed to it.

After House passage of legislation, the most important power of the Rules Committee is either to grant or to avoid a conference with the Senate over differing versions of the bill. The committee can also help revive House-passed bills that were defeated in the Senate. And it can promote final passage of legislation by waiving points of order against conference reports that contain extraneous (non-germane) provisions.

There are provisions by which the full House can overrule the decisions of the Rules Committee either before or after floor action on a bill. But these procedures are difficult and complex and are rarely used successfully.

In addition to its legislative power, the Rules Committee also helps

---

[34]On the Rules Committee see James A. Robinson, *The House Rules Committee* (Indianapolis: Bobbs-Merrill, 1963); Douglas M. Fox, "The House Rules Committee's Agenda-Setting Function, 1961–1968," *Journal of Politics* 32 (1970): 440–43; Douglas M. Fox and Charles Clapp, "The House Rules Committee and the Programs of the Kennedy and Johnson Administration," *Midwest Journal of Political Science* 14 (1970): 667–72; Spark M. Matsunaga and Ping Chen, *Rulemakers of the House* (Urbana: University of Illinois Press, 1976); and Bruce I. Oppenheimer, "The Rules Committee: New Arm of Leadership in a Decentralized House," in Dodd and Oppenheimer, *Congress Reconsidered*, 96–116. On the Rules Committee in the mid1980s see Andy Plattner, "Rules under Chairman Pepper Looks Out For the Democrats," *Congressional Quarterly Weekly Report* (Aug. 24, 1985): 1671–75.

settle jurisdictional disputes between standing committees, it helps kill bills that in fact few members of the House want to be forced to vote on publicly, it approves the creation of select committees, it helps regulate travel by committee members, and it proposes general rules governing the House.

From its creation in the nineteenth century until 1910, the Rules Committee was virtually the personal vehicle of the Speaker. He appointed its members and served as its chairman. From 1910 until the late 1930s, although the Speaker could no longer sit on the committee and had lost the power of making committee appointments, the committee continued to be an instrument loyal to the wishes of the Speaker and other majority party leaders. The committee members from the majority party believed their main function was to assist the leaders of their party in the achievement of their legislative objectives.

From the late 1930s until the early 1960s, however, a group of conservative southern Democrats on the committee allied with the Republicans (who were all conservatives) to kill a number of liberal Democratic initiatives on domestic legislation. This legislative deadlock made the committee the focus of hot political division between liberals and conservatives. In 1961 the House agreed to increase the size of the committee temporarily in order to give the Democratic leaders a better chance of control of the committee. The House made the increased size permanent in 1963.

Since 1963, the Rules Committee has ceased stifling major liberal Democratic initiatives in the House and has become a generally reliable arm of the leadership of the House Democratic party. Occasionally the committee will hold up House consideration of a major bill, as it did with a land-use bill and a mass transit conference report in 1974, but it is surprising to find the committee opposing the wishes of the Speaker. To help solidify the formal hold of the Speaker on the committee, although he still cannot be a member, the House Democrats gave the Speaker the power to appoint all Democratic members of the committee (a safe majority of the committee) beginning in 1975. Different chairpersons have different personal styles but they are, above all, loyal to the Speaker. However, on many fairly minor issues the Speaker may not have a position. In those cases, members of the committee are important in their ability to help other individual members of the House gain their legislative goals.

# CONFERENCE COMMITTEES[35]

When the House and Senate pass two different versions of the same bill, a conference committee is appointed to reconcile the differences and present a final product that both houses must ratify before sending the bill to the president for his signature. About 10 to 15 percent of all bills—including most of the important ones—go to conference. This committee is typically composed of a small number of relatively senior members from the relevant standing committees and subcommittees in each house. In the 1980s the use of the budget reconciliation process produced very large conferences—280 members in 1981 and 242 members in 1985. But the 1981 conference actually met in 50 subgroups and the 1985 conference met in 31 subgroups. The real work was done in these small bodies.

Both parties are represented on the conference committee. The decision making is not by majority vote of the whole committee but is by agreement of the majority of each of the two delegations. In the last few years many conferences have been open to the press and public. However, conferences can still meet behind closed doors.

Some committees routinely appoint the same members to all conferences. Others appoint the senior members of the relevant subcommittee (plus, usually, the chairperson of the full committee and the ranking minority member). Some appoint all of the members of the relevant subcommittee. The senior members of the House and Senate dominate the conference process, although in recent years there has been increasing participation by junior members.

It is expected that the delegations from each house will "fight to win" in any disagreements between the two contingents. However, it is also assumed that disagreements will have to be compromised so that a final bill can be produced that will be acceptable to both houses. The conferees know that they will have to bargain and cannot expect to win all points in dispute. Sometimes, particularly in the Senate, committee leaders will accept amendments on the floor that they really do not favor so that later on, in conference, they will have

---

[35]On conference committees see David J. Vogler, *The Third House* (Evanston: Northwestern University Press, 1971); Gilbert Y. Steiner, *The Congressional Conference Committee* (Urbana: University of Illinois, 1951); Ada C. McCown, *The Congressional Conference Committee* (New York: Columbia University Press, 1927); Fenno, *The Power of the Purse:* Chapter 12; Gerald S. Strom and Barry S. Rundquist, "A Revised Theory of Winning in House-Senate Conferences," *American Political Science Review* 71 (1977): 448–53; John Ferejohn, "Who Wins in Conference Committee?," *Journal of Politics* 37 (1975): 1033–46.

trading chips that they can give away in order to save some provision they really care about.

Conference committees usually have considerable leeway in reaching final agreement. On some occasions they may even insert new legislative language in the bill, provisions contained in neither the House nor the Senate bill. On a few bills, however, they will receive specific instructions from their parent chamber on provisions on which they must insist.

Usually the conference reports are routinely accepted in both houses. Occasionally, one or both houses will reject a conference report; this necessitates a new conference committee (even though it may contain the same individuals). Conference committees almost always reach agreement; when they do not, the bill may die in conference; or the bill may be returned to the two houses in hopes that revisions will be adopted that allow the conference committee to agree. The few seemingly irreconcilable disagreements stem either from an issue on which basic House and Senate attitudes are poles apart or from personal rivalries.

Several studies of the three decades following World War II found that the Senate got more of its provisions adopted in conference committee than the House. However, this does not mean that the Senate dominates the congressional impact on public policy. On all appropriations bills and on many other bills the House acts first, which means that the Senate frequently is left in the position of amending the House bill and reacting to the agenda set by the House. One study of "who wins" in conference concluded that the chamber that acted second had an advantage in terms of agreement on specifics.[36] But, of course, this may be more than offset by the influence implied by acting first and thus setting much of the agenda for eventual compromise. Perhaps the most intriguing suggestion is that conferees find a way to accommodate the most strongly held preferences of both houses. This seems to be the case in such widely diverse fields as water resource development, foreign aid, and defense appropriations, for example.[37]

The vital role that can be played by conference committees is well illustrated by a conference in the summer of 1973. It worked for three months to produce a highway bill acceptable to a large number of

---

[36]Strom and Rundquist, "A Revised Theory of Winning in House-Senate Conferences."
[37]See Ferejohn, "Who Wins in Conference Committee?"; Randall B. Ripley, "Congressional Government and Committee Management," *Public Policy* 14 (1965): 28–48; and Arnold Kanter, "Congress and the Defense Budget," *American Political Science Review* 66 (1972): 129–43.

# THE TAX-BILL CONFERENCE, 1986

"Who benefits and who pays?" This was no mere rhetorical question that Rep. Dan Rostenkowski (D-Ill.) addressed to the members of the conference committee as they began consideration of the tax-reform bill. His words summed up the essence of politics, reminding committee members that every change made in the bill would have consequences, and that in the end, all the changes would have to balance.

Through its nearly continuous ministrations on behalf of various pleaders, Congress had by the mid1980s brought the U.S. tax system to a point where it had more deductions, loopholes, exemptions, and special-interest tax breaks than a dog has fleas. The tax code was unquestionably in need of an overhaul—the question was whether the very body that created the problem by its penchant for giving in to special-interest pressures could be entrusted to do the repair work.

In the House, Rostenkowski, chairman of the Ways and Means Committee, embraced tax reform and especially tax relief for middle-class taxpayers with the zeal of a crusader. Under his leadership, the committee produced a sweeping reform bill that survived lobbyists' protests and floor debate and emerged virtually unscathed from the House at the end of 1985.

The Senate took up the issue in 1986, following the leadership of Senator Bill Bradley (D-N.J.). After the traditional route of trying to retain special-interests tax breaks while reducing individual rates failed to produce a workable bill, Finance Chairman Bob Packwood (R-Ore.), became a convert to radical reform and led the committee to adopt unanimously a package that proposed even lower tax rates than the House version. Packwood sheltered the bill during floor debate from amendments mainly by insisting that "revenue-neutrality" be observed as it had been in the House (that is, no change could reduce revenue unless compensating sources were found). The bill, with very few changes, was accepted 97 to 3 by the Senate in June 1986.

By forswearing amendments, the Senate increased pressure on the conference that was to follow. Lobbyists forsook the Senate floor and began courting prospective conferees, hoping for one last chance to reinstate their favorite tax breaks.

The conference committee assembled in mid-July. On a number of substantive issues, the House and Senate versions were remarkably similar. Key topics dividing them were the level of tax rates for individuals and businesses, the amount of tax burden that would be shifted from individuals to businesses, and sources of revenue from business to offset tax cuts. In general, the House version favored individual taxpayers while the Senate version favored businesses. Rostenkowski (chairman of the conference), Packwood, and President Reagan (who had made tax reform a major domestic goal in his second term) had pledged to maintain the Senate's top tax rate of 27 percent for individuals (the old law had a top rate of up to 50 percent; the House's top rate was 38 percent). Despite the challenges of finding common ground, the conference began its work with an unusual amount of harmonious expectation that common ground would indeed be found.

Procedurally as well as substantively, the conference was breaking new ground. Rostenkowski had tight control over his ten house conferees, handpicked by him for their loyalty, in disregard of traditional seniority rules for selecting conferees. Packwood's ten conferees were more independent and less likely to be ruled by him in all things. After initial meetings of the full conference, the style of operation quickly shifted to private meetings of separate caucuses of the House and Senate delegations. The extensive use of closed sessions facilitated the work of identifying acceptable compromises and limiting lobbyist influence.

Final agreement was still elusive as a self-imposed deadline of August 16 loomed. Failure to complete work before the three-week congressional recess would leave the conference committee's work in vulnerable condition. As Senator Packwood noted, it was important to get approval before the recess "so that the special interests and lobbyists don't have three weeks to hit on our members to change what is in this most remarkable tax package." Even though business opposition was not agreed on all points, business lobbyists were still a powerful force. Recognizing their vulnerability, the conferees instructed Rostenkowski and Packwood to retreat privately and work out a final agreement together. This was an unprecedented method, but effective. In just over a week of lengthy and intensive sessions the two tax leaders hammered out a package that found the balancing point between the House and Senate versions on tax rates, tax cuts, and reduced deductions. The bill was reported by the conference on August 16.

Conference bills cannot be amended in either chamber, but debate in both House and Senate was lengthy prior to the final votes accepting the 925-page bill. Opponents of the reform set aside worn-out arguments for special-interest provisions and took up dire warnings of the unpredictable effects the reform would have on the economy. Advocates countered with the fairness issue. Nearly all special interests were unhappy, so something had gone right. Dramatic reductions in tax rates had been achieved, nearly all tax breaks had been revised or eliminated, and the perception was widespread among supporters that a more equitable tax system had been achieved. In assessing the victory, Packwood observed: " . . . taxes are about more than money, they are about more than economics. They are about fairness—and this bill is fair."

competing interests and points of view—including those of mass transit proponents (primarily urban lobbyists and environmentalists) and pro-highway interests (road builders, concrete and asphalt makers, tire makers, car makers, and oil companies). Congress had failed to enact a highway bill in 1972 because of some of the same disagreements. When the House and Senate passed new bills in the spring of 1973 the potential for irreconcilable disagreement existed because of the major differences between the two bills. Also complicating the work of the conferees was the threat of a presidential veto if the total amount of money in the bill was too large or if the bill provided for subsidizing operating expenses of mass transit systems.

The most critical point of disagreement between the two houses had to do with whether Highway Trust Fund money could be diverted for use in mass transit facilities. (The fund had been created in 1956 to finance the construction of the interstate highway system. By 1973 about $5 billion was spent each year from the fund, which is replenished by taxes on gasoline, trucks, and other highway "user" taxes.) The Senate position was that the fund could be used for mass transit and the House position was negative. The conferees, over a period of three months, worked out an ingenious compromise that gave everyone a partial victory. In 1974 the inviolability of the trust fund for non-highway uses would be formally preserved (by an elaborate paper shuffle proposed by Jim Wright [D-Tex.], the central figure among the House conferees), in 1975 some limited diversion of money would be allowed for buses only, and in 1976 the Senate position became operative: money could be diverted for rail rapid transit as well as for buses. But the language was also written in such a way as to encourage the formation of a separate mass transit trust fund by 1976 or at least the creation of a single trust fund covering a wide variety of transportation needs.

The conferees also placated the administration by removing anti-impoundment language (but endorsing a court decision forbidding this practice by which the administration can refuse to spend money appropriated by Congress for specific purposes), by keeping spending levels within acceptable limits (in some cases below both the House and Senate versions), and by removing the operating subsidies section from the act. Mass transit proponents and pro-highway interests were at least partially satisfied because both got large subsidies.

In short, the conferees took a situation that looked very bleak and—by writing legislative language that appeared in neither the House nor the Senate bill—produced a winning compromise in three months.

A conference in the summer of 1977 illustrates a case in which energetic and committed persons in both houses got part of what they wanted added to a new program, even though in many cases these parts appeared in only the House version of the bill *or* the Senate version of the bill before conference. This conference was on a new set of programs aimed at providing training and employment for unemployed and disadvantaged youth. The various parts of the package were formally amendments to the Comprehensive Employment and

Training Act of 1973. Most of the ideas represented in the final legislation were generated in Congress rather than receiving any central
direction from the White House.

The details of the legislation are very complex and need not concern
us here. What is evident from an analysis of the final bill, however,
is that almost everyone with an idea got a good part of what he or she
wanted. Table 5–4 summarizes the money authorized in the bill for
five major programs and for four specific programs within those major
categories. The most interesting cases are those four instances in
which one chamber had provided no money. The idea (and money)
originated in the other chamber. In each of those instances the "compromise" reached in conference was to include the program and to
grant well more than half the money contained in the version of the
bill passed in the initiating chamber. Thus 60 percent of the House-
initiated youth incentive entitlement program remained, and 69 percent, 76 percent, and 98 percent of the three Senate-initiated programs
(community improvement projects, native-American and farmworker
set-aside, and in-school youth program) remained. "Compromises" of
this sort became less likely in the 1980s because of increased concern
in Congress—at least at the rhetorical level—with federal deficits.

The conference on the major tax overhaul in 1986 succeeded in
producing a bill that no one at the beginning of the year thought was
possible. The two houses made critical compromises on tax rates (and
it was the low rates that, ultimately, let the bill pass rather easily in
both houses even though a number of familiar, long-standing tax

**Table 5–4.** Authorization of Programs under Youth Employment and
Demonstration Projects Act of 1977 (dollars in millions)

| MAJOR PROGRAM SEGMENT | HOUSE BILL | SENATE BILL | CONFERENCE |
|---|---|---|---|
| National Youth Conservation Corps | 350.0 | 350.0 | 350.0 |
| Youth Incentive Entitlement | 287.5 | 0 | 172.5 |
| Community improvement projects | 0 | 250.0 | 172.5 |
| Secretary's discretionary grants | 215.6 | 225.0 | 143.7 |
| State and local programs | 646.9 | 675.0 | 661.2 |
| *Selected Specific Programs within Major Segments* | | | |
| Native American and farmworker set-aside | 0 | 57.5 | 43.7 |
| Governors' statewide program | 32.4 | 90.0 | 57.5 |
| Direct allocations to local governments | 614.5 | 585.0 | 603.7 |
| In-school youth program | 0 | 135.0 | 132.8 |

SOURCE: *Adapted from* Employment and Training Reporter *8 (June 22, 1977): 538.*

breaks were eliminated) and on the amount of tax burden to be shifted from individuals to businesses (which burden had been shifting in the other direction for several decades). Central to their final success, however, was that for a week near the end of the conference the conferees simply let the chairs of the two full committees—Dan Rostenkowski (D-Ill.) from the House and Bob Packwood (R-Ore.) from the Senate—work out the details and report back to them. The conference at this point became a two-person activity, and both of them were determined to produce a bill.

In December 1987 two conferences met for eight days almost continuously to hammer out total budget and spending plans for the entire federal government for Fiscal Year 1988 (which had already begun on October 1, 1987). These conferences followed basic agreements reached between the Administration and congressional leaders in late November on taxes, spending, and total budget size. Two mammoth bills were the product of this work. One conference provided over $600 billion in a single appropriations bill. For the third time in its history and for the second year in a row Congress was forced to combine what is usually 13 separate appropriations bill into one omnibus bill. At the same time the second conference produced a budget reconciliation bill that cut the federal deficit through a combination of tax increases and spending cuts.

## COMMITTEE SUCCESS ON THE FLOOR

The products of committee labors—the bills they produce—almost always pass on the floor. The great majority pass without amendment. One study of floor activity in the House between 1969 and 1980, for example, showed that between 72 and 82 percent of all legislation passing the House did so with no amendments even offered.[38] Many of the amendments adopted were uncontested. Many were offered by committee chairs themselves, often to cement a winning coalition on the floor. The House floor has become the scene of more legislative activity, but committee handiwork is still overwhelmingly dominant.

Individual committees vary in terms of the ease with which their bills are accepted on the floor. Table 5-5 reports data on the passage of House and Senate committee bills for the period from 1963 through

[38]Steven S. Smith, "Revolution in the House: Why Don't We Do It on the Floor," unpublished paper, 1986. Despite the title, the paper simply shows that the degree of uncertainty on the House floor had increased for committees in general.

**Table 5-5.** Percentage of Committee Bills Passing Unamended, 1963–1971

|  | PERCENT OF BILLS PASSING UNAMENDED | TOTAL NUMBER OF BILLS |
|---|---|---|
| *Senate* |  |  |
| All Senate Committees | 65 | 1174 |
| Top Three Committees |  |  |
|    Rules and Administration | 92 | 25 |
|    Interior and Insular Affairs | 88 | 80 |
|    District of Columbia | 80 | 25 |
| Bottom Three Committees |  |  |
|    Public Works | 57 | 61 |
|    Armed Services | 51 | 61 |
|    Appropriations | 40 | 165 |
| *House* |  |  |
| All House Committees | 70 | 1139 |
| Top Three Committees |  |  |
|    Ways and Means | 96 | 99 |
|    House Administration | 93 | 29 |
|    Veterans' Affairs | 93 | 27 |
| Bottom Three Committees |  |  |
|    Banking and Currency | 54 | 74 |
|    District of Columbia | 47 | 17 |
|    Science and Astronautics | 41 | 17 |

SOURCE: *Data compiled from* Congressional Quarterly Almanacs, *1963–1971.*

1971. The table supports the proposition that the House is somewhat more likely to pass the handiwork of its committees unamended than is the Senate (70 percent of the time as compared to 65 percent). The range of unamended bills is similar in both houses. In the Senate the three committees whose bills got amended most often were all pork-barrel committees. This suggests that senators will tack on amendments to spread the benefits of governmental activity—whether public works, military installations, or appropriations in general—more widely. The parallel pork-barrel committees in the House also ranked low—although not among the lowest three (Armed Services was ninth, Public Works was fourteenth, and Appropriations was seventeenth). In both houses the top three committees were in five cases out of the six either relatively minor committees or specifically concerned with housekeeping in the House and Senate themselves. The only important substantive committee in the top three was the House Ways and Means Committee. This can be explained largely because most bills from that committee were considered under a closed rule that does not allow amendments.

A study of floor activity in the House on general appropriations bills between 1963 and 1982 revealed that the number of challenges to committee positions went up as did the percentage of the time the challenges succeeded even when the floor manager for the majority (the chairperson of the relevant appropriations subcommittee) was opposed.[39] But even in the "worst" year (1979) for the appropriations subcommittee chairs, the House adopted a total of only 23 amendments (spread out over 13 appropriations bills each year) over their protest. In one year (1966) the House adopted no amendment opposed by the floor managers. The years between 1974 and 1980 produced the most amendments of this character. In 1982 the House again rarely prevailed over the floor managers—only two amendments passed.

## CHANGE IN COMMITTEES

Committees of Congress change. They change procedures (both formal and informal), members, and policy preferences. As with Congress as a whole, there is nothing static about the life and performance of committees. Some of the changes are generated from within individual committees. Some changes are imposed by the whole House or Senate. Some are in reaction to changes in the presidency, the bureaucracy, the agenda of government, or developments in society. Many changes are responding to all of these forces at once.

One recent change that has affected all committees in both houses is the opening of sessions, including decision-making meetings, to the public. Both houses adopted "sunshine" rules in 1973. Throughout the 1950s and 1960s until 1973 roughly two out of every five meetings were closed to the public. By 1975 this figure declined rapidly to less than one in every twelve meetings.

One study of four House Committees—Agriculture; Interstate and Foreign Commerce; Government Operations; and International Relations—in 1975–76 concluded that the personnel and procedural changes of the 1970–75 period had had definite effects on them, despite

---

[39]Stanley Bach, "Representatives and Committees on the Floor: Amendments to Appropriations Bills in the House of Representatives, 1963–1982," *Congress and the Presidency* 13 (1986): 41–58.

the different histories, "styles," and jurisdictions of the four.[40] All four of the committees became ideologically less distinctive from one another and from the two parties in the House. The membership of each of the four came to represent the ideological complexion of the House as a whole. Power had become less centralized in the four committees; subcommittee autonomy or at least increased importance for subcommittees was in evidence. At the same time the leaders of the committee, particularly the chairpersons of the full committees and the subcommittees, were more responsible and responsive to the memberships of the committees.

On the floor of the House, the decisions of the committees were being accepted less automatically than before. The whole House appeared to feel more of a stake in the decisions they were ratifying than in previous years. At the same time that subcommittees were winning considerable independent influence from the full committees, their decisions were more likely to be questioned and amended on the floor than previously.

A study of the House Ways and Means Committee at the end of the same reform era also found considerable change in a short period of time.[41] Major reforms included expansion of committee size, the creation of subcommittees for the first time in many years, and an opening of committee decisions to amendment in both the Democratic caucus and on the floor of the House (this was accomplished by changing the "closed rule" practice that had virtually always allowed Ways and Means bills to be considered on the floor without the possibility of amendment). In addition, one critical personnel change occurred in 1975: a new chairperson replaced the powerful chairperson of the previous sixteen years, Wilbur Mills (D-Ark.). The replacement was caused by a personal scandal involving Mills and was not generated by the reformers in the House Democratic party, but the sudden absence of a central figure was important.

The principal results of all these changes were to open and democratize committee procedures, to expand the number of participants in decision-making both within the committee and outside the committee, and to allow some decisions that were not possible before, such

[40]Norman J. Ornstein and David W. Rohde, "Shifting Forces, Changing Rules, and Political Outcomes: The Impact of Congressional Change on Four House Committees," in Robert L. Peabody and Nelson W. Polsby (eds.), *New Perspectives on the House of Representatives,* 3rd ed. (Chicago: Rand McNally, 1977): 186–269.

[41]Catherine E. Rudder, "Committee Reform and the Revenue Process," in Lawrence C. Dodd and Bruce I. Oppenheimer (eds.), *Congress Reconsidered,* 1st ed. (New York: Praeger, 1977): 117–39.

as the removal of the oil depletion allowance. In a sense, the price the committee and the House paid for these changes was that in conference with the Finance Committee of the Senate, House influence waned.

Despite the above changes, a comprehensive reassessment of committees published in 1984 reached the conclusion that continuity was more important in committees than change:

> While member specialization has declined and committees are not so autonomous as they were in the 1960s, most members' legislative activity remains structured by their committee and subcommittee assignments. Committees remain crucial to their personal goals and members continue to calculate carefully the value of particular committee assignments to their personal goal pursuits. Members of both chambers still expect standing committees to commit the time and energy to write nearly all important legislation. And leaders on most legislative issues emerge from committees with appropriate jurisdictions. Floor battles, despite their increased importance, are still rearguard actions for the most part, a means of appeal for those who lose in committee.[42]

## THE OVERALL IMPACT OF COMMITTEES AND SUBCOMMITTEES

The standing committees and subcommittees of Congress are critical in determining the substantive impact of Congress on policy and also in determining which interests will have the most access to the policy process at the national level. Representatives of bureaus and interest groups know this and cultivate their contacts with individual members and staff members on committees and subcommittees important to them. Presidents and party leaders alike can be frustrated by their own relative lack of access to the committee system.

As observed previously, in the late 1970s and into the 1980s full committees became less important in Congress, particularly in the House, than in the 1950s and 1960s. The most important change was the increasing power and autonomy of the subcommittees. At the same time more centralizing forces within the House—especially the Democratic caucus and a strengthened Speaker—sought to diminish committee autonomy, with some success. However, the internal centralizing forces did not have much impact on the subcommittees.

Subcommittees have been vital in the Senate for several decades.

[42]Smith and Deering, *Committees in Congress:* 271–72.

The changes adopted in 1977 represent only a slight curb on subcommittee influence. The tensions between internal centralizing forces and internal decentralizing forces in the Senate are less evident and less severe than in the House. The Senate has operated as a largely decentralized institution for the last three decades. The party leaders have not been demanding. Full committees retain some importance; subcommittees have been consistently important. In part, this difference between House and Senate is simply based on the difference in the number of members in the two bodies.

In general, the committee and subcommittee structure of Congress promotes policy fragmentation much more than policy integration.[43] In many ways this is virtually inevitable. However, some elements of integration can be inserted into the committee decision process by "outsiders." Potentially the most important outsiders are the president (and the institutional presidency) and the party leaders in Congress. The party leaders have the most potential because, although "outsiders" on specific committees, they are the epitome of "insiders" in the House and Senate.

[43]For recent discussions of committees and subcommittees that underscore the accuracy of this generalization see David E. Price, "Congressional Committees in the Policy Process," and Christopher J. Deering and Steven S. Smith, "Subcommittees in Congress," both in Lawrence C. Dodd and Bruce I. Oppenheimer (eds.), *Congress Reconsidered,* 3rd ed. (Washington, D.C.: Congressional Quarterly, 1985).

# 6

# Party Leadership

The two congressional parties in each house have their own leaders, rules, and organizations. Collectively, the leaders are important in shaping and facilitating the work of Congress, although they are often competing with other forces for the attention and loyalty of their members. Leaders rarely dissent from substantive positions held by the majority of their party and they are almost always to be found voting with that majority. They are sometimes able to limit the effects of fragmentation in Congress.

A series of brief statements captures the essence of the place of party leaders in Congress. First, they seek to keep their party members behind them on a number of substantive and procedural matters. Second, they typically get more support on procedural matters than on substantive matters. Third, members typically feel some loyalty to their party and to their leaders. Fourth, leaders cannot command their members. They can only persuade them using both tangible and intangible resources. Leaders hope for unity on the part of their members, but have to labor diligently even to approach that happy state.

# THE GENERAL IMPORTANCE OF CONGRESSIONAL PARTIES

Despite much commentary to the effect that American political parties are weak both in the electorate and in the national legislature, they are, inside Congress, one of the major potential integrating forces. They do not always realize that potential, but sometimes it can be stimulated by leadership from within the House and Senate or from the White House.

Political parties in the House and Senate played a central role in the emergence of the modern Congress in the late nineteenth century. In that period and in the first two decades of the twentieth century it appeared as if an American form of strong party government might become a permanent feature of Congress.

But, at about the time of World War I, support for consistently strong parties and party leaders in Congress waned among the members. Strong parties threatened the independence prized by the members. Consequently, the congressional parties that have dominated in Congress since World War I have only sporadically been strong and effective shapers of the policy impact of Congress.

A candidate who has been elected to the House or Senate is confronted immediately with a congressional party. This party is likely to have a much greater impact on the member than either the national party under whose banner he ran for office or the state and local parties, whose organization may have helped him as he campaigned. Congressional party leaders, caucuses, and committees impinge on his daily life and are responsible for matters crucial to the member's congressional career such as committee assignments. They control floor business, so he must come to terms with his party if he desires success in pushing those bills and policies he favors through Congress. Congressional parties provide essential procedural controls over congressional business. Centrally, they provide order and efficiency in the legislative process.

Congressional parties also possess substantive content. Until the twentieth century, congressional parties generated their own substantive positions, but their attention during the course of a Congress was narrowly focused, mainly on tariffs and internal improvements.

In this century, the leaders of the party of the president have typically (and without exception since 1933) accepted most of his policies and program preferences as their own. The leaders of the president's party in the House and Senate usually lend support to these proposals without seriously questioning them.

When the president's program comes to the committees and the floor in each house of Congress it generally receives support from most of the members of his party. There may be considerable dissent over portions of his program, but the party label they share with the president helps motivate most members to avoid dissent when possible. Party label is both a symbol and a reality that provides a focus for loyal behavior on substantive issues. Shared experiences, friendships, and party machinery all help reinforce the natural feelings of loyalty to the president and his program.

These natural ties to the president on the part of his party's members are most dramatically visible when the House or Senate considers the question of overriding a presidential veto. Typically, many members of the president's party who voted for the bill the first time it went through the chamber will change their vote and support the president's veto. The point is underscored in Table 6–1, which reports the shifts in voting by members of the president's party between original passage of a bill and the vote on a veto override attempt. In all of these cases except one, the shift was in favor of the president, often dramatically so. (In a few of these cases the veto was successfully overridden anyway.) The table includes important votes under four presidents: Nixon, Ford, Carter, and Reagan. The point of the table is not to compare presidents or parties or chambers but to make it clear that the instinct on the part of members to support the president of their party is strong no matter which president is in office, which chamber is involved, or which party is involved.

The party that does not control the White House has a difficult time in generating loyalty to a substantive program. This party can decide either to oppose the president and his party with or without proposing programmatic alternatives or to support partially the president's program or to try to participate in the development of some of it (an exceedingly difficult task). Typically, the party without the presidency has far less programmatic or substantive identity than the presidential party. In 1987 the Democrats, in the majority in both houses and facing a Republican president, made bold noises about their "program," but, in fact, they were unable to move legislative initiatives forward when faced by a hostile president.

There are interactive factors that push party members in the House and the Senate to act in concert. In part there are genuinely shared attitudes about public-policy issues. These attitudes are reinforced by the requests and actions of the party leaders for both parties and of

**Table 6–1.** Pre– and Post–Veto Support of President by His Party, 1973–1986, Selected Votes

| ISSUE, CHAMBER, YEAR | PERCENT OF PRESIDENT'S PARTY SUPPORTING PRESIDENT'S POSITION | |
| --- | --- | --- |
| | ORIGINAL PASSAGE | VOTE ON VETO OVERRIDE |
| PRESIDENT | | |
| *Nixon* | | |
| Vocational Rehabilitation, Senate, 1973 | 5 | 76 |
| Water-Sewer Program, House, 1973 | 31 | 87 |
| Office of Management and Budget Confirmation, Senate, 1973 | 52 | 61 |
| Office of Management and Budget Confirmation, House, 1973 | 89 | 90 |
| Cambodia Bombing Halt, House, 1973 | 66 | 72 |
| *Ford* | | |
| Public Works Employment, House, 1976 | 53 | 59 |
| Public Works Employment, Senate, 1976 | 44 | 68 |
| Aid to Day-Care Centers, Senate, 1976 | 47 | 70 |
| Hatch Act Revisions, House, 1976 | 65 | 84 |
| *Carter* | | |
| Weapons Procurement Authorization, House, 1978 | 26 | 69 |
| Public Works Appropriations, House, 1978 | 18 | 48 |
| Oil Import Fee Abolition, House, 1980 | 17 | 15 |
| Oil Import Fee Abolition, Senate, 1980 | 12 | 22 |
| *Reagan* | | |
| Standby Petroleum Allocation Act, Senate, 1982 | 13 | 62 |
| Supplemental Appropriations, House, 1982 | 50 | 79 |
| Supplemental Appropriations, House, 1982 | 27 | 56 |
| Resolution against Saudi Arms Sales, Senate, 1986 | 41 | 55 |
| South African Sanctions, House, 1986 | 45 | 49 |
| South African Sanctions, Senate, 1986 | 27 | 40 |

the president for members of his party. They are also reinforced because members of a party typically seek out other members of their party for most of their discussion of and advice about policy.[1]

Congressional parties serve to predict voting on the floor of the

[1]See John W. Kingdon, *Congressmen's Voting Decisions,* 2nd ed. (New York: Harper and Row, 1981); and Helmut Norpoth, "Explaining Party Cohesion in Congress: The Case of Shared Policy Attitudes," *American Political Science Review* 70 (1976): 1156–71.

**Table 6–2.** Party Unity on Roll Calls in Congress, 1954–1986

| | | AVERAGE PERCENT OF MEMBERS SUPPORTING PARTY ON PARTY UNITY VOTES[a] | | | |
|---|---|---|---|---|---|
| YEARS | (PARTY OF PRES.) | HOUSE DEMOCRATS | HOUSE REPUBLICANS | SENATE DEMOCRATS | SENATE REPUBLICANS |
| 1954–60 | (R) | 80 | 79 | 78 | 80 |
| 1961–68[b] | (D) | 79 | 81 | 75 | 77 |
| 1969–76 | (R) | 73 | 74 | 74 | 72 |
| 1977–80 | (D) | 75 | 78 | 75 | 72 |
| 1981–86 | (R) | 81 | 78 | 76 | 81 |
| *Mean for entire period (1954–86)* | | 78 | 78 | 76 | 77 |

[a]The numbers represent the percentage of members voting with a majority of their party on all roll calls on which majorities of the two parties oppose each other. The percentages are "normalized" to eliminate the effect of absences.
[b]Data were not available for 1961.
SOURCE: Raw data all come from various *Congressional Quarterly* publications. The annual numbers for 1954 through 1983 are conveniently collected in Norman J. Ornstein and others, *Vital Statistics on Congress, 1984–1985 Edition* (Washington, D.C.: American Enterprise Institute, 1984): 183. The raw numbers for 1984 came from *Congressional Quarterly Weekly Report* (October 27, 1984): 2810; and for 1985 and 1986 from *Congressional Quarterly Weekly Report* (November 15, 1986): 2903.

House and Senate better than any other factor. A study of voting in Congress from 1921 through 1964 concluded that "by any measure party remains the single most important factor in roll call voting."[2] The trend during this time period was toward weaker party unity on controversial issues, principally because of the growing ideological conservatism on the part of a number of southern Democrats. Nevertheless, party remained a relatively strong unifying force in Congress.

The degree of support for one's party in votes on the floor of the House and Senate when a majority of the two parties are opposed to each other is moderately high for the members of all four parties. Table 6–2 summarizes the percent of support in each of the four parties from 1954 through 1986, in five periods coinciding with party shifts in control of the presidency (the Eisenhower years, the Kennedy-Johnson years, the Nixon-Ford years, the Carter years, and the first six Reagan years). The table supports the generalization that the four parties have not varied a great deal either compared to each other or at different periods of time. In no period did any party have less than an average of 72 percent or more than 81 percent of its

[2]Julius Turner, *Party and Constituency: Pressures on Congress*, rev. ed., (Baltimore: The Johns Hopkins University Press, 1970), Edward Schneier (ed.).

members supporting it on votes on which the majorities of the two parties differed. All four parties were least cohesive during the Nixon-Ford years. The two majority parties (the Democrats in the House and the Republicans in the Senate) were the most cohesive in the Reagan years, when there was much journalistic speculation that partisanship was increasing because of the different values, beliefs, and priorities, and the partisan behavior of President Reagan and Speaker of the House "Tip" O'Neill, (D-Mass.).

In 1987, both House parties performed about as they had for the preceding six years of the Reagan era: the party unity score for House Democrats was 81 and for House Republicans it was 74. The Democrats regained control of the Senate for the first time during the Reagan years in 1987. This was a factor in a higher party unity score for Senate Democrats in 1987 than in the preceding six years (81) and a lower score for Senate Republicans, now in the minority (75).

## PARTY LEADERS

The functioning of congressional parties is shaped in large part by the individuals who hold critical institutional positions in those parties. This does not mean that other individuals are prevented from developing influence; it simply means that the most influential are those with formal titles.

### The Positions of Leadership

In the House the principal leaders of the majority party in this century have been the Speaker and majority leader. In recent years the majority whip has also emerged as an important leader. The principal leader of the minority party has been the minority leader, sometimes joined by the minority whip.

In the Senate the principal leader of the majority party is the majority leader. The minority leader is generally the chief leader of the minority party. Whips have become increasingly important in both parties.

Individuals selected for the five principal positions in the two houses (the majority leaders, the minority leaders, and the Speaker of the House) have been relatively senior members of their respective chambers, but they are not chosen on the basis of seniority. Table 6-3 summarizes the mean years of service in the House and Senate for the

**Table 6–3.** Average Seniority of Principal House and Senate
Leaders at Time of Initial Selection, by Party, Twentieth Century
(as of 1987)

|  | SPEAKER (N) | FLOOR LEADER (N) |
|---|---|---|
| House Democrats | 25.9 (10) | 18.9 (17) |
| House Republicans | 22.4 (5) | 16.8 (11) |
| Senate Democrats | —— | 9.2 (11) |
| Senate Republicans | —— | 14.6 (15) |

five principal leaders in the four parties. Only the Senate Democrats
have not consistently chosen a very senior member.

Once selected, the leaders in all of the five principal positions tend
to serve for three or more Congresses. Table 6-4 summarizes the years
of service for those who served in the Twentieth century, excluding
incumbents in 1987. There is no striking variation between the parties.

The Speaker, floor leaders, and whips have been consistently important. A number of other members are given various titles in the whip's
organization, in the caucus, or in various party committees. No doubt,
the central leaders make a number of members feel good about their
importance (and their ability to claim such importance in reporting
to their constituents) by passing out such titles. Minor leaders also
help perform some real party tasks, particularly in the collection and
dissemination of information through the whip organization. One
study of the House Democratic party identified 103 members (out of
a total of 243) who could be called party leaders in the Ninety-seventh
Congress (1981–83).[3] Such flattery may have helped unite the party on
some issues. But the Speaker, majority leader, and majority whip still
made the most important decisions.

## Leadership Succession[4]

The problem of succession from one leader to another is critical for
any institution. Contests over succession can disrupt the institution.

[3]Burdett A. Loomis, "Congressional Careers and Party Leadership in the Contemporary House
of Representatives," *American Journal of Political Science* 28 (1984): 180–202.
[4]On leadership change see Robert L. Peabody, *Leadership in Congress* (Boston: Little, Brown,
1976); and Garrison Nelson, "Partisan Patterns of House Leadership Change, 1789–1977,"
*American Political Science Review* 71 (1977): 918–39. On the backgrounds of leaders see Garrison
Nelson, "Change and Continuity in the Recruitment of U.S. House Leaders, 1789–1975," in
Norman J. Ornstein (ed.), *Congress in Change* (New York: Praeger, 1975): 155–83.

**Table 6–4.** Average Length of Service in Principal Leadership Positions, by Party, Twentieth Century (as of 1987)

|  | SPEAKER (N) | FLOOR LEADER (N) |
|---|---|---|
| House Democrats | 6.7 (9) | 5.7 (16) |
| House Republicans | 5.6 (5) | 8.2 (10) |
| Senate Democrats | —— | 6.6 (10) |
| Senate Republicans | —— | 5.4 (14) |

Smooth transition can facilitate the functioning of the institution, although perhaps at the price of continuing outmoded policies or procedures. In the House and Senate, experience over the last several decades leads to a number of generalizations about change in leadership.

The most striking pattern that emerges is that succession is handled quite differently in the majority party from the way it is handled in the minority party. In the majority party, particularly in the case of a long-standing majority, succession is likely to be smooth and divisive internal contests rare. The longer a party is in the majority the more likely it is to develop established patterns of leadership succession. For example, during the long period of dominance of the House by the Democrats from 1931 to the present (with only two two-year breaks) a pattern has emerged whereby, first, a sitting majority leader virtually automatically succeeds to the speakership when it becomes vacant and, second, the majority whip regularly wins election as majority leader when the job opens.

Beginning in the One Hundredth Congress (1987–89) the House Democrats made the position of party whip elective. Previously, the floor leader had appointed the Whip. There was a contest for the position, although Tony Coehlo of California won rather easily. The next time the floor leadership opens in the House Democratic party it will be interesting to see if the whip is advanced to the post, even though the mode of his selection was different than in the past. Seniority has not been important in choosing the Democratic whip in either mode of selection.

In the minority party, particularly in the House, internal fights of an intense character are likely to occur over leadership positions. These contests are likely to occur at all levels of leadership and are most likely to occur at the times of highest frustration for the minority—for example, after a major electoral disaster.

In general, there are no foolproof indicators predicting which specific individuals in the four congressional parties will be selected leaders. The art of compromise has been highly prized by those both electing and appointing leaders; ideologues have rarely won leadership positions. Individuals selected have had to be concerned with the welfare of their party, but this has not meant that a person could never have deviated from party positions, even on important issues. Thus far only white males who have made their careers in Congress have attained positions of party leadership.

In 1987 both parties in the House chose new leaders. Their behavior illustrated some of the general points made above. In the Democratic party the principal leadership positions needed filling because of the retirement of Tip O'Neill from the Speakership at the end of the Ninety-ninth Congress in 1986. The Democrats, long in the majority and with a tradition of smooth leadership succession, quickly decided on elevating Majority Leader Jim Wright of Texas to Speaker and Whip Thomas Foley of Washington to majority leader, both by acclamation at the caucus of all House Democrats in December, 1986. The third top post, whip, had been made elective rather than appointive. Tony Coehlo of California had sought the job actively since O'Neill had announced his retirement many months earlier. He had ambition, was a loyal party member, and had done a number of favors for many of his colleagues as chairman of the Democratic Congressional Campaign Committee since 1981. He was the front runner for the position for many months before the caucus met and easily defeated two late entrants, Charles Rangel of New York and W.G. Hefner of North Carolina. Coehlo won on the only ballot needed: 167 to 78 for Rangel and 15 for Hefner.

The principal Republican leadership posts of minority leader and whip were not open for the One Hundredth Congress and the incumbents were routinely re-elected. However, the number-three person in the leadership, Jack Kemp of New York, resigned his position as chairman of the conference in late April, 1987, to concentrate more of his energies on his attempt to become the Republican presidential nominee in 1988. The number-four person in the leadership, Dick Cheney of Wyoming, ran unopposed for Kemp's former job. Cheney, well respected throughout his party, thus put himself in position to run for floor leader or whip when either of those positions becomes vacant. Cheney had been chairman of the Republican Policy Committee. That opening generated a heated contest between two Californians, Jerry Lewis and Duncan Hunter. The choice was focused on the two different styles of the candidates in dealing with the majority Democrats. Lewis stressed negotiation; Hunter stressed confrontation. The House Republicans revealed their ambivalence about the best stance by according Lewis a very close 88 to 82 victory.

Lewis had been chairman of the Republican Research Committee. Three competitors for that position were voted on by the conference. They were Mickey Edwards, a sixth-term conservative from Oklahoma; Steve Bartlett of Texas, a third-term conservative; and moderate Steve Gunderson, a fourth-term member from Wisconsin. On the first ballot Edwards got 72 votes, Bartlett got 57, and Gunderson got 42. On the second ballot, after the elimination of Gunderson, Edwards defeated Bartlett 93 to 71. As in the election of Lewis, the winner (Edwards) was more interested in negotiation and the loser (Bartlett) was more interested in partisan confrontation. Again the vote was close. The defeat of Gunderson was unsurprising, since the House Republican party routinely defeats moderates who seek leadership positions.

## CONTEMPORARY LEADERSHIP

Throughout history many patterns of leadership have been used by both parties in the House and the Senate. Since the 1880s the formal leaders of both parties in both houses have been consistently important in helping to determine the timing and character of legislation emerging from the House and Senate.

Examination of leadership patterns and practices in the House and Senate in the 1960s, 1970s, and 1980s reveals both stability and changes in terms of institutional arrangements. Glimpses of some of the chief leaders in office in this period will give a sense of some of the personal variations in approaching the task of leading congressional parties. Table 6-5 lists the principal leaders in January 1987 (and also notes two changes for the House Republicans in May 1987).

### House Democrats[5]

THE GENERAL PATTERN. The House Democrats in the 1960s, 1970s, and 1980s had a leadership pattern in which a three-man group (the Speaker, the majority leader, and the majority whip) formed the core. But, over time, the core leaders—especially the Speaker—have in-

[5]On contemporary House Democrats see Lawrence C. Dodd and Bruce I. Oppenheimer, "The House in Transition: Partisanship and Opposition," in Dodd and Oppenheimer (eds.), *Congress Reconsidered,* 3rd ed. (Washington, D.C.: Congressional Quarterly, 1985): 34–64; Robert L. Peabody, "House Party Leadership: Stability and Change," in Dodd and Oppenheimer (eds.), *Congress Reconsidered:* 253–71; Barbara Sinclair, *Majority Leadership in the U.S. House* (Baltimore: The Johns Hopkins University Press, 1983); and Sidney Waldman, "Majority Leadership in the House of Representatives," *Political Science Quarterly* 95 (1980): 373–93.

**Table 6–5.** Principal Party Leaders, January 1987

*House Democrats*

| | |
|---|---|
| Speaker: | James C. Wright, Jr., Texas |
| Majority Leader: | Thomas S. Foley, Washington |
| Majority Whip: | Tony Coehlo, California |
| Chairman of the Caucus: | Richard A. Gephardt, Missouri |

*House Republicans*

| | |
|---|---|
| Minority Leader: | Robert H. Michel, Illinois |
| Minority Whip: | Trent Lott, Mississippi |
| Chairman of the Conference: | Jack F. Kemp, New York (replaced by Cheney in May 1987, after he resigned) |
| Chairman of the Policy Committee: | Richard B. Cheney, Wyoming (replaced by Jerry Lewis, California, in May 1987) |

*Senate Democrats*

| | |
|---|---|
| Majority Leader: | Robert C. Byrd, West Virginia |
| Majority Whip: | Alan Cranston, California |
| Secretary of the Conference: | Daniel K. Inouye, Hawaii |

*Senate Republicans*

| | |
|---|---|
| Minority Leader: | Robert J. Dole, Kansas |
| Assistant Minority Leader (Whip): | Alan K. Simpson, Wyoming |
| Chairman of the Conference: | John H. Chafee, Rhode Island |
| Chairman of the Policy Committee: | William L. Armstrong, Colorado |

volved a growing number of individuals and party committees in performing leadership tasks. By the late 1970s the three individuals at the center were meeting daily with the chief deputy whip and the caucus chairman. The Speaker attended a weekly meeting of the whip organization, which by the 1980s included over 40 members and had been important for several decades in helping the leadership perform a number of information collection and distribution tasks. He developed a system of task forces to work on major legislation as a way of broadening participation of House Democrats and to build support among a wide range of Democrats for the final product.[6] The Speaker and his chief lieutenants remained at the core of House Democratic activity, but he understood that the junior members of his party expected to be active and influential. He also understood that coalition-building—always the central task of the leaders—necessarily had to be focused more strongly on only Democrats because Republicans were becoming increasingly resistant to supporting Democratic posi-

[6]Barbara Sinclair, "The Speaker's Task Force in the Post-Reform House of Representatives," *American Political Science Review* 75 (1981): 397–410.

tions.[7] Therefore, the Speaker pursued a strategy of including more Democrats earlier in the legislative process as a way of giving them more of a stake in the final product. Speaker O'Neill was well aware of the changed nature of how he had to proceed in order to increase his chances of obtaining success on the House floor. In comparing his task with that of his most illustrious Democratic predecessor, Sam Rayburn of Texas (Speaker for 17 of the 21 years between 1940 and 1961), O'Neill said, "Sam didn't have to put up with these kids."[8]

The Speaker convenes the Democratic Steering and Policy Committee several times a month. This committee, which he chairs, was expanded in 1981 to include a number of party leaders automatically, eight members appointed by the Speaker, and twelve members elected by regional caucuses of Democratic members. In the Ninety-ninth Congress (1985–87) the committee had 30 members. In addition to discussing party policy it also serves as the Democratic committee on committees.

Over all of the party apparatus stands the party caucus, which recently became newly active in the House Democratic Party after many decades of slumber. The caucus discusses and adopts party positions, occasionally instructs Democratic contingents on standing committees on positions they must take, and elects leaders (including committee chairmen). With a relatively weak Speaker the caucus seemed to be autonomous. With an activist speaker (such as O'Neill) the caucus seems much more an organ that interacts with the Speaker—both partially shaped by his wishes and partially shaping the positions he takes.

The core leadership group co-opts committee and subcommittee chairpersons when specific bills are ready for floor consideration. This expanded group then works on the tactical details of scheduling and passing the bill. In the whole process of scheduling and attempting to keep procedural control the Rules Committee has, in recent years, become a reliable arm of the leadership.[9] Speaker O'Neill used the committee's powers to rein in full committee chairpersons who

[7]Barbara Sinclair, "Coping with Uncertainty: Building Coalitions in the House and the Senate," in Thomas E. Mann and Norman J. Ornstein (eds.), *The New Congress* (Washington, D.C.: American Enterprise Institute, 1981): Chapter 6.

[8]A statement reported to me by the most perceptive of all students of the House, the late D. B. Hardeman, after an interview with O'Neill in August 1980. For a good treatment of Rayburn's career in the House and his style of leadership there see D.B. Hardeman and Donald C. Bacon, *Rayburn: A Biography* (Austin, Texas: Texas Monthly Press, 1987).

[9]See Bruce I. Oppenheimer, "The Changing Relationship between House Leadership and the Committee on Rules," in Frank H. Mackaman (ed.), *Understanding Congressional Leadership* (Washington, D.C.: Congressional Quarterly, 1981).

wanted to pursue their own ends without coordinating with the party leaders.

**"TIP" O'NEILL AS SPEAKER.** Thomas P. O'Neill, Jr., of Massachusetts was elected Speaker of the House in 1977, having been nominated by the Democratic caucus to succeed Carl Albert, an Oklahoma Democrat. He retired at the end of the 1986 session, after serving for ten years, the longest continuous speakership in the history of the House.

O'Neill had come to the House in 1953. He had been a loyal member of the party and had come into a leadership position in 1971 when newly elected Speaker Carl Albert and Hale Boggs of Louisiana, the majority leader, had chosen him to be Democratic whip. After Boggs's death in a plane crash in late 1972, O'Neill was elected majority leader by the Democratic caucus. When Albert announced his retirement as Speaker at the end of 1976, there was no opposition to O'Neill as the next speaker. During his two years as whip and four years as majority leader, he had shown himself to be forceful as well as sympathetic and responsive to the membership simultaneously. In addition, he had used the powers of his offices to do a lot of favors for a lot of members who repaid him with their support of his rise up the leadership ladder.

It had been clear during the last years of the Albert speakership that O'Neill was the strongest person on the leadership team. Early in his speakership he gave every evidence of delivering on his pledge before being elected Speaker: "I intend to be a strong Speaker. I believe in strong leadership."[10]

O'Neill openly laid his prestige on the line on important issues such as the adoption of a code of ethics for the House and the House passage of the president's energy program in 1977, and he won. The secret behind his early successes was his ability to talk to all sides on an issue within his party, to help engineer winning compromises, and to assert his preferences in a personal manner that left even those opposed to his positions in agreement that he was a fine person and an effective leader. He was tireless in visiting with members of the House, lobbyists, the president, and other executive branch officials. He even flew to Chicago to talk with the mayor and other officials in an attempt to sell the president's bill allowing same-day registration of voters. He had seemingly boundless capacities for hard work, compromise, and doing a series of personal favors for individuals. Despite

[10]O'Neill, quoted in Michael J. Malbin, "House Democrats Are Playing with a Strong Leadership Lineup," *National Journal* (June 18, 1977): 940. On O'Neill as Speaker see also Tip O'Neill, with William Novak, *Man of the House: The Life and Political Memoirs of Speaker Tip O'Neill* (New York: Random House, 1987).

the decentralization of power throughout the subcommittee system that had occurred in the previous years, O'Neill could operate as the undoubted central figure of the House.

A long-time colleague and astute observer of the House, Richard Bolling of Missouri, offered a good capsule description of O'Neill: "He's an Irish politician. No table pounder. He puts an arm around your shoulders and says he needs you. . . . When he's going somewhere he's like a tank, a kind tank."[11]

O'Neill himself was consistently candid in talking with the press about his own speakership. In an interview in the spring of 1977 he spoke insightfully about the kinds of things he could do to build personal ties and loyalties that would pay off in policy decisions to his liking:

> You know, you ask me what are my powers and my authority around here? The power to recognize on the floor; little odds and ends—like men get pride out of the prestige of handling the Committee of the Whole, being named the Speaker for the day; those little trips that come along—like those trips to China, trips to Russia, things of that nature; or other ad hoc committees or special committees, which I have assignments to; plus the fact that there is a certain aura and respect that goes with the Speaker's office. He does have the power to be able to pick up the telephone and call people. And Members often times like to bring their loyal political leaders or a couple of mayors. And often times they have problems from their area and they need aid and assistance, either legislativewise or administrative-wise. We're happy to try to open the door for them, having been in the town for so many years and knowing so many people. We do know where a lot of bodies are and we do know how to advise people.
>
> And I have an open door policy. Rare is the occasion when a man has a personal fund-raiser or being personally honored that I don't show up at it. I've made more public appearances and visited areas if they believe I can help them. I'm always accessible. These are part of the duties and the obligations of the Speaker, and it shows the warm hand of friendship. . . .
>
> So that's what it's all about.[12]

O'Neill remained true to his basic vision of desirable policy and how to lead the House Democrats throughout his entire tenure as Speaker. In 1981 there was some speculation, by non-admirers in both parties in the House and in the press, that his time had come and gone

[11]Bolling, quoted in Richard L. Lyons, "A Powerful Speaker," *Washington Post,* April 3, 1977.
[12]O'Neill, quoted in Malbin, "House Democrats Are Playing with a Strong Leadership Lineup," 942.

both in terms of style and substance. He was often portrayed as lacking in ideas and the modern "style" necessary to appeal to the supposedly new type of voters and members.

The Democrats did suffer some notable defeats in the House in 1981. They faced a vigorous new Republican president, a united Republican party in the House, and enough conservative dissidents within their own ranks to make its nominal majority vanish. But 1981 was unusual. From 1982 through 1986 O'Neill recouped his fortunes both in the House and with the press. He became increasingly effective in holding Democrats together in the House and slowing down or even stopping President Reagan's momentum on some issues. He also became increasingly accepted by both the print and electronic media as a legitimate and forceful spokesman for the national Democratic party, in part because he was by far the most visible and highest-ranking Democrat in the country. Naturally, he did not always defeat President Reagan. But he played a forceful role in helping House Democrats preserve some social welfare programs in a form closer to their liking than to Reagan's, in helping keep legitimate military aid from the "contras" in Nicaragua for a substantial period of time, and in keeping a partial lid on defense spending. Some bills that passed, such as the major tax bills in 1982 and 1986, were at least as Democratic in origin as they were Republican.

**JIM WRIGHT AS SPEAKER.** Like O'Neill, his successor Jim Wright of Texas is a person making a career in the House. He was first elected in 1954 and became known as an effective legislator. He served as majority leader from 1977 until his election as Speaker for the One Hundredth Congress, which began in 1987. The speakership has specific powers attached to it, yet different incumbents can behave quite differently from each other in terms of what they stress and still be effective. Assessments of Wright's performance in 1987 show that he was very interested in the substantive agenda of the House, and had more knowledge of it and influence over it, than his three immediate predecessors.[13] He chose issues on which he could count on a high degree of support from most of the members of his party. He had to balance his desire to be a legislator in the speakership with the need

[13]For good early assessments of Wright's performance as Speaker in the first part of 1987 see Jeffrey H. Birnbaum, "Under the Democrats, Congress is Reasserting A Legislative Initiative," *Wall Street Journal,* May 15, 1987; Richard E. Cohen, "Quick-Starting Speaker," *National Journal* (May 30, 1987): 1409–13; and Janet Hook, "Speaker Jim Wright Takes Charge in the House," *Congressional Quarterly Weekly Report* (July 11, 1987): 1483–88. For good assessments of his performance for all of 1987 see Richard E. Cohen, "Full Speed Ahead," *National Journal* (January 30, 1988): 238–244; and Susan F. Rasky, "Everyone Has Something to Say about Wright," *New York Times,* December 18, 1987.

to consult widely throughout his party. He was viewed by both Democrats and Republicans as consistently highly partisan. Inevitably, Wright faced the same limits faced by all Speakers: as a fellow Democrat put it in mid-1987, "Even if a Speaker wanted to impose an agenda, he doesn't have the tools to do it. The key point for Jim is, will he consult in a way that gives members the feeling that his agenda is the product of those consultations."[14] Inevitably, too, if Wright serves as Speaker while a president of his own party occupies the White House he will lose much of his independence with regard to the substantive agenda. Instead, he would become primarily responsive to the legislative agenda of the administration.

## House Republicans

THE GENERAL PATTERN. The House Republicans had a more diffuse leadership than the Democrats during the 1960s, 1970s, and 1980s. Nine formal positions carried at least some leadership status in the Republican party during much of the period, even though it was in the minority and much smaller in size than the Democratic party.

The Republican leaders were aided by a whip organization and by the members of the Policy Committee and the Research Committee. The Republicans had a large committee on committees to perform the function of assigning Republicans to standing committees. This committee tended to be relatively independent of the principal individual leaders. The full conference also helped organize the party.

In addition, the norms and traditions of the Republican party in the House also gave unusually heavy weight to the senior Republican members of various standing committee delegations. However, like the Democrats, the newer Republicans in the House were much less deferential to their seniors in the late 1970s and 1980s and pushed for and achieved increased influence. These newer Republicans tended to be quite conservative and ideologically committed, which sometimes made life difficult for their more pragmatically oriented, although equally conservative, party leaders.

ROBERT MICHEL AS MINORITY LEADER. In late 1980 two key events helped shape the fate of the House Republicans for the next few years. Critically, the elections in November brought Ronald Reagan to the White House, more Republicans to the House, and a majority of Republicans to the Senate. Second, as a result of John Rhodes's deci-

---

[14]Quoted in Hook, "Speaker Jim Wright."

sion not to seek re-election as floor leader, the Republican conference in the House (all Republican members) elected Robert Michel to be minority leader.

Michel was a typical House leader of the middle and late Twentieth century in that he had been in the House a long time (24 years), was a loyal party member, had held previous party leadership posts (he had been whip since 1975), knew how to get along at a personal level with virtually every member of his party, and saw himself to a large degree cast as a lieutenant to a president of his own party, a lieutenant who had to offer inducements to his troops to stay behind the president.

In 1981 he enjoyed enormous success in working behind the scenes to line up virtual Republican unanimity to support a variety of Reagan initiatives in the budget and tax fields, matters that were controversial and on which it would have been natural for some Republicans to defect. It is difficult to sort out how much credit should go to Michel for building a cohesive party in support of President Reagan and how much should go to the president and his White House liaison effort. The two efforts worked in tandem. Neither would have been nearly as successful working alone.

Michel kept out of the limelight. He felt free to argue quietly with White House strategists when he felt they were making some mistakes in the way they approached the House. He did not generally pursue confrontation either with the Democrats (some of whose votes he needed, since his party was in a minority) or with the very few dissidents that appeared in his own party from time to time on selected issues. Above all, he worked patiently to build winning coalitions on matters deemed vital by the White House.

Michel's own comments on his style are revealing:

> Each member is a separate entity. You can't treat two alike. I know what I can get and what I can't, when to back off and when to push harder. It's not a matter of twisting arms. It's bringing them along by gentle persuasion. Sometimes they don't realize they're being brought into the orbit. You get down to the end of the walkway and you say, 'Hey, we aren't 2 cents apart, are we?' and he says, 'Well, I guess we aren't.'

> I'm a servant of the president. I like being a good soldier.[15]

> [On the necessity of partnership between the White House and House Republicans, after the victory on the budget in 1981:]

[15]Michel, quoted in Margot Hornblower, "The Master of Gentle Persuasion," *Washington Post*, August 10, 1981.

We had to tell David [David Stockman, Director of the Office of Management and Budget and a former House member] on some things that we are willing to do what we can for you, but it has to be our language rather than the stuff you sent over. Sure we take the lead from the administration and utilize the resources of OMB for computer printouts and stuff like that, but it is still the legislative process that has to work its will. . . . I do not want to see them [White House and OMB personnel] get so smug about it [Republican House support] that they think anything they say is going to be an automatic acceptance on the part of our members. It was so dang tough to put it together and keep them in line.[16]

After 1981, Michel's position as the leader of a seemingly permanent minority (the Republicans had lost control of the House in the 1954 elections and had no hope of recovering it as far as anyone could tell) became increasingly frustrating. President Reagan became less effective; Speaker O'Neill and the Democratic House leaders became more effective; the 1982 elections reduced the number of Republicans, losses that were never recaptured entirely, even in the Reagan landslide of 1984; the White House increasingly did not consult with the House Republican leadership; and the majority status of the Republicans in the Senate put the media and legislative spotlights on them. Michel and the Republicans could make life difficult for the Democrats, they could help the president win an occasional victory in the House, and they almost always had the votes to prevent overrides of Reagan vetoes. But life in a permanent minority offers little continuous satisfaction. Even the usually upbeat Michel appeared to be weary. He used his own case to mirror the frustration inevitably felt in some form by virtually all Republican representatives: "I haven't chaired a subcommittee or full committee in my 30 years in Congress. It's a pretty doggone discouraging and debilitating thing."[17]

## Senate Democrats[18]

THE GENERAL PATTERN. The Senate Democrats operate with only a few leaders. By far the most important is the floor leader. He is aided

---

[16]Michel, quoted in Robert Estill, "GOP House Leader Says Budget Victory Left Feathers Ruffled," *San Diego Union,* July 2, 1981.
[17]Michel, quoted in Janet Hook, "House GOP: Plight of a Permanent Minority," *Congressional Quarterly Weekly Report* (June 21, 1986): 1393. On the fate of the minority party in the House see also Janet Hook, "GOP Chafes under Restrictive House Rules," *Congressional Quarterly Weekly Report* (October 10, 1987): 2449–52.
[18]On party leaders in the contemporary Senate see Roger H. Davidson, "Senate Leaders: Janitors for an Untidy Chamber?" in Dodd and Oppenheimer (eds.), *Congress Reconsidered:* 225–52.

by the whip and by the secretary of the party conference (the name for the whole Democratic membership). There are also four deputy whips, a steering committee, and a policy committee. But the whip, secretary, and deputy whips perform mainly housekeeping chores. The floor leader himself chairs the Steering Committee (which makes committee assignments) and the Policy Committee. He is constrained by the decisions reached in those committees but is simultaneously the most important figure in their deliberations.

**ROBERT BYRD AS FLOOR LEADER—MAJORITY AND MINORITY.** As in the case of the House Democrats, the Senate Democrats also made a major leadership change in 1977. The majority leader from 1961 through 1976, when he retired, had been Mike Mansfield, a gentle, scholarly Montana Democrat, who had succeeded one of the most active and flamboyant of all Senate floor leaders, Lyndon Johnson of Texas. Mansfield's style and philosophy of leadership were the antithesis of that of Johnson (and also of Tip O'Neill): "I don't collect any IOUs. I don't do any special favors. I try to treat all Senators alike, and I think that's the best way to operate in the long run, because that way you maintain their respect and confidence. And that's what the ball game is all about."[19] Mansfield kept the flow of business moving through the Senate but—except on matters affecting Montana, when he became a bulldog—he did not often stamp his own imprint on the substance of what emerged.

Mansfield chose to keep a low profile in most decision-making situations. This was in marked contrast to Lyndon Johnson's style in the 1950s. Where Mansfield was tolerant of dissent, Johnson would often charge disloyalty; where Mansfield refused to apply even mild pressure, Johnson would skillfully "arm-twist" using his full range of resources; where Mansfield was consistently calm and quiet, Johnson would run through a range of moods and appeals, including some dramatic and boisterous ones.

In 1977, Robert C. Byrd, West Virginia Democrat, was elected

[19]Mansfield, quoted in Daniel Rapoport, "Congress Report/It's Not a Happy Time for House, Senate Leadership," *National Journal* (February 7, 1976): 171. For good discussions of Mansfield's leadership see Richard E. Cohen, "Marking an End to the Senate's Mansfield Era," *National Journal* (December 25, 1976): 1802–09; Andrew J. Glass, "Mike Mansfield, Majority Leader," in Norman J. Ornstein (ed.), *Congress in Change* (New York: Praeger, 1975): 142–54; and John G. Stewart, "Two Strategies of Leadership: Johnson and Mansfield," in Nelson W. Polsby (ed.), *Congressional Behavior* (New York: Random House, 1971): 61–92. For an excellent description of Johnson as leader in the Senate see Rowland Evans and Robert Novak, *Lyndon B. Johnson: The Exercise of Power* (New York: New American Library, 1966): Chapters 3–10.

majority leader of the Senate by the Democratic caucus. Just before the vote his only opponent, Hubert Humphrey, withdrew because, much like Tip O'Neill, Byrd appeared unbeatable. He had few enemies. And, also like O'Neill—although with a very different personal manner—he had patiently built up personal indebtedness and commitments through hard work in the Senate for many years. Beginning in 1967 he held two leadership posts: secretary of the Senate Democratic conference (1967–71) and whip (1971–77). His first position—secretary of the conference—did not amount to much when he acquired it, but he made it a position of service to his fellow Democrats. He treated the whip's position in the same way. When the majority leadership became vacant through Mansfield's retirement, Byrd had ten years of favors to draw on in building support.

Byrd's style is to proceed relatively quietly (more like Mansfield than Johnson) but with considerable unrelenting purpose and efficiency in achieving that purpose (more like Johnson than Mansfield). Like most party leaders in both houses, he focuses on providing procedural conditions that allow decisions to be made. He also intervenes in some substantive questions in order to suggest what he hopes will be winning compromises. He has complete mastery of the procedures of the Senate and understands well the personal views and political sensitivities of his colleagues. Although he does not like the term "facilitator," in fact his principal skill comes in facilitating the work of the Senate by manipulating procedures and substantive compromises in tandem.

An effective Senate leader must, of necessity, proceed differently than an effective House leader. A chief reason for this situation is the different rules used by the two chambers. The House is relatively highly structured and tightly controlled by formal rules. The Senate has a number of formal rules, but most of the time the proceedings are governed by the necessity of acquiring "unanimous consent" (that is, one objector can prevent a debate or decision from going forward or can at least stall the proceedings). Byrd himself has remarked of the Senate that "It would be impossible for Jesus Christ to do anything without unanimous consent."[20]

Byrd defined the essential tasks he saw in the job of majority leader: "He facilitates, he constructs, he programs, he schedules, he takes an active part in the development of legislation, he steps in at crucial

---

[20]Byrd, quoted in Adam Clymer, "Leadership Gap in the Senate," *New York Times,* September 28, 1977.

moments on the floor, offers amendments, speaks on behalf of legislation and helps to shape the outcome of the legislation."[21]

In his first year as minority leader (1981) both Byrd and the Democrats in general had problems adjusting to their minority status. Democrats seemed directionless and the Republicans, who held 53 of the 100 seats, won all of the battles. However, over the next five years in minority status (1982–86) Byrd adopted practices that led to increasing cohesion in his party. Under his guidance, through devices such as luncheon meetings and task forces, Senate Democrats became more issue-oriented and also more cohesive in support of certain points of view. Although remaining in the minority (with 45 seats in 1983 and 1984 and 47 seats in 1985 and 1986) they began to pick up enough dissident Republicans while minimizing their own defections to win occasional votes. Byrd easily kept his job as floor leader in late 1984 when challenged by Lawton Chiles of Florida. In late 1986, after the Democrats had regained control of the Senate with 55 seats, Byrd was not challenged for the floor leadership. When the One Hundredth Congress met in 1987, he was again majority leader.

In 1987, Byrd retained his desire to achieve a unified Democratic party in the Senate. He used his undoubted skill in manipulating the rules of the Senate to help push for that result. He also worked closely with Speaker Wright to have the Democrats in both houses coordinate some of their legislative initiatives to the benefit of the party in general. He was determined to make his second stint as majority leader productive.[22]

## Senate Republicans

THE GENERAL PATTERN. In the 1970s and 1980s the Senate Republicans developed a pattern of leadership that had a number of leaders at the top. The floor leader chairs no other party committees. He is the most important single leader but is also aided and constrained by the whip, the chairperson of the conference, the chairperson of the Policy Committee, and the secretary of the conference. The Senate Republicans also have a Committee on Committees with a separate chairperson, although this committee does little beside automatically

---

[21]Byrd, quoted in Richard E. Cohen, "Byrd of West Virginia—A New Job, A New Image," *National Journal* (August 20, 1977): 1294.

[22]For a good assessment of Byrd's performance as majority leader in 1987 see Jacqueline Calmes, "Byrd Struggles to Lead Deeply Divided Senate," *Congressional Quarterly Weekly Report* (July 4, 1987): 1419–23.

# BYRD GIVES TRUANT SENATORS A LESSON

BY JONATHAN FUERBRINGER

Under any circumstances, it is difficult to run the United States Senate. On Fridays, when members are hankering to escape for the weekend, it's even tougher. And with Presidential aspirants pursuing their ambitions out of town, it's well nigh impossible.

Today, the Senate majority leader, Robert C. Byrd, got fed up.

In an unusual display of pique at his own Democratic colleagues, Mr. Byrd, a West Virginian, manufactured unnecessary roll-call votes, which senators do not like to miss, just to penalize those who had left early.

"This Senator is not going to stand supinely by in silence and quaking with fear and let others say, 'Well, I'm going home, let's not have any votes,'" Mr. Byrd said, after losing a key vote on a supplemental appropriation bill because of the absences.

"Let it be a lesson to those who nonchalantly walk off at 1 o'clock on Friday afternoon and think, 'Well, school's out, we don't have any more votes.'"

Mr. Byrd's annoyance caught some members by surprise. "I haven't had a bed check since summer camp," joked Senator Carl M. Levin, Democrat of Michigan, as he scurried back into the Senate chamber for one of the two roll-call votes Mr. Byrd arranged. Both would normally have been taken up as voice votes. Eighteen senators missed the first roll-call and 25 missed the second.

Senator Christopher J. Dodd, Democrat of Connecticut, was sympathetic with Mr. Byrd. "I think you need them sometimes," he said of the votes.

But Senator Patrick J. Leahy, a Vermont Democrat, was annoyed. On the floor, he said the "bed check" votes "would be meaningless." He said senators should not be rated by the number of hours the Senate was in session. Seeing constituents at home, he insisted, is just as important as voting.

Mr. Byrd's annoyance came to the surface after weeks of trying and failing to nudge the Senate ahead on several important bills, including legislation governing Defense Department programs for 1988. Because of a filibuster led by Republicans that bill has been set aside.

Today, the Senate was working on a $9.6 billion supplemental appropriation bill for 1987, which it has been debating, on an off, for nearly a month. Mr. Byrd had hoped to pass it today but the absences forced him to put off final approval until next week.

One of the factors that makes the Senate difficult to run are rules that give individual members the power, if they choose, to block action with filibusters and manipulate procedures.

Also under the informal code of Senate courtesy, many senators can seek to postpone important roll-call votes when they are out of town. Senators prefer not to miss roll-call votes because their truancy might be used against them in a re-election campaign.

The key vote today on which absences hurt was on a measure to waive the spending limit in the budget-balancing law so that the supplemental appropriation bill, which is $2.6 billion over the limit, could be approved.

The waiver, which required 60 votes, failed by five, 55 to 34. Seven Democrats, who were counted on to support the waiver, were not in town. Among them were three Presidential hopefuls, Paul Simon of Illinois, Joseph R. Biden Jr. of Delaware and Albert Gore Jr. of Tennessee. Among the others were two former candidates, Edward M. Kennedy of Massachusetts and John Glenn of Ohio.

"We've got enough Presidential candidates out who I think will give us the votes" next week, said Sena-

tor J. Bennett Johnston, the Democrat from Louisiana who was managing the debate on the supplemental appropriation bill.

Mr. Byrd said he was annoyed because he thought he had reached an agreement with his colleagues not to work, or at least not to have votes, on Mondays in exchange for working on Fridays. "If I'm going to make a commitment I expect senators to keep their commitment," he said.

"I don't expect to get kudos from everybody, maybe anybody," Mr. Byrd added, acknowledging that his tactic would not be popular.

"I understand I'm not very well liked around here anyhow," he said. "But I didn't get elected to be liked here. I got elected because I thought I could do a job."

Source: Jonathan Fuerbringer. "Byrd Gives Truant Senators a Lesson," *New York Times,* May 30, 1987. Copyright © 1987 by The New York Times Company. Reprinted by permission.

ratifying what seniority dictates. The Senate Campaign Committee, and its chairperson, has also taken on increased importance among Senate Republicans because it now collects and disburses millions of dollars.

**ROBERT DOLE AS FLOOR LEADER.** In 1984, when Majority Leader Howard Baker of Tennessee announced his retirement from the Senate, a number of Republican Senators began exploring the possibility of running for the post. Five finally did run: Robert Dole of Kansas, Ted Stevens of Alaska, Richard Lugar of Indiana, Pete Domenici of New Mexico, and James McClure of Idaho. None of these individuals was a sure bet to win. On the first ballot in the Republican conference in late 1984 the eventual winner, Robert Dole, got only 14 votes out of the 53 cast. His opponents got 12, 10, 9, and 8, respectively. The senator with the fewest votes was dropped after each ballot until one individual had a majority. On the fourth and final ballot Dole beat his final remaining opponent, Stevens, 28 to 25.

In common with all party leaders in the modern Congress, Dole was a professional politician and a long-time member of Congress. He had held elective office continuously since 1951, served eight years in the U.S. House of Representatives beginning in 1961, and had come to the Senate in 1969. At the time of his election as floor leader he had been in the Senate for 16 years. He had also been Gerald Ford's vice presidential running-mate in the losing national campaign of 1976.

As majority leader in 1985 and 1986, he worked for the ends adopted by the Reagan Administration. Above all, he wanted to win in the Senate. At the same time he wanted to enhance his own chances of becoming the Republican nominee for president in 1988. He was a very partisan floor leader, not much interested in gaining the good will of the Democrats, including their floor leader. He wanted Republican positions to win and he especially wanted to make individual Republican senators look good, particularly those faced with re-election campaigns in 1986. He structured floor debate to spotlight the interests and contributions of various individual Republican members. He did this to help Republicans retain the majority in the Senate after the 1986 elections. He campaigned, at least electronically, for fellow Republican incumbents at the same time he was seeking re-election in Kansas himself. However, his hopes were dashed when the Democrats regained their majority.

He proved to be a superb coalition builder among the members of his own party. He maneuvered well on the floor and even got involved in complicated deal making within committees. He put together packages that helped him get what he wanted. For example, when it became clear in 1986 that the president could not avoid some legislation creating sanctions against South Africa, Dole tied the Senate's version of that bill to approval of military aid for the "contras" seeking to oust the Sandinista government in Nicaragua—a high priority goal for Reagan and one that had met congressional rebuffs before. Dole calculated, correctly, that senators who did not want contra aid could not afford, politically, to vote against sanctions against South Africa.

Dole kept his own counsel. He met rarely with committee chairpersons as a group. Rather, he worked with one or a few Republican senators at a time to arrange the compromises he thought would produce victory. Inevitably, given the fixation of Congress on budget and spending matters in 1985 and 1986, he became intimately involved in the detailed compromises necessary to produce omnibus budgets and continuing resolutions—catch-all bills that allow Congress to extend a large number of spending items at the same rate all at once. Dole realized that the Senate is a highly individualistic institution and set out to work with individuals so that a winning vote would emerge from any specific bargain he was able to put together.

His passion for winning and his partisanship were best summarized by Dole himself in responding to charges of unfairness by Byrd in August 1986. He said, "I did not become Majority Leader to lose," and added, "I didn't get elected Majority Leader to be dictated to by the minority."[23]

## LEADERSHIP FUNCTIONS

The leaders of all four congressional parties perform (or at least have the potential of performing) five major functions.

First, the leaders help organize the party to conduct business. Essentially this means that they participate in the selection of new leaders and the decisions concerning who will sit on which committees. This choice determines which individuals will be sitting in the most critical institutional positions when policy decisions are made.

In the House Democratic party, the caucus nominates the winning candidate for Speaker as long as it is the majority party and elects its floor leader and whip. Until 1975 the caucus also elected Democratic Ways and Means members. Usually, the Speaker can determine who the majority leader will be if he announces his preference publicly or lets it be widely known privately, although some Speakers have refrained from making their choice known. The Speaker could also usually endorse winning candidates for Ways and Means vacancies, although occasionally the caucus chose someone other than the Speaker's candidate. The Speaker and the majority leader appointed the whip until late 1986. The central leadership serves on the Steering and Policy Committee, which makes all committee assignments. The Speaker serves as chairman. It is reasonable to assume that most major committee assignments are pleasing to the Speaker and his lieutenants. Prior to 1975 the influence of the leaders over committee assignments had to be much more selective because of the process for assignments that was then used.

In the House Republican party the conference elects the minority leader, the minority whip, and the chairperson of the conference. The Committee on Committees is constituted entirely through the state delegations—with one member of the committee coming from every state that has at least one Republican in the House. The minority leader (and the other central leaders too) have minimal influence on

[23]Dole, quoted in Richard E. Cohen, "Dole's High-Risk Game," *National Journal* (September 6, 1986): 2111. See also Jacqueline Calmes, "Majority Leader Dole: Determined to Do It All," *Congressional Quarterly Weekley Report* (September 6, 1986): 2075–79.

the decisions of the Committee on Committees and on the choice of other leaders.

In both Senate parties the leadership seems disposed not to play a very active role in helping with the leader and committee choices in the party. Every individual senator seems to fend for himself or herself. Little central direction is evident in organizational terms in either party.

The second of the five functions that the leaders of all four congressional parties perform is the scheduling of business to come to the House and the Senate floors. In the House the Speaker and majority leader make these decisions, although they occasionally consult the minority leader to make sure that his sense of fairness is not violated. In the Senate the majority leader routinely consults the minority leader. If they agree, they have great flexibility because the Senate usually proceeds in an ad hoc fashion under so-called unanimous consent, which is based on agreements among everyone present to proceed in a specified way (time of debate, day of debate, control of time, allowable amendments) regardless of any formal Senate rules. The scheduling decisions made in both houses are not neutral. They can be used to influence the chances of success or failure of specific pieces of legislation. For example, if the majority party leaders fear a close vote they will postpone floor consideration if they know that some of their reliable supporters have to be absent. Or they may move floor action to a day on which some known opponents have to be absent.

Third, the leaders are responsible for promoting attendance on the floor of the House and the Senate. Both of the parties in the House do this primarily through their whip organizations, which are responsible for informing all party members that a critical vote is at hand and that their presence on the floor is required. This is done through an established telephone network between staff members in the regional whips' offices and staff members in the offices of individual congressmen who are responsible for knowing the whereabouts of the "boss." In the Senate, neither party routinely uses their whip apparatus that exists on paper. Consequently, a senator who is interested in a particular piece of legislation will frequently do his own "whipping" to increase attendance. Beginning in 1977 the Democratic whip became more active.

Selectivity is, of course, exercised in this attempt to increase attendance. For example, the whip organization of one of the House parties may well not contact a known opponents of the leaders' position when a critical vote is imminent.

Fourth, the leaders are constantly engaged in the collection and distribution of information. Reliable information is a precious commodity in both houses. In the House the whip organizations in both parties serve as focal points for this function. They solicit members' attitudes on selected upcoming bills and disseminate the leaders' preferences and limited information on the content of proposed legislation to party members. In the Senate, however, individual senators particularly interested in a bill usually wind up doing their own "headcounts" and their own distribution of substantive information. Beginning in 1977, the official whips for both parties became more active in conducting headcounts.

Fifth, the party leaders in both houses maintain a liaison with the White House on policy matters. This involves the leaders of the president's party more frequently than the leaders of the other party. Between the late 1930s and the late 1960s the leaders of the president's party met with him weekly. President Nixon had less frequent meetings with the Republican leaders in Congress. Presidents Ford, Carter, and Reagan held more frequent meetings. There may also be meetings on an emergency basis. The members of the opposition party may be invited from time to time for specific briefings and consultation. The leaders can serve as mediators between the president and the rank-and-file members, helping to facilitate the flow of policy-related information and preferences in both directions.

All five of these functions can be performed in such a way as to enhance the possibility of attaining specific desired policies and programs. The leaders' central task is to persuade members to support their policy preferences on the floor of the House and the Senate. The leaders usually take their substantive cues from a committee delegation and then exercise their persuasive powers to gain ratification for that position, rather than attempting to push a personal position on their party in an authoritarian manner. They may also take major cues from the president or, in the case of the House Democrats, from the party caucus.

One relatively minor function the leaders perform, which should, logically, be more important, is to maintain contact with the leaders in the other house to facilitate both the flow of business and the adoption of common party positions in the two chambers. In recent years there has been increased interaction between the leaders, by party, across the houses on both a routine basis and on an ad hoc (usually signifying a crisis) basis.[24]

---

[24]See Walter Kravitz, "Relations between the Senate and the House of Representatives: The Party Leadership," in Commission on the Operation of the Senate. *Policymaking Role of Leadership in the Senate* (Washington: Government Printing Office, 1976): 121–38.

The leaders are also responsible for some administrative chores—simply making the House and Senate function as organizations that must meet payrolls, monitor expenses, buy supplies, and so on. In the mid-1970s both houses undertook studies of their ways of conducting business (some of which smacked of quill pens and 1789). The two commissions (the House Commission on Administrative Review and the Commission on the Operation of the Senate) both issued a number of specific recommendations for modernizing and streamlining the business arrangements. In late 1977, however, the House rejected the proposals of its commission.

## THE PRINCIPAL LEADERSHIP RESOURCES FOR AFFECTING LEGISLATIVE RESULTS

The party leaders in both houses have four principal resources at their disposal as they labor to influence the policy statements and actions emerging from the Senate and the House. They may not, however, always use all of these resources.

The first is their ability to use the rules of the House and the Senate. Leaders, out of desire and necessity, develop considerable expertise in manipulating the intricacies of the rules.

In the House, the majority party leaders, particularly the Speaker, are in a very strong position to use the rules to further their policy ends. The minority leaders in the House have some obstructive powers, but the House rules generally put the majority party in a consistently dominant position. For example, the Speaker can be selective in placing legislation on the "suspension calendar," a device for expediting relatively non-controversial bills (bills brought to the floor on this calendar are debated for only forty minutes and require a two-thirds vote for passage). Many bills of low visibility would die if they were not moved through the House quickly in this fashion. This means that the Speaker is in a good position to build credits for the future, to reward past loyalty, or to punish past disloyalty by either granting or ignoring a member's request to place a low visibility bill on the suspension calendar. The Speaker can also use his procedural powers to prevent action he thinks would be unwise for his party. In late 1983, for example, Speaker O'Neill used his control over the House calendar to prevent the House from considering a controversial immigration bill he feared might pass. In the previous year he and the majority leader had prevented action by agreeing to schedule the bill so late in the session that there was no time to consider it. His political judgment was that the opposition of Hispanic interest groups and the Hispanic members of his own party in the House made the bill a minefield for the Democratic party.

In the Senate, the leaders of both parties have influence over the use of the rules. The legislative process in the Senate is highly flexible because of the use of unanimous consent agreements. The leaders play a central role in arranging these agreements, thereby enhancing their ability to collect IOUs for the future and to reward or punish past behavior.

The second resource possessed by the leaders of both houses is their control over a number of forms of tangible preferment, which include appointments to special and select committees, commissions (such as those overseeing service academies), and delegations to foreign meetings (such as the NATO parliamentarians); appointments to standing committees; help in pushing specific bills; and help aimed at re-election. The granting or withholding of such preferments is used selectively to improve the chances that the leaders will succeed when they ask for specific policy actions.

The leaders' control over assignments to standing committees is, with the partial exception of the House Democrats, less direct than their control over other appointments. But even indirect influence can be important.

In the House at present, as has been noted, the Speaker and his lieutenants are in a position to name the Democrats on the Rules Committee and to influence initial assignments to other committees, although they often refrain from using the maximum influence they could.[25] Even before these formal powers were given to the leaders in the mid-1970s they expanded the number of seats on the most desirable committees to help add to their resource base.[26] And the leaders would intervene selectively in the assignment process even during the period when they had little formal role to play. In the 1950s, for example, Speaker Sam Rayburn saw to it that the Democratic membership on the Education and Labor Committee was reoriented from conservative to reliably liberal. Since at least the 1960s the Democratic Committee on Committees has paid some attention to party loyalty in making assignments—those members more loyal to the party are

[25]See Waldman, "Majority Leadership in the House of Representatives" and Kenneth A. Shepsle, *The Giant Jigsaw Puzzle* (Chicago: University of Chicago Press, 1978).
[26]Louis P. Westefield, "Majority Party Leadership and the Committee System in the House of Representatives," *American Political Science Review* 68 (1974): 1593–1604. For a somewhat different view see Bruce A. Ray and Steven S. Smith, "Committee Size in the U.S. Congress," *Legislative Studies Quarterly*, 9 (1984): 679–95.

more likely to receive their preferred assignments when they request transfers.[27]

In 1981 Democratic representative Phil Gramm of Texas played a leading role in helping the Reagan administration and its Republican and conservative Democratic supporters in Congress pass a major omnibus and tax package that dramatically reduced spending on domestic social programs and simultaneously dramatically reduced taxes. His behavior enraged Democratic leaders of the House and the majority of the party, which had opposed the Reagan initiatives. In early 1983, after Gramm had been re-elected as a Democrat for his third term, the House Democratic caucus, with the strong support of the party leaders, voted not to reappoint him to a seat on the Budget Committee, the position he used in 1981 and 1982 to thwart party aims. Gramm immediately resigned from the House, successfully sought re-election to his House seat as Republican in a special election, and then in the fall of 1984 was the successful Republican candidate for a U.S. Senate seat from Texas.

There is also good evidence that the weakening of the seniority system in the House Democratic party helped lead to increased party loyalty on the part of senior members either seeking to retain committee chairs or aspiring to them.[28]

The House Republican leaders have less influence over standing committee assignments. The Committee on Committees is selected and operated so that, typically, a few senior conservatives from the states with the largest Republican delegations effectively make the assignment decisions. This means that the Republican delegations on the most important committees are heavily weighted in the conservative direction.

In the Senate, the leaders have only minor influence on committee assignments. This is particularly true in the Republican Party where the Committee on Committees makes initial assignments on the basis of seniority. With only minor exceptions, if two individuals apply for the same opening the more senior person automatically gets it. The influence of the Republican leaders can be seen only occasionally when they might ask a more senior senator to apply for an opening in order to keep an undesirable senator off the committee. The Democratic Steering Committee, which is the Committee on Committees,

[27]See Randall B. Ripley, *Party Leaders in the House of Representatives* (Washington: Brookings, 1967): 59–61.
[28]Sara Brandes Crook and John R. Hibbing, "Congressional Reform and Party Discipline: The Effects of Changes in the Seniority System on Party Loyalty in the US House of Representatives," *British Journal of Political Science* 15 (1985): 207–26.

is not bound by seniority and the majority leader chairs the committee. But his degree of influence is related to his degree of aggressiveness.

The leaders of all four parties can facilitate or impede committee and floor consideration of specific bills.

An additional tangible preferment is campaign help, which leaders can help channel to particularly supportive and valuable incumbents. All four of the congressional campaign committees distribute a substantial number of dollars, although the amounts are still much smaller than those coming from other sources such as Political Action Committees and individual contributions. Republicans have much more money flowing through their congressional campaign committees than do Democrats, but the latter's resources are not trivial. Maverick incumbents may get little or no aid from these committees.

The leaders of all four parties can also personally campaign for a few incumbents each year. It is very flattering for a rank-and-file congressman to have the Speaker or the majority leader speak in his or her district during a campaign. These appearances are rare and are highly valued by those who benefit.

The third resource the leaders can use to affect policy statements and actions is psychological preferment. This simply means that the leaders, particularly in the House, are in a position to give cues on how highly they value an individual member. These cues, once given, help establish a member's reputation. A member with a high reputation is likely to be more successful legislatively than a member who is not so highly regarded. House members know they need the respect and good will of their colleagues to help their legislative careers. They are, therefore, extremely sensitive to the leaders' cues. Skillful leaders can help sway behavior by the content and timing of the cues and by selective publication of those cues to appropriate audiences. The increased independence of subcommittees and the rapid rise of junior members to importance on subcommittees has made them somewhat less dependent on the good will of the leaders. But since many of the most important friendship ties within legislatures stay inside a single party, the approval of the party leaders always retains considerable importance.[29]

Senators also need respect and good will in the Senate if they are to be deemed successful legislators. On the other hand, senators can

---

[29]For a suggestive study of friendship in a state legislature and its relation to party label see Gregory A. Caldeira and Samuel C. Patterson, "Political Friendship in the Legislature," *Journal of Politics* 49 (1987): 953–75.

also command wider attention than that accorded to House members and many may not worry excessively about their perceived legislative effectiveness. They can also attain gratification by being public figures in their states or regions or even nationally. Almost any senator can command good newspaper space in his state and with a little extra effort can be quoted and pictured regionally or nationally. This opportunity is not open to most House members, which means that they are very sensitive to their standing in the House. Senators who want above all to be considered effective legislators are susceptible to psychological preferment manipulated by the leaders. Senator Mansfield did not use this tactic, although his predecessor, Lyndon Johnson, was masterful at it. The Republican leaders in the 1960s, 1970s, and 1980s and Senator Byrd were somewhere between Mansfield and Johnson in their level of activity.

The fourth resource that can be used by the leaders in seeking specific legislative action is their dominance over the communications processes internal to the House and Senate. The leaders are in a unique position to control what is learned by members about the schedule and rules affecting pending legislation and about the legislative intentions of the president, key members, and the leaders themselves. Particularly in the House, members of both parties routinely look to their party leaders for reliable information on such matters. They are not, however, heavily dependent on their party leaders for information on the substance of legislation; for that they rely on the standing committee members from their party. Even in the Senate, a skillful leader can make the senators of his party (and even of the other party) come to him or his staff members for the most current and most reliable information.

## THE IMPACT OF THE LEADERS

### The Leaders and Individual Members

EXPECTATIONS OF MEMBERS AND THE NATURE OF LEADERSHIP. The members of the House and Senate have definite expectations about the intrusion of the party leaders into their lives as legislators. House members are more likely to consider aggressive leadership legitimate than are senators. Senators acknowledge the legitimacy of their leaders stating party positions on at least some legislative matters, appealing for unity and loyalty on important bills, and distributing and collecting information on scheduling and substance. They do not, however, accept coercion as legitimate, nor do they think that the party leaders should interfere with the business of standing committees, aside from urging them to keep on schedule. Most House members accept the same tasks as legitimate for the leaders to perform but they are more willing than senators to accept the coercive activities of leaders as legitimate.[30] This difference is rooted both in history and tradition (the simple fact that House leaders have usually been more aggressive than their Senate counterparts) and in the perceived necessities of managing a body of 435 people as opposed to a body of only 100 people.

The leaders understand that they must lead through a complicated process of interaction with the members. They can state preferences and apply a variety of pressures to get maximum support. But their job is persuasion. They do not have sanctions available that will always produce compliance. Leaders feel the need, however, to be restrained in the use of the sanctions they do possess because they realize the party membership can balk if it feels it is being subjected to unfair pressure. Members of Congress are keenly aware that they have been elected largely on the basis of their own resources and wits, and they inevitably feel a strong pull toward their constituencies. Likewise, members prize their own independence and resent what they consider to be unfair attempts at coercion to achieve unity for its own sake or even for a specific policy goal. When the pull of constituency or the dictates of conscience conflict with the demands of the party leaders, the member's decision can go either way. The most successful leaders acknowledge the existence of these cross-pressures and undertake a constant balancing act between demanding partisan unity and loyalty and deferring to constituency interests and the dictates of individual judgment.

Senate leaders have, at least for several decades, been engaged largely in "taking in other people's laundry"—that is, managing the processes in the Senate so as to facilitate adoption of the preferences of a large proportion of their colleagues (and also of the White House). In recent years, particularly since the reforms in the early 1970s, House leaders have also had to move more in the direction of paying attention to a wider circle of House members in identifying and catering to individual preferences. The House Democratic leaders have been particularly active in trying to provide more services to more members and in trying to include as many of their members as possible

---

[30]See Ripley, *Party Leaders in the House.*

in coalitions they seek to build.[31] Adapting to changed circumstances is necessary, but the basic task of the leaders in both houses—to produce winning coalitions whenever possible—has remained constant. Leaders have to bargain, compromise, and rely in large part on mutual good will in developing coalitions. That also has been a constant fact of life for leaders in both houses for many decades.

THE TECHNIQUES OF THE LEADERS. The party leaders of both houses have a number of specific techniques they can employ to gain the support of their members for specific legislative ends, although they must constantly decide how aggressive to be in using them. Among these techniques are the following:

1. Using personal contact to ask for such actions as favorable roll-call votes, votes in committees, certain kinds of speeches on the floor, absence or presence on the floor.
2. Promulgating permanent or temporary changes in the rules, procedures, and practices of the House or Senate that will make favorable legislative outcomes easier to achieve.
3. Using influence over committee assignments to achieve a desired ideological balance on a committee.
4. Encouraging the development of unanimous positions by standing committee contingents before floor debate begins.
5. Announcing official party positions on pending legislation by a letter to all members, by a statement from a policy or steering committee, or by the adoption of an official party position in one of the caucuses or conferences.
6. Co-opting key members into the leadership circle for the duration of a given legislative struggle.
7. Stimulating key intra-party groups, such as state delegations, to unify behind specific positions.
8. Influencing the distribution of tangible rewards such as federal patronage, federal projects, and electoral aid.
9. Distributing information selectively to the members on substance and procedure.
10. Giving special concessions to a few key members of the opposition party when a winning coalition cannot be formed from within a single party.

[31]Barbara Sinclair, "Majority Party Leadership Strategies for Coping with the New U.S. House," *Legislative Studies Quarterly* 6 (1981): 391–414; Roger H. Davidson, "Congressional Leaders as Agents of Change," in Mackaman, *Understanding Congressional Leadership;* and Christopher J. Deering and Steven S. Smith, "Majority Party Leadership and the New House Subcommittee System, in Mackaman, *Understanding Congressional Leadership.*

11. Manipulating floor proceedings by scheduling critical business at the most propitious time, arranging for influential speakers, managing the pattern of voting, and helping arrange the optimum time and amendment limits for a particular bill.

# CONGRESSIONAL LEADERSHIP AND THE TRADE BILL, 1986

Democratic leaders in the House vowed that comprehensive trade legislation would be a priority in 1986. Several factors spurred the Democrats on:

- The trade deficit was growing larger every year—like a runaway train, it seemed unstoppable.
- Increasing numbers of domestic firms were going out of business, unable to compete with cheaper imported goods.
- President Reagan's veto of trade legislation at the end of 1985 was a stinging memory. Congress had lacked the votes necessary to override the veto.
- In the election year, trade was a popular issue—jobs and economic well-being were irresistible issues for legislators regardless of party affiliation. As Rep. Ed Jenkins (D-Ga.) said, "it will give everyone political cover . . . it will get you through November 1986."
- Democrats were operating in a vacuum of presidential leadership. The administration refused to draft its own bill and threatened to veto any bill containing protectionist provisions.

In February, Speaker O'Neill (D-Mass.) called a meeting of the chairpersons of the committees that were working on aspects of trade legislation. He told them he was making the majority leader, Jim Wright (D-Tex.), responsible for crafting a trade strategy that incorporated work of all of the committees—Ways and Means, Banking, Commerce, Energy, Education and Labor, and Agriculture. (Wright early on had to defuse a turf battle between Energy and Ways and Means over trade assistance for the telecommunications industry.) The leadership laid out a schedule for the bill, expecting a mid-May completion.

Both the House leaders and Ways and Means Chairman Dan Rostenkowski (D-Ill.) recognized the need to strike a balance between the ardently vocalized views of free-traders and protectionists. The bill from Ways and Means, the traditional leader in trade legislation, became the skeleton on which pieces of bills from the other committees were hung. The bill was comprehensive, covering exchange rates, third-world debt, education, retraining, and trade negotiations, and it was not designed to protect specific industries (although it contained many special deals for a range of imported goods including kiwis, teddy bears, and red pepper sauce). The bill focused on opening up new markets and assisting U.S. exports instead of simply closing U.S. markets to imports. A key amendment sponsored by Richard Gephardt (D-Mo.) required U.S. trade retaliation against countries that maintained consistently large trade surpluses, particularly Japan, Taiwan, and West Germany. Objections to this "get tough" amendment and to limitations on presidential discretion over trade matters led many Republicans to reject the bill.

The House passed the bill 295 to 115 on May 22. All but four Democrats supported it, and a third of the Republicans also supported it. A distinct regional pattern was present in the voting, with delegations from the South and Northeast supporting it, while representatives from states more dependent on free international trade, such as the Pacific Northwest, resisted the bill. President Reagan condemned the House action, calling it "kamikaze" legislation that would "plunge the world into a trade war, eroding our relations with our al-lies and free world trading partners."

In the Republican-controlled Senate, leadership was also a key factor, but now it was working against the legislation, not for it. The leaders knew the president would veto any bill containing protectionist measures, but they could not persuade the administration to draft its own bill or to work with the Senate Finance Committee to develop a joint bill. In the absence of White House support, Finance Committee Chairman Robert Packwood (R-Ore.) was unwilling to take the initiative. The committee met and reviewed a staff draft in desultory fashion, but no vote was taken and no report was issued. The Congress adjourned without a trade bill. Following the November elections, the Democrats, once more in control of the Senate, vowed that a strong trade bill would again be a legislative priority for the new year.

CONDITIONS FOR SUCCESS.[32] Not all leaders are equally successful in achieving what they want as they seek to stimulate certain kinds of behavior from the members of their party. The leaders of the minority party are, by definition, dependent on some support from members of the majority party. Their hand is strengthened when the president is also of their party, but the problem of insufficient numbers remains. The leaders of the majority party, who presumably have the numbers on their side, must labor to maximize the unity of their members and prevent defections that could cause losses. In general, majority party leaders have greater chances of legislative success when their majority is large, when it is a relatively new majority, and when there is supportive activity coming from the president and the White House.

The leaders of both parties have increased chances for success on issues not terribly visible or salient to constituents. This leaves mem-

[32]Randall B. Ripley, *Majority Party Leadership in Congress* (Boston: Little, Brown, 1969): 184–187; Lewis A. Froman, Jr. and Randall B. Ripley, "Conditions for Party Leadership: The Case of the House Democrats," *American Political Science Review* 59 (1965): 52–63; Barbara Deckard Sinclair, "Determinants of Aggregate Party Cohesion in the U.S. House of Representatives, 1901–1956," *Legislative Studies Quarterly* 2 (1977): 155–75; and Waldman, "Majority Leadership in the House of Representatives": 378–80.

bers freer to succumb to the blandishments of the leaders. Leaders are also more likely to prevail with specific requests at relatively invisible points in the legislative process. If a member perceives that his position might cause some negative reaction in his constituency, he would feel insecure in honoring a leadership request on a final roll call on the floor. His action in a committee, however, is likely to go unnoticed at home by either the press or public, whereas his action on the floor is likely to be reported. Leaders are also more likely to gain converts on issues that are defined in procedural terms than on issues that are defined in substantive terms. For example, a motion to adjourn may really be a motion that will kill a bill. A person who may mildly favor the bill can still claim that position and yet vote with his party leaders in favor of adjournment and rationalize his action—if it is ever questioned—as "only procedural." The relative visibility of actions on procedurally-defined issues is lower than on the substantively-defined issues and this allows members to adhere to the requests of the leaders without worrying in detail about constituency reaction.

## The Leaders and Standing Committees and Subcommittees

The party leaders are the main centralizing forces in the legislative process, the standing committees and subcommittees the main decentralizing forces. Leaders and committees must necessarily interact in conducting the business of the two chambers. The exact nature of the interaction, however, can vary, as can the relative importance of leaders and committees on critical items of substance.

In many ways leaders and committees are interdependent. As party leaders seek specific legislative ends they must rely on the standing committees for a number of things: the detailed substance of bills, the timetable within which bills are ready for floor consideration, the transmission of leaders' legislative preferences to the members of the committee during committee deliberations, and aid in the transmission of those preferences to all party members during floor consideration. Committee leaders must rely on the party leaders for scheduling business for the floor and working for its passage or defeat, for communicating important information about members' preferences to the committee, and for helping distribute committee opinions to noncommittee members.

THE NATURE OF LEADER-COMMITTEE INTERACTION. There are three important points of interaction between party leaders and committee leaders. The first involves assignments to committees. Who sits on a committee may, in many instances, determine what emerges from that committee. The custom of seniority limits leaders' potential impact on committee assignments to sitting members who desire to change assignments or to new members. In the case of freshmen members and new assignments the leaders of both parties are generally disposed to exercise only minimal influence unless vital issues are at stake.

By virtue of changes made in the 1970s, (and spelled out in previous sections of this book), the House party leaders have moved into a position to prevent individuals from becoming chairpersons or ranking minority members if they can persuade a majority of the party that such individuals are undesirable for those jobs.

Both parties in the House have the machinery for rejecting an unacceptable product of the seniority system in the top spot of any standing committee. The Democrats have used their machinery. The Republican conference members and Democratic caucus members could, of course, ignore the preferences of the formal party leaders either to retain or reject a chairperson or ranking minority member. But it seems likely that members who have come to those positions through seniority will not be deposed if they have the strong support of the party leaders. If the party leaders should ever agree on the necessity of rejecting a nomination for a top position based on seniority, they would probably stand a reasonably good chance of carrying either the caucus or the conference with them.

A second major point of interaction between party leaders and the committee system involves the scheduling of floor activity that, of necessity, has implications for the scheduling of committee business. If the party leaders of the majority party have an overall program in mind (and this is particularly likely to be the case if their party also controls the White House) they are going to need to spread the program out over the life of a Congress. They cannot afford to have all of the important legislation come to the floor in the last two months of a session or, worse yet, the last two months of a Congress. The leaders consult with chairpersons about the major items on the agenda both to get some reading on when reports might be expected and to make some requests either to speed up or, less frequently, slow down committee consideration and action.

Similarly, committee chairpersons have their own agenda to consider. Therefore, they make timing requests of the leaders for floor consideration on specific dates.

A third point of interaction between party leaders and committees involves the substance of legislative proposals. Party leaders may well be too busy with scheduling matters for the floor and working for their passage (or defeat) to have preferences on the substantive details of legislation. If they are working together with representatives of the White House or individual executive departments or agencies, however, they may have detailed requests on some matters. And some leaders have strong personal interests that they pursue. For example, when Sam Rayburn (D-Tex.) was Speaker he followed the work of the Ways and Means Committee on trade (he wanted fewer restrictions) and the oil depletion allowance (he wanted it preserved unchanged) and did not hesitate to intervene if he felt it necessary.

Leaders in the last few decades have tended to keep their intervention in the work of standing committees to a minimum. They have been much more likely to allow the committee to produce its substantive product by whatever natural processes exist in the committee and then work with the senior members of the committee for the passage (or defeat or amendment) of the committee's handiwork.

A rule adopted in 1973 by the House Democratic caucus increases the likelihood of more substantive input by the leaders into the work of committees. This rule allows fifty or more members of the party to bring to the caucus any amendment proposed to a committee-reported bill if the Rules Committee is requesting a closed rule. If the proposed amendment is supported by a majority of the caucus then the Rules Committee Democrats will be instructed to write the rule for floor consideration so that that specific amendment could be considered on the floor. In effect, this prevents closed rules on bills if a majority present at a Democratic caucus opposes such a rule. Leeway for leadership intervention is present here if the Speaker and/or majority leader and/or majority whip should decide to side with the members who want to force floor consideration of a specific amendment not favored by the committee (including at least some of the Democrats on the committee).

In the 1970s the practice of referring individual bills to more than one committee became fairly common in the House. This also increased the potential for substantive impact on the part of the Speaker and Rules Committee.[33]

**THE IMPACT OF LEADER-COMMITTEE INTERACTION.** The nature of the interaction between leaders and standing committees is critical

---

[33]On the practice and its impact see Roger H. Davidson, Walter J. Oleszek, and Thomas Kephart, "One Bill, Many Committees: Multiple Referrals in the House of Representatives," *Legislative Studies Quarterly* 13 (1988): 3–28.

to the performance by Congress of its lawmaking function. In general, the nature of the interaction can be viewed along a spectrum ranging from virtual committee autonomy at one end to leader activism at the other. In a situation of committee autonomy the central party leaders rarely intervene in such matters as committee assignments, the scheduling and timing of committee business, and the substance of matters before committees. In a situation in which leader activism is predominant there is a considerable amount of such intervention. There are, of course, a number of mixed patterns along the spectrum.

Some facets of lawmaking for domestic policy and the domestic aspects of foreign policy (for example, defense procurement, or "buy American" or "ship American" provisions in foreign-aid legislation) are different than for the non-domestic aspects of foreign policy. What is the same, however, is that the committee autonomy pattern leaves the congressional party leaders out of an important substantive role in policy of either kind.

When domestic policy is at stake (and also the domestic aspects of foreign policy) the existence of committee autonomy promotes the dominance of subgovernments. Leader activism, on the other hand, promotes increased influence not just for the leaders but also for the president and presidency when the leaders are in accord with presidential policies and for rank-and-file senators and representatives. This increased influence restrains the influence of the subgovernments. The subgovernments may or may not produce good or reasonable policy decisions but, in any event, they cannot be expected to consult more than a narrow range of interests in making their decisions. The increased influence for non-subgovernment members that is facilitated by leader activism allows for a broader range of interests to be articulated and consulted.

Another value that can best be served by leadership activism is coherence of the legislative program. This means that some order is apparent in the welter of proposals presented to Congress—both in terms of substance and in terms of timing. Leadership activism leaves room for an activist president, but in no way does it place Congress in a subordinate position to the president. It simultaneously affords maximum influence for the party leaders and all members. In addition, it puts some restrictions on the influence of the members of the issue-specific subgovernments. If the program is set—both in substance and in timing—by these subgovernments, then little relationship will be seen between programs that are in fact competing for scarce resources or have other logical ties. In the leader activism pattern the centralizing forces can spell out those relationships so that the decisions can be made on the basis of more rather than less information and there is a chance for greater coherence of all legislative results considered together.

The major difference between the situation just described and the situation when non-domestic aspects of foreign policy are at stake is the enormous impact of the president and institutional presidency. Presidential influence over Congress is no longer as much of a problem for the president except on those occasions when he needs a treaty ratified or a new program approved. He may have more problems in relation to appropriations requests. Another major difference is that interest groups play only a very limited role. The chief actors in this policy arena are the president and institutional presidency, the foreign policy bureaucracy, key committee members on the Senate Foreign Relations, House Foreign Affairs, and the two Appropriations Committees, the party leaders, and the individual members of the House and Senate. Controversy involving Congress can, however, erupt in this area despite the power and prestige of the presidency. Congressional conflict with the Reagan administration's preferences with regard to sanctions against South Africa and aid for the Nicaraguan "contras" are cases in point.

An alliance between members of the foreign policy bureaucracy and senior committee members may have considerable influence on the routine aspects of foreign policy, particularly when a pattern of committee autonomy exists. Such an alliance may even limit presidential influence on such matters, although it seems as if the alliance is much less close between the foreign policy bureaucrats and committees and subcommittees than it is in many domestic areas (including the domestic aspects of foreign policy). The major subgovernment in foreign policy may, in fact, consist of the presidency and foreign policy bureaucracy with all congressional elements, including the key committee and subcommittee members as well as the party leaders, relegated to relatively minor roles.

In a pattern of activism the leaders increase their potential for influence in the foreign policy arena. In the event of a major disagreement between a committee and the president, the committee itself will have a stronger hand if backed by at least some of the central party leaders—especially if the leaders are from both parties. Leader activism does not necessarily diminish the potential for influence on the part of committees, except perhaps in some of the routine matters that are left mostly to the interaction of committees and subcommittees and the foreign policy bureaucracy. The difference is that in domestic policy and the domestic aspects of foreign policy these routine matters, when aggregated, constitute the bulk of policy both in amount and importance. But in the foreign policy arena routine matters are not as important.

─────

Leaders are partially free agents who can shape their own styles and actions. But they are also products of the institutional context they face.[34]

If Congress is assessed in terms of its potential for important and swift policy action, the party leaders necessarily play a critical role. On those occasions when Congress has been at its most active, the party leaders have usually been aggressive—both in their own right and in responding to an aggressive president. When the leaders are the most constrained in their actions, either of their own volition or by virtue of matters over which they have little control, Congress is most likely to be proceeding on a "normal" course of handling most matters in a disaggregated and incremental fashion. The performance of the leaders offers an index to the overall mood and performance of Congress. Since the leaders can help shape the environment in which they work, the choices they make on how they use their resources, what techniques they employ, and how they perform their functions can help determine the nature of congressional influence on public policy.

[34]See Joseph Cooper and David W. Brady, "Institutional Context and Leadership Style: The House from Cannon to Rayburn," *American Political Science Review* 75 (1981): 411–25; and the chapters by Charles O. Jones, Roger H. Davidson, and Burdett A. Loomis in Mackaman (ed.), *Understanding Congressional Leadership,* 117–79.

# 7

## Other Internal Influences: State Delegations, Groups, Caucuses, Staff, and Support Agencies

Members of the House and Senate receive a constant barrage of advice—both solicited and unsolicited—on which policies to support from their standing committee colleagues and from the party leaders. The committees and leaders are the most consistently important internal congressional forces shaping public policy. There are, however, other forces inside Congress that also serve as important sources of advice and direction for individual members as they seek to cope with a staggering workload in a limited amount of time. State delegations, a wide variety of intra-party and inter-party groups and caucuses, staff members working both for individual members and for committees, and four central support agencies all perform this function. Individual members and groups of members also use the delegations, groups, caucuses, and the staff over which they have control to enhance their influence. The relative sizes of the two houses dictate that state delegations and groups and caucuses have particular importance in the House and that staff members have added importance in the Senate.

## STATE DELEGATIONS

In Congress, particularly in the House, states serve as an identifiable symbol around which members sometimes cluster. State delegations, usually divided on a partisan basis, provide cues for some individual behavior.[1] They also provide a vehicle for members to increase their chances of achieving everything from desirable committee assignments to favorable policy and program decisions.

Sometimes state delegations meet on a bipartisan basis. Occasionally senators from the same state will be included, regardless of party. But these bipartisan, bicameral meetings are relatively rare and involve only questions relating to direct federal benefits for the state or region in which the state is included. Ordinarily, the influential state delegations are in the House alone.[2]

State party delegations vary greatly in the frequency of their meetings, the extent to which they help socialize new members, the amount of interaction they have outside of meetings, the topics they discuss in their meetings, and whether they seek unity in voting on the floor of the House. They vary greatly in cohesion.

Two conditions promote state delegation cohesion: stable membership and a relatively high proportion of members desiring to make their careers in the House. Socioeconomic homogeneity of districts is not necessary for cohesion to be high. Such homogeneity, however, may be necessary for unified bloc voting to occur. Homogeneity of ideology or positions on public policy questions is not necessary for

[1]For general insights into the functioning and importance of state delegations see Richard Born, "Cue-Taking within State Party Delegations in the U.S. House of Representatives," *Journal of Politics* 38 (1976): 71–94; Charles L. Clapp, *The Congressman* (Washington, D.C.: Brookings, 1963): 41–45; John H. Kessel, "The Washington Congressional Delegation," *Midwest Journal of Political Science* 8 (1964): 1–21; Leo M. Snowiss, "Congressional Recruitment and Representation, *American Political Science Review* 60 (1966): 627–39; and Tom Watson, "State Delegations: Power's Payoffs and Pitfalls," *Congressional Quarterly Weekly Report* (January 3, 1987): 24–28.
[2]The concept of "state delegation" in the Senate is meaningless since there are only two senators per state. Senators from a state cooperate explicitly with House members from the same state only sporadically. Various interest-based caucuses, both within the House and occasionally including senators, absorb what might be thought of, in principle, as regional interests. Political scientists, reasonably so, use region as an analytical category for understanding congressional behavior, especially on roll calls, but regional considerations only rarely serve to motivate concrete individual behavior in Congress in the late Twentieth Century.

a delegation to function effectively to help members attain a variety of goals such as achieving good committee assignments, promoting the flow of federal benefits to the state, and creating a reliable set of informants on a variety of substantive questions.[3]

Most members of the House constantly seek information on the substance of the great number of matters they have to consider, on the procedure by which those matters are considered, and on the preferences and intentions of others both in the House and outside of it. Given the vast workload, the complexity of the rules, and the large number of policy actors, members value time-saving devices that can provide them with reliable information.

State party delegations are a means of providing a lot of information to members quickly.[4] A large delegation is likely to have members on most important committees in the House. A member from such a delegation is in a good position to minimize the amount of time he needs to spend in collecting information about bills emerging from the committee structure.

Delegations also communicate voting cues to members on the floor of the House. There are several reasons for members to accept the cues. One is simply that they respect the opinion of the individual in the delegation to whom they turn for the cue. A second is that if all of the members of a state party delegation vote the same way they protect themselves from criticism at home. Third, they are aware that they enhance their bargaining potential within the House if they maintain an alliance. If they can deliver a predictable number of votes, for example, on a given measure important to some other group or set of individuals in the House then they are in a position to ask for reciprocal action on something of particular importance to them, such as an amendment to a public works bill adding a project in their state.

State party delegations also serve as agents of socialization. In the discussions between more senior delegation members and more junior members the norms and traditions of life in the House are transmitted. The delegations can also make life a bit more pleasant socially.

State delegations work to channel the benefits distributed to indi-

[3]Barbara Deckard, "State Party Delegations in the U.S. House of Representatives: A Comparative Study of Group Cohesion," *Journal of Politics* 34 (1972): 199–222; Barbara Deckard, "State Party Delegations in the United States House of Representatives—An Analysis of Group Action," *Polity* 5 (1973): 311–34.

[4]See Arthur G. Stevens, Jr., "Informal Groups and Decision-Making in the U.S. House of Representatives," (Ph.D. dissertation, University of Michigan, 1970); and Alan Fiellin, "The Function of Informal Groups in Legislative Institutions," *Journal of Politics* 24 (1962): 72–91; and Fiellin, "The Group Life of a State Delegation in the House of Representatives," *Western Political Quarterly* 23 (1970): 305–20.

vidual members of the House and to states, regions, and districts. For the individual representative, one of the most important benefits is committee assignments. Delegations that have members serving on important committees strive to ensure that their seat on that committee is retained within the delegation whenever it becomes open. A number of seats on important committees are, in effect, reserved for members from specific states.[5]

Delegations work to gain support for projects important to their states and regions. They also work for programmatic amendments that have broader impact. They use important positions on committees and unity in floor voting as bargaining chips with other members, other state delegations, and the party leaders. Even relatively small delegations can increase their influence if they stick together and bargain as a unit.[6]

## OTHER GROUPS AND CAUCUSES

Most members of Congress are, by nature, "joiners." They often build initial electoral support at home through memberships in Kiwanis clubs, churches, lodges, and the like. Their instincts to form and join groups carry over into their life on Capitol Hill. Groups get formed both within parties and on a bipartisan basis. Some are focused on single issues. Others seek to move the centers of gravity of one of the four congressional parties to the "right" or the "left." Constituent interests receive additional representation, at least symbolically, through a variety of groups and caucuses.[7]

[5]Charles S. Bullock III, "Influence of State Party Delegations on House Committee Assignments," *Midwest Journal of Political Science* 15 (1971): 525–46; David E. England and Charles S. Bullock III, "Prescriptive Seats Revisited," *American Journal of Political Science* 30 (1986): 496–502.

[6]For good evidence that state delegations do, in fact, tend to vote together see David B. Truman, "The State Delegation and the Structure of Voting in the United States House of Representatives," *American Political Science Review* 50 (1956): 1023–45; Truman, *The Congressional Party* (New York: Wiley, 1959): 249–69; Stevens, "Informal Groups and Decision-Making"; and Aage R. Clausen, "State Party Influence on Congressional Party Decisions," *Midwest Journal of Political Science* 16 (1972): 77–101.

[7]For overviews by political scientists of the caucus phenomenon in recent years see Arthur G. Stevens, Jr., Daniel P. Mulhollan, and Paul S. Rundquist, "U.S. Congressional Structure and Representation: The Role of Informal Groups," *Legislative Studies Quarterly* 6 (1981): 415–37; Burdett A. Loomis, "Congressional Caucuses and the Politics of Representation," in Lawrence C. Dodd and Bruce I. Oppenheimer (eds.), *Congress Reconsidered,* 2nd ed. (Washington, D.C.: Congressional Quarterly, 1981): Chapter 9; and Susan Webb Hammond, Daniel P. Mulhollan, and Arthur G. Stevens, Jr., "Informal Congressional Caucuses and Agenda Setting," *Western Political Quarterly* 38 (1985): 583–605.

# HOW CAROLINA DEMOCRATS MAKE 6 VOTES ADD UP

BY JONATHAN FUERBRINGER

In the House of Representatives, the six Democrats from North Carolina make up one of the smaller delegations. But in the realm of impact, these quiet legislators carry a big stick that they have used successfully to defend the issue most important to them: tobacco.

Their work has done much to keep alive a troubled program of tobacco price supports and much to hold down the cigarette tax in years when the two could have been easy targets.

Further, the group's collegial politics is a good example of how a small delegation can gain influence in the House while larger delegations are often divided, and thus less influential, on issues important to their states.

## THEY OFTEN MOVE AS A BLOCK

The legislative success enjoyed by the six North Carolinians—Walter B. Jones, Charlie Rose, Charles Whitley, Stephen L. Neal, W. G. Hefner and Tim Valentine—is notable for its combination of party loyalty, personalilty, hard work and horse trading. The six tend to vote in a block even on some issues that might normally split them and go against the grain back home.

"If we all stick together and stay in a block," said Mr. Rose, "its easier to explain that this is part of our missionary work."

What they have got in return, with an assist from the five Republican members of the North Carolina House delegation and the state's two Senators, is support for tobacco—strong support. In 1986 Congress helped the industry, both the companies and the farmers, by approving a redesigning of the price support program. And while the cigarette tax has been raised to 16 cents a pack, Democratic leaders in the House say that a further increase this year, a proposal that might be taken up by the House in a few weeks, is unlikely to pass.

"The main commodity of a Congressman is cooperation," said Mr. Rose, explaining how he and his fellow Democrats approached their work. "We cooperate with the leadership and remind them from time to time of our needs."

## 'WE ULTIMATELY NEED THEM'

Mr. Whitley added: "We try and stick together and know what is important to the Democratic leadership, frankly with the idea that we ultimately need them on tobacco."

What does the leadership say?

"They are perceived to be team players and more responsible," said Representative Jim Wright, Democrat of Texas, the majority leader. "And because of that it follows that when they ask for support they have a more attentive ear. They have realized that it is the Democratic majority that has worked with them."

Representative Thomas S. Foley of Washington, the Democratic whip, adds, "There is no doubt that they get the attention of the leadership in the House on tobacco." . . .

The group voted with Speaker Thomas P. O'Neill Jr. and against President Reagan on aid to the rebels fighting the Government in Nicaragua. They supported loan guarantees for New York City and the Chrysler Corporation. Despite the revolt of most Southern Democrats in 1981, they voted with the Democratic leadership against the spending cuts Mr. Reagan pushed through the Congress.

And while the delegation's votes have not been unanimous in every case, they have usually been close enough to unanimity to provide considerable help for the leadership.

In fact, the North Carolinians can often unite on an issue important in some other state. They have helped New York City legislators by supporting rent control legislation and they have backed Californians who have pushed for money for a subway in Los Angeles.

The six are on several important committees and concentrated in Agriculture, other important factors in their success. . . .

While the six believe in cooperation, as they put it, colleagues say they are too subtle to talk openly of trading votes. "They never ask for a quid pro quo," said Representative Charles E. Schumer, Democrat of Brooklyn, who has received support from the North Carolinians. "They're too smart for that."

**Source:** Jonathan Fuerbringer, "How Carolina Democrats Make 6 Votes Add Up," *New York Times,* September 10, 1986. Copyright © 1986 by The New York Times Company. Reprinted by permission.

In recent years there has been a great proliferation of many different types of groups and "caucuses" in both houses, especially in the House. In part, this is a reflection of the general fragmentation of politics in the United States and especially the rise of the "single interest" groups. It is also a reflection of the continued movement of Congress in recent decades toward fragmentation. Increased support for issue-oriented caucuses and groups has been available through money contributions from businesses, trade associations, labor unions, and even federal agencies in recent years, space donated by the House and Senate (a practice limited by the House in late 1981), and additional money channeled from basic office and staff allowances given to all senators and representatives.

In one listing of "informal congressional groups" in Congress in 1984, 92 groups appeared.[8] Some were in a single house and single party (the Democratic Study Group and the House Republican Study Committee were the largest in the House), some were bipartisan in a single house (the Northeast-Midwest Congressional Coalition in the

[8]Roger H. Davidson and Walter J. Oleszek, *Congress and Its Members,* 2nd ed. (Washington, D.C.: Congressional Quarterly, 1985): 364–65.

# CALIFORNIANS' ENERGY, NUMBERS MAKE THEM A POWER IN HOUSE

BY TOM KENWORTHY

Late last year, California's Democratic House delegation drew up a list of legislative priorities for the 100th Congress. A key item was a dramatic increase in the federal commitment to battling AIDS, which has plagued California more than any other state except New York.

The campaign began in earnest in February, when at the urging of Rep. Barbara Boxer of San Francisco, the House Budget Committee devoted one of its four field hearings to AIDS. The following month, when committee Democrats met privately to write a budget resolution, Boxer and her two California colleagues on the panel made it clear they would oppose any budget that did not include a major boost in AIDS funding.

By mid-April, the full House had adopted a fiscal 1988 budget that would double the amount to be spent on AIDS research and education while cutting the growth of overall domestic spending by $9 billion. The $970 million allocated for AIDS was 82 percent higher than the amount sought by the Reagan administration and represented the largest increase in the $1 trillion federal budget.

The successful drive to increase AIDS funding clearly owed something to Congress' heightened awareness of a national health emergency. But it also illustrates the growing clout of the California delegation, which is increasingly viewed as the most influential in the House.

California's evolution into a House power is also an object lesson in how things get done in Washington. Bright, shrewd, hard-working and cohesive, California Democrats are gaining the seniority to climb the leadership ladder and possess the political agility to skip some rungs.

"As it has become more Democratic on the congressional level, California has become more and more effective," said Christopher Matthews, who was an aide to former House Speaker Thomas P. (Tip) O'Neill, Jr. "They don't stay in the pocket; they're always out there scrambling."

Through sheer size, California's House contingent would play a major role. At 45 members—more than 10 percent of the House—it is the largest state delegation and will grow again after 1990 census. Twenty-seven of them are Democrats.

But California's legislative prowess is not just a function of its bulk. Despite some handicaps—Democrats and Republicans rarely pull in harness and lawmakers from other states occasionally rebel against its influence—the California delegation has the potential to dominate the House as Texas did during the two decades after World War II.

The key to legislative dominance is longevity, and California's Democrats have achieved extraordinary job security at the time when retirements have thinned the ranks of senior House members.

Thanks to a clever redistricting map fashioned by their late chairman, Rep. Philip Burton, Democrats picked up six additional congressional seats following the 1980 census, and now outnumber Republicans 27 to 18. (The year before redistricting the Democrats only had a 22 to 21 edge over the Republicans.) But more importantly, the seats are safe. In 1984, the year of Reagan's ree-lection landslide, only one Democrat lost. Last year, only six Democrats received less than 65 percent of the vote, and the closest of their races was a 57-to-43 runaway.

As a result, a bevy of relatively young California Democrats, many first elected to the House in the 1970s after earning their spurs in local and state government, has moved into positions of authority and is poised to advance further.

In the 100th Congress, House Democrats from California hold 27 committee and subcommittee chair-manships, as well as the No. 3 spot in the Democratic leadership. Name almost any policy area in Congress and at least one Californian is posi-tioned to affect the outcome.

**Source:** Tom Kenworthy, "Californians' Energy, Numbers Make Them a Power in the House," *Washington Post,* June 12, 1987. © *The Washington Post.*

House was the largest with 196 members; it was also large in the Senate with 40 members); and some were bicameral. One of the most impor-tant of these was the Military Reform Caucus.[9] Some of these groups were very limited in scope. The Congressional Mushroom Caucus in the House (with sixty members) probably had little impact on the general welfare of the nation, but there are probably obscure policies on mushrooms that please its members mightily. The House had many more caucuses than the Senate. The following pages discuss a few of the most important groups, especially in the House.

## The House

THE DEMOCRATIC STUDY GROUP (DSG).[10] The DSG began in 1957 as a loose alliance of liberal Democrats. It immediately set up a whip organization, which functioned sporadically until 1959 when the DSG was formally established. The group has developed into a sturdy institution with an elected chairperson, a sizable full-time staff, a budget raised through the dues of members and others who subscribe to the DSG's legislative research services, and a whip organization.

[9]David C. Morrison, "Caucusing for Reform," *National Journal* (June 28, 1986): 1596–1602.
[10]Mark F. Ferber, "The Formation of the Democratic Study Group," in Nelson W. Polsby (ed.), *Congressional Behavior* (New York: Random House, 1971): 249–67; Kenneth Kofmehl, "The Institutionalization of a Voting Bloc," *Western Political Quarterly* 17 (1964): 256–72; and Arthur G. Stevens, Jr., Arthur H. Miller, and Thomas E. Mann, "Mobilization of Liberal Strength in the House, 1955–1970: The Democratic Study Group," *American Political Science Review* 68 (1974): 667–81.

Membership size has fluctuated. Forty members attended the organizational meeting in 1959. By 1975–76 there were about 225 dues-paying members. This number grew to about 250 by 1979–80, shrunk to about 200 in 1981–82, and was at 228 in 1985–86.

The DSG members form task forces and issue reports on various substantive legislative topics. The DSG staff produces a large volume of research documents: summaries of projected legislative activities; analyses of bills that include summaries of both pro and con arguments; analyses of topics broader than single bills; and roll-call analyses.

The DSG whip organization performs much as the regular party whip organizations perform. Its main task is to get a good DSG turnout on the floor when critical votes are being taken. DSG members tend to vote together on the floor. This is hardly surprising, since ideological and policy agreement is the basis for self-selected membership in the first place. Because of its size and skill in working in the House, the DSG has been an important force on a variety of issues.

In the 1964 congressional campaign, the DSG moved into a new area of endeavor when it gave financial aid to the campaigns of liberal Democratic candidates.

FROM "BOLL WEEVILS" TO CONSERVATIVE DEMOCRATIC FORUM. A group of conservative Democrats has met with some regularity since the end of World War II in order to generate both discussion and positions on a wide variety of legislation. This group, popularly called the "Boll Weevils" (a southern pest destructive to cotton) had a fluctuating and publicly unidentified membership until 1981. In the 1960s about 30 to 35 House Democrats usually attended meetings. At the end of 1972 the Democratic Research Organization—supposed to be a conservative counterweight to the DSG—was formed and was modeled on the DSG in terms of its organization and operations.

Until the 1980s, the Democratic leaders in the House were basically unwilling to deal with the "Boll Weevils," most of whom they viewed as uncompromisingly opposed to core Democratic policy positions. Only occasionally, would the leaders attempt to mute the "Weevils" through direct negotiations.

In late 1980, after the election results made it clear that the nominal Democratic majority in the House and their leaders would have to face a very conservative Republican president and a very conservative Republican Senate, a group of 30 or so of the "Weevils" formed a new group called the Conservative Democratic Forum. (Membership had increased to 47 by June 1981, and included three members not from a southern or border state, one of whom became a Republican later in the summer.) They asked for and got a meeting with Speaker O'Neill, and from that meeting stemmed increased representation for them on the Democratic Steering and Policy Committee and on some of the most important standing committees in the House. These concessions, however, did not prevent them from siding with the Republicans to hand O'Neill and the majority of Democrats decisive and stunning defeats on every major budget and tax contest that reached the House floor during 1981.

The defection of the Conservative Democratic Forum [CDF] again and again to the Republican position in 1981 and 1982, coupled with the unpopularity of Phil Gramm (a Texan, and a Democrat until 1983), the single most visible member of the CDF in that Congress, led to a dramatic reduction in influence in 1983 and 1984. Membership fell from 47 to 38; recruitment of new members was difficult; and alliances with the Republicans to sustain the Reagan position in the House were either not attempted or generally unsuccessful. At the same time the Democratic leaders made overtures to CDF members to give them an increased voice in party counsels. By 1985–86 the CDF was again more active (although with only 35 members) but as a body to present a more conservative view of issues *within* the Democratic party in the House, rather than in opposition to it and in alliance with the Republicans. The CDF began to have weekly meetings and opened them to other Democrats who were interested in getting some additional information through them. By 1987 the CDF no longer resembled the Boll Weevils of the 1960s and 1970s and the first two years of the Reagan presidency. It sought to sway Democratic party positions in a more conservative direction rather than simply seeking their defeat. It had become respectable rather than avowedly maverick.[11]

THE REPUBLICAN WEDNESDAY CLUB AND "GYPSY MOTHS." Since the beginning of the New Deal, the House Republican Party has been overwhelmingly conservative in orientation. It has also been in the minority since 1931 with the exception of four years (1947–48 and 1953–54). There have always been a few moderate and even liberal members of the party in the House but they have not had much weight in party decisions or councils. A small group (beginning with seven members) formed the Wednesday Club in 1963 to talk about issues

[11]Jacqueline Calmes, " 'Boll Weevils' Now Welcome in House Democratic Fold," *Congressional Quarterly Weekly Report* (April 26, 1986): 909–13; Alan Ehrenhalt, "Changing South Perils Conservative Coalition," *Congressional Quarterly Weekly Report* (August 1, 1987): 1699–1705.

from a liberal Republican perspective. This group continues to meet and issue papers. By 1986 it had 35 members but it possesses minimal influence.

In 1981 a shifting, informal, group of fifteen to twenty-five moderate to liberal Republicans from the upper midwest and northeast began meeting as a result of some Reagan budget cuts that worried them because of the disproportionate impact of the cuts on their constituents. The name "gypsy moth" was applied to the group and it stuck. (Gypsy moths are also destructive pests—they attack the foliage of shade trees.) The group felt that they got some key items restored during the summer 1981 budget reconciliation process, although they also felt the president betrayed them when he announced a second round of budget cuts that hit some of the programs they thought they had helped preserve in part (programs such as medicaid, student loans, and aid to Conrail, Amtrak, and mass transit.) Like the Wednesday Club, the Gypsy Moths had very limited impact on their party or on public policy. A minority of a minority party in the House is, by definition, in a feeble position.

THE CONGRESSIONAL BLACK CAUCUS.[12] The Congressional Black Caucus was formally organized in 1971. Its membership is limited to black members of Congress (they have all been in the House in recent years) and the Delegate to the House from the District of Columbia. A white House member applied for membership in 1975 but was turned down specifically on grounds of his race. The caucus staff and the members follow legislative concerns particularly important to blacks. Caucus unity on voting on issues is high, not just because the members are all black but because they are also all liberal Democrats. The caucus is unusual in that it is more important outside Congress than inside. It has sought, with considerable success, to be recognized as a leading national black organization that is legitimate in speaking for the concerns of black persons in a general sense.

Individual black members have achieved increasing personal importance in the House as they have become more senior. In 1985–86 black members chaired five standing committees and two select com-

[12]See Marguerite Ross Barnett, "The Congressional Black Caucus," in Harvey C. Mansfield, Sr. (ed.), *Congress against the President,* Volume 32, No. 1, of *Proceedings of the Academy of Political Science:* 34–50; Charles P. Henry, "Legitimizing Race in Congressional Politics," *American Politics Quarterly* 5 (1977): 149–76; Nadine Cohodas, "Black House Members Striving for Influence," *Congressional Quarterly Weekly Report* (April 13, 1985): 675–81; and D.D. Fears, "A Time of Testing for Black Caucus as Its Members Rise to Power in House," *National Journal* (April 27, 1985): 909–11.

mittees. Two of these committees—Budget as well as Education and Labor—are important. The existence of the caucus did not bestow importance on these members. Seniority and the abilities of the individuals to behave skillfully in the House setting combined to make them both visible and influential.

## The Senate

The Senate has never generated as many caucuses and groups as the House. The caucus fad also caught on in the Senate in the 1970s and 1980s, but Senate caucuses have had only marginal policy importance.

The two most important intra-party groups were both conservative. A group of right-wing Republican senators formed the Senate Steering Committee in 1974. This group has the formal trappings of an organization: staff, space, a budget. The small membership proceeds informally. A group of moderate to conservative Democrats—which never adopted a formal name—began to meet in 1981. They proceed quietly. From the beginning, this group did not seek to sabotage Democratic positions but rather to influence them from a conservative perspective.

## CONGRESSIONAL STAFFS[13]

In the 1970s the numbers of both personal and committee staff members expanded rapidly. And, while the rate of growth slowed in the 1980s, each member of both houses now has a sizable personal staff. Most members also have committee staff members who are personally responsible to them or at least to a relatively small subcommittee on

---

[13]For two recent broad treatments of congressional staff see Harrison W. Fox, Jr., and Susan Webb Hammond, *Congressional Staff: The Invisible Force in American Lawmaking* (New York: Free Press, 1977), and Michael J. Malbin, *Unelected Representatives: Congressional Staff and the Future of Representative Government* (New York: Basic Books, 1980). See also Malbin, "Delegation, Deliberation, and the New Role of Congressional Staff," in Thomas E. Mann and Norman J. Ornstein (eds.), *The New Congress* (Washington, D.C.: American Enterprise Institute, 1981): Chapter 5. On the place of staff in the functioning of Congress see Warren H. Butler, "Administering Congress: The Role of Staff," *Public Administration Review* 26 (1966): 3–13. For a more recent study of staff in the Senate alone, which concludes that staff is "ubiquitous and important in the policy process," see Norman J. Ornstein and David Rohde, "Resource Usage, Information and Policymaking in the Senate," in a compilation of papers prepared for the Commission on the Operation of the Senate, *Senators: Offices, Ethics, and Pressures* (Washington: U.S. Government Printing Office, 1977): 37–46.

which they sit. Individual members of both houses have become, in effect, managers of "enterprises." By the late 1970s "each elected member hires and presides over the work of between 18 and 125 or so individuals, depending on chamber, state, and committee or subcommittee responsibilities."[14]

Only since World War II has Congress shown consistent concern for developing professional staff—both for individual members and for committees. At the beginning of the post-war period personal and committee staff numbered about 2,000 people. There were about 18,000 people in comparable positions in 1985. When a variety of other staff positions in support and housekeeping agencies for Congress are added, more than 24,000 individuals can reasonably be counted as constituting total congressional staff.

These staff members are essential in managing the extremely heavy workload of Congress. Without them neither the individual members nor the committees could perform adequately. The presence of adequate staff does not guarantee good congressional performance, but without adequate staff Congress would lose much of its capacity to be consistently important in shaping public policy.

The presence of such large staff resources means, inevitably, that a large proportion of the legislative activity of Congress is undertaken by staff instead of elected members. The existence of members as "enterprises" underscores the fragmentation of Congress because each individual enterprise must negotiate with a set of other enterprises in order to achieve results. These negotiations are more complicated than those just between individual members simply because more people are involved.

It is worth noting that Congress has by far the largest professional staff of any national legislature in the world. Staff has grown in major western European legislatures since World War II but remains small compared to Congress. For example, the congressional staff of 18,000 working for individuals or committees compares to a staff of about 800 for the British House of Commons, a staff of close to 2,000 for the West German Bundestag, and a staff of about 1,800 for the two houses of the French Parliament.[15]

[14]Robert H. Salisbury and Kenneth A. Shepsle, "Congressional Staff Turnover and the Ties-That-Bind," *American Political Science Review* 75 (June 1981): 394. See also the article by the same authors, "U.S. Congressman as Enterprise," *Legislative Studies Quarterly* 6 (1981): 559–76.
[15]See Samuel C. Patterson, Gerhard Loewenberg, and Malcolm E. Jewell, "Editors' Introduction: Parliamentary Staffs in the United States and Europe," *Legislative Studies Quarterly* 6 (1981): 489–94. For details on the three European cases see the articles in that issue of *Legislative Studies Quarterly* by Michael T. Ryle ("The Legislative Staff of the British House of Commons"), Stanley Campbell and Jean Laporte ("The Staff of the Parliamentary Assemblies in France"), and Werner Blischke, ("Parliamentary Staffs in the German Bundestag").

## Personal Staff

Congress began to provide money for individual senators and representatives to hire personal staff members for their Washington offices in the late nineteenth century. Since that time there has been a steady increase in the funds allocated for this purpose. Table 7-1 summarizes the growth of personal staff in both houses from 1930 through 1986.

The amount of money senators receive for their staffs varies according to the size of the state the senator represents. In 1987 the range of the annual staff allowance to each senator was from about $716,000 to over $1.4 million, depending on the population of the state. The two California senators had the largest allocations. There are no limits on the number of people who can be hired with this money. In 1975 junior senators were instrumental in amending the rules of the Senate to provide over $100,000 additional for each senator to hire three more staff members explictly designated to help them with their committee work. These staff members are formally on committee staffs but, in effect, work as personal staff members.

In 1986, there were almost 3,800 personal staff members working for senators. Virtually all senators had year-round offices in their states (most had more than one such office) and employed over one-third of all their staff members in those offices. State offices have expanded greatly in size in recent years. In 1972, for example, only about one-eighth the Senate personal staff members worked in the states.

In 1987 each House member received a staff allowance of about $406,000 and could hire up to 22 staff members with that allowance. House rules also permit the use of staff money to hire persons who are then assigned to informal groups and caucuses. Senate rules do not permit such pooling of resources. In 1986 House members had hired about 7900 personal staff. Well over 40 percent of these staff members were assigned to offices "back home" in the districts. This proportion has grown substantially in the last few decades—from an estimated 14 percent in 1960. About half of the House members had more than one office in their districts. The impact in both houses of increasing staff in the districts has been to make evident the increased attention to errand-running for constituents on the part of members.[16]

Party leaders in both houses are also given money with which to hire extra staff members for their leadership offices.

[16]Steven H. Schiff and Steven S. Smith, "Generational Change and the Allocation of Staff in the U.S. Congress," *Legislative Studies Quarterly* 8 (1983): 457–67; and Glenn R. Parker, *Homeward Bound: Explaining Changes in Congressional Behavior* (Pittsburgh: University of Pittsburgh Press, 1986).

**Table 7–1.** Number of Personal Staff Members in Congress, Selected Years, 1930–1986

| YEAR | SENATE | HOUSE |
|---|---|---|
| 1930 | 280 | 870 |
| 1935 | 424 | 870 |
| 1947 | 590 | 1,440 |
| 1957 | 1,115 | 2,441 |
| 1967 | 1,749 | 4,055 |
| 1972 | 2,426 | 5,280 |
| 1976 | 3,251 | 6,939 |
| 1980 | 3,746 | 7,301 |
| 1983 | 4,059 | 7,606 |
| 1986 | 3,774 | 7,920 |

SOURCE: Norman J. Ornstein and others, *Vital Statistics on Congress, 1987–1988* (Washington, D.C.: Congressional Quarterly, 1987): 142.

**THE JOB OF PERSONAL STAFF MEMBERS.** Personal staff members are asked to undertake a great variety of jobs. In general, three kinds of skills are represented in the typical office: clerical-bureaucratic support skills, technical-professional legislative skills, and political skills. Clerical-bureaucratic work dominates what goes on in a member's office. The mail must be answered, constituent casework pursued, visitors received, files kept, and phones answered. The substance of proposed legislation and other legislative matters also need staff attention but since the same individuals are usually required to perform in all three areas, the demands of clerical-bureaucratic support work often leave little time for legislative problems. On the political front, members need some staff people who know the political situation in their state or district and who can advise and work for successful re-election campaigns. Preparing for re-election is a continuous process, particularly in the House. Members of both chambers also need staff members who know the political situation inside both Congress and segments of the bureaucracy.

In general, personal staff has limited time to devote to legislative business.[17] Shifting more staff to the home district has been explicit recognition of this fact and, perhaps, an attempt to free more time for Washington-based staff to pay attention to legislative matters.

**THE ORGANIZATION OF PERSONAL STAFFS.** Senators and representatives organize their offices in a variety of ways. Some have all of their

[17]John S. Saloma III, *Congress and the New Politics* (Boston: Little, Brown, 1969); and Harrison W. Fox, Jr., and Susan Webb Hammond, "The Growth of Congressional Staffs," in Mansfield (ed.), *Congress against President*, 119.

top assistants report directly to them; others have a more hierarchically structured office. House offices tend to have a single top aide who combines skills in bureaucratic, legislative, and political areas. The others on the office staff are likely to be more exclusively concerned with bureaucratic-clerical matters.

Most Senate offices are organized functionally; duties are more clearly divided and defined than in House offices (largely because senators have much larger staffs). Typically, there are one or more professionals in charge of public relations, casework, legislation, political affairs, and office administration. The professionals are, of course, aided by a number of clerical employees.

One central purpose for any pattern of organization, either in the House or the Senate, is to handle routine matters expeditiously so that the members and their top staff aides have time to deal with more important matters involving the substance of policy. Sometimes, however, the pressure of the routine consumes virtually all of the time of the staff member and perhaps of the member too.

THE LEGISLATIVE IMPACT OF PERSONAL STAFF. Staff members in the offices of individual senators and representatives can and do have substantial legislative impact, despite the limited time available for legislative work. This is particularly true of the top assistants to senators. For the most part, the average senator is not the genuine legislative expert that many House members are, given their limited and specialized responsibilities. Senators are far fewer in number than House members and have a larger number of committee and subcommittee assignments. As a result, they must spread themselves much thinner in terms of substantive expertise. Also, senators usually have more external demands on their time in terms of requests for speeches, television and radio appearances, newspaper interviews, and other such activities that do not as often involve the average representative. The typical senator therefore needs help, especially in the areas about which he knows very little and has little time to learn. For this help, he frequently turns to his staff members. Studies of the treatment of individual issues and bills in Congress provide a great deal of evidence of the legislative importance of senatorial aides.

Staff members can increase their legislative impact if they are aggressive in advising the individual for whom they work and in challenging the views of that individual at least some of the time. They can also enhance their influence if they have a sense of exactly the proper time to release critical information or a point of view to a member. One Republican staff member in the Senate put it well: "At the point when a senator gets to a committee meeting, particularly the executive sessions, and at the point when he goes to the floor to listen to the last few chords of debate and cast a vote, there an assistant who is either well read or at least well prepared and is able to pick out the salient points and say which does what to whom, when and how can make a big difference in the final decision of the senator."[18]

Members become particularly reliant on personal staff for legislative assistance on new problems they have not faced before and on matters on which they have not become expert themselves. Junior members are more likely to rely heavily on personal staff for legislative help than senior members both because they are less experienced and expert personally and because they have less access to committee staff. Minority party members are also more likely to rely heavily on personal staff than majority party members because they have less access to committee staff.

Staff members for members from states with small populations (in the case of the Senate) or for members from states and districts geographically distant from Washington are most likely to be important legislatively. Senate staffs for members from large states are beseiged by an unusual amount of mail, casework, and personal visits that makes it difficult to free any time for legislative work. Staffs in either house whose member's state or district is relatively close to Washington have an inordinate amount of time eaten up by visits from constituents.

## Committee Staff[19]

In the mid-nineteenth century congressional committees gradually began to hire clerks to help them with their work, but formal professional staffs were slow to develop. By the time of World War II only the two Appropriations Committees and the Joint Committee on

[18]Quoted in Randall B. Ripley, *Power in the Senate* (New York: St. Martin's, 1969): 197.
[19]On committee staff see Clapp, *The Congressman,* 256–264; James D. Cochrane, "Partisan Aspects of Congressional Committee Staffing," *Western Political Quarterly* 17 (1964): 338–48; George Goodwin, Jr., *The Little Legislatures* (Amherst: University of Massachusetts Press, 1970): 142–52; Kofmehl, *Professional Staffs of Congress;* John F. Manley, "Congressional Staff and Public Policy-Making: The Joint Committee on Internal Revenue Taxation," *Journal of Politics* 30 (1968): 1046–67; Samuel C. Patterson, "The Professional Staffs of Congressional Committees," *Administrative Science Quarterly* 15 (1970): 22–37; David E. Price, "Professionals and 'Entrepreneurs': Staff Orientations and Policy-Making on Three Senate Committees," *Journal of Politics* 33 (1971): 316–36; Ripley, *Power in the Senate:* 200–12; Edward I. Sidlow and Beth Henschen, "The Performance of House Committee Staff Functions: A Comparative Exploration," *Western Political Quarterly* 38 (1985): 485–94; and Beth M. Henschen and Edward I. Sidlow, "The Recruitment and Career Patterns of Congressional Committee Staffs: An Exploration," *Western Political Quarterly* 39 (1986): 701–8.

Internal Revenue Taxation had well-developed professional staffs. A provision of the Legislative Reorganization Act passed in 1946 made clear the intention of Congress that professional staffs be developed for all committees—it provided for four professional staff members and six clerical staff members for each committee and allowed the size of committee staffs to expand beyond that number. In 1970 Congress increased the formal allotment of professional members to six. In 1974 the House expanded the basic allotment for each standing committee (except Appropriations and Budget) to eighteen professional staff members and twelve clerical staff members. Senators provided up to 300 new committee staff members for themselves (three under the control of each senator) in 1975.

Table 7-2 summarizes the growth of committee staff in both houses from 1930 through 1986.

Staffing of committees reflects the partisan nature of Congress. On virtually all committees, majority and minority party members have separate staff. Formal authority for selecting committee staff members rests in part with the chairperson. Some subcommittee chairpersons and ranking minority members of both full committees and subcommittees also have the power to hire and fire committee staff members. In the Senate every senator has at least three committee staff members spread across his assignments personally responsible to him. In 1977 the Senate provided that the minority party had to be given at least one-third of the funds and office space for the staff on each committee.

Those with the power of appointment in both houses naturally want

**Table 7–2.** Number of Committee Staff Members in Congress, Selected Years, 1930–1986

| YEAR | SENATE COMMITTEES | HOUSE COMMITTEES |
|------|-------------------|------------------|
| 1930 | 163   | 112   |
| 1935 | 172   | 122   |
| 1947 | 232   | 167   |
| 1955 | 386   | 329   |
| 1965 | 509   | 571   |
| 1972 | 844   | 817   |
| 1976 | 1,201 | 1,680 |
| 1980 | 1,191 | 1,917 |
| 1983 | 1,075 | 1,970 |
| 1986 | 1,075 | 1,954 |

SOURCE: Norman J. Ornstein and others, *Vital Statistics on Congress, 1987–1988* (Washington, D.C.: Congressional Quarterly, 1987): 146.

their staff to be personally loyal and responsible to them. Partially as a result of this method of selection, the distinction between personal staff and committee staff—particularly in the Senate—is blurred. Consequently, committee staff members often perform what amount to non-committee chores for individual senators and, to a lesser extent, representatives. These chores may include working on constituency matters or even re-election campaigns.

Committee staff positions are generally well regarded on Capitol Hill and throughout the executive branch. Many committee staff members have had experience either in the executive branch or on the personal staff of one or more senators or representatives. There has been growing stability in the personnel on committee staffs. As is the case with the legislators they serve, seniority among committee staff members helps them develop influence in their jobs.

**THE JOB OF COMMITTEE STAFF MEMBERS.** Committee staff perform a variety of duties. They organize the hearings that the committee conducts. They personally conduct research on topics relevant to committee investigations. They draft bills and amendments, and prepare the language of committee reports. They help legislators prepare for floor debate either by distributing materials to all members or by briefing the members of the committee who are primarily responsible for conducting the debate. They participate in the preparation for meetings of conference committees and in the writing of conference reports. Committee staff members also serve as the committee's principal liaison agents with both the executive branch and interest groups.

A survey of committee professional staff members in 1974 (126 in the Senate and 130 in the House) revealed that the most important activities in which they engaged were acting on requests for information; legislative research, bill drafting, and reading and analyzing bills; and engaging in investigation and oversight.[20] The first activity was dominant in the reported use of time by House committee members. The three activities were more nearly equally important in the Senate. This again suggests an important House-Senate difference: House members become personally more genuinely expert in their committee work than senators.

Committee staff members also perform some tasks not related to the business of the committee. These tasks are performed for the members who are responsible for their appointments. Use of committee staff on

[20]Fox and Hammond, "The Growth of Congressional Staffs," 119.

work outside the committee is accepted by the staff members themselves because of the highly personal nature of their appointments, and by other committee members because of the partisan nature of staff appointments.

The job of committee staff members has been described in terms of four principal functions they perform: intelligence, integration, innovation, and influence.[21] In performing the intelligence function, committee staff members collect and filter a great deal of information before passing it on to committee members.

Committee staffers perform an integration function in several senses. Most committee staffs are harmonious internally. They generally work closely with staff members from the committee or committees in the other chamber that have the same jurisdiction. This helps bridge the bicameral gap. It also means that conference meetings usually go smoothly. Staff members also help promote integration between committees and the related pieces of the executive branch. They work closely with staff members in the bureaucracy and may have served there before coming to Congress.

Some committee staff members innovate by seeking out new problems for attention or by proposing new solutions to problems already identified. The more highly specialized a committee staff is the more likely are its members to be innovative in dealing with policy.[22]

Committee staff members are influential both because of the vital tasks they perform and because of the trust they build up in their relationships with members of the House and Senate.

In performing their tasks and functions, committee staff members interact with a number of individuals. Primarily they are responsible to their appointing authority—which, in the case of the majority party's staff on House committees, means that they are primarily loyal to the chairperson of the committee or of the subcommittee. The minority party's staff in the House, usually very small, is loyal and responsible principally to the ranking minority member. Senior members of House committees are, therefore, likely to have the most access to committee staffs. Junior members of committees tend to be distrustful of committee staffs and rely more heavily on their personal staffs for legislative help. In general, the typical member of the House does not rely heavily on committee staff members.

Since 1975, senators have had more access to committee staff be-

[21]See Patterson, "The Professional Staffs of Congressional Committees," 26–29.
[22]Eugene Eidenberg, "The Congressional Bureaucracy," (Ph.D. dissertation, Northwestern University, 1966).

cause, in effect, even the most junior senator has one committee staff member personally responsible to him on every committee. The general statements about dominance of committee staff by senior members applicable to the House would also have been applicable to the Senate until 1975. Since then the situation has changed: senior senators still have many more staff members at their disposal, but all senators have substantial help at the personal level. The most influential staff members are, however, still most likely to be responsible to the more senior senators.

Committee staff members also work closely with both executive branch officials and lobbyists. Lobbyists view staff as prime contacts. The growth in the size of staff has increased the workload for lobbyists.[23]

Committee staff members, like senators and representatives, operate within the constraints of relatively well-developed norms as they perform their jobs. Although the norms vary from committee to committee both for members and for staff members, six norms are widespread.[24] These norms include: limited advocacy (the staff person is expected to restrain himself in advocating his own policies, conclusions and proposals), loyalty to chairpersons, deference to members of Congress, anonymity, specialization (committee staff are expected to become experts in a particular subject), and limited partisanship.

Committee staffs are organized in a variety of ways, but three patterns predominate.[25] One pattern has a single staff director who is in charge of both the professional staff and the clerical staff and who reports to the chairperson. A second pattern has two staff directors (one for the professional staff and one for the clerical staff) who each report to the chairperson. In the third pattern, a staff director for the clerical staff reports to the chairperson; each of the professional staff members also report directly to the chairperson.

PARTISANSHIP AND COMMITTEE STAFF MEMBERS.    For policy-related committee staff positions chairpersons usually hire individuals from their own party who share their general policy orientation.

---

[23]See Lester W. Milbrath, *The Washington Lobbyists* (Chicago: Rand McNally, 1963); and Kay Lehman Schlozman and John T. Tierney, *Organized Interests and American Democracy* (New York: Harper and Row, 1986): Chapter 12.
[24]See Patterson, "The Professional Staffs of Congressional Committees," 29–31.
[25]Ibid., 32–33.

Ranking minority members appoint members who share their party and political orientation. Partisanship is muted on many committees. Committees that regularly deal with divisive partisan issues, (for example, House Education and Labor) however, are likely to have staffs with definite partisan orientations, because the appointing authorities on those committees are likely to be strong partisans.

Even though hiring is on a partisan basis, retention of professional staff members may be non-partisan. A large number of staff members survived the party turnovers in Congress in 1947 (from Democrat to Republican), 1949 (from Republican to Democrat), 1953 (from Democrat to Republican), and 1955 (from Republican to Democrat). There is no necessary conflict between partisanship and professionalism. Individuals whose hiring and tasks are imbued with partisanship may simultaneously be first-rate professionals. In general, congressional staffs have become increasingly professional.

In recent years, Republican members of the House, seemingly condemned to perpetual minority status, have become increasingly concerned about the small numbers of committee staff members assigned to the minority. Republican senators shared this concern until they became the majority party from 1981 to 1987.

The 1970 Legislative Reorganization Act provided for at least three minority employees on most committees. The Republican capture of the White House for eight years beginning in early 1969 resulted in more access to executive branch staff for Republicans and lessened somewhat their drive for more minority staff. However, their concern did not disappear and again became stronger in 1977 with the return of the White House to the Democrats. In late 1974 and early 1975 the House came close to earmarking some special money for minority staffing (one-third of specially authorized staff funds) but the new Democratic majority after 1974 decided not to agree to such earmarking. In 1977 the Senate adopted a broad resolution affecting committees. One provision required that the staff of each committee reflect the size of the majority and minority contingents of senators on the committee and that, if the minority members requested, it, at least one-third of the funds for hiring the staff of the committee would be placed under minority control (except those members designated by the chairperson and ranking minority member as working for the whole committee). This provision, coupled with the 1975 provision giving all senators three committee staffers spread among their assignments, significantly improved the access of the minority party to committee staff in the Senate.

THE LEGISLATIVE IMPACT OF COMMITTEE STAFF. Committee staff members, like personal staff members, have considerable impact on legislation. This impact varies from committee to committee. One study of staff behavior on three different Senate committees (Finance, Labor and Public Welfare, and Commerce) concludes that two kinds of behavior can be observed among equally competent staff members on different committees.[26] "Policy entrepreneurs" dominated the Labor and Public Welfare and Commerce Committee staffs. These individuals were not shy about consulting both their own policy preferences and political considerations as they carried out their jobs. Much of the time they did not pretend to be neutral. On the other hand, the staff of the Finance Committee was dominated by "professionals" who valued neutral expertise highly and downplayed both their own preferences and politics.

A study of the staff of the Joint Committee on Internal Revenue Taxation concluded that it is "powerful," but that its power is largely based on the adroitness with which the staff members take cues from the members of the committee itself.[27]

Committee staff members cannot initiate public policy without regard to the wishes of their nominal and actual superiors. On the other hand, they have considerable quasi-independent impact on some committees and on some specific bills. Staff members with more seniority are likely to have more independent substantive impact than staff members with less seniority. Likewise, those who are closest personally to the chairperson of a subcommittee or committee are more likely to be important: Staff members on subcommittees are in a particularly favorable position to develop influence because they work with only a few members on a limited agenda. Those working on technical matters that are hard for the members to understand are likely to be independently important.

## The Place of Congressional Staff in the National Government

Congressional staffs are a permanent feature of the governmental landscape in Washington. Given the demands on the time of the elected members of the House and Senate, they inevitably develop

---

[26]Price, "Professional and 'Entrepreneurs'," 335.
[27]Manley, "Congressional Staff and Public Policy-making."

some independent influence. Congress expanded professional staff as a major way of seeking to offset the superior numbers and informational base of the executive branch. Some people, including some members, have been worried about large congressional staffs on several grounds. First, large staffs have the potential of becoming uncontrollable bureaucracies. Second, as staffs get larger there is probably a greater likelihood that staffers will simply perform chores for individual members that have little or no relation to legislative business. Third, it is impossible for the size of congressional staffs ever to match the size of the executive bureaucracy with which they interact. Rather than simply expanding the size of congressional staffs, then, attention should be directed toward improving their training and skills and increasing the resources available to them.

Thoughtful members and staff members alike express concern about the development of independent influence on the part of staffers. Staff members are, of course, not elected but speak in the name of individuals who are. And their views are usually accepted as those of the elected officials by other participants in the political system, including representatives of the media.

Perhaps the most serious problem is that professional staff members in Congress may join with civil servants in the executive branch and representatives of interest groups to dominate policy in a variety of specialized areas. None of these individuals directly represents any segment of the electorate. All may be highly professional and highly competent, but the complexity of modern government means that they may in fact carry out large portions of government business without any meaningful intervention from elected representatives—either the president or the members of the Senate and House. Bad policy may not necessarily result, but a growing bureaucratization of Congress may reduce its representative character. Both the genius of Congress and its greatest weakness is that it contains large numbers of amateurs and semiprofessionals in the policy business who may ask questions and reach decisions that bureaucrats, operating on strict grounds of efficiency, would not reach. The bureaucratization of Congress could also result in an erosion of both its political character and its representative character.

## SUPPORT AGENCIES

In the last few decades, collective staffing for Congress has expanded considerably through the upgrading of personnel and redefinition of mission by two old agencies—the General Accounting Office and what is now called the Congressional Research Service of the Library of Congress—and through the creation of two new agencies—the Office of Technology Assessment in 1972 and the Congressional Budget Office in 1974. Collectively, these four agencies have come to be called congressional support agencies.[28]

### General Accounting Office[29]

The General Accounting Office (GAO) was created in 1921. Over the years its functions have expanded. In broad terms it simultaneously tried to remain independent of both Congress and the executive branch in order to conduct audits, investigations, and program analyses while also serving Congress directly. Trying to maintain both stances has often plunged GAO into the midst of controversy. It has been criticized both as not very useful to Congress and as too responsive to political pressures emanating from Congress. Reflecting its dual purpose, GAO has power to initiate studies as well as being expected to respond to congressional requests.

GAO performs five major functions: it conducts independent audits and reviews of executive branch agencies and programs (some of these ask evaluative questions about the effectiveness of programs); it sets government-wide accounting standards; it gives a variety of legal opinions; it settles claims against the government; and it conducts studies in direct response to congressional requests (and those requests may come from Congress as a whole through statutes or from individual committees or individual members of the House or Senate).

The total staff of GAO is about 5,000. Some individuals work directly with congressional committees on loan from GAO. The use

[28]On all four agencies see Ernest S. Griffith, "Four Agency Comparative Study," in a compilation of papers prepared for The Commission on the Operation of the Senate, *Congressional Support Agencies* (Washington: U.S. Government Printing Office, 1976): 95–148.
[29]See Joseph Pois, "The General Accounting Office as a Congressional Resource," in *Congressional Support Agencies,* 31–54; Frederick C. Mosher, *The GAO: The Quest for Accountability in American Government* (Boulder, Co.: Westview Press, 1979); and Mosher, *A Tale of Two Agencies: A Comparative Analysis of the General Accounting Office and the Office of Management and Budget* (Baton Rouge: Louisiana State University Press, 1984).

of GAO products in Congress varies a great deal from committee to committee. Some routinely rely on GAO findings in helping them make evaluative decisions that affect the future of programs. Others seem more inclined routinely to ignore GAO reports. Over the years, however, GAO has gained a larger clientele in Congress and has consequently had a larger impact on congressional decisions.

## Congressional Research Service[30]

The predecessor agency of the Congressional Research Service (CRS), the Legislative Reference Service (LRS), was created in 1914, primarily to provide traditional reference library services (short-run, limited factual statements and bibliographic searches) to members of Congress. There was some expansion of the size and responsibilities of the LRS before 1970, but until the Legislative Reorganization Act of 1970 it performed mainly in this mode. Then in 1970 Congress mandated a new emphasis on broader-scale policy research done by the newly named Congressional Research Service, especially for committees.

Beginning in 1970 the CRS began to grow—both in size and in terms of its workload. It had 332 staff members in 1970. By 1979 it had 847 positions and has stabilized at about that size. In 1986 it had 860 positions. It responds to about 300,000 congressional inquiries a year and also conducts a number of major research projects for committees. It does not have investigative capacity or power but must rely on published materials and on file materials, including its own extensive files. It must also be careful not to appear to be advocating positions. Since it is equally responsible to all members of Congress, neutrality and objectivity must be apparent to the members of Congress as they peruse the work of the CRS.

The CRS has the staff capacity to do research in almost any substantive area. Its central problem is the tension between the short-run demands of members of Congress who want immediate help with a speech or with answering the request of a constituent and the more time-consuming demands of genuine policy-relevant research. In many ways the incentives are loaded in favor of serving the short-run interests first because they do have short deadlines and also because the members' own interests are oriented more toward short-range help than toward long-range analysis.

[30]See James D. Carroll, "Policy Analysis for Congress: A Review of the Congressional Research Service," in *Congressional Support Agencies,* 4–30.

## Congressional Budget Office[31]

The Congressional Budget Office (CBO) was created in 1974 as an integral part of the new congressional budget process. It was to have a highly qualified staff working in the areas of economic forecasting, fiscal policy analysis, and cost projections. In effect, its domain was the economic aspects of all federal policies and programs—a vast domain indeed. Its staff was to work closely with the two budget committees created by the same act (one in each house) and was also to be particularly responsive to the revenue (Ways and Means and Finance) and appropriations committees. Other committees and members could also request information and special studies, although their requests for special studies would necessarily take a lower priority than those coming from the primary constituents.

The director of CBO is appointed for four years by the Speaker and President pro tempore of the Senate, although in fact the recommending power of the two budget committees is paramount. The director can be removed by a resolution of either house at any time. After considerable debate and political maneuvering Alice Rivlin, an experienced economist with admirable professional credentials, was named the first director. In 1983 the CBO acquired its second director, Rudolph Penner, an economist with extensive academic and government experience. In early 1988, House and Senate budget leaders had trouble agreeing on a successor to Penner.

CBO was allowed to expand to 203 in its second year after filling its 193 person staff quickly. Its size has fluctuated between 201 and 222 since then. It began issuing a number of different kinds of reports soon after its establishment. Many of these reports get considerable attention. In general, there is agreement that the staff of CBO is highly competent. Given its policy domain and given also the aggressive stance taken by Rivlin, it is not surprising that CBO is visible and sometimes controversial. During the Ford presidency some congressional Republicans felt that CBO's criticisms of the president's proposals were partisan. Early in the Carter presidency the president's energy program was the subject of a highly critical CBO report that said that his projected savings were far overstated. Speaker O'Neill was known to be upset by this report. The CBO and President Reagan

[31]See William M. Capron, "The Congressional Budget Office," in *Congressional Support Agencies,* 75–94; Joel Havemann, *Congress and the Budget* (Bloomington, Indiana: Indiana University Press, 1978): Chapter 6; and Douglas H. Shumavon, "Policy Impact of the 1974 Congressional Budget Act," *Public Administration Review* 41 (1981): 339–48.

and his staff had numerous visible disagreements over a series of economic assumptions and projections. The CBO was particularly unpopular with the Reagan administration because it quickly and accurately predicted dramatically higher budget deficits as part of the results of the president's economic program, despite much more rosy administration forecasts. The tension continued between CBO numbers and administration numbers on many economic questions. CBO tries to be objective and it lets the political fallout from its analyses descend without regard for the origin of proposals analyzed. By nature it is likely to remain a visible and controversial support agency, despite its relatively small size.

## Office of Technology Assessment[32]

The Office of Technology Assessment was created by a 1972 statute and began operations in early 1974. Its primary function according to the statute is "to provide early indications of the probable beneficial and adverse impacts of the applications of technology and to develop other coordinate information which may assist the Congress."

Broad policy decisions for OTA are made by the Technology Assessment Board, which is made up of six senators, six representatives, and the director of the agency. The director is appointed by the board for a six-year term and the congressional members are equally split between the parties. The chairmanship of the board rotates between the House and Senate contingents. The statute also specifies a Technical Assistance Advisory Council, which thus far has not had much importance.

Issues come to OTA through requests from congressional committees or from the board or from the director after consulting with the board. OTA is set up to be primarily and directly responsible to congressional committees and especially to those members of the board who choose to be active.

The professional staff of OTA peaked at 164 in 1978. In 1986 it was at 143. The policy board had established seven broad areas for organizing its work: energy, food, health, materials, oceans, transportation, and technology and world trade. In general, despite completion of

[32]See E.B. Skolnikoff, "The Office of Technology Assessment," in *Congressional Support Agencies,* 55–73.

some reports, many members of Congress were not aware of OTA and of its actual or potential utility.

## INFORMATION AND POLITICS

All the topics discussed in this chapter revolve around the needs of members of the House and Senate to acquire information as they make up their minds on an intimidating array of substantive matters. In Congress information is never neutral. Whoever controls the provision of information helps shape outputs. This is not to say that members do not seek "facts" as they make up their minds, but "facts" are always colored by a whole range of other factors, such as guesses about constituency attitudes, political ideologies, and personal ambitions.

Over the years, individual members and committees of Congress have constructed the range of institutions and practices detailed in this chapter. Members have sought the company and views of other members from their state or region. Like-minded groups of members have created formal organizations such as the Democratic Study Group that mingle information, research, and ideology. Both personal and committee staff have proliferated at a rapid pace in recent years. And additional support agencies have also grown and prospered. All of these parts of the congressional stew help Congress make policy decisions.

In some ways the demand for information is insatiable. Given the agenda of the federal government—which is, by definition, also the agenda of Congress—the members can never know everything that is relevant to their work. Congress has provided itself with good staff resources. How can those resources be best organized to focus on those aspects of policies and programs that would benefit most from their attention? Policy decisions cannot be made on apolitical grounds. Given the representative nature of Congress, attempts to make decision-making "technocratic" are bound to fail. Attempts to remove politics from congressional decision making are counter to the spirit of the institution; fortunately, they have no hope of success. This is not to say that pointed, relevant information and analysis are useless. Many members genuinely seek and use expert analysis. But, ultimately, the decision-making calculus of any member includes many factors other than such analysis, no matter how expert.

Some perhaps hope that more and better information and analysis provided to Congress will help overcome its natural tendency to policy fragmentation. Perhaps some marginal integration can be achieved if the sources providing information and analysis are themselves more integrated and coordinated. However, both by necessity and by choice, many of these sources will remain tied to fragmented patrons—state or regional groups, ideological and interest-based organizations and caucuses, committees and subcommittees, and individual representatives and senators. These ties help intensify both organizational and policy fragmentation rather than alleviating it.

# III

# The External Environment for Congressional Policy-Making

# 8

## Congress, Interest Groups, and Constituents

This chapter examines the interaction of members of Congress with interest groups and with constituents, two of the most salient features of the external environment in which Congress is placed. Both of these sets of actors are important in influencing Congress in the shaping of public policy. Interest groups articulate their policy concerns with clarity and persistence. Constituents sometimes state their policy concerns, although generally with less clarity and persistence than groups. Members, however, seek to anticipate constituent reactions and their views even when they are not clearly stated.

Interest groups and constituents have long been important and have usually had a fragmenting impact on policy. In recent years members of Congress have paid even more attention to both. Interest groups have come increasingly under the control of institutions rather than individual members.[1] This has made them more persistent and, critically, has given them more money. The change in federal election law

[1] Robert H. Salisbury, "Interest Representation: The Dominance of Institutions," *American Political Science Review* 78 (1984): 64–76.

in the 1970s allowed these groups to spend a lot of that money on election campaigns (see Chapter 3) through Political Action Committees. They have increased their clout even more in this way.

At the same time, members of Congress have paid increased attention to serving constituents through specific "casework."[2] If a member becomes increasingly entrenched in a constituency in part through such casework it may leave him or her a bit more free to engage in "policy entrepreneurship." Increased attention to constituency needs, however, is not necessarily accompanied by increased attention to the policy views of constituents. In fact, there may be an inverse relationship.

Interest groups have a number of channels for communicating both directly and indirectly with members. They do not necessarily dominate the resolution of issues in Congress, but they help set the congressional agenda. Constituencies and constituents also claim considerable congressional attention. Sometimes they enhance their access and influence by working with an interest group. Other times they simply go directly to the member. Much of the time they do not have to take an active stance because members anticipate their views and make assumptions about them.

Constituents who want to communicate with members of Congress through an organization, logically could do so either through an interest group or through a political party. However, local political parties do not contact members of Congress on policy matters.[3] The absence of that organizational channel enhances the role of interest groups a bit more.

## MEMBERS AND INTEREST GROUPS

Interest groups enter the policy-making process through their lobbying activities. They represent their views directly through a variety of contacts with members of Congress and congressional staff members. They also represent those views more indirectly by stimulating a variety of constituency activity. Interest groups are very important in

[2]Glenn R. Parker, *Homeward Bound: Explaining Changes in Congressional Behavior* (Pittsburgh: University of Pittsburgh Press, 1986). See also Jon R. Bond, "Dimensions of District Attention over Time," *American Journal of Political Science* 29 (1985): 330–47; Glenn R. Parker, "Stylistic Change in the U.S. Senate, 1959–1980," *Journal of Politics* 47 (1985): 1190–1202; and Glenn R. Parker and Suzanne L. Parker, "Correlates and Effects of Attention to District by U.S. House Members," *Legislative Studies Quarterly* 10 (1985): 223–42.

[3]David M. Olson, "U.S. Congressmen and Their Diverse Congressional District Parties," *Legislative Studies Quarterly* 3 (1978): 239–64.

helping finance campaigns for the House and Senate through their Political Action Committees (the importance of which was discussed in Chapter 3).[4]

## The Setting for Interaction

Whom do interest groups represent? In a book published in 1960, E.E. Schattschneider estimated that 90 percent of the adult population cannot get into the "pressure system" (his label for a number of organized groups pursuing special interests in the political arena simultaneously).[5] He observed that the pressure system was skewed in favor of the more well-off in society—especially business interests— and against groups representing the less affluent and broader public interests. His observations were affirmed as accurate for the 25 years following 1960 by subsequent research: "Taken as a whole, the pressure community is heavily weighted in favor of business organizations: 70 percent of all organizations having a Washington presence . . . The over-representation of business interests takes place at the expense of two other kinds of organizations: groups representing broad public interests and groups representing the less advantaged. . . . [T]he socioeconomic tilt of the Washington pressure system is unambiguous. The professionals and managers who might be considered to be 'haves' constitute at most 16 percent of American adults; they are represented by 88 percent of the economic organizations."[6]

There are two parties involved in every legislative lobbying activity—the lobbyist and the legislator—and they interact, usually to their mutual benefit. The relationship that is often portrayed of vulture-like lobbyists preying on helpless legislators is distorted. Lobbyists, to be sure, seek favors and assistance for their particular interests. But they are required to register and publicly identify themselves as lobbyists. Also, legislators seek out lobbyists for the information on substance, on bureaucratic intent, and (less often) on constituency preferences that they can provide. The exchange of mere information for influen-

[4]For a thorough assessment of interest-group behavior see Kay Lehman Schlozman and John T. Tierney, *Organized Interests and American Democracy* (New York: Harper and Row, 1986). Chapter 12 focuses on "Lobbying Congress."

[5]E. E. Schattschneider, *The Semisovereign People* (New York: Holt, Rinehart and Winston, 1960).

[6]Schlozman and Tierney, *Organized Interests,* 68, 70. See also Grant McConnell, *Private Power and American Democracy* (New York: Knopf, 1966); and Kay Lehman Schlozman, "What Accent the Heavenly Chorus? Political Equality and the American Pressure System," *Journal of Politics* 46 (1984): 1006–32.

tial favors may at first seem an uneven trade, for legislators are in a postion to do more than the lobbyist in terms of magnitude of favors granted. But the congressional system values the acquisition of a great deal of information and this necessity balances out the exchange of favors for knowledge. At any rate, interest groups continue to flourish and their major offering continues to be information, although campaign contributons and well-financed electoral "hit list" activities have become more extensive in recent years. It also needs to be noted that legislators often take the lead in promoting a legislative action and are joined later by lobbyists. Legislative ideas originate with legislators, not just lobbyists.

Members generally view themselves as being free to act on the basis of their own judgment despite lobbying from interest groups. They feel pressure, but they assert they can withstand it. Lobbies rarely dominate a congressional vote in the sense of simply dictating an outcome. Rather, they work with members to achieve as much as they can. Few members question the legitimacy of interest groups and lobbying. In fact, a large proportion work actively to facilitate the interests of specific groups.[7]

## Types of Interest Groups and Lobbyists

There are many different types of interest groups—ranging from the large and well-financed to the miniscule and impoverished. There are also many types of lobbyists—ranging from full-time professionals to part-time amateurs.

Under the rubric "interest group" the large national associations (composed of both individual and organizational members) come to mind first—groups such as the National Association of Manufacturers, the U.S. Chamber of Commerce, and the American Federation of Labor-Congress of Industrial Organizations. There are also a number of industries that have their own national groups that engage in lobbying activities. Examples include the American Petroleum Institute, the Manufacturing Chemists Association, and the National Coal Association. Some individual corporations, at least on some issues, constitute interest groups by themselves. For example, when aerospace companies compete for major contracts they actively lobby on their own behalf.

Interest groups do not represent only industry, commerce, and

[7]Roger H. Davidson, in *The Role of the Congressman* (New York: Pegasus, 1969).

labor. There are groups that represent smaller units of government: the National Association of Counties, the National League of Cities, and the U.S. Conference of Mayors, for example. A number of states, counties, and cities maintain their own representatives in Washington too. Some national groups represent professions and act as interest groups when they become involved in the legislative process. The American Medical Association and American Bar Association fall in this category. Some professional or semi-professional groups specifically represent employees of other governmental units. For example, there is a National Association of State Aviation Officials, a National Association of Public Health Officials, and an Airport Operators Council (most airports are owned by a municipality).

There have always been interest groups that have asserted that they were working in the "public interest." Among older groups the League of Women Voters serves as a good example. In the 1970s two new organizations became highly visible and quite effective in representing what they claimed was the "public interest." One of these groups was Public Citizen and the other was Common Cause. Both lost membership and budget in the late 1970s and 1980s. They remained active lobbies but were no longer as important in the 1980s.

The group of active lobbies is not static. As issues and social and economic conditions change, the configuration of active and influential groups also changes. A good example is provided by the emergence of effective lobbies for the elderly in recent years, a phenomenon primarily the result of the general aging of the U.S. population. On issues such as medicare, social security, and retirement age, organizations representing the elderly have proved to be very important. The largest group working in this area is the American Association of Retired Persons, whose membership grew from three million in 1971 to more than eleven million in 1977 and to thirteen million by 1982.

In the late 1970s a number of well-funded so-called "single issue" groups emerged and began to play an important role in some congressional campaigns and in some congressional decision making. They relied heavily on direct mass mailing to constituencies if they wished to target a member for defeat. They expressed interest—forcefully and publicly—only when their single issue was on the congressional agenda. The most visible of these groups were those with views on legalized abortion. The groups opposing abortion were particularly visible. A number of "traditional" groups have also had one main interest to pursue, but the new "single interest" movement was different in that the amount of money at their disposal had increased dramatically, the direct-mail technique both for raising money and for conveying viewpoints had been refined, and many of the issues on which they focused—like abortion—were particularly emotional and tended to produce two unalterably opposed points of view rather than the more "normal" compromises. Congress normally shies away from such issues because there is perceived to be little room for compromise. Even a very conservative Congress in 1981 avoided the so-called "social agenda" that included abortion, busing, and school prayer, because a number of fiscal conservatives saw little payoff in addressing these issues that could only produce vitriol and the potential for loss of the votes from one side or the other at the polls.

In 1982 the New Right lobbies got two of their favorite items—abortion and school prayer—on the congressional agenda. But they lost on both issues in September 1982 in the Senate. In retrospect, they had made little headway in converting traditional, fiscal conservatives and moderates in Congress to their causes. When these individuals joined the traditional liberals and when the New Right lobbies were opposed by increasingly active lobbies on the other side of these issues, the New Right issues lost. They declined in visibility in Congress after 1982.

Interest groups also come and go in the foreign policy area depending on what issues are on the national agenda. In the 1980s, for example, a number of interest groups both supporting and opposing Reagan administration policy in Nicaragua, and Central American generally, formed and were active and visible. Other foreign-policy matters stay on the agenda for a long period of time and help generate groups that also last longer. One of the most potent lobbies of this description is the American Israel Public Affairs Committee (AIPAC), which lobbies on behalf of what it considers pro-Israel positions. In recent years a lobby attempting to push pro-Arab positions has developed, in part to counteract the influence of AIPAC.[8]

"Membership" in an interest group is an elusive concept. All groups claim to represent the maximum number of members they can. In some groups the members are quite inactive; in others they are quite active. Different groups also have different kinds of members. When the most important interest groups in the housing field are examined, for example, their members include such diverse entities as commercial banks, individual urban planners, firms in mortgage banking, both firms and individuals engaged in home building, individuals and firms

[8]Christopher Madison, "Arab-American Lobby Fights Rearguard Battle to Influence U.S. Mideast Policy," *National Journal* (August 31, 1985): 1934–39.

involved in redevelopment, mutual savings banks, individual realtors organized in local real estate boards, municipalities and state leagues of municipalities, mayors of large cities, and savings and loans companies.

Interest groups often ally with one another for specific legislative battles. These alliances may be more or less permanent in some instances. For example, even before they merged their staffs in late 1969 the National League of Cities and the Conference of Mayors cooperated on virtually all issues. Other alliances may be formed over a single issue and may, in fact, unite groups that have fought each other in the past and may do so in the future. For example, during the controversy over the supersonic transport airplane in the early 1970s environmentalist groups such as the Sierra Club, Friends of the Earth, and the League of Conservation Voters opposed the efforts of the aerospace companies such as Boeing to gain congressional approval of the project. However, in 1973 the environmentalists were joined by a number of aerospace companies such as Boeing, Rohr Industries, and LTV in working for passage of a highway bill that allowed highway trust fund money to be used for mass transit. The environmentalists favored the bill as a way to reduce the polluting effects of the automobile and the environmental and aesthetic damage resulting from what they considered excessive roadbuilding. The companies favored the bill because the aerospace industry was in considerable economic trouble and a number of firms had turned to the manufacture of mass transit equipment such as subway cars in an effort to survive.

In 1977, in the struggle over a bill to guarantee a fixed percentage of oil-import shipping to American-built and operated tankers two unusual coalitions emerged. Pushing for the bill was an alliance of unions (including both maritime and non-maritime unions and the AFL-CIO itself) and maritime business interests. The coalition opposed to the bill included oil companies, a Nader organization (Congress Watch), The League of Women Voters, the American Farm Bureau Federation, and the U.S. Chamber of Commerce. On both sides the groups often opposed each other on other issues but on this one issue they found common ground and could unite.

In 1986, during the attempt to reauthorize and strengthen the statute controlling the use of pesticides, two very large alliances of groups took positions on various proposals and also entered into direct negotiations with each other. One of these alliances was called the National Agricultural Chemicals Association. It had 92 chemical companies as constituent units. The other alliance was named the Campaign for Pesticide Reform. It included 41 different environmental, public health, labor, and consumer groups.

Even single industries don't stay monolithic on all issues. Any large industry has a number of different interests and different kinds of companies will pursue those different interests—sometimes directly conflicting with the interests of other companies. A good example is provided by the oil industry, where the interests of the large, international oil companies (the "majors") and the smaller companies (the "independents") often clash. The majors have more resources and personnel with which to lobby but the independents often prevail. One target of lobbying put it colorfully: "When the call goes out to Texas the sky gets dark with Lear jets if they don't like what's going on here." A lobbyist added that independents get more attention than the slick lobbyists for the majors because "a 50-year-old millionaire in his 10-gallon hat and his boots is a far more interesting, captivating, and effective human being."

The American Petroleum Institute seeks to keep the oil interests working together but is not always successful. As one lobbyist said, "Getting a consensus is not easy." The job of the oil lobbyists is also complicated by the fragmentation of Congress. One experienced lobbyist put it well: "It used to be that you could take a bottle of bourbon into a back room for a drink with a committee chairman and cut a deal with him. No more. You could still cut the deal, but he can't make it stick with his committee, or sometimes even his staff."[9]

The largest interest groups maintain substantial Washington offices with a number of full-time lobbyists. Some even have their own buildings, usually located close to government offices. Small groups maintain a minimal Washington office—a staff of one professional lobbyist, one secretary, and a mimeograph machine is typical of a number of operations. Some groups and companies prefer not to maintain an office of their own but, instead, hire a "Washington lawyer" to represent their interests. These individuals specialize in lobbying and do very little legal work in the narrow sense. Some law firms in Washington are wholly devoted to this kind of work; others have some individuals specializing in it while others pursue more usual legal work. Some "Washington lawyers" are former government figures themselves (ex-senators and ex-secretaries of departments, for example). Others who serve as full-time lobbyists for an association, corpora-

---

[9]All quotations in the previous two paragraphs come from Richard Halloran, "Capital's Diverse Oil Lobbyists: Much Criticized, Often Effective," *New York Times,* August 9, 1979.

tion, or union are retired military officers, ex-employees of the bureaucracy, and former congressional staff members. Perhaps the most prized catch for an interest group is an ex-senator or ex-representative. These individuals are particularly valuable because of their personal and professional contacts on Capitol Hill. They also have a number of potentially useful contacts in the executive branch.

## Patterns and Techniques of Lobbying Activity

There are several general features that characterize almost all lobbying activity. First, it should be stressed that the lobbyists' major task is mobilization of those who already believe rather than conversion of the infidels.[10] Lobbyists do not, by and large, concentrate on changing members' minds. Instead, they seek out persons whom they have identified as supporters and work to reinforce their views, providing them ammunition to use in pursuing the cause in which they all believe.

Second, Washington lobbyists have a broader job than simply soliciting tangible actions—legislation, appointments, investigations—from members of the House and Senate. The lobbyists also seek to use members of Congress to influence the bureaucracy, to get information, and to achieve favorable publicity for an organization. The typical request from the lobbyist to the legislator seeks help for personal, business, or professional problems; Lewis Dexter calls the handling of such requests by legislators "casework." Most of these casework requests are not something the legislator can directly solve; usually the best he can do is to intercede with a bureau in the executive branch.[11] Such intercession can take many forms—ranging from one perfunctory telephone call by a congressional staff member that results in nothing to repeated personal requests from a member that are likely to result in the desired bureaucratic response.

Lobbying itself—that is, asking for explicit congressional action rather than information or indirect intervention in the bureaucracy— occurs principally when there is some likelihood that Congress can

---

[10]See Raymond A. Bauer, Ithiel de Sola Pool, and Lewis A. Dexter, *American Business and Public Policy* (New York: Atherton, 1963); Randall B. Ripley, "Congress Champions Aid to Airports, 1958–59," and "Congress and Clean Air: The Issue of Enforcement, 1963" in Frederic N. Cleaveland and associates, *Congress and Urban Problems* (Washington, D.C.: Brookings, 1969); and Schlozman and Tierney, *Organized Interests.*

[11]Lewis A. Dexter, *How Organizations Are Represented in Washington* (Indianapolis: Bobbs-Merrill, 1969).

and will act, when the interested lobbies have enough resources (mostly personpower) to spend on the enterprise, and when the bad effects of lobbying (indignant opponents, for example) are not likely to outweigh the good effects. Unless an interest group takes these factors into account it is probably wasting its resources and perhaps harming its own cause.

The specific techniques that lobbyists employ as they pursue favors and information in Congress are numerous.[12] They make personal contacts with members of the House and Senate and staff members who work for individual representatives and senators and committees. On relatively noncontroversial issues they focus on contacts with staff members and on influencing substantive outcomes in committees. On more controversial issues they are more eager to contact members personally and shift their attention to influencing outcomes on the floors of the House and Senate.[13]

Communications with members and staff members can be made in person or by phone. Personal efforts may well involve a social aspect— such as the lobbyist taking the staff member out for lunch or a drink. Lobbyists can also work indirectly through other individuals thought to be important to or influential with specific members—key constituents (for example, an important publisher or campaign contributor), representatives of allied interest groups, key bureaucrats, or, most important, other members of the House and Senate.

Lobbyists provide useful information to members and can often package this information in directly usable ways—as, for example, by preparing a speech for the member to deliver that espouses the interest group's viewpoint, thereby saving the time of the member and his staff. Lobbyists also testify before congressional committees that are holding hearings on bills. They prepare their testimony and distribute it widely in written form both before and after delivering it. They also respond to questioning, often in colloquies that are prearranged with sympathetic members of the committee. Their prepared testimony and the oral interchanges are also printed in the record of the hearings issued by the committee.

---

[12]For discussions of techniques see Charles L. Clapp, *The Congressman* (Washington: Brookings, 1963): Chapter 4; Harmon Ziegler, *Interest Groups in American Society* (Englewood Cliffs, N.J.: Prentice-Hall, 1964); Dexter, *How Organizations Are Represented in Washington;* David B. Truman, *The Governmental Process* (New York: Knopf, 1951); Lester W. Milbrath, *The Washington Lobbyists* (Chicago: Rand McNally, 1963); Norman J. Ornstein and Shirley Elder, *Interest Groups, Lobbying and Policymaking* (Washington, D.C.: Congressional Quarterly, 1978); and Schlozman and Tierney, *Organized Interests,* Chapter 12.

[13]John M. Bacheller, "Lobbyists and the Legislative Process: The Impact of Environmental Constraints," *American Political Science Review* 71 (1977): 252–63.

# TRENCH WARFARE: LOBBYING ON SUPERFUND, 1984 AND 1985
BY RONALD BROWNSTEIN

On Oct. 9, 1984, two months after the House approved a five-year reauthorization of the federal superfund used to clean up hazardous waste dumps, Rep. Dennis E. Eckart, a young liberal Democrat from Ohio, dropped into the *Congressional Record* a statement condemning the industry lobbyists who had killed the bill in the Senate. . . .

A little over nine months later, Eckart stood up at the conclusion of a House Energy and Commerce Committee mark-up session and delivered an emotional speech denouncing unnamed environmental lobbyists for their "insatiable appetite" and "character besmirchment." The objects of his ire, Leslie Dach of the National Audubon Society and A. Blakeman Early of the Sierra Club, had just finished distributing a press release denouncing the superfund bill that Eckart had co-sponsored and the committee was about to approve, by 31-10.

A year earlier, the same committee, by 38-3, had approved a superfund bill enthusiastically welcomed by the environmentalists and opposed by industry. Now, in July 1985, it had approved a bill that industry accepted and environmentalists called "a summer break for polluters."

How the committee changed direction so sharply is a complex story of ambition, national politics, internal congressional maneuvering and, at every turn, heavy and persistent lobbying. In the long battle over superfund, lobbyists have been visible at every step, advising harried congressional staffers on numbing

technical issues, routinely reviewing proposed legislation, drafting and forwarding proposals of their own.

With billions of dollars and broad questions of public health and environmental protection at stake, superfund has attracted (as of 1984) at least 122 lobbyists representing trade associations for the oil, chemical, insurance and other industries and dozens of individual companies, and at least eight representing environmental and public interest groups.

Day after day in the offices of Energy and Commerce Committee members, these lobbyists have waged quiet trench warfare over all of the obscure parts of the sprawling superfund bill. But even with all this effort, both sides in turn were swept along by basic political forces on the major question: how tough a superfund bill to pass. In 1984, industry lobbyists were blown away in the House; in 1985, the environmentalists so far have failed on many of their major goals.

This year, the chemical and oil lobbyists generally made the same arguments they did last year. What changed was that committee members who wanted a bill backed by environmentalists, in part for political reasons, in 1984 were more inclined to accept those industry arguments in 1985. "There were [political] forces that went well beyond the superfund last year that determined the issue," said William M. Stover, vice president for government relations at the Chemical Manufacturers Association (CMA). "Those forces aren't there this year, and that is why the debate has moved differently."

Once that general direction each year was set, the lobbyists played a clear and crucial role, sanding down the fine points that can mean millions of dollars. . . .

## PROLOGUE: 1984

Authorization for the superfund, which Congress originally approved in 1980, doesn't expire until the end of this month. But in 1984, environmental groups and [James] Florio, [D–N.J.] who chairs the Energy and Commerce Subcommittee on Commerce, Transportation and Tourism, which has jurisdiction over the program, thought the climate was right to push a major bill right away. . . .

While the superfund bill raced through the House, industry lobbyists felt they were on the outside looking in. "In the House, we were essentially rolled," said an oil lobbyist. "Once the deal was cut, there was very little opportunity for input." The insurance and chemical industries worked hard for a successful floor amendment to eliminate the new federal right to sue for damages. But the House passed the overall bill, 323-33, on Aug. 10.

In the Senate, the situation was reversed. Aware that the Democrats were hoping to embarrass Reagan with a superfund bill loaded with implicit criticism of EPA, the Republican leadership held the bill. Environmental lobbyists urged their members to write and call, and they prowled the Senate office buildings, pressing staff.

But it was all like throwing Ping-Pong balls against a battleship. In early October, the Republicans brushed aside an attempt to attach superfund to the continuing spending resolution and went home for the election, leaving the issue to stew for another winter.

## SETTING THE STAGE

Almost immediately after the November election, environmental lobbyists began meeting to plan for 1985. The environmental coalition held weekly Wednesday morning meetings at the Sierra Club's Capitol Hill office. . . .

As they surveyed the legislative scene last winter, environmental lobbyists felt confident that the House would again pass the 1984 version of the bill, with some strengthening amendments—including a larger fund and provisions establishing a community's "right-to-know" which chemicals are being used at local factories.

But as the winter wore on, it became apparent that the situation had changed. In early February, just after the National Campaign coalition announced a nationwide petition drive supporting a strong superfund, a delegation of environmentalists went to see Eckart, whom they expected to be a staunch ally. Eckart told them he was trying to write his own compromise bill. That struck some of those in the room as ominous: Didn't they already have a compromise—last year's bill?

The environmentalists trooped over to see key members of Dingell's staff [John Dingell, (D–Mich.), chairman of House Committee on Energy and Commerce] and urged them to press for an early introduction of legislation based on the previous year's bill, but Dingell's aides didn't commit. That again struck some as ominous.

Lobbyists from the oil and chemical industries making the rounds at the committee picked up the same message. But over the winter, they spent most of their time negotiating among themselves, and with the Senate, over how to pay for the superfund.

From the start, financing has been the key superfund issue for the two industries. . . . Under current law, 87.5 percent of superfund financing comes from a tax on petroleum and chemical feedstocks, with the remainder appropriated from general revenues. The industry feared that if the size of the fund sharply increased, so would its taxes. The House had taken that route in 1984.

Both industries were looking for ways to pay for an enlarged superfund without raising their feedstock taxes. . . .

This time, the tax lawyers came back with a tax on manufacturers that was broad-based. . . . The tax was based on the theory that not only oil and chemical companies, but all business—indeed all society— benefited from chemicals.

With those internal negotiations completed, API sat down with the CMA to develop a joint position. Though the two groups share many members, this took time. Eventually the groups reached a joint position calling for a $5 billion fund and a freeze on the feedstock tax, with the broad-based tax triggered if Congress wanted a larger fund.

That happened soon enough: on March 7, the Senate Environment and Public Works Committee approved a $7.5 billion superfund. Around that time, API sent a delegation of oil company chief executives to discuss their idea with Lloyd Bentsen, D-Texas, a member of the Senate Finance Committee, which had jurisdiction over the superfund tax.

Bentsen had been interested in a broad-based tax since the previous

fall, and so at the meeting, he didn't need to be sold on one. What he wanted was assurance that if he got out in front of a parade, the oil industry would be marching behind him. It was clear from the meeting it would be, and because the oil people had also interested Sen. Malcolm Wallop, R-Wyo., it was clear Bentsen would have a good political base. Bentsen signed on.

Staffers for the two Senators developed the proposal into a bill, changing many of the particulars but retaining the oil industry's basic concept. The Senators introduced their bill on April 18, and, a month later, the Finance Committee, with strong industry support, approved by a 19-1 vote a superfund paid for with the current feedstock tax and the new broad-based levy. Later, the Energy and Commerce Committee would recommend that the Ways and Means Committee use a similar scheme.

## THE DEAL

While the Senate moved, the House stalled. Eckart approached the Republicans and some moderate Democrats trying to write his own consensus bill, but gave up in early spring. Florio, who had begun discussions with other subcommittee members back in February, didn't introduce his bill until early May. But Florio couldn't muster a majority on his subcommittee.

Finally, some subcommittee members not aligned with Florio quietly approached Dingell to convene a meeting to get the bill moving. In mid-May, Dingell gathered together the subcommittee. . . .

A few days later, Dingell decided to move. Dingell approached Eckart and the Republicans to begin writing a bill that could clear the subcommittee. . . .

The group was sworn to secrecy during the drafting. But at that juncture they didn't need to communicate much with the outside lobbyists. They already knew what the environmentalists wanted. . . .

And business interests, informally dividing up responsibility, had made their positions clear. Chemical companies had focused on pushing their tax plan, opposing citizen suits to force emergency private cleanups of imminent health hazards and obtaining releases from future liability during cleanup settlements. Oil interests had made their case on how to clean up leaking underground gasoline tanks. The insurance industry, after an unsuccessful early push to change the liability standards, had been largely absent from the debate.

The staff group completed its work the second week in June. On June 11, the staff brought in a group of environmental lobbyists to show them the draft bill. Two days later, the lobbyists came back with a two-page list of 39 specific objections. . . . The staff began meetings with the subcommittee's liberals that were, if anything, even more heated. The subcommittee members were talking too.

The staff group passed the bill out to industry at the same time. It wasn't everything they wanted, but the industry lobbyists realized anything less stringent than last year's bill was "a godsend," a committee aide said. The lines were drawing fast. . . .

As the committee finished its work, emotions ran high again. Shortly before the final vote, Early and Dach rushed out a press release indicting the bill on 11 counts. When he saw the release, Eckart was livid. Though Eckart wasn't mentioned by name, the release said "the polluters couldn't have written a better bill for themselves." Eckart stormed up to Dach, snapped the lapels of Dach's suit and told him, "You've made a big mistake." Then he delivered a barbed response to the press release, citing his 92 percent voting record from the League of Conservation Voters (LCV) and accusing the environmentalists of misrepresenting the bill (a charge Eckart, Dingell and other coalition Members still make). . . .

## WHY?

Was it lobbying that changed the committee's course?

Industry lobbying didn't change much over the winter. "We did the same things we always do," said an oil lobbyist. (One of those is to give money; companies directly affected by superfund gave $9.8 million in the 1984 election to House and Senate candidates.) Staffers said they relied on industry and environmental lobbyists mainly as technical resources.

A committee source sympathetic to the environmentalists said the groups didn't do enough to convince Members that a vote against them would be painful back home. "On these issues, environmentalists deliver pain, industry delivers money. The Members began to perceive the environmentalists couldn't deliver that much pain on superfund," the source said.

That assessment is probably too harsh. In 1984, the groups' efforts were magnified by election-year politics that prompted many legislators to accept a more liberal bill than they felt comfortable with; in 1985, they drifted back. . . .

Dingell's own motivations are, as

usual, more complex. It wasn't lobbying that moved Dingell; both sides say he is virtually immune from pressure because of his secure seat. His partisans say he moved because Florio was stuck, with the expiration date creeping near; his critics say the committee chairman wanted to demonstrate to Florio—and the other liberal subcommittee chairmen—who was in charge. Dingell, sources say, was also uncomfortable with some of the provisions in last year's bill, particularly those limiting EPA's discretion. Only Dingell knows the real answer, and these strands of thought may be inextricably intertwined in his mind.

**Source:** Ronald Brownstein, "Trench Warfare," *National Journal* (September 14, 1985): 2047–2049, 2053. Copyright 1985 by *National Journal,* Inc. All Rights Reserved. Reprinted by Permission.

Lobbyists and their employers often attempt to influence critical assignments to committees that handle legislation of importance to them. They make representations to the members of the relevant committee on committees about which members, or at least which type of member, would be satisfactory. They also work to get specific committees to conduct hearings they think would highlight information favorable to their positions.

Lobbyists try to stimulate mail supporting their position. This can be done on a selective basis (for example, for a few corporation presidents or union leaders) or it can be a mass campaign (for example, from as many members of a union or a chamber of commerce as possible). In general, the selective mailing is likely to attract more attention from the senators and representatives than the mass mailing. Mass mailings are generally obviously that and usually require minimal effort on the part of the individual mailer. Members often ignore or at least discount them.

The provision of money for campaigns is the most important election-time service rendered by the interest groups. They can also be helpful by conducting voter registration drives and by providing campaign workers and campaign literature.

It should be noted that not all interest groups are equally skillful in using the techniques identified above. Even the most effective lobbyists can be rebuffed or make mistakes. Among the most common errors committed by lobbyists are the misidentification of potential friends, sympathizers, and opponents; inattention to important stages in the legislative process; and the use of tactics that aggravate potential supporters. Interest groups—particularly the large ones—can also be rendered impotent by conflicts within their own membership. For example, different individual unions may take opposing views, thus making it impossible for the AFL-CIO to take a strong position. An inept lobbyist can alienate even a natural ally. Groups are at their most effective when their representatives are, in fact, "reinforcing, providing ammunition for, and serving their sympathizers in the Congress."[14]

## Conditions for Interest-Group Influence

Interest groups and members of Congress can both gain from one another. The nature of the relationship between groups and members varies depending on the kind of policy question at stake. Although interest groups do not consistently dominate congressional decision making they are often important. A number of conditions enhance their influence.[15]

In many cases there may not be two competing groups or coalitions of groups on an issue. Only one point of view may be presented in lobbying. Under such conditions that group or coalition is likely to get much of what it wants.

If the groups on one side of a controversy are unified and coordinated on the major issues they want to push or if they can cover up any disagreements, they will enhance their chances of success. When a single group or a few groups acting in concert can demonstrate the primacy of their interest in a particular area, they gain both visibility and effectiveness. For example, the walnut growers are represented by a single highly organized group. They are likely to get what they want legislatively. By contrast, chicken farmers are dispersed over the entire nation and have no effective single group to speak for them. Therefore they have difficulty in achieving their legislative ends.[16]

If there are key members of the House and Senate (for example, a subcommittee chairman) who actively believe in the interest group's

---

[14]Dexter, *How Organizations Are Represented in Washington,* 72.

[15]For an interesting theoretical statement about the nature of the relationship between lobbyists and legislators see Michael T. Hayes, *Lobbyists and Legislators: A Theory of Political Markets* (New Brunswick, N.J.: Rutgers University Press, 1981). See also Hayes, "The Semi-Sovereign Pressure Groups: A Critique of Current Theory and an Alternative Typology," *Journal of Politics* 40 (1978): 134–61.

For empirically-based discussions of the role of interest groups (and other actors) in both the formulation and implementation of different types of policy see Randall B. Ripley and Grace A. Franklin, *Congress, the Bureaucracy, and Public Policy,* 4th ed. (Chicago: Dorsey Press, 1987); and Ripley and Franklin, *Policy Implementation and Bureaucracy,* 2nd ed. (Chicago: Dorsey Press, 1986).

[16]On these two groups in the Eighty-sixth Congress (1959–60) see Clem Miller, *Member of the House* (New York: Scribner's, 1962): 137–40.

# LOBBYING AND THE FARM CREDIT SYSTEM, 1987

BY WARD SINCLAIR

It doesn't quite live up to the flash and dash of the crowd from Gucci Gulch, as the wags call the well-heeled petitioners at the House Ways and Means Committee, but the daily gathering outside 1300 Longworth is giving it the old college try.

The congressional cognoscenti know that 1300 Longworth House Office Building is the province of the Agriculture Committee, where elected men frequently gather to debate the merits of arcana such as deficiency payments, marketing loans and acreage bases.

That is the stuff that draws farmers in ball caps and lobbyists whose sartorial habits are more in tune with pipe-rack clothing stores than Italian designers. But since last week, the committee has been plowing different turf and, as a result, a different kind of lobbying crowd has planted itself outside the door.

These are money people—bankers, insurance executives, computer salesmen. Not only do they frequently fill the corridor outside Room 1300. They jam the hearing room itself and spill over into an adjacent room, where sound is piped in from the main chamber for easy listening. They all are here because they want something. A piece of the action. A break, a tidbit.

A former congressional aide who now works for the teetering Farm Credit System (FCS) put it bluntly: "The sharks are circling." Another executive of a farmer organization observed it this way: "The banks finally have learned where the Agriculture Committee is, to their dismay."

The committee, emitting regular grunts of self-conscious uncertainty about its ability to craft a banking regulation bill, has been working since last week on legislation to prop up the nearly broke FCS with a multibillion-dollar infusion of federal funds (no one yet knows where it will come from) and new rules for the FCS to live by.

Rep. Edward R. Madigan (R-Ill.), ranking Republican on the committee, retains sanity in this atmosphere by exercising his wry sense of humor. In a burst of mirth earlier this week, when the debate was getting zany, Madigan sent a note to an Illinois reporter at the press table. It was written as an amendment and said, in rough paraphrase, "A wet bird will not fly at night."

Which speaks for itself, obviously.

Every day as the committee convenes, an assistant treasury secretary, Charles O. Sethness, takes a seat down front. He smokes cigarettes and frequently shakes his bearded head in undisguised dismay at the panel's insistence on putting things in the bill that the White House doesn't want.

Alongside him are a half-dozen functionaries from the Farm Credit Administration, regulator of the FCS. Behind them is an uncountable phalanx of FCS officials who come on expense account from such venues as Amarillo, Wichita, Columbia and points beyond, to hear the fate of their system debated.

In the hallway outside, one hears such phrases as "our language" and "under our amendment." As committee members enter and leave the hearing room, small squadrons of the financial lobbyists waylay them to whisper advice or to press sheets of paper into their hands. Back in their offices, committee members are flooded with phone calls from farmers, FCS officials and bankers who want this or that in the final bill.

The pressure is intensified by the insistence of House Speaker Jim Wright (D-Tex.) that the committee finish its work this week before the summer recess so the reform bill can go to the floor immediately after Labor Day. It is further intensified by the administration's objections to including aid for Farmers Home Administration borrowers and the creation of a second market for farm real estate mortgages.

The committee keeps battling the fine print and through it all, Chairman E (Kika) de la Garza (D-Tex.) maintains an air of optimism about his panel finishing its markup on time. Few of the hallway experts think the chairman will be able to meet his deadline.

Well, sometimes they're right and sometimes they're not. Sometimes they're in another world. Over lunch in the Longworth cafeteria yesterday, one lobbyist gave another his "three criteria" for scoring points at the committee: "It has to be noncontroversial, the administration has to support it . . . and you have to want it." Plainly, this could not have related to an FCS bailout.

They finished lunch and went back to duty stations at Room 1300.

**Source:** Ward Sinclair, "The New Crowd at 1300 Longworth," *Washington Post,* August 5, 1987. © *The Washington Post.*

---

position, the chances of success are greatly enhanced. The same is true when a lobbying effort is made in a field where the power of Congress vis-à-vis the executive branch is unusually strong. Former Assistant Secretary of the Treasury Stanley S. Surrey makes this point in relation to tax legislation:

> The Congress regards the shaping of a revenue bill as very much its prerogative. It will seek the views of the executive. . . . But control over the legislation itself, both as to broad policies and as to details, rests with the Congress. Hence a congressman, and especially a member of the tax committees, is in a position to make the tax laws bend in favor of a particular individual or group despite strong objection from the executive branch. Under such a governmental system the importance to the tax structure of the institutional factors that influence a congressman's decision is obvious.[17]

The visibility of the issues for which groups lobby is another important factor affecting their impact. On issues regarded as routine by Congress without much wide public visibility, interest groups become

---

[17]Stanley S. Surrey, "How Special Tax Provisions Get Enacted," in Randall B. Ripley (ed.), *Public Policies and Their Politics* (New York: Norton, 1966): 53.

entrenched in the decision-making process in Congress and the executive branch. In these relatively invisible areas, interest groups are likely to have maximum impact. Their impact is also high when they seek single, discrete amendments to bills as opposed to advocating a large legislative package. As the visibility of issues increases and public attention to issue areas grows the impact of interest groups tends to diminish.

In early 1986, for example, lobbyists for the dairy industry quickly and relatively quietly were instrumental in getting Congress to amend a section of a general farm bill it had passed only a few months earlier, at the end of 1985; to exempt milk producers from a number of the budget cuts in price supports that would have been required by the Gramm-Rudman Act to reduce the federal deficit, legislation also passed late in 1985. The lobbyists argued, effectively and without public notice, that conferees working on the farm bill in 1985 had made this pledge to them and now they needed the delivery of appropriate statutory language. Congress agreed and produced the desired amendment quickly. Similarly, also in 1986, the relevant lobbies pushed for, and Congress quickly passed, some technical legislation allowing banks in the Farm Credit System to alter their accounting procedures in various ways designed to pump more money into farm credit without doing so through direct and obvious spending; a move that would have been difficult in the budget-cutting and budget-vigilance mood that year. Relative invisibility of the issue as it was framed allowed rapid action that went unchallenged and pleased the interested groups and their congressional supporters.

Another factor that works in favor of an interest group is support for or, at least, no opposition to its aims from the relevant executive branch agency in its representations to Congress.

Groups sometimes state views on matters remote from their primary interests. But an interest group is likely to have greatest impact on issues that coincide with the interests the group purports to represent directly. AFL-CIO lobbyists may be very influential in advising on matters concerning the working conditions of factory workers, but they receive less attention from legislators when they advocate a higher tariff for tung nut imports or when they make a broad pronouncement on foreign policy.

Interest groups are likely to be most consistently important on issues defined either as distributive or as regulatory with the potential of being converted to self-regulatory (which turns out to be another form of distribution in most ways). They are less influential on redistributive issues.

Interest groups will usually have a greater impact on amendments than on entire pieces of legislation. This is because amendments are generally technical and thus less widely understood and salient to only a few people.

On such issues conflict can usually be limited. As the field of conflict widens, more participants enter the fray and any single participant is likely to be less influential. The fewer the participants, the greater their influence.[18]

## The Defensive Nature of Lobbying

Much lobbying is defensive—that is, aimed at preventing changes in the existing situation or at least preventing more than minimal change when some change is inevitable. In many policy areas there are well-established patterns of special privilege and entrenched interests that will resist any change not to their benefit. Given the complexity of the decision process in Congress and the executive branch, those taking a negative position, rather than those urging something new to be done, have an advantage.[19]

In general, successful defensive lobbying in one year does not necessarily remove an item from the congressional agenda for future years. Legislation in a given area may eventually be forthcoming, but skillful defensive lobbying can postpone it and probably produce some amendments that weaken a measure when it finally passes. For example, in 1972 defensive lobbying was credited with defeating a number of major initiatives: no-fault insurance, extended minimum wage coverage and a higher minimum wage figure, the establishment of a consumer protection agency, the opening of the highway trust fund for mass transit purposes, the inclusion of small businesses in a new occupational safety law, strip-mining regulation, and gun control.[20]

In the years since 1972 only a few of these initiatives, in weak form, succeeded. A higher minimum wage was achieved in 1977 but coverage was not expanded. The highway trust fund was opened to mass transit uses in 1973, and a strip-mining bill with important limits was passed in 1977. No-fault insurance, a consumer protection agency, inclusion of small businesses under occupational safety regulations, and gun control went nowhere.

[18]Schattschneider, *The Semisovereign People.*
[19]See Dexter, *How Organizations Are Represented,* 62; and Truman, *The Governmental Process,* 391–92.
[20]"Opponents of Major Legislation Score Success," *Congressional Quarterly Almanac* (1972): 1074–80.

The history of attempts to pass federal strip-mining legislation, finally successful in 1977, affords a good example of defensive lobbying that prevented a bill for a number of years and then succeeded in obtaining some key weakening amendments when passage did come. Congressional consideration of federal regulation of strip mining began in 1968, when a Senate committee first held hearings. By 1972 the House passed a bill but the Senate did not act. In 1974 President Ford pocket-vetoed a bill that Congress had passed (that is, he vetoed it after Congress had adjourned and so it had no chance to override the veto). In 1975 Congress passed another bill, which Ford vetoed, and an override attempt in the House failed by three votes. In 1976 the House Rules Committee twice prevented bills from reaching the floor (they would have been vetoed had they passed). Throughout this period a coalition of mining interests, led by coal, prevailed.

When success finally came in the form of legislation that passed Congress and was signed by President Carter in 1977, the years of successful opposition had resulted in some key changes in the legislation. For example, the bill addressed only coal mining and left other types of mining alone (although other mining, such as that for copper, also uses stripping techniques). This was a move to reduce the political weight of the opponents of the bill by concentrating only on coal. And even in the provisions dealing with coal mining, several provisions were weaker than House proponents would have liked because of the persistent opposition and arguments of the coal interests. For example, the provision relating to strip mining on alluvial valley floors in the West was weakened so that such mining was not banned but only somewhat restricted. Similarly, relatively small operators were given a temporary exemption from the environmental provisions of the act.

In 1986 a good example of defensive lobbying is provided by the opponents of a bill that would have set federal standards for product liability lawsuits. Manufacturers wanted such a law since it would give them a single standard nationwide. However, a powerful group of interests opposed the creation of federal law in this area because they benefitted from the state domination of the system. These groups represented trial lawyers, unions, consumer groups, and state officials (attorneys generals and judges). This coalition was unusual in that it combined people whose living depended on lots of state lawsuits (lawyers and state officials) and those who took the view that the law in at least many states was likely to be more generous to those suing manufacturers than would a federal law enacted in the Reagan era (unions and consumer groups).

Another example from 1986 and 1987 underscores a slightly different point: when some form of legislation is inevitable, defensive lobbying consists in trying to get the legislation to be as palatable as possible. In 1957 Congress had enacted legislation that limited the liability of the then-new nuclear power industry to $650 million for any single nuclear accident. The following three decades saw the industry mature, the occurrence of the Three Mile Island accident, the rise of anti-nuclear lobbies, and inflation that made 1957 dollars worth about four times more than 1987 dollars. An upward shift in the liability limit was not preventable no matter how hard the nuclear industry lobbyists tried. However, in 1986, they were able to fend off a proposal to remove all limits on liability. In 1987 the House passed a bill approving a $7 billion limit on liability of nuclear utilities in the case of an accident. This was viewed as a victory by the nuclear industry because the House was much more hostile than the Senate and the industry could live with a $7 billion liability limit. One of the lobbyists for the anti-nuclear groups summed it up well from the opposing point of view: "We got beat up pretty badly. They went right down the line with the nuclear industry."[21]

## The Impact of Interest Groups on Congressional Decision-Making: An Assessment

In the final analysis, the impact of interest groups "depends more on the harmony of values between the groups and the legislators than it does on the ability of a group to wield its 'power' either through skillful techniques or presumed electoral influence."[22] For example, the Welfare Rights Organization facing a predominantly conservative Congress will make much less headway on issues important to it than it will under a predominantly liberal Congress.

What are the implications of interests groups' activity for representative government? A measure of skepticism and distrust is not entirely misplaced. Much national public policy reflects the special interests represented by the various groups. And competing groups may all get part of their preferences written into statutes, even if that results in "irrational" public policy—that is, policies that contain built-in contradictions and simultaneously aim at opposing ends. Unchecked, interest groups present dangers. They participate in cozy

[21]Quoted in Robert E. Taylor, "House Clears $7 Billion Liability Cap in Victory For Nuclear Power Industry," *Wall Street Journal*, July 31, 1987.
[22]Zeigler, *Interest Groups in American Society*, 274.

subgovernment arrangements that essentially make policy in many areas without oversight from other sources. They provide a large amount of issue-related information to legislators that is one-sided. Their very existence usually works for the maintenance of the status quo: they play an important role in keeping the agenda of Congress looking pretty much the same from year to year. They buttress Congress's preference for familiar, nonthreatening solutions to familiar issues. However, when other forces change the broad public agenda, interest groups must adjust. For example, the overwhelming concern in the 1980s with budgetary matters—especially the size of the federal deficit and the size of the national trade imbalance—confronted interest groups with some constraints they could not evade. Some favorite spending programs had to succumb in whole or in part. Similarly, the passage of a major tax overhaul in late 1986 removed favored tax treatment for a variety of interests such as financial institutions (for example, loss of deductibility of Individual Retirement Account contributions) and the real estate industry (through severe limits on tax shelters). However, other interests were protected: municipalities through retention of tax-free status for their bonds, and the construction, real estate, and mortgage-banking interests through retention of the deductibility of interest payments on mortgages and local property taxes from individual tax returns.

Any system of government that is representative must allow interest groups to have their say, although participants must realize that the groups do not necessarily represent all legitimate interests. Interest groups do not possess untrammeled influence, however. Congressmen receive information that is biased, but they often are exposed to opposite views from competing lobbyists. It may not be possible to eliminate the coziness of subgovernment arrangements in many policy areas, but the entry of new people into a subgovernment helps new ideas to emerge. In addition, a watchful press is important in checking the activities of interest groups. The extensive role of specific lobbies in financing both presidential and congressional campaigns, for example, are often revealed by diligent journalists.

Congress itself made a presumably comprehensive attempt to regulate lobbying in Title III of the Legislative Reorganization Act of 1946. This act is based on the assumption that the collection and publication of information about the identification of lobbyists and spending for lobbying activities will be sufficient to keep the activities within reasonable bounds. There is no evidence supporting this assumption. In addition, the act requires the filing of data only when a group is engaged in spending *principally* for the purpose of influencing legislation. This means that many groups that spend considerable sums and hire a number of representatives for legislative purposes but can interpret their principal activities to be for other purposes do not file the required reports. In short, the information collected is only partial, is presented in raw form, and seems to have little effect on lobbying. A major revision of the lobby disclosure provisions failed to pass in 1976. A number of additional efforts since 1977 have also failed.

## MEMBERS AND CONSTITUENTS

Representation in several senses, partially discussed in Chapter 1, is at the heart of relationships between members and their constituents.[23] Members view their constituents in a variety of ways. They sometimes see them through the filter of interest groups. For example, a House member might think of his district having 5,000 members of the United Auto Workers, 2,000 members of railway unions, 3,000 members of civil service unions, 1,000 members of the National Farmers Organization, 2,000 members of the American Farm Bureau Federation, seven corporate members of the National Association of Manufacturers, 4,000 members of the Sons of Italy, 3,000 members of the National Rifle Association, and 2,000 members of the Sierra Club. Or he might see them as being affiliated with the major economic institutions of the district: 3,000 employees of the Burlington Northern, 5,000 employees of John Deere, 2,000 employees of General Foods, 14,000 employees of the federal government, and 5,000 employees of the state government.

Members might also think in terms of the general socioeconomic characteristics of their districts: highly urban or highly rural, large or small ethnic and black populations, well-educated or poorly educated, well-paid or poorly paid, predominantly Protestant or predominantly Catholic, highly identified with the Republican party or the Democratic party. Members may not realize that they are using these categories but, in fact, they instinctively do so. Interviews with members include statements such as the following: "My people are mostly poor Czechs and Germans." "I've got a lot of blacks and poor white Appalachians." "Most of my folks own their own farms or own their own businesses in small towns. They have all lived in those counties a long time."

[23]See Heinz Eulau and Paul D. Karps, "The Puzzle of Representation: Specifying Components of Responsiveness," *Legislative Studies Quarterly* 2 (1977): 233–54.

They might also think of at least a few of their constituents as individuals: the editor of the district's largest newspaper, the party county chairperson, the managers of the largest plants, the presidents of the largest unions, and other such local notables are likely to be known as individuals by a member.

A study based on close observation of seventeen House members from 1970 through 1976 concluded that members see four different kinds of constituencies when they think about their districts.[24] First they see a geographical constituency, consisting of all of their constituents, and they also see some basic differentiations. They are generally aware of whether their district is homogeneous or heterogeneous in terms of population characteristics. Second, members see a re-election constituency made up of the people the member thinks vote for him. Third, members identify a primary constituency, those supporters among the re-election constituency who are viewed as being the most reliable, active, and strongest. Finally, members have a personal constituency, those strong supporters who interact often with the member on a personal basis.

Regardless of the filter he or she uses, the member of Congress is sure to be thinking of his constituents almost all of the time. "This bill has important benefits for the folks back home and I have to work for its passage." "How will my vote on this controversial roll call be received at home?" "What are the responses from the questionnaire I sent home last week looking like?" "Will I have time to get home this month for some speaking and unofficial campaigning?" Constituencies are important to members for a variety of reasons. The most basic, of course: it is constituents who elect and re-elect members.

## Interaction between Constituents and Members

Members of the House and Senate have a number of methods of communicating with their constituents. They appear on radio and television. They send newsletters to their constituents and solicit opinions through mailed questionnaires. Other means by which the member informs his constituents include: promoting newspaper coverage of his activities; writing reports or columns for newspapers; sending committee reports and government publications; establishing film and

[24]Richard F. Fenno, Jr., "U.S. House Members in Their Constituencies: An Exploration," *American Political Science Review* 71 (1977): 883–917. See also Fenno, *Home Style: House Members in Their Districts* (Boston: Little, Brown, 1978).

record libraries on government activities and programs; speaking in the district at public functions such as service club meetings and high-school graduations; acting personally as a host for visitors from the constituency; and responding to constituent mail. There are other communications that don't contain information about legislation but that help the member to enhance his image: for example, most members write letters of congratulation and condolence and send such useful items as free seeds and booklets on baby care to constituents.[25]

Members receive information from their constituents through a number of sources, including letters, telegrams, phone calls, personal visits to members and their staffs, and appearances before committees. The mail is the most important vehicle for transmitting constituents' opinions to members. Organized letter-writing campaigns from constituencies, often generated by an interest group, are considered less important by congressmen than letters from individual constituents. An organized campaign is usually recognizable by the set phraseology or standard form of the letters.[26]

On a number of important issues there is little mail from constituents. The level of issue-specific information available to constituents varies from issue to issue. Well-formed constituent opinion does not exist on most matters. Even those opinions on issues transmitted to members of Congress are likely to be vague and poorly expressed. As a result, much of the time members do not have clear indications of constituency opinion; in fact, much of the time such opinion does not exist.

Even when constituent opinion is expressed, two distortions accompany it. First, it tends to come from individuals who already agree with the position of their representative or senator. Second, members tend to interpret what they hear as being supportive of views they already hold. This is relatively easy since many communications from constituents are unclear and ambiguous. In short, on most issues constituency is only a weak or nonexistent constraint on members' legislative behavior. Clear expressions of mass opinion on specific issues are rare. Most of the time, members represent their own images of the nature of their district or state, including opinion they think

[25]In general, the choices members make about communications are related to their goals and political situations. See Diana Evans Yiannakis, "House Members' Communication Styles: Newsletters and Press Releases," *Journal of Politics* 44 (1982): 1049–71; and Albert D. Cover, "Contacting Congressional Constituents: Some Patterns of Perquisite Use." *American Journal of Political Science* 24 (1980): 125–35.

[26]See Lewis A. Dexter, "What Do Congressmen Hear?" in Nelson W. Polsby (ed.), *Congressional Behavior* (New York: Random House, 1971).

# DAVID PRICE: CONGRESS UPDATE

## A NEW FACE IN WASHINGTON

After six months of unpacking and organizing, our new Congressman has set up his offices and is hard at work in the historic 100th Congress. David wouldn't be there right now were it not for your efforts, and we especially wanted you to know who's working with him, what his goals are and how he plans to serve his constituents.

## READY TO SERVE YOU—THE DISTRICT OFFICES

One of a Congressman's most important jobs is serving the people back home—a goal to which David is deeply committed. His three district offices, located in Raleigh, Chapel Hill and Asheboro, are headed by district manager Joan Ewing. Having served as administrative assistant for Congressman Andrews in Washington for four years, she has plenty of experience at cutting through bureaucratic red tape and helping Fourth District residents.

These offices are the people's direct links to Washington. Fourth District residents having problems with Social Security checks, Medicare or Medicaid, disability claims, the IRS or veterans benefits, may contact David directly through them for quick efficient help. They assist constituents with passports, visas and immigration matters, and they help select appointees to U.S. military academies. Families and groups planning to visit Washington should contact their nearest office to arrange special passes to the Congressional galleries and for tours of the White House. . . .

## ELECTION '88: ALL SYSTEMS GO!

This spring many of you received a letter from David asking for contributions to help pay off his campaign debt. A great many responded and, thanks to you, David and Lisa have now paid off the bank loan they took out to help fund the campaign. With this task out of the way, the Price Committee is ready to start building its base for 1988. It's not too early to start replenishing the campaign coffers and we are accepting contributions for the coming race. . . .

## PRICE ON THE ISSUES— GETTING DOWN TO BUSINESS

Last year, when David produced his 22-page "Price on the Issues" document, he wasn't just making empty campaign pledges. In his first few months in Washington, he's been hard at work putting his promises into practice.

**Dumping the Nuclear Waste Dump:** In February, along with fellow North Carolina freshmen Jamie Clarke and Martin Lancaster, David introduced legislation to repeal the law requiring the Department of Energy to select an eastern United States location for the disposal of high-level nuclear waste. Two North Carolina sites, one in Wake and Franklin Counties, are being considered for construction by the DOE. At the same time, David has worked to eliminate congressional appropriations for work on the second site, and is one of a group of interested Congressmen and Senators seeking to re-write the nation's nuclear waste policy.

**Education:** In keeping with his pledge to be a national spokesman for education, David has been a leader in opposing the severe cuts in education proposed by the Administration. This month, he joined with Martin Lancaster in introducing legislation to amend the Tax Reform Act to relieve the tax burden of students receiving college loans and scholarships. And as one of two freshmen House members appointed to the Congressional Task Force on Illiteracy, he is planning field hearings in the Fourth District to study and search for solutions to North Carolina's illiteracy problem.

**In-District Concerns:** From his seat on the Small Business Committee, David is working to ensure that small and medium sized businesses get a fair shot at bidding for government contracts and that they receive prompt payments for the services and products they provide. He is arranging to bring the Committee to the Fourth District for hearings on these issues. David was instrumental in securing an experimental radar system for Raleigh-Durham Airport that allows the simultaneous use of parallel runways, thus assuring the timely opening of the new American Airlines hub.

## DAVID PRICE'S COMMITTEE ASSIGNMENTS

**Banking, Finance and Urban Affairs:** In his post on this major committee, David will help set federal policy governing the country's banking and financial institutions—a key part of North Carolina's expanding economy. Federal housing legislation passes through this committee, which also deals with key aspects of trade issues.

**Science, Space, and Technology:** It seems natural that a representative from the district that houses part of the Research Triangle Park and several major universities would serve on this committee. As a member, David will help guide the nation's policy in these areas, handle the budget for the National Science Foundation and oversee the space program. David has also been appointed as a freshman member to the Task Force on United States Technology Policy, the House group charged with formulating national policy to help the United States reclaim its traditional position as the world leader in technological and manufacturing innovation.

**Small Business:** As a member of this committee, David will address federal issues pertaining to small businesses and provide a voice for area small businessmen in Washington.

**Note:** David Price, a Democrat from North Carolina, defeated an incumbent Republican in 1986 for a House seat. These excerpts are from a political newsletter to his supporters about six months after he took office (July 10, 1987).

exists. Members shape and create those images.[27] Opinion in the constituency can be important, but the process by which "opinion" is constructed and transmitted to members is far from straightforward.

Some members of Congress let the expressed opinions of a few individual constituents speak for the opinion of the entire constituency. These are people the member trusts and considers to be representative. Although they may transmit no opinion other than their own, the important point is that the member values those opinions, accepts them as representative, and interprets them as endorsements of positions already held. The identity of these individuals varies widely from case to case. They may include prominent industrialists, editors, union leaders, local politicians, or rather obscure people who just happen to be old friends.

## Congressional Workloads and Constituency Service

There is conflicting evidence on how much of their time and resources congressmen allocate to constituency service, broadly defined. In fact, different members proceed very differently in their constituencies. A pioneering study by Richard Fenno concluded that each member of Congress has a "home style" and that each home style is at least partially unique. Three aspects of home style seemed to vary: how the member allocated both his personal resources and those of his office, how the member presented himself at home, and how the member explained his personal activities in Washington, as well as the activities of Congress, at home.[28] Constituencies are important to virtually all members but each member proceeds differently.

Discussions with members of the House in 1959 led Charles Clapp to assert that legislators spent most of their time dealing with constituency-related aspects of their jobs. His generalizations from 30 years ago are still accurate:

A congressman is administrator, educator, and errand boy, as well as legislator. In each of these roles he is mindful of his constituents. He

[27]Lewis A. Dexter, *The Sociology and Politics of Congress* (Chicago: Rand McNally, 169): Chapter 8. A study of the content of opinion represented in congressional mail compared to general district opinion concluded that the mail adequately represents only the opinion held by a member's "primary constituency"—the most reliable, active, and strongest of the member's supporters. See John S. Stolarek, Robert M. Rood, and Marcia Whicker Taylor, "Measuring Constituency Opinion in the U.S. House: Mail Versus Random Surveys," *Legislative Studies Quarterly* 4 (1981): 589–95.

[28]Fenno, "U.S. House Members," and *Home Style*.

organizes his office with them, rather than his legislative responsibilities, in mind. Though he considers his work in behalf of individuals as less fundamental to his job than work on legislation, he nonetheless gives it precedence. He both derives satisfaction from it and is dismayed by it. It often is an onerous chore, but it meets a real need, brings him valuable information, and is the activity most likely to "pay off" at the polls. He resents the time it takes, but he will not slight it.[29]

Systematic surveys have found that members claim legislative work to be more time-consuming than constituency service. In a study by Roger Davidson, only 16 percent of the legislators listed constituency service as their primary activity (although 59 percent listed it as their secondary activity); 77 percent claimed legislative work to be their primary activity. Constituency service was less important to senior members than to junior members because senior members felt less need to strive for electoral safety (which they had already achieved) but junior members were still building it.[30]

An elaborate survey of workloads in the Eighty-ninth Congress showed that the average member spent only 28 percent of his or her time on constituency service; legislative work consumed 65 percent of his or her time.[31]

The House Commission on Administrative Review in 1977 published data based on a survey of House members conducted in mid-1977 on how members spent their time. They presented their data in terms of an "average" day of eleven hours and twenty-six minutes of work in Washington. When those figures are converted to percentages, the commission reported that the average Representative spent 39 percent of his or her time on the floor of the House and in committee and subcommittee and conference committee work, 29 percent of the time in his or her office, 18 percent of the time at other locations in Washington, and the remaining time (14 percent) in miscellaneous other activities. Except for the first category, much of the time was spent on constituent business. And, of course, a number of days were spent in the district devoted wholly to constituent business. The Commission's observation on these data is more important than the exact figures:

Members are extraordinarily busy people. An average day for legislators is so filled with diverse activities that little time is available for concentrated attention on any single issue. Legislators have exhaustive schedules

---

[29]Clapp, *The Congressman,* 103; see also 50–53.
[30]Davidson, *The Role of the Congressman,* 99; Clapp, *The Congressman,* 52.
[31]John S. Saloma III, *Congress and the New Politics* (Boston: Little, Brown, 1969).

that keep them running back and forth from their offices to floor sessions, committee meetings, or receptions and events in various parts of Washington. Legislators, too, are regularly flying or driving back and forth between Washington and their congressional districts.[32]

A careful study of the activity of Congress with regard to "casework" [defined as "intervention for individuals, groups or organizations (including businesses) that have requests of, grievances against, or a need for access to federal (and occasionally state or local) government departments or agencies"] and "projects" [defined as "assisting state and local governments in their attempts to secure federal grants from agencies that possess discretion in allocating such funds"] finds that senators and representatives personally spent an average of three to six hours per week on such work in the late 1970s and early 1980s.[33] Some members spent more time; staff members, of course, spent a great deal of time.

If the work of the representative or senator is divided between legislative work and constituency support, the job of congressional staff is much less divided—staff work is principally devoted to constituency service. A survey of congressional staff in the Eighty-ninth Congress showed the average office spent 25 percent of its time in direct constituency service, 41 percent of its time answering the mail, 10 percent of its time on education and publicity, and only 14 percent of its time on legislative support.[34]

Politically, time spent on constituency service is well spent. The payoff at the polls and in terms of constituency opinion is substantial. As one careful study concluded:

> Representatives undertake constituency work with a variety of motives, but by their own testimony the electoral incentive is significant, especially for those in marginal seats, who are the largest providers of constituency

---

[32]Commission on Administrative Review, *Administrative Reorganization and Legislative Management,* House Document No. 95–232, Vol. 2 (September 28, 1977). The data are from pages 17–19. The quotation is from page 17. For a study that concludes that variations in the amount of casework for constituents undertaken by any individual member may be largely idiosyncratic (and, therefore, depend mostly on the choices of members and their staff) see John R. Johannes, "The Distribution of Casework in the U.S. Congress: An Uneven Burden," *Legislative Studies Quarterly* 5 (1980): 517–44. A collection of papers examining the House as an organization and stemming, in large part, from the work of the Commission on Administrative Management was published as Joseph Cooper and G. Calvin Mackenzie (eds.), *The House at Work* (Austin, Texas: University of Texas Press, 1981).

[33]John R. Johannes, *To Serve the People: Congress and Constituency Service* (Lincoln, Nebraska: University of Nebraska Press, 1984). The definitions come from p. 2; a table summarizing personal time spent by members appears on p. 152.

[34]Saloma, *Congress and the New Politics,* 185.

service. Representatives believe that casework has both a positive and a negative electoral component: they can gain votes by extra efforts and lose votes by not living up to expectations. Analyses corroborate these beliefs: the activities representatives undertake affect their reputations.[35]

## Constituency Impact on Member Behavior

Constituency impact on the behavior of members of the House and Senate falls into three broad categories. First, there are those instances in which the economic interests of the district push a member into a specific position. For example, in 1977, members of the House from sixteen northeastern and midwestern states (the "frostbelt") formed a coalition to work for changing federal aid formulas they felt were discriminatory against their area in favor of the "sunbelt" states of the South and West. This coalition continued to be active in the 1980s. One specific study found a strong relationship between federal spending for agriculture, education, and space and roll call voting patterns in the Senate. Senators coming from states receiving high benefits in these areas would only rarely vote against bills providing those benefits.[36]

Even in the budget-cutting fervor in Congress in the 1980s many "pork barrel" enterprises were protected, including those for some of the chief conservative congressional allies for President Reagan's efforts to cut spending for social programs.

The second area for constituent impact is on a few issues on which enough constituents are so concerned that a wrong move by a member could cost him his seat. If in the 1940s or 1950s a southern member had come out in favor of strong civil rights legislation, he almost surely would have been defeated. By the 1970s and 1980s, however, a member from a district with a large black population (which, because of the effect of the federal Voting Rights Act of 1965, now voted) was much more likely to be responsive to perceived interests of black constituents. Electoral problems might now arise from unresponsiveness to the interests of black constituents.[37] If a member from a strongly unionized district came out in favor of the Taft-Hartley Act, limiting union power, in 1947, he might have been defeated in 1948. If

[35]Bruce Cain, John Ferejohn, and Morris Fiorina, *The Personal Vote: Constituency Service and Electoral Independence* (Cambridge, Mass.: Harvard University Press, 1987): 213.

[36]Lance T. LeLoup, "The Impact of Domestic Spending Patterns on Senate Support: An Examination of Three Policy Areas," *American Politics Quarterly* 5 (1977): 219–36.

[37]On the change in the relationship between black population and behavior of members of Congress see Charles S. Bullock, III, "Congressional Voting and the Mobilization of a Black Electorate in the South," *Journal of Politics* 43 (1981): 662–82.

a member from a middle-class suburban area came out in favor of massive busing to achieve school integration with an adjacent metropolitan area, he might be defeated. If a member from a sparsely populated western state vigorously espoused the cause of gun control, he might well lose his seat. If a member from a heavily Roman Catholic district supported abortion on demand he or she would have severe electoral problems.

But this kind of issue is relatively rare. On most issues the member has a great deal of freedom to maneuver because most of his constituents are uninformed or unconcerned about the issue. There is good evidence that members try to anticipate issues that may cause them problems in their constituencies and they try to avoid trouble in voting by guessing the safe route to take.[38]

The third kind of constituency impact occurs principally in the mind of the senator or representative. He or she thinks that representing constituents is important and therefore attempts, usually by intuition rather than by gathering data, to reflect the opinion of the constituency on a given issue or to hypothesize what the constituency would favor if it were asked to voice an opinion. In making these calculations, a number of subtle processes occur. Most members seek information that confirms them in their previously held beliefs. They can distort information they receive or simply rely, almost unconsciously, on a previously held image of constituency opinion. Constituency opinion is a very real phenomenon in the minds of members even if they guess at its content. It concerns them constantly.

Members are, of course, aware of the voting habits of their constituents—both for Congress and in general. Typical statements from members might include the following: "Registration in my district is two to one Democratic but a smart Republican can still carry it." "The district is competitive. My constituents always split their tickets and elect some candidates from both parties." "My people don't much like political parties. You are better off not harping on party."

As members internalize all of these various understandings and pressures, both perceived and real, they may lean toward one of two poles in terms of how they articulate the effect of constituency on their behavior. At the one pole are members who perceive themselves to be "delegates"—individuals who are simply instructed in one way or another by their constituents how to behave and how to vote and who willingly do it. At the other pole are members who perceive them-

---

[38]Morris P. Fiorina, *Representatives, Roll Calls, and Constituencies* (Lexington, Mass.: Lexington Books, 1974).

selves to be "trustees"—they consider constituency opinion and make-up as they understand it but they take final responsibility for reaching decisions on the grounds that they hold the welfare of their constituency in trust and should do what is best for the constituency regardless of the constituents' own perceptions or misperceptions.[39] Most members generally behave on the basis of some middle position. The categories of "delegate" and "trustee" are not very useful empirically except to indicate that members have a wide range of choice both about what they perceive and how those perceptions influence them.

External events and conditions can also change the way in which members think about the importance of constituency opinion. For example, there is evidence that southern Democrats and eastern Republicans increased their rate of defection from their respective dominant party positions in House roll calls in the 1960s because the tumultuous events of the 1960s—especially violence surrounding civil rights and anti-Vietnam war activities—made politics more salient to their constituents. Members tried to be more responsive to what they thought was dominant opinion in their constituencies on a number of issues.[40]

Students of Congress have not found definitive ways of measuring the impact of constituency. Instead, they have focused on making inferences about the impact of constituency—both in terms of opinion and in terms of socioeconomic and partisan categories—by examining roll call votes. There are some limits to the use of roll calls for this purpose. They can, however, provide some evidence about variations in the impact of constituency.

Constituency attitudes vary in impact from issue to issue and can be reflected in members' behavior on roll call votes in several ways. Figure 8–1 provides an overall scheme. The critical variables are the member's own attitude, the way he perceives the constituency's attitude, and his willingness to deviate from that perception in his behavior. After investigating roll call votes in three issue areas—civil rights, social welfare, and foreign involvement—Warren Miller and Donald Stokes concluded that the local constituency has a measure of control over member behavior. The pattern of constituency-representative relations varied from issue to issue: in the civil-rights issue domain the correspondence between roll call behavior and constituency attitudes

---

[39]On representational roles see Davidson, *The Role of the Congressman,* Chapter 4.
[40]Barbara Sinclair Deckard, "Political Upheaval and Congressional Voting: The Effects of the 1960s on Voting Patterns in the House of Representatives," *Journal of Politics* 38 (1976): 326–45.

**Figure 8–1.** The Linkages between Constituency Attitudes and Representatives' Roll Call Behavior

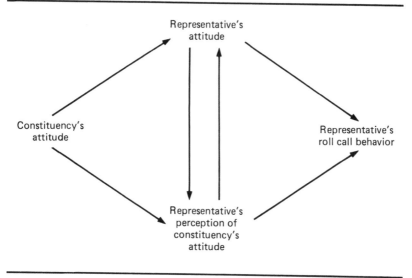

SOURCE: Warren E. Miller and Donald E. Stokes, "Constituency Influence in Congress," in Campbell and others, *Elections and the Political Order:* 361.

was greatest (and quite high), in the area of foreign affairs it was least (and quite low), and it fell in the middle in the area of social welfare.[41]

Another way to attempt to explore the impact of constituents is to sort out the groups that tended to vote for a member and to see if that member is particularly responsive to the presumed interests of those groups. An analysis using this method studied the voting of senators in 1963–64 and found that senators indeed seemed to be particularly responsive to the interests of individuals voting for them. The party affiliation of the senators was also highly important.[42]

Still another—and the most common—way to explore the impact of constituents is to aggregate their characteristics by district and then examine the difference that variations in these characteristics seem to

[41]Warren E. Miller and Donald E. Stokes, "Constituency Influence in Congress," in Angus Campbell and others, *Elections and the Political Order* (New York: Wiley, 1966). For arguments that Miller and Stokes may have understated the amount of opinion representation in Congress in their study see Robert S. Erikson, "Constituency Opinion and Congressional Behavior: A Reexamination of the Miller-Stokes Representation Data," *American Journal of Political Science* 22 (1978): 511–35; and Robert Weissberg, "Collective vs. Dyadic Representation in Congress," *American Political Science Review* 72 (1978): 535–47.

[42]Gregory B. Markus, "Electoral Coalitions and Senate Roll Call Behavior: An Ecological Analysis," *American Journal of Political Science* 18 (1974): 595–607.

make in the behavior of the members. A number of such studies have been done—always with roll call voting as the measure of member behavior. Some conflicting findings have emerged.[43] But there are also areas of agreement:

First, certain kinds of constituencies tend to elect Democratic members and others tend to elect Republican members. In general, districts represented by Democrats are poorer and more urban than districts represented by Republicans. They also have a larger proportion of non-white population. There is an important regional variation that should be noted, however: southern Republican districts are more urban than southern Democratic districts. They remain "whiter" than Democratic districts but there is virtually no difference in the percent of owner-occupied housing units.

A second conclusion of most studies is that constituency characteristics are wedded to ideological differences among congressmen. Democrats and Republicans generally differ in their views, particularly on domestic policy, with the Democrats being generally more liberal and the Republicans generally more conservative. Within the parties, however, differences between the districts represented by individuals are not always systematically predictive of which party members will be the more liberal or more conservative or more or less loyal to the party.[44] A few variables are more predictive of ideological differences than others. For example, among urban southern Democrats in the Eighty-eighth Congress the percent urban population in the district was highly correlated with party unity, support for a larger federal role, and support for President John Kennedy's programs. Among this subset of congressmen, those from the more urban districts were the more liberal, loyal Democrats. Among rural southern Democrats, the percentage of black population in the district was negatively correlated with party unity, support for a larger federal role, and support for the president's programs. The rural southern Democrat with the greatest proportion of blacks in his district tended to be the most conservative and least loyal to his party's legislative

[43]See, for example, Thomas A. Flinn and Harold L. Wolman, "Constituency and Roll Call Voting: the Case of the Southern Democratic Congressmen," *Midwest Journal of Political Science* 10 (1966): 192–99; Lewis A. Froman, *Congressmen and their Constituencies* (Chicago: Rand McNally, 1963); Julius Turner and Edward V. Schneier, Jr., *Party and Constituency: Pressures in Congress* (Baltimore: The Johns Hopkins University Press, 1970); W. Wayne Shannon, *Party, Constituency and Congressional Voting* (Baton Rouge: Louisiana State University Press, 1968); Duncan MacRae, Jr., *Dimensions of Congressional Voting* (Berkeley: University of California Press, 1958); Aage R. Clausen, *How Congressmen Decide* (New York: St. Martin's, 1973); and Fiorina, *Representatives, Roll Calls, and Constituencies.*
[44]Ripley, *Party Leaders in the House of Representatives*, 157–158, 211–212.

positions.[45] The whites in the districts with the largest number of blacks reacted to that "threat" in part with conservative politics.

When constituency characteristics are weighed against the influence of party affiliation, party generally emerges as the stronger force. One classic study specifically found party differences to be more explanatory than differences in urbanness or ethnic or racial composition of districts.[46]

A recent study presented more differentiated findings. When the impact of party and constituency were compared on five policy dimensions, constituency was found to be relatively potent on questions of international involvement and civil liberties but party was found to be more important on questions of agricultural assistance, social welfare, and government management.[47]

It may be that the "dispute" in the roll call literature between party influence and constituency influence is ultimately pointless since the type of district helps determine the party of the congressman. In most cases party influence and constituency influence as measured by aggregate constituency characteristics such as race, home-owning patterns, income, and urbanization push in the same direction. Given the four levels of constituency Fenno has found members to perceive, it is also inaccurate to talk about "constituency" as if it can be measured adequately by aggregate characteristics. Such measures may capture one meaning of constituency, but others are ignored. Constituency interests are obviously important, but the customary methods of measurement are questionable.

———

Neither interest groups nor constituents set the agenda for Congress, although they influence it. Likewise, neither of them determine policy outcomes, although they can influence them. They both help set the bounds within which Congress operates. Their presence is tangible in a variety of ways. Skillful lobbyists can achieve at least part of their aims. Constituent interests—whether explicitly articulated by constituency spokespersons or operating in the imagination of the member—find eager supporters in the House and Senate.

[45]See Flinn and Wolman for these data and a discussion of them.
[46]Turner and Schneier, *Party and Constituency.* See also Demetrios Caraley, "Congressional Politics and Urban Aid," *Political Science Quarterly* 91 (1976): 19–43, for findings that party affiliation is more important than constituency characteristics in explaining voting on urban aid measures.
[47]Clausen, *How Congressmen Decide.*

It is also quite clear that members have the latitude, if they have the will, to use interest groups and lobbyists for their own ends and to lead constituency opinion much of the time rather than just following it. To portray members as captives of interest groups or constituencies is inaccurate. Some may lean in that direction. Some lean in the other direction. But the choice is theirs.

To the extent that members pay attention to the policy preferences of interest groups and constituents, those preferences, because they are numerous and diverse, push in the direction of greater policy fragmentation rather than greater policy integration.

# 9

# Congress, the President, and the Presidency

"In a sense, no relationship between president and Congress is ever normal, for the country passes from one special pattern of association to another, each influenced by the unique personality of a president, a particular configuration of congressional leaders, and the political setting of the time."[1] The presidential-congressional relationship is

[1] James L. Sundquist, *The Decline and Resurgence of Congress* (Washington, D.C.: Brookings Institution, 1981): 483.

For a good review of the literature on the president as a legislative leader see John F. Manley, "The Presidency, Congress and National Policy-Making," in Cornelius P. Cotter (ed.), *Political Science Annual, Volume 5* (Indianapolis: Bobbs-Merrill, 1974): 227–73. For additional recent useful analyses of the congressional-presidential relationship see, in addition to the Sundquist book, George C. Edwards III, *Presidential Influence in Congress* (San Francisco: Freeman, 1980); Louis Fisher, *The Politics of Shared Power: Congress and the Executive* (Washington, D.C.: Congressional Quarterly, 1981); William S. Livingston, Lawrence C. Dodd, and Richard L. Schott (eds.), *The Presidency and the Congress* (Austin, Texas: Lyndon B. Johnson School of Public Affairs and Lyndon Baines Johnson Library, 1979); Steven A. Shull, *Presidential Policy Making: An Analysis* (Brunswick, Ohio: King's Court, 1979): Chapters 3 and 7; and Anthony King (ed.), *Both Ends of the Avenue: The Presidency, the Executive Branch, and Congress in the 1980s* (Washington, D.C.: American Enterprise Institute, 1983). For a review of the literature on legislative-executive relations in general—including the leading material on the President and Congress—see Bert A. Rockman, "Legislative-Executive Relations and Legislative Oversight," in Gerhard Loewenberg, Samuel C. Patterson, and Malcolm E. Jewell (eds.), *Handbook of Legislative Research* (Cambridge, Mass.: Harvard University Press, 1985): 519–72.

complex and constantly changing. Yet there are patterns in the relationship, there are tendencies, and there are factors that can be identified as partial causes for changes in the relationship and the legislative results that stem from those changes.

Some observers see trends and major changes in the events of the moment. In the last two decades alone there have been those who have proclaimed the seemingly permanent rise of the "imperial presidency," culminating in the Johnson and early Nixon years; the dominance of Congress and the submergence of the president, spotted in the Ford and Carter years; a new era of presidential dominance and congressional subservience, descried in the first Reagan year of 1981; and the reassertion of Congressional power in the waning Reagan years, particularly after the Iran-contra affair was revealed. Genuine cycles in American politics are not this short; nor do major changes occur overnight. Events of the day are sometimes important and they *may* be part of a longer-term trend. But an event or even a few years of events generally do not permanently alter major aspects of American political life, including the critical relationship between president and Congress.

The above caution is not expressed to diminish the interest of the reader in short-term variations related in large part to central individuals. The excesses of Johnson and, especially, Nixon were important in generating a congressional reaction. The ineptness of Carter was important in helping produce a situation in which there seemed to be no guiding core to domestic policy. The skills of Reagan and his lieutenants in 1981 were important in helping explain a series of key congressional endorsements. Some missteps in 1982 on the part of the same individuals help explain increasing congressional reluctance to go along with the administration's announced first preferences on some matters. The scandal arising in late 1986 when it was revealed that the United States had sold arms to Iran, coupled with a Democratic party that had just recaptured the Senate, produced a situation in which President Reagan was less likely to get his way in the One Hundredth Congress (1987–88). But broader questions about relationships and impacts cannot be answered only by glimpses of interesting individuals at work.

## THE PRESIDENTIAL-CONGRESSIONAL RELATIONSHIP: AN OVERVIEW

In many ways the twentieth century has been a century of presidential domination of the national government. Congress has been consistently more important than is generally recognized, but it is true that on the greatest issues facing the American people the role of Congress has seemed to pale in comparison to that of the president. However, with the growing unpopularity of the Vietnam War in the late 1960s and early 1970s and the revelations of presidential abuse of power under Nixon, the will in Congress to be more assertive was strengthened. A war powers act passed in 1973 and a budget reform act passed in 1974 were designed to give Congress more power on the major issues of war and peace and governmental impact on the economy.

At the end of the first year of the presidency of Jimmy Carter a number of members of Congress, including the leaders, expressed a great deal of satisfaction that the balance between president and Congress had been restored to a healthier level. Speaker O'Neill said, "Congress is asserting its legitimate powers. I don't think there's any question about the fact that there was an erosion of power in Congress that started in the last years of Sam Rayburn's life. That erosion has been reversed." House Majority Leader James Wright observed that measures such as the new budget process and the War Powers Act had improved the congressional position: "This was a relatively major shift back toward the direction of power-sharing. We define the stream banks through which executive power may flow."[2]

The relationship between Carter and Congress for four years was typified by a fair measure of presidential impotence, especially considering that he had large Democratic majorities in both houses with which to work. Some began to wonder if congressional aggressiveness had not gone too far and presidential weakness had not become dangerous. However, in 1981 Ronald Reagan demonstrated that the president could play the central legislative role.[3] Reagan needed lots of skill and some luck to get his way with Congress—and Congress was far from a cipher even in 1981—but the post-Watergate changes instituted by Congress had not reduced the potential of the presidency for giving legislative and policy guidance. Problems remain for any president in working with Congress, but they are not new problems created in the 1970s.

Events in 1982 further demonstrated that the advent of Ronald Reagan had not permanently altered presidential-congressional relations. In that year President Reagan and his advisers responsible for congressional relations demonstrated that the 1981 performance was unique to that year and that the tone of presidential-congressional

[2]Both quotations come from Martin Tolchin, "Power Balance Tips to Congress from President," *New York Times,* October 9, 1977.
[3]Norman J. Ornstein (ed.), *President and Congress: Assessing Reagan's First Year* (Washington, D.C.: American Enterprise Institute, 1982).

relations could change very quickly. In 1981 the Reagan performance can be characterized as follows:

- a small, highly focused agenda (reduced spending and taxes) repeatedly stressed by the president;
- a willingness on the part of the administration to compromise and to trade resources in its control for votes of individuals in the House and Senate;
- a much less convincing performance when the administration wandered away from the budget and tax focus, as it did, for example, in putting a lot on the line in preventing congressional blockage of the sale of the AWACS plane to Saudi Arabia;
- a moderately strong performance overall as measured by congressional approval of administration positions (not as strong as President Johnson in 1964 or President Eisenhower in 1953, but stronger than any other first-year performances in the last three decades—notable in part because the House remained nominally in the hands of the opposition);
- normal support from the four different congressional parties when compared to predecessors in their first year in the 1950s, 1960s, and 1970s.

But in 1982 this general (although not universal) pattern of focus and relatively high success was not repeated. By the time of the pre-election congressional recess in Autumn 1982, the Reagan performance was proceeding along the following lines:

- an expanded agenda with much less focus. Cuts in social programs remained central, but the first presidential budget was acceptable to almost no one in Congress. A much-revised proposal won support during the budget reconciliation process. The message on taxes shifted during the course of the year from one of no tax increases to one in which the administration reluctantly became identified with the Congress-led effort to increase taxes by the single largest increment in our national history. Non-fiscal matters also came onto the agenda but received only sporadic bursts of attention. The most broad-ranging was the proposal by the president to send many federal functions back to state control (with only partial funding that would diminish over time) in the name of "new federalism";
- increasingly divided Republican reaction to the president's proposals and performances;
- increasingly skeptical or hostile reaction from more and more Democrats (some of whom had simply kept quiet in 1981 and nursed private doubts);

- a liaison effort by both the president and his liaison office that seemed a good deal less polished and professional than it did in 1981;
- defeat by Congress on one veto override involving spending;
- nominal presidential support for ultra-conservative "social issue" proposals on abortion and school prayer that met defeat in the Senate;
- presidential support for a constitutional amendment requiring a balanced budget that met defeat in the House.

By late 1982, Ronald Reagan had begun to look like most of his predecessors: a person holding an office with potential for legislative leadership who could not consistently sustain a pattern of success. Normal congressional behavior means that no president is going to be recognized as *the* legislative leader on all major issues or even a majority of them for very long.

From 1983 on, the Reagan administration made no attempt to set a comprehensive agenda for congressional action. Not only was the overall focus gone, but the level of presidential activism in dealing with Congress diminished. In 1981 and 1982 the Reagan administration had set a large economic agenda for the country. Even that centerpiece was gone in 1983 and subsequent Reagan years, save for the constant theme song from the White House that federal spending on social programs must continue to be reduced. Both the president personally and the institutional presidency still became heavily engaged in struggles over specific bills. Sometimes the administration won—as it finally did in 1986 when Congress reversed its previous stance and authorized military aid to the contras seeking to oust the Sandinista government in Nicaragua. Sometimes the administration lost—as it did when Congress overrode a presidential veto of sanctions against South Africa in 1986, when the Senate refused to confirm Robert Bork for a Supreme Court vacancy in late 1987, or when the House voted against aid to the Nicaraguan contras in February 1988. In other cases, such as the major tax revision in 1986, the president and presidency played a marginal role and Congress shaped the details of the final product. In yet other cases Congress simply set its own agenda and enacted what it could agree on, with a minimum of presidential participation, except for a signature on the final product. In 1985–86 this characterized congressional action on a major immigration bill, on a variety of environmental measures such as the extension of the "superfund" program for cleaning up toxic waste dumps, and on a five-year education bill that raised the limits on federal loans and grants available to college students.

In a few areas, Congress seized the initiative only to be successfully thwarted by a presidential veto. But a few of those decisions got turned around later. For example, the Clean Water Bill, which included about $18 billion for sewage treatment, was passed unanimously in late 1986 in both houses and pocket-vetoed by President Reagan. By February 1987 Congress had already enacted the same bill over another presidential veto.

In 1981 a number of observers reached the conclusion that Reagan was an unusually effective president in dealing with Congress. In fact, his peak effectiveness was limited to that year. Even in 1982, when dealing with the same Congress that had been quite pliant the year before, the Reagan effort lost focus and effectiveness. In subsequent years conditions changed and help to explain diminished effectiveness. In 1983–84 the Democrats substantially increased their majority in the House and became bolder in dealing with Reagan. In 1987–88 the Democrats had the advantages of having recaptured the Senate majority and of dealing with a president who was both aging personally and damaged politically by the Iran-contra revelations. The 1985–86 period is the hardest to explain in that the 1984 election had produced an overwhelming re-election victory for Reagan, had increased Republican membership in the House (although still well short of a majority), and had retained Republican control of the Senate. Yet the president never put together a compelling legislative program. In fact, primarily he was opposed to any new taxes, to new legislation in the social arena, and to increased spending (or even spending at the same rate) for many programs. Historically, presidents with "negative" agendas have not appeared to be forceful legislative leaders. Reagan stood out as the first president since Calvin Coolidge to have a personal and political agenda that looked primarily negative. The media (and, through them, that part of the public that follows such matters) and Congress itself had both come to expect a number of legislative initiatives. Reagan offered mainly a "hold the line" posture on spending and taxes. His few positive ideas were very controversial, as in the case of aid to the Nicaraguan contras.

Despite experience that varies from issue to issue, year to year, and president to president, the chief executive is the single leader with the most potential for producing a legislative program. The president and Congress are not equal at some points in the policy process, particularly the development of coherent policy statements. A single individual with considerable formal power can inevitably declare a position and follow through on it more skillfully and rapidly than a multi-headed body like Congress. Adlai Stevenson III (D-Ill.), who retired from the Senate in 1980, put it bluntly: "The Congress has never been

# THE PRESIDENT WINS IN CONGRESS: CONTRA AID, 1985–1986

United States government support for opponents (contras) of the Sandinista government in Nicaragua has been a highly controversial and visible policy repeatedly debated by Congress and the president. Early in his first term, Reagan made support for the "freedom fighters" a primary component of his administration's foreign policy. Fighting communism was an issue that Reagan was deeply committed to personally. Obtaining the necessary support from Congress required continuing legislative requests and battles, marked by cutoffs, restrictions, and resumptions of assistance, narrow margins in votes of support, and overall uncertainty regarding the continuation of whatever aid was approved by Congress. The House Speaker and the president locked horns over this issue repeatedly in intensely partisan struggles.

In the early 1980s Reagan relied on the CIA and its contingency funds to pursue a policy of covert aid in support of the contras aimed at overthrowing the government in Nicaragua. In 1984 word leaked out about the CIA's role in mining Nicaraguan harbors. The CIA's role came under intense congressional scrutiny, especially from members of intelligence committees who felt outraged that they had not been consulted. The administration's policy suffered a serious setback when Congress voted a cutoff of all aid to Nicaragua. The CIA's funds ran out in May, 1984.

Reagan repeatedly undertook the public initiatives necessary to restore funding for the contras. Early in 1985, the president used his weekly radio broadcast and a news conference to increase public awareness about the plight of the resistance movement. The Senate voted narrowly with the president. The president carried on a major battle in the House to secure funding. The House voted heavily against the president in April but changed course dramatically and voted with the president in June. Several factors helped explain the change in the House. First, and most important, the president compromised on the type of assistance, sacrificing military aid and restricting his request to $27 million in nonmilitary or humanitarian aid. Second, the CIA and Defense Department were excluded from administering the aid. Third, Congress was smarting from partisan taunts and accusations from some administration officials that the Democrats were soft on communism. Fourth, the President lobbied individual members of the House personally and with great energy, targeting moderate Republicans fearful of opposing the president too frequently and southern Democrats whose constituents were fearful of a flood of refugees overwhelming their districts.

The limited aid approved in 1985 was a start from the president's point of view. But it expired in March of 1986, and the president resumed immediately the fight to get more funds and fewer restrictions. The battle in the House in 1986 was again very intense. Only on the third try was the vote favorable to the president. The House resisted two attempts in March and April to provide military aid for the contras. The votes were close, and the president voiced his "solemn determination to come back again and again until the battle is won." He was as good as his word. He asked the Speaker for permission to address the House, which was refused. The Speaker countered with an invitation to address both houses jointly, which the president refused, choosing instead to speak from the Oval Office prior to the final vote in June. The president again personally lobbied undecided members. The following day the House narrowly (221 to 209) accepted a proposal for resumed funding. Only 51 Democrats voted for the proposal, and all but 11 Republicans did. The package contained $30 million in humanitarian aid, $70 million in military aid, and $300 million in economic aid for the region. The restrictions against CIA participation were dropped.

Debate in the Senate, which had backed the president in previous years, was also intensely partisan. Consideration in August was possible only after convoluted parliamentary maneuvers that sought to extricate contra aid and sanctions against South Africa from filibuster threats. Republican leaders in the Senate worked energetically and successfully to insure that none of the Democrat-sponsored amendments aimed at killing the contra aid would pass.

The President signed the bill resuming the flow of public funds on October 24, 1986. Shortly thereafter, news about the Iran-contra scandal became public, and aid to the contras faced intensified congressional debate.

capable and never will be capable of formulating any policy sense. In its finest moments, it supports strong Presidents. It has been my misfortune to serve in the Congress for a decade in which Congress had no president to support, no one strong."[4]

Once the congressional disadvantage in initiation is acknowledged, then the president and Congress face similar kinds of tensions as they ponder how to deal with each other. Both must decide on the level of activism they will adopt as their basic legislative stance, and to what extent they will cooperate with the other branch. Some presidents and some Congresses are relatively restrained in the legislative tasks they set for themselves and in the energy they display in working toward the achievement of those tasks. Other presidents and Congresses set goals and expend much energy in the pursuit of them. And, of course, the minority parties in Congress might take very different stances from each other.

The decision about relative activism or relative restraint is much more conscious and explicit for the president than it is for Congress, simply because one person can decide something with greater clarity

[4]Quoted in *Wall Street Journal,* November 5, 1980.

than 535 people. But leaders of different Congresses also express different attitudes toward the legislative task; their statements offer a fairly accurate guide to the level of activism likely to be espoused by the Congress. For example, in the Eighty-ninth Congress (1965–1966) the leaders of the majority party made it clear that they were eager to have Congress cooperate with President Johnson in working on a very full legislative agenda. But those same leaders in the Ninetieth Congress (1967–1968) were equally clear in their position that Congress should proceed at a more deliberate pace, thus helping the government and the nation digest the new programs that had been created in the preceding Congress. Similarly, the Republican leaders were unabashedly eager to support the full presidential agenda announced by Reagan in 1981 and 1982. In subsequent Reagan years they were more selective in their support.

Leaders do not make these choices simply on the basis of whim. They assess a variety of factors in pondering the choices along the spectrum from activism to restraint. These factors include the political strength of the president, the general appeal of the issues he espouses, the political and party situation in both Congress and in the country at large, and perceptions of "objective" needs both domestically and in foreign affairs. Leaders must also make careful assessments of how their own members in Congress are likely to react to requests they make of them and pressure they put on them in working for (or against) a presidential legislative program. All of these factors are in constant flux; it is not surprising, therefore, that the same leaders in two successive years or even shorter periods of time might make different choices.

Presidential access to Congress depends on a number of variables, the most important of which are the president's view of his legislative role, his skill at implementing his vision of the role both personally and through the institutional presidency, the willingness and ability of the leaders of the president's party to transmit and obtain his legislative wishes from the committee system and the rank-and-file members on the floor, and the president's direct access to the leaders of his party, the other party, the committees, and the rank-and-file members. Presidential will, style, and institutions are all important elements affecting the outcome of the policy process, but they are balanced against a variety of congressional wills, styles, and institutions. Success is never guaranteed to a president, even when a sizable majority of his party controls both the House and Senate.

Presidents' backgrounds help explain some of the variations in personal relationships between them and the members of Congress. Lyndon Johnson, a formidable leader in the Senate before becoming president, was praised by many as an authentic genius in interacting with key members of the House and Senate so as to get desired results (until the Vietnam escalation soured his relations with Congress). His performance in 1964 and 1965 contrasts with those of his predecessor, John Kennedy, and his successor, Richard Nixon. Kennedy and Nixon had served in both the House and Senate but neither had risen to leadership positions and neither seemed to enjoy legislative life very much. Both were reluctant to deal personally with members after they became president and neither possessed a great deal of skill at it. In his last year in office Nixon's relations with most members of Congress simply ceased.

President Ford did not have the flair or reputation for leadership in Congress during his long service in the House that Johnson did during his period of Senate leadership. Nevertheless, he was a career congressman until he was nominated to be vice-president by Nixon after Spiro Agnew resigned in the autumn of 1973. He began his presidency indicating that he expected close and cordial relations with individual members of Congress even though he knew there would be policy disagreements. In his first address to Congress, just three days after becoming president following Nixon's resignation, he expressed admiration both for Congress as an institution and for the members of Congress as individuals. Given the values inculcated by twenty-five years of service in the House, Ford felt little discomfort in dealing with members of Congress, even though the majority often did not agree with his policy stances.

President Carter exhibited considerable tentativeness and lack of skill in dealing with Congress throughout his presidency. He never seemed to understand the utility of consultation, even if it were only to keep key members of Congress informed of upcoming presidential actions. He had consistent problems in setting clear priorities and in following through with actions designed to enhance the chances of success for his initiatives. He seemed addicted to policy switches without telling members beforehand. Apparently, his experience in dealing with the Georgia legislature while governor had not taught him very much about how to deal with Congress.

By contrast, Ronald Reagan seemed to have learned some lessons about dealing with legislatures through his experience in California as governor. Several members of Congress when Reagan became president in 1981 had been in the California legislature during his gubernatorial days. They testified that he had been inept in legislative relations in his first term but had learned a great deal by the second term. And those lessons were put to immediate use when he reached the White House. He quickly adopted a style that appealed to members in both congressional parties on whom he depended for legislative success. The style was based on accessibility, no surprises, and clear priorities.

In 1981 this style brought considerable rewards to the president in terms of key congressional victories, particularly on budget matters and taxes. In 1982, however, the same style served Reagan less well. In part, the focus was less clear and/or began to seem single-minded and too restrictive to many members of Congress, including some Republicans. In addition, the undoubted "good fellow" image of the president began to wear thin when coupled with seemingly incoherent and uncoordinated foreign and domestic policies. In 1983 and subsequent years his problems multiplied and much of the time he was no longer an effective legislative leader. He had spurts of effectiveness, however, as when, in 1986, he wheedled military aid for the contras out of Congress and narrowly prevented an embarrassing defeat on arms sales to Saudi Arabia. By 1987 and 1988 he appeared to be out of touch with his own administration as the Iran-contra hearings and related events revealed a president who was not quite sure what he knew about foreign-policy matters of major importance. Members of both parties in both houses were severely critical of his performance. Even in this weakened condition, however, the president and administration retained the power to keep the spotlight on their activities and away from Congress. In the summer of 1987, the reflagging of the Kuwaiti tankers, their escort by ships of the U.S. Navy, and the initiative to bring peace to Central America through an offer to end aid to the contras if the contras and Sandinistas in Nicaragua could reach a ceasefire, helped keep Congress off-balance. The administration demonstrated considerable skill in getting Democratic Speaker Jim Wright, in effect, to co-sponsor the Nicaraguan initiative.

The brief overview presented thus far of presidential performance as legislative leader over the last several decades underscores the accuracy of the quotation that opened this chapter. Presidents each have special relationships with Congress. Those relationships vary between presidents and within presidencies. The factors that help produce those variations are complicated; however, they are not random. Those focusing on presidential-congressional relations need to look at systematic variations as well as idiosyncratic variations in the relationship.

# PRESIDENTIAL TECHNIQUES FOR DEALING WITH CONGRESS

## Individual Techniques

If a president decides on an aggressive approach to Congress on legislative matters he has a number of techniques at his command.

First, he can set much of the agenda for Congress by making a series of specific proposals. Presidents have always submitted some preferences. In the last few decades the "program of the president" has emerged as the largest part of the legislative agenda for Congress, even in those cases in which Congress and the White House are controlled by different parties. Since the early 1930s presidents have routinely assumed they would submit a large program to Congress.

Presidential proposals are contained in the annual state of the union message, the annual budget message, the annual economic message, and a great variety of special messages. The use of this technique is now virtually automatic and represents the minimum effort any president is likely to make. Congress has become dependent on these messages.

Size of agenda, timing of its presentation, and clarity of priorities in it are all important in helping the president deal effectively with Congress.[5] Presidents Carter in 1977 and Reagan in 1981 present a clear contrast on these matters. Carter's agenda was always too large, his timing seemed to be almost random, and priorities never emerged with clarity.[6] One calculation was that Carter had made 43 major recommendations to Congress. These included such diverse items as the expansion of public service jobs, extending and improving benefits for Vietnam war veterans, supporting the creation of a federal strip mine law, giving preferences to American ships in transporting oil, providing federal funding for congressional campaigns, gaining ratification of the Panama Canal treaties, and creating "sunset" legislation limiting the life of federal programs. At the end of 1977 Carter himself concluded that he had "asked for too much too soon."

[5] On presidential domestic agenda-building throughout the 1960s and 1970s see Paul C. Light, *The President's Agenda: Domestic Policy Choice from Kennedy to Carter* (Baltimore: Johns Hopkins University Press, 1982).

[6] For a detailed examination of Carter's first year see Randall B. Ripley, "Carter and Congress," in Steven A. Shull and Lance T. LeLoup (eds.), *The Presidency: Studies in Policy Making* (Brunswick, Ohio: King's Court, 1979): 65–82. For a thorough assessment of the entire Carter period in terms of executive-legislative relations see Charles O. Jones, *The Trusteeship Presidency: Jimmy Carter and the United States Congress* (Baton Rouge, La.: Louisiana State University Press, 1988).

In 1981 Reagan presented a small agenda in terms of numbers of requests (although large in terms of consequences and ambition), timed its presentation skillfully, and kept hammering at his few major priorities all year without being distracted very often by other large-scale matters. His principal requests were neatly packaged in an omnibus budget bill and in a far-reaching tax bill. In his last congressional victory of 1981 (in December) on a four-year farm bill, Reagan got what he wanted because he and the administration skillfully controlled the agenda in such a way that the contents set different farm interests against each other rather than allowing them to ally and parcel out something for everyone. Under these conditions the farm interests' congressional supporters were willing to settle for much less than usual. Even the House Democratic whip, Thomas Foley (D-Wash.), a former chairman of the Agriculture Committee, was willing to support the bill as the best that could be obtained.

Second, the president can seek to garner popular support for his proposals by making public statements in support of them. Presumably, if popular support develops it will be transmitted in one way or another to the members of Congress and increase their willingness to support the proposals. All presidents make appeals to the public but vary a great deal in the frequency with which they use this method. Franklin Roosevelt, for example, sought popular support for a great variety of programs, especially through the medium of his "fireside chats" on radio. Presidents Truman and Eisenhower were considerably more restrained than Roosevelt. John Kennedy was selective in his addresses to the people, focusing on a few issues like medical care for the aged and economic policy.

Lyndon Johnson returned to a more Rooseveltian posture, speaking often and with great force on a wide variety of issues, notably aid to education and civil rights early in his presidency and in defense of his policies in Southeast Asia late in his presidency. President Nixon did not make public statements on every issue but concentrated on a few, such as Southeast Asia policy, revenue-sharing, and economy in government. In his first year in office, President Carter made a major continuing appeal to the public on his energy program. He labeled it the "moral equivalent of war" and criticized the level of profits of the oil companies in the course of seeking support for his program. In succeeding years he seemed less able to focus public attention on matters he thought important. President Reagan, in his first year, appealed almost exclusively to the public to support his initiatives to cut both domestic spending and taxes. After 1981, he made fewer public appeals on a broader range of issues and seemed to get much less response. Throughout his presidency he made a short weekly radio address on a wide variety of topics. Each Reagan presentation was countered by a broadcast by a congressional Democrat selected for expertise on the topic chosen by Reagan. Except for his strong support for aid to the contras, Reagan generally supported general themes (for example, less government regulation and less social program spending) rather than specific legislative initiatives.

Presidents can also seek to magnify their public appeal by having other respected and well-known citizens publicly endorse their views. On critical matters of foreign policy, for example, recent presidents have sought and received the public support of living ex-presidents. Business leaders, labor leaders, and other such individuals are also approached by presidents for their public support. A president often finds it particularly useful to seek endorsement for a proposal from a well-known national figure from the opposition party. Presidents Kennedy and Johnson used this technique often in trying to build support for foreign aid proposals. President Carter enlisted the support of leading Republicans, including former president Ford and former secretary of state Kissinger in working for ratification of the Panama Canal treaties.

Third, the president can take a hand in allocating projects and patronage to encourage Congress to back his proposals. The executive branch has many resources at its disposal: jobs, post offices, courthouses, dams, federal contracts, support of relatively obscure but lucrative legislative amendments, and other tangible rewards. Because of civil service laws the president's power over the dispensation of federal jobs (the "spoils system") is quite limited. But he and his departmental secretaries still have about 6,700 positions at their disposal. These include about 3,500 top jobs throughout the executive branch exempt from civil service, White House employees, ambassadors to foreign countries, federal judgeships, U.S. attorneys, U.S. marshals, and many part-time positions on commissions and boards. Even if the last category is deleted, the president is the effective appointing authority for close to 5000 highly desirable positions. The Senate must ratify many of the president's nominations for these positions. President Carter was reluctant to use his control over jobs ("patronage") to further party and policy ends. Most presidents have not been reluctant.

President Reagan, to some extent in connection with his budget preferences and to a much larger extent in connection with his tax bill in 1981, made a series of tangible promises and deals about matters important to key blocs of members. In the case of the budget bills he restored some cuts critical to some wavering Republicans. These included modest, but politically important, additional money for the Export-Import Bank, youth training programs, nutritional aid for infants and pregnant women, and counseling for Vietnam veterans. In the case of the tax bills, deals were made that added additional benefits to the tax code for specific interests important to enough members to allow them to vote for the whole package. Extra breaks for oil producers were especially helpful in getting southern Democratic support.

In commenting on the president's victory on a key vote on the budget in late June 1981 a Louisiana Democrat, John Breaux, one of 29 Democrats who supported the president to give him the victory, said, "I went with the best deal." Someone asked if that meant he had "sold" his vote. Breaux answered no, but "It can be rented." Another Democrat, a non-defector, said of the same vote: "The Democratic cloakroom had all the earmarks of a tobacco auction."[7] In close votes important to President Reagan throughout his terms of office, he continued to bargain concretely for undecided votes. Such tactics helped him to win contested judicial nominations, MX missile deployment, aid to the Nicaraguan contras, and arms sales to Saudi Arabia in the Ninety-ninth Congress (1985–86), for example.

Fourth, the president can give three kinds of personal attention to members of the House and Senate. First, he can simply talk personally with members—a highly flattering and somewhat intimidating act— to persuade them in person on the basis of argument and personal appeal. Presidential style is critical in making these contacts effective. The testimony of one Southern Democratic House member about his contrasting experiences with Presidents Carter and Reagan is telling:[8] On Reagan:

I wasn't there more than a couple of minutes, but I didn't feel rushed and I'm not quite sure how I was shown the door. A photographer shot the usual roll of pictures; the President gave me a firm, friendly handshake. He patted me on the back and told me how much he needed and appreciated my support. He said I should call if I need help on anything. And that was it.

---

[7]The Breaux quotation comes from Ward Sinclair and Peter Behr, "Horse Trading," *Washington Post,* June 27, 1981. The other quotation, from House Budget Committee Chairman James Jones (D-Okla.), is from Dale Tate with Andy Plattner, "House Ratifies Savings Plan in Stunning Reagan Victory," *Congressional Quarterly Weekly Report* (June 27, 1981): 1127–29.
[8]These two quotations come from Allen Schick, "How the Budget Was Won and Lost," paper prepared for an American Enterprise Institute conference (Jan. 7, 1982), 13.

On Carter:

> The last time I was in the Oval Office, Jimmy Carter was there, and I came with another member to discuss a bill we were working on in committee. We had hardly gotten seated and Carter started lecturing us about the problems he had with one of the sections in the bill. He knew the details better than most of us, but somehow that caused more resentment than if he had left the specifics to us.

A second type of personal attention involves consultation. President Carter suffered because he was perceived never to be interested in consulting with members of Congress whose interests were vitally affected by many of his decisions. Again, Reagan's skill stands in contrast. For example, when he pondered during December 1981 and January 1982 whether he would include a recommendation for new taxes to offset growing federal deficits he consulted with congressional proponents holding both points of view before making up his mind. However, he ignored their pro-tax advice and, after several months of deadlock, was forced to support huge tax increases, although he still resisted altering the third year of the personal tax cut enacted in 1981.

The third type of personal attention involves seemingly minor matters such as inviting members to meals at the White House, having them conspicuously present at bill signing ceremonies, calling them on the phone, writing complimentary letters that are released for publication, sending them autographed pictures, and boosting their egos in a number of other ways. President Johnson was particularly skillful in using this technique, especially in the first years of his incumbency. President Carter's White House barbecues were aimed at establishing "folksy" rapport with members of Congress.

President Reagan used such items as "Presidential cufflinks, social invitations to the White House and tickets to the Presidential box at the Kennedy Center" in his efforts to win Democratic defectors for his budget priorities.[9] He also showed little courtesies that mean a lot to members. He got off on the right foot with Ways and Means Chairman Dan Rostenkowski (D-Ill.), for example, by shifting the date of his first major policy address to Congress by one night because Rostenkowski had a previous out-of-town engagement.

Presidential snubs can also be used to put pressure on members through negative personal attention. When moderate Republican James Jeffords of Vermont protested about social spending cuts in 1981

[9]Martin Tolchin, "Reagan Used Shortcut to Slash Budget; Stockman Legislative Plan Bore Fruit," *New York Times,* June 28, 1981.

he found that a routine request for a White House tour ticket for a constituent had been rejected. "Things hit bottom when Rep. Jeffords and 11 other wavering Republicans were bundled off for an eyeball-to-eyeball session with the President. At the White House door, 11 of the 12 were ushered inside by smiling functionaries. The 12th, Jim Jeffords, was discreetly pulled aside. . . . While his colleagues trooped into the Oval Office, Mr. Jeffords was shunted to a siding . . . to talk to a lowly aide."[10]

Fifth, a president can get personally involved in the inevitable compromise and bargaining process that takes place once a presidential proposal has arrived on Capitol Hill. By making critical compromises at just the right time the president can help to insure the success of most of the initiative. Presidents Kennedy and Johnson used this technique extensively, especially in courting the support of Senate Minority Leader Everett Dirksen on matters such as civil rights, foreign aid, the nuclear test ban treaty, and support for United Nations bonds. President Carter had continuing problems because he refused to compromise. In 1982 President Reagan's aversion to compromise also became clear and caused him to get nowhere, even with his own party, with his initial proposals on the Fiscal Year 1983 budget and federal tax policy early in the year. Similar unwillingness to compromise doomed his efforts to kill the Clean Water Bill in 1987. When Reagan and his top advisors were willing to bargain, as with the major tax bill in 1986, the president could get part of what he wanted.

Sixth, a president can give direct campaign help to particularly supportive members of the House and Senate from his own party. He can help channel funds. More important, he can make personal appearances both to sway voters and at fund-raising events. He can aid supportive members of the opposition party who are seeking re-election by not working on behalf of their opponents.

Seventh, the president has the power to veto (disapprove) legislation coming to him from Congress.[11] This power is defensive, however, and is not a good basis upon which to build presidential legislative influence in a positive sense. It is most often resorted to by presidents whose party is in the minority in Congress. Before the post-Civil War

---

[10]Dennis Farney, " 'Gypsy Moths' Feel Reagan Is Up a Tree Without Their Vote," *Wall Street Journal,* October 1, 1981.

[11]For analyses of conditions under which vetoes take place see Jong R. Lee, "Presidential Vetoes from Washington to Nixon," *Journal of Politics* 37 (1975): 522–46; and David W. Rohde and Dennis M. Simon, "Presidential Vetoes and Congressional Response: A Study of Institutional Conflict," *American Journal of Political Science* 29 (1985): 399–427.

**Table 9-1.** Regular Vetoes and Overrides, 1945-1986

| PRESIDENT AND YEARS | NUMBER | NUMBER OVERRIDDEN | PERCENTAGE OVERRIDDEN |
|---|---|---|---|
| Truman, 1945-53 | 180 | 12 | 7 |
| Eisenhower, 1953-61 | 73 | 2 | 3 |
| Kennedy, 1961-63 | 12 | 0 | 0 |
| Johnson, 1963-69 | 16 | 0 | 0 |
| Nixon, 1969-1974 | 26 | 7 | 27 |
| Ford, 1974-77 | 48 | 12 | 25 |
| Carter, 1977-81 | 13 | 2 | 15 |
| Reagan, 1981-86 | 31 | 6 | 20 |

SOURCE: Roger H. Davidson and Walter J. Oleszek, *Congress and Its Members,* 2nd ed. (Washington, D.C.: Congressional Quarterly, 1985): 294, for Truman through Carter. Figures for Reagan were compiled from various Congressional Quarterly Weekly Reports.

era the power was used only sparingly. From 1789 through 1986 Congress overrode about 7 percent of all regular vetoes. Pocket vetoes (those made when Congress was out of session and so could not attempt to override) were almost as numerous as regular vetoes. Table 9-1 summarizes the experience of post-World War II presidents in using regular vetoes.

## Reagan in 1981: The Use of Multiple Techniques

Skillful presidents do not simply use one technique at a time or one technique on an issue. They mix and match a variety of techniques on anything of major importance to them. In 1981 Ronald Reagan demonstrated that he understood the dynamics of Congress both overall (for example, his framing of an agenda that had only a few items on it) and in individual struggles over major policy decisions. A good way to show the importance of the cumulative impact of a variety of techniques is to contrast a fight that was handled skillfully from the White House—that over a major tax bill that was passed in a form that adhered to the most important priorities of the administration—and one that was not handled well—that over the sale of $8.5 billion worth of arms to Saudi Arabia, most visibly five AWACS radar planes. The former issue, taxes, represented a major administration triumph and was passed easily in the Senate and by a larger majority than expected in the House. The AWACS issue, which did not require new legislation but only required that the administration keep both houses from voting against it (that is, the administration only had to win in one

# THE PRESIDENT LOSES IN CONGRESS: HIGHWAYS, 1987

In mid-March of 1987, the House and Senate voted by extremely wide margins (407 to 17, 79 to 17) to adopt HR 2: a five year, $88 billion highway construction and mass transit reauthorization bill. President Reagan objected strenuously to provisions of the bill he labelled pork barrel items: numerous special demonstration projects, increased funding for mass transit, and higher authorization levels than his administration had requested. He vetoed the bill on March 27.

The president's opposition was grounded on his instinctive personal reaction to the bill as a budget-buster rather than on the more politically sensitive advice of his aides. He told Chief of Staff Howard Baker, the former Senate minority leader: " . . . I'm going to veto that thing because it is vastly overbudget and it ought to be vetoed." Many in and out of Congress felt the president was trying to restore his image as an active manager and leader in the wake of the Iran-contra revelations and the Tower Commission's report that raised questions about his detached management style.

The issue over which he chose to go to battle could hardly have been more popular with Congress. There was real demand for highway funding since the Ninety-ninth Congress had failed to complete action on the reauthorization. HR 2 contained demonstration projects scattered among members' districts and states that would support local economies and provide jobs. The mass transit aid appealed to urban interests, while increasing the speed limit on rural interstates attracted rural votes. The prospect of passing a substitute bill if the veto stood was very dim. As Senator Bob Kasten (R-Wisc.) said: "I don't support all of the demonstration projects and the mass transit spending increases, but my highway people really need to have their funding in place."

The vote to override in the House was 350 to 73. Reagan wrote the House off as a lost cause and concentrated his efforts in the Senate. The Senate held two votes on the override. On the first vote, 65 to 35, only two Democrats voted with the president, while only thirteen Republicans voted against him. One of the two Democratic votes was that of the majority leader, Robert Byrd, who did so simply to avoid a 66 to 34 loss (67 votes were needed to override) to enable reconsideration. Byrd secured reconsideration and a second vote was scheduled. Intense pressure was directed to the fourteen senators viewed by their respective parties as defectors. The Democrats overwhelmed their one delinquent—Terry Sanford from North Carolina. He agreed to change his vote.

Meanwhile, the president and the minority leader, Robert Dole (R-Kan.), were lobbying the nonconforming Republican senators to try to get at least one of them to reverse his previous vote. The president made an extremely rare personal appearance on Capitol Hill on April 2, taking both Democrats and Republicans by surprise. Of the visit, Senator Patrick Moynihan (D-N.Y.) quipped: "We have two theories. The first is that he wouldn't be here if he didn't have an extra vote. The second theory is that if had an extra vote, he wouldn't be here." The president met with all 46 Senate Republicans and then separately with the specially targeted thirteen. He put each of them on the spot in the public meeting, asking them to defend their support of the highway bill, much like a parent admonishing willful children. The participants reported that the pressure was intense and painful. But despite the bind—many of those present had been elected with White House support—not one agreed to change his vote, either individually or collectively. Minority Leader Dole threw in the towel, and the group returned to the Senate Chamber, where the Democrats had been waiting, and the vote proceeded. The final count, 67 to 33, provided exactly the margin needed to override.

Afterward, defending the president, Senator Dole said: "we fought the good fight" but "no minds were changed." The president did "precisely the right thing . . . he came to the Hill, he pleaded his case . . . he did not make any deals." Other Republicans were less understanding. Their sense of loyalty to the president and the party was strained by anger that Reagan had chosen to provoke a needless confrontation with Congress on a issue of irresistible popularity. One anonymous Republican senator called it "an act of extraordinary political stupidity." Many observers felt Reagan simply misjudged the strength of support, or chose to ignore that support, and that he badly erred in launching a public and highly visible appeal to secure the votes to sustain the veto in the Senate.

house to be allowed to complete the sale), was won narrowly at the last minute in the Senate after the administration had suffered a drubbing in the House. The outcome was nearly disastrous for the administration; it may well have been negative in the long run in terms of calling into question a number of foreign policy issues and skills.

It is instructive to compare administration efforts on the two bills in terms of use of some of the specific techniques just discussed:

- The tax proposal was put on the Reagan agenda early in the session of Congress and it was made clear that it was the number one priority in the whole program of the president to restore the economy to health. The AWACS issue, by contrast, snuck up on the administration. It was ill-defined and most of the definition came from forces and interests outside of the White House. The administration seemed unaware of the repercussions of the issue. The administration seemed to ignore the issue until a variety of positions had been taken by those who ordinarily might be led by the administration on a matter of foreign policy.
- The president used frequent and skillful public appeals for support on the tax issue. These appeals, in fact, stimulated considerable public support that found its way into the consciousness of the senators and representatives who would have to vote on the matter. AWACS was

injected into public debate by opponents of the sale before the president made an appeal for public support. He made appeals, but it was clear they were in reaction to impending defeat, rather than because the sale was somehow central to a foreign policy strategy or vision held by the administration.

- On both efforts the administration used specific tangible chips in the trading for votes, although they felt obliged to deny they had done so in the case of AWACS because they somehow felt that foreign policy issues would be sullied by "politics as usual." The deals had the desired impact, particularly in the House on taxes and in the Senate on AWACS.

- A variety of personal attention was showered on Congress by the president in the drive for a major tax bill. The president initially adopted his basic idea for the bill from congressional Republicans, who had developed a bill in 1980 that had gone nowhere at that time. He consulted with the leaders of this group in developing his own ideas. He talked with members both just to persuade them and also to give them minor tangible personal attention. In the case of the AWACS sale the president did not consult ahead of time and used personal attention only late in the debate, apparently primarily relying on a simple appeal to members (all senators, since he gave up on the House) to support the president on a foreign policy matter mainly just because it was foreign policy and he was the president.

- The tax bill was altered in the proceedings, particularly in the House, as a way of guaranteeing passage. These compromises were significant, although the heart of the bill—a large cut in personal income taxes phased in over a three-year period—remained. In the case of AWACS there was virtually no room left for compromise because of the way in which the issue evolved. Some attempts were made along the lines of getting the Saudis to agree to American crews for the planes, joint crews, or some form of continuing American presence. They rejected such ideas. The point is, however, that negotiations with the Saudis had reached a stage that made compromise purely between president and Congress and within Congress impossible. The administration was stuck with a win-or-lose situation.

The skillful mix of techniques by the president and his lieutenants and the party leaders in Congress paid off handsomely on the tax bill. The basic "supply-side" vision of the president was put into the internal revenue code by a vote of 89 to 11 in the Senate (with only one Republican defection) and a vote of 238 to 195 in the House (with only one Republican defection and 48 Democratic defections). On AWACS the administration stumbled to a narrow victory. After losing 301 to 111 in the House—where they made virtually no effort to win—they barely got through the Senate 52 to 48. Only the switch of a number of freshmen Republicans at the last minute saved the president from a bad defeat. Even so, 12 Republicans voted against their president. These losses were offset by 11 Democrats who voted for his position.

### Reagan in 1982: A Changed Context and Presidential Stumbling

In 1982 the president's ability to move Congress in policy directions he favored appeared to disintegrate. Why?

Part of the explanation comes from the president and his advisers not working as adroitly in stroking individual members and committees and party leaders in Congress. When the president presented his Fiscal Year 1983 budget in early 1982, for example, he ignored warning signs that even most Republicans would reject it on a variety of grounds. He did not consult systematically with those around him and he did not seem to see the necessity of getting key figures in his own party in line before making the proposal public. He simply threw it on the table. It was rejected almost unanimously and was a dead issue almost from the time of its presentation to Congress.

Following this embarrassing beginning, both the president and different factions, leaders, and committees in Congress went through an elaborate process that resulted, after several months, in face-to-face, well-publicized negotiations between congressional leaders from both houses, presidential aides, and the president personally. The negotiations failed in late April after a month of intensive bargaining. A key reason for the failure, however, was that the president did not approach Congress in a bargaining spirit. Rather he was, by most accounts, willing to give very little in return for a lot of give on the part of Congress, particularly the House Democrats.

Congress continued working on a budget reconciliation plan on its own after that and finally passed it. The president claimed credit for the final version simply by endorsing one that did, in fact, pass. But this version was considerably different from his preferences announced in the winter. The bill called for an enormous increase in taxes. Key members of both parties in both houses had to convince the president to support this increase. He did and claimed credit for the resulting narrow passage of the bill. But it was, in reality, a bipartisan Congressional success in which the president participated late, although energetically, despite the fact that he shifted policy preferences drastically to do so. Simultaneously the reality of the reconciliation numbers in terms of gross spending, revenues, and deficits was open to serious question. The administration insisted the bill would result in a Fiscal Year deficit of about $100 billion. At the same time the Congressional Budget Office estimates were running at least $30 to $50 billion higher. In the midst of this kind of uncertainty it appeared that almost no one—certainly not the president—knew very definitively what he or she was doing in terms of predicting end results.

What happened? Why did a president who appeared to have some keys to influencing congressional behavior in 1981 appear to have lost or forgotten those keys in 1982? In part, of course, the president and his aides had become embroiled in a variety of issues, including major problems of foreign policy, that distracted them from giving the kind of focus to budget and tax matters in 1982 that they had given such matters in 1981. In part, perhaps, the president and his people may have been getting tired and/or sloppy. Or they may have been taking their own press clippings from 1981 too seriously and may have convinced themselves that they did not need to do the patient homework that characterized some of their principal successes in 1981.

Equally important in explaining the difference between President Reagan's performance in 1981 and 1982 were a series of contextual factors. Congress is not a static institution, nor does it sit in a static environment, nor do its members necessarily perceive the same facts the same way at any two different points in time. Above all, 1982 was an election year and members—both dissident conservative Democrats and Republicans—who could afford to believe the president's promises about the effect of adopting his budget and tax proposals in 1981 had to begin worrying about actual performance as perceived by voters. What they saw was not heartening. Especially, they saw an economy that was not only sluggish but getting worse. Unemployment rose and stayed at record post-World War II levels. In addition, at least some saw a president that seemed insensitive to the need on the part of many individual Congressional members, including conservatives, to build broad electoral coalitions. They viewed him as intent on cutting off programs in such profusion as to put the members in the position of being alienated from too many groups in society all at once. Such alienation can prove fatal on election day.

## Reagan in 1983 and Later: A Sporadic Performance

President Reagan's performance after 1982 resembled the erratic performance of that year. Never again did he and his administration regain the focus of 1981. In addition, political reality changed with the

Ninety-eighth Congress (1983–84) having a more heavily Democratic House than the Ninety-seventh Congress (1981–82). The House Democrats were searching for a way to build a record that would help win the White House in 1984 and became more united and more partisan.

Reagan won re-election overwhelmingly in 1984 but the composition of Congress changed little. The Ninety-ninth Congress (1985–86) achieved a fair amount legislatively, but in most areas the president did not play a major role. His major interventions sometimes came on relatively trivial matters such as individual judicial nominations. When the president and Congress engaged in head-on fights each won some of the time—with the president winning on Saudi arms sales, aid to the Nicaraguan contras, and the MX missile and Congress on sanctions against South Africa in 1986, for example.

In 1987 the same pattern emerged. Congress achieved a fair amount, but usually with minimal presidential leadership. Several of the most notable presidential interventions resulted in defeats. In October the Senate defeated the Reagan nomination of Judge Robert Bork to a vacant seat on the U.S. Supreme Court, 58 to 42. This was a bitter defeat for the president. His second nominee, Douglas Ginsburg, self-destructed in a few days when it was revealed he had smoked marijuana on several occasions during the period he was a law professor at Harvard University. Reagan finally found a winner in his third nominee, Judge Anthony Kennedy, who was confirmed 97 to 0 in early February 1988.

Also in early 1988 the president put a good deal of credit on the line to get congressional passage of a bill providing $36 million in aid to the Nicaraguan contras (with $3.6 million designated as "lethal" aid). The House defeated the bill 219 to 211. The Senate passed the bill (after the House defeat) 51 to 48, but that was a meaningless gesture.

## INSTITUTIONAL SUPPORT FOR PRESIDENTIAL RELATIONS WITH CONGRESS

The president is a powerful individual in dealing with Congress. But he lacks the time to pursue his congressional relations single-handedly, and the volume of work and the scope of subjects prevents him from having a personal grasp of all that is going on. Over the years, two parts of the institutional presidency—the White House congressional liaison office and the Office of Management and Budget—have become important presidential agents in seeking congressional support for the president's program.

## The White House Liaison Operation[12]

A central part of the relations between the presidency and Congress involves extensive personal contact. The liaison office in the White House is in business to provide such contact. The liaison staff spends a great deal of time communicating with members and staff members of the House and Senate. The chief of White House liaison also is supposed to coordinate a large network of department agency liaison offices scattered throughout the bureaucracy. But many of the latter proceed with considerable autonomy.

Presidents Franklin Roosevelt and Harry Truman both used assistants in the White House to deal with Congress. Under President Eisenhower the liaison staff was expanded: more individuals were added and duties were divided. Different individuals were responsible for the Senate and for various regional groupings in the House. The whole operation was overseen by a close and trusted adviser to the president, Bryce Harlow.

President Kennedy appointed Lawrence O'Brien as his chief liaison officer. O'Brien expanded and centralized the operation inherited from Harlow. His major innovation was to require the legislative liaison offices in all departments and agencies to report on Monday to O'Brien's office on their activities completed during the past week and projected for the coming week. O'Brien's staff digested these reports and briefed Kennedy before his weekly Tuesday breakfast with the Democratic leaders of the House and Senate. The president was kept personally informed, and liaison activities were coordinated. This arrangement allowed the president to give the leaders of his party the sense of helping control the flow of information to the House and Senate.

Subsequent presidents kept the essentials of the Kennedy-O'Brien operation, although, of course, the personnel changed.

At the beginning of 1973 the Nixon liaison operation underwent several changes. The liaison staff in the White House was given responsibility for dealing with interest groups as well as for dealing with Congress. This underscored formally the White House strategy of trying to orchestrate interest-group campaigns in ways favorable to its own policy ends. A greater degree of control over departmental liaison

---

[12]For good treatments of White House congressional liaison by scholars see Eric L. Davis, "Congressional Liaison: The People and the Institutions," in King (ed.), *Both Ends of the Avenue,* 59–95; Abraham Holtzman, *Legislative Liaison* (Chicago: Rand McNally, 1970); John F. Manley, "Presidential Power and White House Lobbying," *Political Science Quarterly* 93 (1978): 255–75; and Joseph A. Pika, "White House Boundary Roles: Marginal Men Amidst the Palace Guard," *Presidential Studies Quarterly* 16 (1986): 700–15.

personnel and operations was also asserted by the president and the White House liaison staff by making these individuals presidential appointees who would be supervised directly by the White House. This change was intended to increase the coordination of executive branch lobbying and counteract the centrifugal forces in the bureaucracy that sometimes set departmental objectives that differ from presidential objectives. Nixon planned to increase the frequency of his meetings with the Republican leaders of Congress. He also planned to invite the Democratic leaders for more ad hoc meetings. During early 1973 these meetings did, in fact, increase. But the breaking of the Watergate scandal in mid-1973 and the aftermath that eventually led to Nixon's resignation resulted in reduced contact during his last year in office.

President Ford was on friendlier terms with Congress personally than Nixon and also paid more attention to his White House liaison operation. The operation resumed the less hierarchical and more informal aspect of pre-Nixon days.

The Carter liaison effort got off to a very bad start, in part because no one on the staff had any experience in dealing with Congress and so made a series of blunders. The effects of the bad start lingered throughout the Carter presidency, although the operation improved over time.

The Reagan liaison office got off to a fast start in 1981, in part because it relied on experienced professionals who had worked both on the Hill and in the White House in previous years. The Reagan operation was also somewhat more informal than the Carter operation. Despite some key personnel changes the liaison office continued to function quite well during the rest of the Reagan presidency. Reagan had problems with Congress, but they were neither caused nor enhanced by a faulty liaison operation.

## The Office of Management and Budget[13]

OMB was created in 1970 as the successor to the Bureau of the Budget, which had been created in the Treasury Department in 1921 and was

[13]On various aspects of OMB functioning in relation to executive-legislative relations see Richard E. Neustadt, "President and Legislation: The Growth of Central Clearance," *American Political Science Review* 48 (1954): 641–71; Richard E. Neustadt, "Presidency and Legislation: Planning the President's Program," *American Political Science Review* 49 (1955): 980–1021; and Robert S. Gilmour, "Central Legislative Clearance: A Revised Perspective," *Public Administration Review* 31 (1971): 150–58.

moved to the newly organized Executive Office of the President in 1939. OMB plays a number of management and substantive roles for the president. In relating to Congress it is in constant contact on the details not only of the budget and appropriations bills but also on the details of a broad range of substantive legislative questions.

Any agency that wants to submit proposed legislation to Congress must first clear it with OMB. If OMB decides that the proposal of the agency is "not in accord with the program of the president" then the agency cannot formally submit its proposal, although a member of Congress in favor of the proposal may still submit it on his or her own. The White House feels free to intervene in the OMB legislative clearance process to assemble and pursue its own legislative priorities.

OMB also gets heavily involved, along with the White House and relevant agencies, in generating the ideas that eventually are packaged annually as the program of the president.

## CONSTRAINTS ON PRESIDENTIAL LEGISLATIVE ACTIVITY

Despite the power and resources he commands and despite his substantial institutional support, the president still faces a number of practical limits as he seeks to influence the course of legislation in Congress. He is limited, for example, by the complexity of the government in which he must operate. The size of the enterprise is awesome. The president presides over close to three million civilian employees, another three million people in the armed services, 13 departments, more than forty independent agencies and regulatory commissions, and an elaborate set of institutions collectively called the presidency. He also has to interact with two other elaborate sets of institutions: Congress and the judiciary. He is additionally limited by his own popularity and both past and projected future electoral strength.[14]

A president cannot be too imperious in setting forth his program. He must request and persuade; he cannot demand and command. A president and his advisers who get the reputation for being too demanding must be prepared to suffer a negative reaction. For example, President Nixon and his closest White House advisers had poor relations with Congress much of the time. Congress felt it was being

[14]See Jon R. Bond and Richard Fleisher, "The Limits of Presidential Popularity as a Source of Influence in the U.S. House," *Legislative Studies Quarterly* 5 (1980): 69–78; and Kathryn Newcomer Harmon and Marsha L. Brauen, "Joint Electoral Outcomes as Cues for Congressional Support of U.S. Presidents," *Legislative Studies Quarterly* 4 (1979): 281–99.

pushed around and/or ignored as Nixon tried to accomplish his policy goals. When the Watergate scandal broke, congressional opinion was that now Congress could and would recoup both lost prestige and power. The Watergate affair provided the opportunity for Congress to reassert itself, but such a move would have occurred even without Watergate, for many members of Congress indicated that President Nixon and the White House staff had gone too far in trying to legislate without Congress. Senate Majority Leader Mike Mansfield described the situation:

> It's my belief that before Watergate broke, the Congress was really on the ropes; that our influence was diminishing and that the influence of the men around the President was increasing.
>
> However, they pushed too far with their espousement of executive privilege, claiming it was applicable to all 2.8 million government employees; too far in the area of impoundment; too far in vetoing legislation and too far in lack of consultation with the Congress.
>
> So when the Watergate thing really broke open, I would assume it had a part in pushing ahead a movement that was already under way.

Senate Minority Leader Hugh Scott also expressed his displeasure with the way in which the White House had consulted with him and other members of the Republican leadership in Congress. "They never invite me for the take-offs, but they damned well want me there for the crash landings."

Still another Republican senator, one thought of as a supporter of Nixon programs, complained that top White House staff members such as John Ehrlichman and H. R. Haldeman "had the attitude that Congress was more fun and games than reality. So when Watergate broke, there was less room for maneuver by the White House because of the alienation process which had preceded it."[15]

The Watergate scandal and related problems of the Nixon administration made members of Congress more aware of a desire to limit the presidency. But the basic fact of the president being in a position of asking rather than commanding has always been true. Had Watergate not intervened, the congressional reaction to Nixon's presidential style would not have been as extreme and he probably could have achieved some of the centralization and some of the subordination of Congress he desired. But Watergate underscored limits already present, and

---

[15]The quotations from Mansfield, Scott, and the unnamed Republican senator come from Andrew J. Glass, "Congress Report/Watergate Diminishes Nixon's Leverage, Forces Series of Legislative Compromises," *National Journal* (July 21, 1973): 1049–56.

transformed some of them from potential to actual. The practical limits on the presidency grew because of Watergate, but they were not invented at that time. What was, perhaps, "invented" because of Watergate was a willingness on the part of liberal Democratic intellectuals to criticize the power of the presidency in principle—a criticism rarely made by them for the preceding forty years. From the congressional point of view, the presidency had become bloated and arrogant under Nixon. Several moves were made to add language to legislation reducing the White House and Office of Management and Budget expenditures, staff sizes, and number of high-paying jobs. None of these measures became law but one of the first things President Ford did upon assuming office was to make some changes in these two staffs that went a long way toward meeting congressional criticism. Had the Nixon administration somehow managed to finish its term, such restrictions might well have been put into statutory form.

President Carter began his term in 1977 as an "outsider" to Washington. He had, in fact, made a virtue of his status in the campaign in 1976. In his first year in office many members of Congress saw him as aloof and self-righteous in making legislative "demands." Carter never did find the key to persuading Congress. He was alternately blamed for being aloof and inflexible and for being too "folksy" and ready to compromise too quickly. One of the most annoying habits of Carter, especially to members of his own party in the House and Senate, was that he announced some of his "compromises" unilaterally without really engaging in bargaining or informing the interested members of Congress of what he was about to announce.

Ronald Reagan showed early in his presidency in 1981 that he understood both the need to stroke congressional egos and the value of private discussions before public announcements. He did not always adhere to the most fruitful practices after 1981 but he did not engage in behavior that members of Congress characterized as imperious. Some members of his administration were much less skilled in congressional relations, however. Members revealed some of their frustrations with presidential subordinates during their investigations into the Iranian arms scandal in 1986 and 1987. Members of both parties expressed dismay with the anti-congressional imperiousness of some key Reagan aides.

The president and the institutional presidency are virtually excluded from many policy areas because of the close-knit relationships within numerous low-profile subgovernments. The more routinized a policy area becomes, the less the possibility that the president will have much impact on it. Less routine matters generally break out of

# CONGRESSMAN LEE HAMILTON REFLECTS ON THE 1987 IRAN-CONTRA HEARINGS

There was too much secrecy and deception in government. Information was withheld from the Congress, other officials, friends and allies, and the American people. Information provided was misleading and evasive. Critical decisions were taken by a handful of people. The Congress and responsible officials, even the President, were cut out of the process.

There was too little regard for the rule of law. False statements to the Congress are violations of law, as the Attorney General reminded us. Key decisions were made and carried out without written legal analysis, and without written notice to Congress as the law requires. . . .

These hearings have been about how the United States governs itself, and particularly how it runs its foreign policy. For this inquiry, the key question now is how we make our system of government work better.

The conduct of foreign policy in our democracy is difficult, because the Constitution gives important powers to the President and the Congress. The scholar Edward Corwin said the Constitution "is an invitation to struggle for the privilege of directing American foreign policy."

The Congress is a check on the Executive, but also a partner; the Congress is sometimes a critic, yet its support is essential if our policies are to succeed; the Congress sometimes has divisive foreign policy debates, but when debate ends, the country needs decisiveness and unity.

Some believe that a decision-making process that calls for shared powers and public debate just will not work in a dangerous world. They argue that sometimes bypassing normal checks and balances, through procedural shortcuts and secrecy, are necessary to protect our freedoms. They argue that the President and those who work for him, must be given near-total power. Their views have been stated here with great force and eloquence.

But these hearings make another point: Shortcuts in the democratic process and excessive secrecy in the conduct of government are a sure road to policy failure. These hearings show us that policies formed under democratic scrutiny are better and wiser than policies formed without it. . . .

[T]he President and the Congress need to exhibit a greater sensitivity to their respective roles. The President is the preeminent foreign policy-maker. Only he can make the hard decisions. The buck does not stop anywhere else. The President's decisions must be clean and crisp. Otherwise, as we have seen in these hearings, confusion follows and those who work for him cannot carry out his policies successfully. The President must understand that our system works better if he engages in consultation before, not after, policy has been formulated.

The Congress also needs to get its house in order. It must strengthen its ability to protect secrets. It must show a willingness to engage in consultation. It must avoid interference in day-to-day policy implementation.

And it must take its share of responsibility for shared decisions on tough issues. The Congress must strike a balance between responsible criticism and necessary cooperation with the President. . . .

A deep respect for the shared powers of the Congress and the President is the predicate for making the Constitution work. President John Adams said, "A legislative, an executive and a judicial power comprehend the whole of what is meant and understood by government. It is by balancing each of these powers against the other two, that the efforts in human nature towards tyranny can alone be checked and re-strained, and any degree of freedom preserved in the Constitution."

The separation of powers produces a healthy and creative tension. We believe—and these hearings teach us again—that through the process of open and democratic debate, better and stronger policies emerge. The democratic process is often time-consuming and frustrating. It is never tidy and precise. But we believe there is no better way; the alternatives are unacceptable.

The Constitution and the rule of law work if we understand them, and if those in public life practice prudence, discretion and honesty.

---

As the public hearings by House and Senate committees on the sales of arms to Iran and diversion of the proceeds to the Nicaraguan contras ended on August 3, 1987, the chairperson of the special House committee, Lee H. Hamilton (D–Ind.), made the above comments.

---

these subgovernments and a wider range of participants becomes involved. Only then is there much opportunity for presidential access and leverage. But any president is likely to have minimal impact on such items as allocation of sugar quotas to foreign nations, the details of defense procurement, or the interpretation and application of patent policy.

Policies and programs tend to change very slowly and by small increments or decrements. In the very complex world of American public policy, both the necessity for compromise among many actors and the technical nature of many policies make marginal change from an existing situation the most likely (but not an inevitable) outcome of any policy debate. The incremental nature of policy change means that under normal conditions the president cannot hope to alter dramatically a large number of policies simultaneously and quickly. He usually must choose to stress only a few areas and, even then, efforts to achieve dramatic change will meet with resistance. Of course, innovative congressmen meet this same resistance when they attempt to initiate substantial policy change.

In 1981 Reagan got credit for making dramatic shifts in American public policy. There is limited truth in this portrayal of what he achieved. He led the way in reducing the spending growth rate (and in some cases actual spending) for a variety of social programs and increasing the growth rate for defense spending. The tax cut on which he insisted was very large and based on theories of the economy not tried for many decades. But, in fact, total federal spending kept growing and the deficit grew at a greatly accelerated rate. Reagan had unquestionably charted some new directions in 1981, ones that were partially unfamiliar in the post-1933 era. But much that was familiar also remained largely in place in the federal policy and program cupboard. As his presidency wore on, both Reagan and Congress became obsessed with efforts to control deficits. But they usually had profound disagreements on how to do it.

## THE CRITICAL ROLE OF THE MAJORITY PARTY

The relationship between the presidency and party leaders in Congress is critical in helping determine the policy-making role of Congress at any given time. Inevitably, the majority party is the most important. Even if the majority party suffers from internal dissension, it still has the potential for dominating congressional performance. And although the leaders cannot dictate outcomes in Congress, they play a mediating role between the presidency and the rank-and-file members of Congress and, occasionally, the standing committees and subcommittees, thus setting the tone for congressional response to presidential wishes.[16]

The importance of the majority party leader-presidential relationship was underscored in 1977 by the relations between President Carter and Speaker O'Neill and Senate Majority Leader Byrd. The Carter-O'Neill relationship developed into a close one, and the Speaker helped initiate the president into the most productive ways of doing business with the House, often running interference for him and preventing mistakes on his part. In June, 1977, Carter autographed a picture of himself for O'Neill: "To my friend Tip O'Neill— thanks for another lesson in good politics." The relationship between the two led to successes in getting the president's energy program through the House nearly intact, in reaching an agreeable compromise

---

[16]See James L. Sundquist, "Congress and the President: Enemies or Partners," in Henry Owen and Charles L. Schultze (eds.), *Setting National Priorities: The Next Ten Years* (Washington: Brookings, 1976): 583–618.

with the House over water projects (proving that presidents can at least make a dent in pork barrels), and in reaching a mutually agreeable compromise over the level of funding for the Department of Health, Education, and Welfare, and the Department of Labor (a compromise that avoided what would have been a politically destructive veto and override attempt in which the Democrats could only have looked bad no matter what happened).[17]

By contrast, Carter did not have such a relationship with Robert Byrd in the Senate. As his first year wore on he took his legislative lumps in that chamber without the wise counsel and reliable support of the key figure in it. The lack of a close, supportive relationship helps explain why the Senate proceeded to gut the president's energy program, with the president apparently helpless and the majority leader showing little leadership.

In the remaining years of the Carter presidency the relationship with Byrd remained cool and the relationship with O'Neill deteriorated. Carter's failure to enlist the loyal support of these two leaders accounted in part for the mediocre record Carter had in getting what he wanted from Congress.

In 1981 the Senate was, in many ways, the key to Ronald Reagan's ability to win the few big fights he defined for himself on the Hill. It had gone Republican in the election of 1980 for the first time since 1953–54. More important, Howard Baker (R-Tenn.), the majority leader, became a close and skillful ally of Reagan's and could deliver the Senate with ease on virtually any matter (only AWACS was close and that was not Baker's fault—in fact, he helped save the day by his own private appeals, especially to freshmen Republican senators). Baker welded a strong partisan majority and abandoned much pretense of bipartisanship. With the Senate solidly pro-Reagan in 1981 this left the administration free to concentrate on the House, where the problem was stickier. Relationships with the leader of the nominal majority (Democratic Speaker O'Neill) were not particularly productive. But Robert Michel, the Republican floor leader, showed considerable skill in keeping the Republican minority almost unanimous on the big issues about which the president cared. This meant that the number of "Boll Weevils" and other dissenting Democrats that had to be won over in order to carry the day in the House turned out to be within the realm of possibility time after time. The nominal Demo-

---

[17]For a good story on the Carter-O'Neill Relationship in 1977 see Martin Tolchin "An Old Pol Takes on the New President," *New York Times Magazine,* July 24, 1977.

cratic majority was around 50. If the Republicans held solid, 25 to 30 Democratic defections were enough to secure Reagan victories.

After 1983, Reagan became less able to win in the House. The 1982 elections had produced more Democrats. In addition, some Democrats who had been dubious about the political wisdom of opposing the very popular Reagan in 1981 and even 1982 became more self-confident in taking positions that differed from his. Even the overwhelming Reagan re-election victory in 1984 did not produce many more House Republicans. Nor did that victory serve to intimidate Democrats. By 1987–88 Reagan had an uphill fight in Congress, now controlled completely by Democrats. Throughout the period from 1983 on, Reagan had good relations with the leaders of his party, but he never developed close working relations with the Democratic congressional leaders.

## PRESIDENTIAL IMPACT ON CONGRESSIONAL POLICY-MAKING: AN ASSESSMENT

A number of aggregate measures have been used to examine variations in the magnitude of presidential impact on congressional policy-making.[18] One of these, which was devised and used by *Congressional Quarterly* from 1954 through 1975, is simply the percentage of presidential requests passed by Congress. This measure is, of course, approximate. Many presidential requests may be passed in form but altered dramatically in substance by the congressional amending process. Even more important, the percentage of requests granted does not take account of the extent of those requests or their content or whether they represent intelligent responses to national needs. *Congressional Quarterly* was dubious enough about the measure that it abandoned it after 1975.

The only years in which a president was able to get more than 50 percent of his proposals enacted were in 1954, when Eisenhower still had a Congress controlled by his party and in four of the five years that Lyndon Johnson was president. Eisenhower, Kennedy, and Johnson all suffered declines in their ability to get what they wanted as their terms wore on. Nixon did not have any notable success with the Democratic Congress he faced; 1971 represented the least success of any president in the period.

[18]See Steven A. Shull, "Assessing Measures of Presidential-Congressional Policy Formation," *Presidential Studies Quarterly* II (1981): 151–57.

Presidential impact on congressional policy behavior can also be analyzed in terms of congressional voting support for the president and shifts in favor of the president's proposals. There is considerable evidence that many members of Congress will support the foreign policy initiatives of the president if they share the same party label even though they might well oppose those same initiatives if the president belonged to the other party. For example, a number of Democrats inclined to be skeptical of such programs as foreign aid under Republican presidents supported such programs under Democratic presidents. Likewise, a substantial number of Republicans inclined to oppose such programs as foreign aid under Democratic presidents supported them under Republican presidents.[19] On the other hand, the president does not seem to have this same kind of pull on domestic issues.[20] There is also evidence that support for presidential proposals increases as individual members of Congress perceive his popularity to be strong among their electoral supporters.[21]

Another measure, also developed by *Congressional Quarterly,* is the success rate of the president on votes on the House and Senate floor on which he has taken a clear position. Figure 9-1 summarizes this success measure from 1953 through 1987.

With the exception of Kennedy, presidents won fewer votes as their terms wore on. The declines were considerable in the cases of Eisenhower, Johnson, Nixon, Ford, and Reagan and quite slight in the case of Carter. The highest rate of success on House and Senate votes for any president came in 1965 when Lyndon Johnson won 93 percent of all votes on which he took a position. The low points came near the end of the terms of Eisenhower (52 percent in 1959), Nixon (51 percent in 1973), Ford (54 percent in 1976), and Reagan (44 percent in 1987). Carter's record is quite consistent and about average, although considering he had a Congress of his own party his record is not strong compared to the opening years of Eisenhower (who had a narrowly Republican Congress), Kennedy and Johnson (both of whom had Democratically controlled Congresses), or Reagan (who had a Republican Senate but still had a Democratic House with which to contend).

---

[19]See Aage R. Clausen, *How Congressmen Decide* (New York: St. Martin's, 1973); and Mark Kesselman, "Presidential Leadership in Congress on Foreign Policy," *Midwest Journal of Political Science* 5 (1961): 284–89, and "Presidential Leadership in Congress on Foreign Policy: A Replication of A Hypothesis," *Midwest Journal of Political Science* 9 (1965): 401–6.
[20]Clausen, *How Congressmen Decide:* Chapter 8.
[21]George C. Edwards, III, "Presidential Influence in the House: Presidential Prestige as a Source of Presidential Power," *American Political Science Review* 70 (1976): 101–13; and Douglas Rivers and Nancy L. Rose, "Passing the President's Program: Public Opinion and Presidential Influence in Congress," *American Journal of Political Science* 29 (1985): 183–96.

**Figure 9–1.** Presidential Success on Votes in Congress, 1953–1987

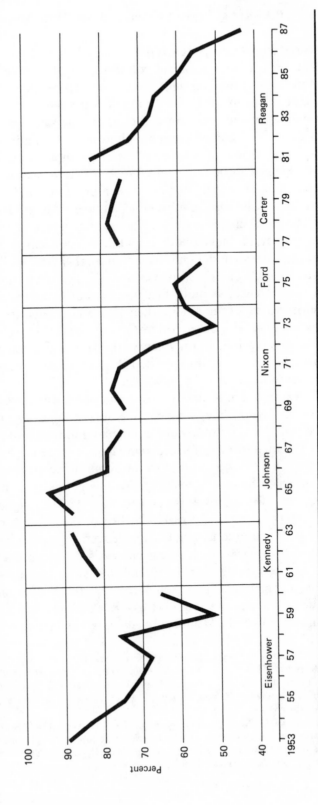

SOURCE: *Congressional Quarterly Weekly Report* (January 16, 1988): 95.
NOTE: 1974 is a composite of separate scores for Nixon and Ford. The separate scores were almost identical.

Naturally, the higher scores all tended to come in years in which the presidency and Congress were controlled by the same party and the lower scores tended to come in years in which there was a split government, although both Eisenhower and Nixon had some good years when confronted with a Democratic Congress. Eisenhower in 1955 and 1958 and Nixon in 1970 and 1971 all equaled or surpassed Johnson in 1968 and Carter in 1980—two low points for presidents in dealing with a Congress controlled by their own party. Reagan's start in 1981 was quite strong—surpassed only by Eisenhower's first two years and Johnson's first two years. But his support declined steadily over his first seven years.

Table 9-2 summarizes support for individual presidents from each of the four congressional parties—their own party in each house and the opposition party in each house.

These aggregate, quantitative measures of success and support only give us some general hints about the impact of presidents on Congress.

**Table 9–2.** Support by Congressional Parties for President's Position on Roll Call Votes, 1954–1987

| PARTY PRESIDENT, (YEARS)[a] | HOUSE | | SENATE | |
| | PARTY OF PRESIDENT | OPPOSITION | PARTY OF PRESIDENT | OPPOSITION |
| --- | --- | --- | --- | --- |
| Eisenhower, R (1954–60) | 68 | 54 | 80 | 52 |
| Kennedy, D (1961–63) | 83 | 41 | 75 | 47 |
| Johnson, D (1964–68) | 81 | 49 | 71 | 56 |
| Nixon, R (1969–74) | 73 | 53 | 73 | 50 |
| Ford, R (1974–76) | 65 | 41 | 72 | 48 |
| Carter, D (1977–80) | 69 | 42 | 74 | 52 |
| Reagan, R (1981–87) | 69 | 34 | 78 | 43 |

[a]Eisenhower was, of course, president beginning in 1953, but data were calculated for his presidency only beginning in 1954.

SOURCE: Calculated from raw data in Norman J. Ornstein and others, *Vital Statistics on Congress, 1987–1988* (Washington, D.C.: Congressional Quarterly, 1987): 206–207, for 1954 through 1986; and in *Congressional Quarterly Weekly Report* (January 16, 1988): 94 for 1987 and for correcting one figure for 1986.

*Note that entries on the table are percentages that indicate the number of congressional votes supporting the president divided by the total number of votes on which the president took a position. The effect of absences are eliminated. The yearly scores for presidents are averaged to produce a single figure for the years of each presidency.*

An important substantive impact of the president is his contribution to the content of legislation. He sets the bulk of the legislative agenda for Congress with his various annual and special messages. Even before specific actions are taken the president, in effect, decides much of what is and is not most important for Congress to consider.[22]

The agenda-setting power, however, does not necessarily diminish the important substantive contributions Congress can make to legislation. Congress and its leaders can still be creative in approving, amending, and criticizing the proposals of even a very active president. And some congressional initiation, even though difficult, is not impossible. An empirical study of the relative substantive inputs of president and Congress to a broad range of legislation concluded that the congressional contribution was very large.[23]

─────

As indicated in Chapter 1, the image of a fixed sum of "power" or "influence" for which the Congress and president compete is misleading. This implies that both cannot be "strong" or "weak" together, whereas in fact they can. It also implies that there are no other competitors for legislative influence, whereas there are—especially the bureaucracy and interest groups.

The president has become a more visible policy-maker in this century. Congress has in many ways become more important simultaneously, simply because the range of matters with which the federal government deals has increased both in scope and in importance. The "seesaw" image of relative influence is false. Experience in this century suggests that active, influential legislative leaders in Congress can co-exist successfully with an active, influential legislative leader in the White House. Legislative creativity may be present simultaneously within both the White House and the Capitol.

The president is one of the primary forces working on Congress that can help bring some integration to congressional policy deliberations. However, he can only achieve a limited amount in pushing in the direction of integration. The forces of fragmentation are strong. Presidents are under severe constraints as they deal with Congress. This

[22]On the control of the agenda by President Reagan in his first two years see Barbara Sinclair, "Agenda Control and Policy Success: Ronald Reagan and the 97th House," *Legislative Studies Quarterly* 10 (1985): 291–314.
[23]Ronald C. Moe and Steven C. Teel, "Congress as Policy-Maker: A Necessary Reappraisal," *Political Science Quarterly* 85 (1970): 443–70.

chapter has portrayed the most important of these constraints. Above all, it should be reiterated that a great deal of public policy is not subject to much presidential influence or even to much congressional influence above the committee or subcommittee level. Subgovernments make policy in many substantive areas regardless of the policy positions or activities of the president or the congressional leaders.

# 10

Congress and the
Bureaucracy

Among modern nations a large bureaucracy is an important feature
of the central government. The United States is no exception. There
are almost three million civilian employees and over two million
uniformed military personnel directing and operating programs cost-
ing over $1 trillion a year and affecting the lives of all citizens in many
ways. Just as individual citizens have had to accommodate to the
reality of such a bureaucracy, so has Congress. The basic congressional response to the fact of a large, expert bureaucracy administering
hundreds of programs has been to seek influence by cooperating with
the bureaucracy most of the time and challenging it only now and
then. Congress might well be overwhelmed in a situation of perpetual
conflict. Conflict occurs, but cooperation is a more common characteristic. In the recesses of the thousands of relationships between the
congressional members and their staff and the bureaucrats a great deal
of American public policy is decided.

So much emphasis is usually placed on presidential-congressional
relations that the role of the bureaucracy is often shortchanged, both
in journalistic accounts of the workings of American government and

in more analytic treatments. But the bureaucracy is, in fact, at the heart of what American government can and does achieve. It limits both the president and Congress and is, at the same time, limited (although not always directed) by them.

## CONGRESS, THE BUREAUCRACY, AND SUBGOVERNMENTS

A large proportion of the interaction between Congress and the bureaucracy represents the ongoing activities of subgovernments: clusters of individuals with shared policy interests and easy access to each other who make most routine policy decisions. Subgovernments dominate distributive policy decisions, whether domestic or involving foreign policy and national defense issues. They also dominate competitive regulatory policy. They play a moderately important role in protective regulatory policy and are at least sporadically important in framing policy in redistributive areas. Given that there is also a natural tendency for all domestic issues and even many foreign policy and defense issues to be defined or redefined as distributive if possible, the importance of subgovernments is enhanced even more.[1]

The basic institutional units in typical subgovernment interactions are standing subcommittees from the House and Senate and various executive branch units below the departmental level such as bureaus, agencies, services, and administrations. Much of the detailed business of the government is carried on between these units, often with the participation of interest group representatives. Larger units such as the entire House or Senate, the White House, or the office of a departmental secretary get involved in details much less frequently. In general, only highly visible and politically sensitive issues are likely to receive attention from the larger units. Relatively less visible matters are often handled completely by a bureau speaking for the entire executive branch and a subcommittee speaking for the entire House and Senate. Individual members of the House and Senate and their staff members also get involved with the bureaucracy, usually because of a pending "case" involving a constituent.

[1]For considerable empirical evidence supporting the generalizations in this paragraph, see Randall B. Ripley and Grace A. Franklin, *Congress, the Bureaucracy, and Public Policy,* 4th ed., (Chicago: Dorsey, 1987). For an argument that "issue networks" for "expanding national policies" also exist and constitute an "overlay" for subgovernments see Hugh Heclo, "Issue Networks and the Executive Establishment," in Anthony King (ed.), *The New American Political System* (Washington, D.C.: American Enterprise Institute, 1978): Chapter 3.

Not only do subgovernments exist in fact, but most individuals both in Congress and in the bureaucracy believe that they should exist. They also generally believe that a high degree of interest-group access to both Congress and the bureaucracy is appropriate. The belief system of the individuals who make policy sustains the legitimacy and predominance of subgovernments.[2]

A classic case of a subgovernment is described by Douglass Cater:

> . . . consider the tight little subgovernment which rules the nation's sugar economy. Since the early 1930's, this agricultural commodity has been subjected to a cartel arrangement sponsored by the government. By specific prescription, the sugar market is divided to the last spoonful. . . .
>
> Political power within the sugar subgovernment is largely vested in the chairman of the House Agricultural Committee who works out the schedule of quotas. It is shared by a veteran civil servant, the Director of the Sugar Division in the U.S. Department of Agriculture, who provides the necessary "expert" advice for such a complex marketing arrangement. Further advice is provided by Washington representatives of the . . . producers.[3]

Richard Neustadt adds the necessary caveat that this system of subgovernments does not cover areas in which there are "jurisdictional entanglements" and "mingled programs" involving several agencies in the bureaucracy. In these areas congressional participation may be much more sporadic.[4]

The occasions for contact between Congress and the bureaucracy are many. The principal formal point of contact involves subcommittee or committee appropriations hearings that are, in most cases, held annually for agencies and programs. These hearings are taken very

---

[2]For important and creative work that provides the evidence for the statements in this paragraph see Joel D. Aberbach and Bert A. Rockman, "The Overlapping Worlds of American Federal Executives and Congressmen," *British Journal of Political Science* 7 (1977): 23–47; and Aberbach and Rockman, "Bureaucrats and Clientele Groups: A View from Capitol Hill," *American Journal of Political Science* 22 (1978): 818–32.

[3]Douglass Cater, *Power in Washington* (New York: Random House, 1964): 17–18. For a discussion of subgovernments and ways in which their influence might be reduced, see Roger H. Davidson, "Breaking up Those 'Cozy Triangles': An Impossible Dream?" in Susan Welch and John G. Peters (eds.), *Legislative Reform and Public Policy* (New York: Praeger, 1977): 30–53. On the nature of relations between Congress and the bureaucracy also see Morris P. Fiorina, *Congress: Keystone of the Washington Establishment* (New Haven: Yale University Press, 1977) and Fiorina, "Congressional Control of the Bureaucracy: A Mismatch of Incentives and Capabilities," in Lawrence C. Dodd and Bruce I. Oppenheimer (eds.), *Congress Reconsidered* (Washington, D.C.: Congressional Quarterly, 1981): Chapter 15.

[4]Richard E. Neustadt, "Politicians and Bureaucrats," in David B. Truman (ed.), *The Congress and America's Future* (Englewood Cliffs, N.J.: Prentice-Hall, 1965): 108.

seriously both in Congress and in the bureaucracy. Considerable preparation for them goes on in both institutions. Authorization hearings for executive programs are usually less frequent than appropriations hearings, but they are also regarded by participants as very important. In addition to the hearings there are also numerous year-round contacts in the form of lunches, phone calls, and personal visits between personnel from the agencies and members and staff members in the House and Senate.

One relatively recent development affecting contact between Congress and the bureaucracy has been the proliferation of formal liaison units throughout the executive branch.[5] A few agencies had legislative liaison units in the 1920s and 1930s. But the White House and most of the executive departments did not begin developing formal liaison apparatus until after World War II. White House liaison became a "big-time" operation during the Eisenhower presidency. Every department had a formal liaison staff early in the Kennedy administration. By fiscal 1963 the ten departments then in existence employed 500 liaison employees, almost half of them in the Defense Department. No department employed fewer than 13. The independent agencies (those not in a departmental hierarchy) employed an additional 233 liaison employees.[6]

By 1978 it was estimated that the executive branch employed about 1,000 lobbyists and paid them about $24 million to undertake the presentation of agency cases to Congress. In 1981 comparable figures for only the largest federal agencies showed a total of about 1,000 people and total liaison budgets of about $35 million. The largest were the Department of Defense with 211 staff and a budget of about $7.5 million, and the Department of Health and Human Services, with 178 staff members and a budget of almost $7 million.[7] These lobbyists used to be able to concentrate on a few committee and party leaders in making their cases. The growing fragmentation and dispersion of power in both houses made their task more complex. As the chief lobbyist for the Department of Transportation put it in 1978: "Ten years ago if you wanted a highway bill, you went to see [former House Public Works Committee chairman John A.] Blatnik [D-Minn.], the

[5]On this topic in general see Abraham Holtzman, *Legislative Liaison* (New York: Rand McNally, 1970).

[6]G. Russell Pipe, "Congressional Liaison: The Executive Branch Consolidates Its Relations with Congress," *Public Administration Review* 26 (1966): 17.

[7]Shirley Elder, "The Cabinet's Ambassadors to Capitol Hill," *National Journal* (July 29, 1978): 1196–1200. The quotation in the text from the Department of Transportation lobbyist is from the same source. For 1981 figures see *The Washington Post*, June 24, 1982.

speaker, and the chairman of the Rules Committee. There would be a small collegial discussion—and all the political decisions would be made. Now there's no one person to see. . . . You have to deal with everybody."

Liaison efforts at the subdepartmental (agency or bureau) level have also grown. Some departments, such as Health and Human Services, have formal liaison units for each of their principal administrative subdivisions. Sub-departmental units in other departments may not have a formal liaison staff but some of their officials will, in fact, spend time engaged in liaison activities.

## RESOURCES FOR INTERACTION

Members of Congress and the bureaucracy each possess resources the other values. When relations are smooth, a continuous trading of these resources goes on. When disagreements arise, withholding or punitive use of resources can occur. Typically, the advantages of smooth relations far outweigh any advantages to be gained in conflict. The incentives to strive for smooth relations are, therefore, great.

### Congressional Resources

In most instances Congress determines whether a program will live or die. A few small programs can be established by executive order of the president if there is vague statutory authority from some time in the past. But most programs require explicit congressional authorization and virtually all programs—certainly those of any size or permanence—require congressional action in terms of appropriations. Not only can Congress say either yes or no to a program at the time of its establishment, it also holds the power of life or death throughout the existence of any program. Inertia is powerful, of course; once a program is established it is not lightly terminated by Congress. But the power to terminate, either by refusal to renew authorization or the refusal to appropriate funds, is firmly lodged in Congress and nowhere else.

The allocation of money to all federal agencies, usually through the appropriations process, but also through the creation of trust funds and methods of funding other than appropriations, is controlled by Congress. The control of money is the single most important resource Congress has in its dealings with the bureaucracy.

Congress can also, both by statute and by informal means, help shape the content of programs administered by the bureaucracy. Specific actions can be prohibited; others can be encouraged. In recent years Congress has been aggressive in seeking new ways of assuring itself of this continued power even in the face of proliferation of executive agencies and personnel.[8] Two means have been particularly effective—the requirement in many cases that programs be authorized annually (virtually all programs also receive annual appropriations) and the requirement for a number of programs that formal committee agreement be solicited and received before specific actions can be taken by the bureaucracy (this is the so-called "legislative veto" or "committee clearance"). The requirement for annual authorizations means that some agencies and programs are subject to four separate congressional reviews each year—those by the relevant House and Senate authorizing committees and those by the relevant House and Senate appropriations subcommittees.

As the legislative veto developed, beginning in the 1930s, it came to take a number of forms. Most included one of four basic requirements.

1. That an agency report proposed administrative actions in advance to a committee.
2. That an agency "come into agreement" with a committee before a given action is undertaken.
3. That an executive proposal lie before Congress for a fixed period of time before it can be implemented. If Congress, or part of it, (the provisions can vary) disapproves of the specific proposal, then the executive is prevented from going forward with its plans. A variation of this requirement does not provide for explicit congressional disapproval, but rather assumes that, if Congress does not like a particular executive proposal, positive action will be taken to circumvent it rather than vetoing it. This technique is used, for example, in relation to the closing of military facilities.
4. That Congress or some part of it (provisions vary) must give positive approval before the executive can proceed with a planned action.

In June 1983 the U.S. Supreme Court ruled unconstitutional a one-house legislative veto involving immigration decisions by the Attorney General. The House had vetoed a decision by the Immigration and Naturalization Service suspending the deportation of a Kenyan student of Indian descent who had overstayed his student visa. The student (Jagdish Chadha) filed suit to challenge the constitutional

[8]Neustadt, "Politicians and Bureaucrats," 105-6.

power of Congress to overrule an administrative agency in this way. The Supreme Court sided with Chadha when the case reached them. In addition, the Court affirmed two lower court decisions invalidating another one-house legislative veto and a two-house legislative veto two weeks later. The Supreme Court appeared to be saying that all legislative vetoes were unconstitutional because they did not allow for the full participation of the president and both houses of Congress as specified in Article I of the Constitution.

Despite these Court decisions, however, the legislative veto has remained alive and well. Congress amended some previous provisions to get around some of the technical objections of the Court. In most cases both Congress and the affected agencies have continued to abide by the provisions of legislative veto provisions that remain in several hundred statutes. Even where formal statutory requirements have been amended or deleted, both Congress and executive branch agencies have not altered their behavior. Remarkably, Congress has continued to enact legislative veto provisions in new statutes, including more than 50 in the 16 months immediately following the supposedly sweeping and definitive Supreme Court decision.[9] The *Chadha* case has, in reality, altered little in congressional-executive branch relations.

Congress often approves what the executive proposes, but it is also capable of exercising its power of denial. For example, between 1946 and 1968 Congress rejected twenty-two plans offered by four different presidents for reorganizing parts of the executive branch.

In addition to these techniques for shaping content, Congress can simply write specific statutory details in authorization or even appropriations legislation. Such language is theoretically forbidden in appropriations bills, but the practice occurs nonetheless. Informal contacts between members and staff members of the House and Senate and bureaucrats also afford numerous opportunities for substantive congressional input in shaping programs.

Congress has power over the structure of the bureaucracy. Not only do the House and Senate have veto power over reorganization plans offered by the president, they can also write specific organizational provisions into statutes. In this way they have considerable control over where in the bureaucracy a given program or agency is lodged. It was congressional pressure and activity, for example, that kept the

---

[9] Louis Fisher, "Judicial Misjudgments about the Lawmaking Process: The Legislative Veto Case," *Public Administration Review* 45 (1985): 705–11. See also Elder Witt, "High Court to Clarify Sweep of Its Legislative Veto Ruling," *Congressional Quarterly Weekly Report* (December 6, 1986): 3025–30. On the *Chadha* case itself see Barbara Hinkson Craig, *Chadha: The Story of an Epic Constitutional Struggle* (New York: Oxford University Press, 1988).

bureaucratic responsibility for air and water pollution in motion for a decade. The responsibility was located in at least four different bureaus for short periods until creation of the Environmental Protection Agency.

In this case Congress was trying to instill some aggressiveness into the bureaucracy in the area of abatement enforcement. Congress can also have considerable impact on the internal structure of individual bureaus or agencies. Personnel within the executive branch, both at an aggregate and an individual level, are subject to congressional influence. At the aggregate level, Congress provides the money for salaries. Congress also often sets limits on the number of slots open for an agency's top-level executives such as assistant secretaries and "supergrade" civil servants.

At the individual level, Congress will sometimes specify the status of a specific job. For example, when the Department of Housing and Urban Development was created, Congress stipulated that one of the five assistant secretary positions allocated to the department be filled by the Federal Housing Commissioner. This signaled congressional devotion to the FHA program and warned the new HUD secretary that he should not try to downgrade it.

Also, at the individual level, members of Congress support specific persons for specific open jobs in the bureaucracy. They concentrate their attention on top jobs.

The Senate has to ratify a number of presidential appointments. The Constitution, in Article II, section 2, speaks of the "Advice and Consent" of the Senate as necessary for a number of positions—both those specified in the Constitution and those later established by law with a ratification provision. How much "advice" the president seeks varies, but the "consent" in the form of a majority vote is necessary. The Senate now considers well over 100,000 nominations every two years, although many of these are military officers and are handled in batches without controversy. Few presidential nominations are rejected outright on the floor of the Senate, but a larger number are killed in committee. In other cases a nomination will cause so much controversy that the president will withdraw it. Some nominations are never confirmed simply because the Senate adjourns with some still pending.

The most important offices requiring Senate ratification include cabinet and subcabinet positions, ambassadorships, and federal judicial officials, including Supreme Court justices, district and appeals court judges, and U.S. marshals and attorneys. High officials who serve on an interim basis before confirmation must proceed very cautiously in making decisions. Rejection of an important nominee is embarrassing to the administration and may also frustrate the achievement of some policy goals. Presidents invest heavily in getting approval of nominations for this reason. In 1985 and 1986, for example, President Reagan and his top people invested a great deal of time and effort in getting Senate confirmation of four appointments in the judicial area. The president succeeded, after 13 months of struggle, in getting Senate approval of Edwin Meese as attorney general. The Senate, however, turned down the nomination of Bradford Reynolds to the number three position in the Department of Justice. In two hotly contested cases involving nominations to federal judgeships, the Senate supported Reagan in the case of Clarence Manion but rejected Jefferson Sessions. In 1987 the Senate rejected one Reagan nominee for Supreme Court, Robert Bork, in a fiercely contested fight. In early 1988 the Senate unanimously approved a noncontroversial nominee, Anthony Kennedy, for the same seat.

Over time, the Senate has been relatively active in defeating or forcing the withdrawal of Supreme Court nominations—over 20 percent of all presidential nominations have failed in one way or another. It has been much more reluctant to intervene in presidents' choices of cabinet members, and since the Civil War only four cabinet nominations have been defeated on the Senate floor. However, at the subcabinet level the Senate has been more active. For example, in 1975 the Senate did not defeat any presidential nominees on the floor but did defeat three in committee and returned two to the president without committee action. The president also chose to withdraw a few nominations. In 1976 the Senate again followed the same pattern of not rejecting any on the floor but of killing some in committee, leaving some in limbo by virtue of taking no action, and, in effect, forcing presidential withdrawal of others.

Congress also participates, both formally and informally, in the removal of some executive officials. To force removals Congress can bring great political pressure and can abolish specific jobs by statute. It also intervenes to prevent removals or demotions on some occasions.[10]

Finally, Congress has the power to investigate the activities of bureaus, both through normal authorization and appropriation hearings and also through specific hearings on individual programs or even individual changes in personnel. Just as important, Congress can also deliberately refrain from conducting a thorough probe of the activities of an agency.

---

[10]Louis Fisher, "Congress and the Removal Power," *Congress and the Presidency* 10 (1983): 63–77.

Broader probes raise important policy issues, as well as personnel issues. Various investigations of intelligence activities in the mid-1970s had this effect. In 1986 and 1987 congressional investigation into the role of the White House, the National Security Council, the Central Intelligence Agency, and other agencies in the sale of arms to Iran had similar effects.

## Bureaucratic Resources

The projects and activities that a bureau administers are important to members of Congress, either because of their views regarding the importance and utility of particular programs or because they perceive that their constituents' interests are affected by a bureau's activities.

The decisions that bureaus make about the physical locations of their projects and activities are important to senators and representatives, who are generally anxious to increase the number of federal projects and activities in their respective districts and states. Occasionally, they may want to make sure that a controversial project or activity, such as a Job Corps camp or toxic waste dump, is *not* located in their constituency.

One careful study of bureaucratic decisions about model cities grants, military employment location (base closings), and water and sewer grants concluded that "bureaucrats appear to allocate benefits strategically in an effort both to maintain and to expand their supporting coalitions. . . . But the allocational strategies that bureaucrats select are not the same for all programs. Each is specially tailored to fit a program's peculiar situation in Congress . . . and to reward those congressmen who are especially important to a particular coalition's success."[11] Another study of federal grant practices concluded that agencies making grants were quite willing to cooperate with members of Congress in timing announcements of grants for specific constituencies so as to be most useful politically.[12]

Bureaus are responsible for the handling of individual "cases"—instances in which some person or persons disentangle themselves from the aggregate mass of bureau clients and beneficiaries to demand special, personalized attention. These cases, of course, involve constituents.

Bureaus possess vast amounts of program information that is useful

[11]R. Douglas Arnold, *Congress and the Bureaucracy* (New Haven: Yale University Press, 1979): 207.

[12]J. Theodore Anagnoson, "Federal Grant Agencies and Congressional Election Campaigns," *American Journal of Political Science* 26 (1982): 547–61.

to members of the House and Senate in many ways. Members can use this information to increase their knowledge about programs, to aid decision making, and to improve personal performance in committee work. An adroit use of information can increase a member's intellectual reputation and, thereby, his or her status with fellow members and even with some voters.

Departmental legislative liaison personnel help the bureaucracy in the use of these resources but they do not provide a substitute for direct contact between the bureaus and committees. Neither do they get involved in the appropriations process, perhaps the single most important area of congressional-executive interaction. The best study of legislative liaison in the executive branch concludes that liaison personnel are important because they help members meet their own perceived self-interest and needs. Specifically, liaison personnel can provide access to the secretary of a department for a member who needs it; they can help provide individual members with a substantive point of view about programs; they provide "collaborators" for members who are legislative activists; and they can help members meet constituent needs.[13]

## THE JOINT SHAPING OF PUBLIC POLICY: INITIATION AND SUPPORT

Much public policy is jointly shaped by interaction between the bureaucracy and members of Congress. Even if one branch dominates the development of legislation in a specific substantive area, there are still many occasions for intimate interaction as that area is administered. In many cases, the basic statutes themselves are jointly developed. For most fields, there are three areas where shared policy development is possible: 1) in the development of substantive legislation; 2) in the development of appropriations legislation; and 3) in the development of projects, rules, regulations, procedures, and the other details of day-to-day administration. Many of the conditions for shared influence vary in each of these fields. In general, however, party control cuts across all three areas: the chances for relatively smooth relations and shared influence between Congress and the bureaucracy are enhanced if the majority of both houses and the White House are controlled by the same party; the chances are diminished if there is split control.

[13]Holtzman, *Legislative Liaison,* 51–53. See Chapters 7 and 8 for a lengthy discussion of the strategies and tactics used by liaison officers.

## Authorizing Legislation

One of the classic questions in the scanty literature on bureaucratic-congressional relations is: who initiates? For some reason the answer to this question has been viewed as highly significant, although the significance is usually never analyzed except in terms of either applauding or bemoaning the supposed demise of Congress. Also, much of this literature seems to assume that it is only in the initiation of authorizing legislation that Congress can have a significant impact on the shape of national policy.

The "who initiates" question is important only if the answer indicates that over time one branch or the other is effectively shut out of any role in shaping authorizing legislation. The best evidence seems to indicate that, regardless of the source of initiation, the other branch—whether it be Congress responding to bureaucratic initiative or the bureaucracy responding to congressional initiative—ordinarily makes some important changes.

Instances both of congressional initiation of authorizing legislation and of major congressional impact on executive branch initiatives are numerous. For example, a study of ninety major laws between 1890 and 1940 attributed major initiative to Congress in about 40 percent of the cases, to the president in about 20 percent, to both jointly in about 30 percent, and to interest groups in about 10 percent.[14] An updating of this study for the years from 1940 through 1967, using the same impressionistic standards, arrived at the same basic conclusion: that Congress was still extremely important in the development of authorizing legislation. In the words of the authors, "Our conclusion challenges the conventional wisdom that the president has come to enjoy an increasingly preponderant role in national policy-making. . . . The evidence suggests that Congress continues to be an active innovator and very much in the legislative business."[15]

An impressionistic review in 1975 by a journalist assigned to cover Congress for *The Washington Post* credited Congress with initiation in a number of policy areas: Medicare, Social Security disability insurance, pension reform, the eighteen-year-old vote, political campaign reform, air pollution (including that from automobiles), reduction and cessation of the U.S. role in Indochina, chemical additives in food, the creation of a consumer protection agency, mandatory automobile safety standards, food programs for the poor, and increases in the

---

[14]Lawrence H. Chamberlain, *The President, Congress and Legislation* (New York: Columbia University Press, 1946).
[15]Ronald C. Moe and Steven C. Teel, "Congress as Policy-Maker: A Necessary Reappraisal," *Political Science Quarterly* 85 (1970): 467–68.

minimum wage.[16] He also added references to major investigations initiated by Congress, including those of the drug industry, multinational corporations, organized crime, and labor racketeering.

Instances of joint collaboration between parts of Congress and parts of the bureaucracy on specific authorization bills are legion.[17] A few illustrations underscore the general point.

In the housing field in recent years much of the bill drafting was done jointly by staff members from the General Counsel's office in the Department of Housing and Urban Development and its predecessor, the Housing and Home Finance Agency, who collaborated with the staff director of the Housing Subcommittee of the House Committee on Banking and Currency.[18]

In the consumer protection area the same kind of relationship between bureaucrats and congressional staff members developed. "There has been a great deal of staff contact between Senator Nelson's subcommittee investigating prescription drugs and the Food and Drug Administration. The Commerce Committee staff worked with the Federal Power Commission on gas pipeline safety. There has been a whole range of these ad hoc contacts . . ."[19] In this field the ad hoc contacts also tend to vanish once the issue is off the congressional agenda. This is probably because consumer protection is a relatively new field and there are jurisdictional instabilities in both the executive and legislative branches. In other fields, where jurisdictions are clearer and more well established, contacts are also likely to be more permanent.

In the air pollution field, even though Congress has taken the initiative, there has been informal cooperation from the executive branch staff. This cooperation has come despite formal bureaucratic positions that often ran counter to congressional initiatives. For example, in 1962 legislative and technical experts from the Public Health Service and the General Counsel's office in the Department of Health, Education, and Welfare worked with a representative of the United States Conference of Mayors (an interest group representing roughly the 100 largest cities in the country), and a few senators and representatives and their staffs to produce draft legislation even though the

[16]Spencer Rich, "Congress Has Lead in Major Programs," *The Washington Post,* February 14, 1975.

[17]For a number of additional examples see Chapters 4–7 of Ripley and Franklin, *Congress, the Bureaucracy, and Public Policy.* See also Gary Orfield, *Congressional Power: Congress and Social Change* (New York: Harcourt Brace Jovanovich, 1975).

[18]Harold Wolman, *Politics of Federal Housing* (New York: Dodd, Mead, 1971): 107.

[19]Mark V. Nadel, *The Politics of Consumer Protection* (Indianapolis: Bobbs-Merrill, 1971): 115.

Public Health Service formally was opposed to some of the provisions they were drafting.[20]

In the tax field, the staff of the Treasury Department works closely with members of the relevant congressional committees (Senate Finance, House Ways and Means, and the Joint Committee on Taxation) in developing details of tax code revisions. The process that resulted in passage of a major tax bill in late 1986 began in earnest with the release in November 1984 (after the presidential election) of a draft proposal from the Treasury Department. This draft was responsive to the concerns of a number of members of the House and Senate who were especially interested in tax reform. President Reagan was lukewarm to the Treasury plan, in part because it seemed more responsive to forces in Congress than to the administration itself. Treasury experts continued to work closely with members of the House and Senate and expert congressional staff members. The key development in a two-year story that allowed a dramatic change in the tax code in the final bill came in the spring of 1986 when the chairman of the Senate Finance Committee, Robert Packwood (R-Ore.) devised a strategy of rejecting many special tax breaks all at once to allow a bill that produced genuine change, especially in a highly visible reduction in the top marginal tax rate. Packwood and six of his senatorial colleagues (three from each party) met privately with each other, with staff, and also with the deputy secretary of the treasury to put together the core of what finally passed the Senate committee unanimously and the Senate itself almost unanimously. The final bill, agreed on in conference committee and by both houses, closely resembled the handiwork of this core group of senators, congressional staff, and Treasury staff.

## Appropriations

Both agencies and subcommittees approach the matter of appropriations in predictable ways. Executive officials, above all, seek to reduce uncertainty in the process. They want to know, as early as they can, how much money they have to spend and they want to be able to predict how much they will have in the future so they can plan ahead. Typically, officials seek to reduce uncertainty by seeking the confi-

[20]Randall B. Ripley, "Congress and Clean Air: The Issue of Enforcement," in Frederic N. Cleaveland and associates, *Congress and Urban Problems* (Washington: Brookings, 1969): 224–78. See also Charles O. Jones, *Clean Air: The Policies and Politics of Pollution Control* (Pittsburgh: University of Pittsburgh Press, 1975).

dence of the appropriations subcommittee members to whom they are responsible. In seeking confidence they are especially careful in preparing for the hearings of their subcommittees so that they appear to be "on top" of their job. They also are assiduous in maintaining personal contacts outside of the formal hearings.

The members of the appropriations subcommittees, especially in the House, start with the view that all budgets can be cut. Their basic suspicion of bureaus and bureaucrats is overcome when they gain a level of confidence in particular individuals. They are particularly rigorous in investigating proposed increases, proposed new programs, and programs with little client support. Well-established programs with a satisfied and politically potent clientele do not receive such rigorous scrutiny.[21]

Not all subcommittees and agencies interact as described above. Ira Sharkansky has shown how both the agency and the committee can behave otherwise in examining the interaction between one House appropriations subcommittee and four of the agencies for which it is responsible over a period of a dozen years. He summarizes the behavior of the subcommittee as follows:

> Evidently, the legislators vary their oversight activity among agencies. They devote more than the average amount of supervisory and control efforts to the agencies that spend the most money, whose requests have increased the most rapidly, and whose behavior toward the subcommittee has deviated most frequently from subcommittee desires. In a sense, they allocate their time and staff assistance to agencies most "in need" of supervision and control.[22]

Writing from the perspective of the agencies, Sharkansky concluded that agencies vary in the level of assertiveness with which they approach appropriations subcommittees; that those agencies with greater public and administration support are more assertive; and that administrators are not totally guided to their levels of assertiveness by subcommittee attitudes and behavior, which usually appear fuzzy anyway.[23]

[21]Richard F. Fenno, Jr., *The Power of the Purse* (Boston: Little, Brown, 1966), especially parts of Chapters 6, 7, and 11. See also Robert D. Thomas and Roger B. Handberg, "Congressional Budgeting for Eight Agencies, 1947–1972," *American Journal of Political Science* 18 (1974): 179–87.

[22]Ira Sharkansky, "An Appropriations Subcommittee and Its Client Agencies: A Comparative Study of Supervision and Control," *American Political Science Review* 59 (1965): 628.

[23]Ira Sharkansky, "Four Agencies and an Appropriations Subcommittee: A Comparative Study of Budget Strategies," *Midwest Journal of Political Science* 9 (1965): 254–81.

## Day-to-Day Administration

Congressional influence on the bureaucracy does not end once authorization and appropriations statutes have been passed. Interaction continues on a daily basis as agencies administer their programs. Some examples can provide the flavor of the interaction. The following discussion of the Office of Education is illustrative:

> Perhaps more important than formal amendments, however, congressional influence on administrative behavior is manifest in the nature of questions put to officials in hearings; in subcommittee requests for information; in press statements and in public speeches attacking or questioning existing practices within an agency; in letters or telephone calls to the Commissioner or to the Secretary of HEW. Agencies live by congressional favor, and congressional power is variable. For this reason, the views, opinions, and attitudes of key legislators (especially committee and subcommittee chairmen and their immediate staffs) are powerful influences on administrative behavior. Francis Keppel (the Commissioner of Education) spent agonizing months trying to fill top level vacancies because Congressman Adam Clayton Powell insisted upon a number of Negro appointees. A great deal of time of top officials is taken up in the laborious and often harrowing processes of meeting both the legitimate and illegitimate calls of Congress for program review.[24]

When a subgovernment is firmly entrenched there is likely to be intimate congressional involvement in administration. Theodore Lowi describes the situation in the agricultural field, where he identifies ten different "self-governing systems" dealing with different sets of programs:

> Each of the ten systems has become a powerful political instrumentality. The self-governing local units become one important force in a system that administers a program and maintains the autonomy of that program against political forces emanating from other agricultural programs, from antagonistic farm and nonfarm interests, from Congress, from the Secretary of Agriculture, and from the President. To many a farmer, the local outpost of one or another of these systems *is* the government.
>   The politics within each system is built upon a triangular trading pattern involving the central agency, a Congressional committee or sub-

[24]Stephen K. Bailey and Edith K. Mosher, *ESEA: The Office of Education Administers a Law* (Syracuse: Syracuse University Press, 1968): 185.

committee, and the local district farmer committees (usually federated in some national or regional organization).[25]

Bureaucrats who disagree with the policies of a president and his appointees can use their ties with Congress to protest. Alternatively, members of Congress who disagree with the presidential policies can seek out dissident bureaucrats. The lack of interest of the Nixon administration in pursuing civil rights in a number of fields spurred congressional-bureaucratic cooperation highly critical of the administration. For example, in 1969 a Senate subcommittee in effect conspired with pro-civil rights bureaucrats in the Equal Employment Opportunity Commission to harass the administration on its handling of a discrimination case involving three textile companies in the south. A similar kind of alliance was formed with regard to job discrimination policy in the Department of Transportation and succeeded in getting some equal opportunities actions taken that otherwise would not have been forthcoming.[26] Similar bureaucratic-congressional alliances kept some pressure on the Reagan administration not to cease civil-rights enforcement.

Several studies lead to general statements about when a congressional committee is more or less likely to pursue its oversight of an agency's daily activities vigorously.[27] Oversight is promoted by the existence of autonomous subcommittees; ample committee staffs; perceptions of partisan advantage on the part of the majority party members; and perceptions that service to constituents can be enhanced by such activity. Oversight is also most likely on the part of committees that are highly prestigious and oriented toward a relatively large amount of legislative output. Oversight is most vigorously pursued when a committee is considering major revisions in policy.

Vigorous oversight is discouraged if there are close, mutually rewarding contacts between members and agency officials that might be

[25]Theodore J. Lowi, "How the Farmers Get What They Want," in Theodore J. Lowi and Randall B. Ripley (eds.), *Legislative Politics U.S.A.,* 3rd ed. (Boston: Little, Brown, 1973): 188.
[26]Orfield, *Congressional Power,* 82–84.
[27]See John F. Bibby, "Committee Characteristics and Legislative Oversight of Administration," *Midwest Journal of Political Science* 10 (1966): 78–97; and Seymour Scher, "Conditions for Legislative Control," *Journal of Politics* 25 (1963): 526–51. On oversight in general see Morris S. Ogul, *Congress Oversees the Bureaucracy: Studies in Legislative Supervision* (Pittsburgh: University of Pittsburgh Press, 1976); and Ogul, "Congressional Oversight: Structures and Incentives," in Lawrence C. Dodd and Bruce I. Oppenheimer (eds.), *Congress Reconsidered,* 2nd ed. (Washington, D.C.: Congressional Quarterly, 1981): Chapter 14; Sundquist, *The Decline and Resurgence of Congress,* Chapter 11; Loch Johnson, "The U.S. Congress and the CIA: Monitoring the Dark Side of Government," *Legislative Studies Quarterly* 5 (1980): 477–99; and Mathew D. McCubbins and Thomas Schwartz, "Congressional Oversight Overlooked: Police Patrols versus Fire Alarms," *American Journal of Political Science* 28 (1984): 165–79.

disrupted by such activity. Aggressive oversight is also avoided if it seems to members that a great deal of negative reaction from interest groups, important to them and part of an existing subgovernment, is likely.

## CONFLICT OVER PUBLIC POLICY

Much of the time, most members of Congress have strong incentives to get along with the various parts of the federal bureaucracy. In most policy areas congressional-bureaucratic relations proceed relatively smoothly and inconspicuously.

But conflict does occur. When congressmen—particularly members of relevant committees and subcommittees—perceive their interests to be threatened they will react by seeking to bring agency policy into line with their preferences. The motivation for the conflict may be programmatic or political, but the effect is the same: Congress and the executive branch engage in conflict over substantive policy statements and actions. Either side may prevail in these conflicts. The bureaucracy has considerable resources with which to pursue its point of view. But in cases in which congressional feeling is intense, Congress usually prevails, at least in symbolic ways that mollify the protesting members.

In a conflict situation those members (again usually organized in committees or subcommittees) who are involved use all of the resources available to them in order to prevail. A number of examples illustrate how conflicts can be resolved.

The harshest punishment Congress can administer in settling a conflict is to kill an existing program. Congress administered that fatal stroke to the Area Redevelopment Administration in 1963, even though it had only been created in 1961. The principal reason for this action was that a number of members had become convinced that, despite clear provisions in the law, the ARA was encouraging industries to relocate in redevelopment areas. In the eyes of those members and their constituents from districts losing such industries, the ARA was engaging in "piracy."[28] After being assured by the administration that such abuses would not occur in the future, Congress reestablished the ARA program in 1965 under a different name—the Economic Development Administration.

Congress can demand and obtain major programmatic concessions

[28]See Randall B. Ripley, *The Politics of Economic and Human Resource Development* (Indianapolis: Bobbs-Merrill, 1972): Chapter 2.

in exchange for extending the life of a program. For example, in dealing with a small juvenile delinquency program during the Kennedy administration, Edith Green, chairwoman of the House sub-committee with jurisdiction over the program extracted the following concessions to put the program more in line with her vision of it in return for extending the program in 1963:[29]

1. The extension was changed from three years to two years and was, by informal agreement, considered the terminal extension.
2. Funds were authorized for only one year, which meant that annual justification of the program before Congress would be necessary.
3. New projects would not be comprehensive in scope but rather would be limited demonstration projects. The director of the Office of Juvenile Delinquency provided a written statement for Green to read into the record to make this agreement explicit.
4. A special amendment was added to the bill requiring, in effect, that a project be started in the District of Columbia.

Congress can redefine the jurisdictional authority of a regulatory agency so that it no longer has the power to make decisions in a particular area. This was the case when the Federal Trade Commission first sought to move against cigarette advertising. An irate Congress simply removed the FTC's jurisdiction that would have allowed it to accomplish what it wanted to do. It was not until several years later that a weakened version of the original FTC position was allowed to be implemented.[30]

The FTC was a general target for increasing congressional intervention in the late 1970s because its critics, supported by business interests, felt that the FTC had become too aggressive in its antitrust activities.[31] For four years in a row (beginning in 1977) Congress did not pass an authorization bill for the FTC. Thus it could not receive regular appropriations. Finally, in the spring of 1980 the FTC actually had to close for three days because no money had been provided in any form. New legislation was passed after this symbolic slap that

[29]John E. Moore, "Controlling Delinquency: Executive, Congressional and Juvenile, 1961–1964," in Cleveland et al., *Congress and Urban Problems:* 166–67. Atypically, one thing that had offended Green was that the program sought to put a project in her home district before the local officials had submitted what she considered to be a good plan. She refused to play politics with the program, even though it meant losing some federal money at home.

[30]See A. Lee Fritschler, *Smoking and Politics,* 3rd ed. (Englewood Cliffs, N.J.: Prentice-Hall, 1983).

[31]For a summary of various aspects of the continuing controversy between Congress and the FTC see Randall B. Ripley and Grace A. Franklin, *Policy Implementation and Bureaucracy,* 2nd ed. (Chicago: Dorsey, 1986): 166–71; and Ripley and Franklin, *Congress, the Bureaucracy, and Public Policy,* 140–42.

gave Congress a much larger role in overseeing FTC decisions in the future. A two-house legislative veto of FTC rules was inserted into the authorization statute and the president was denied any role in it. This was the first time Congress had inserted such a veto procedure for a so-called independent regulatory commission.

Congress made its first use of this legislative veto in 1982 in disapproving an FTC rule involving sales of used cars. In 1982 and 1983 political controversy continued as Congress intervened to rein in the agency. Finally, after a number of Reagan appointments had turned the agency into a much less aggressive pro-consumer body by 1984 and 1985, Congress eased up on the agency and passed a reauthorization bill. The great reduction in business complaints about the FTC explains a great deal of the changed congressional attitudes.

Congress can determine what standards a program will be allowed or required to use in evaluating its operation. When the Army Corps of Engineers wanted to implement new, more accurate cost-benefit standards for determining which water projects it should undertake, Congress passed an amendment to the Transportation Act of 1966 prohibiting the implementation of more rigid standards and preserving the standards that would maximize the number of Corps projects throughout the country, despite the dubious economic validity of some of them.[32]

Congress can reverse an organizational edict issued by an agency if it feels pressure to do so. In 1968 HEW sought to decentralize programs authorized under the Elementary and Secondary Education Act of 1965. This decentralization would have spread responsibility for the programs to HEW field establishments and would have diminished the power of the Office of Education officials in Washington. The move was opposed by "the education lobby." Wilbur Cohen, Secretary of HEW at the time, told how the chairman of the relevant Senate appropriations subcommittee reversed the HEW decision:

> When we went up to Senate Appropriations, the committee reduced the Office of Education's budget by about $2.4 million. So I paid a visit to Sen. (Lister) Hill (D.-Ala.), and I said, 'What goes?' And he replied, 'The National Education Association doesn't want that program decentralized.' I said, 'If I rescind that order, will you give me that money back?' And he said, 'Yeah.' So I rescinded that order and I doubt whether to this day it's been reissued.[33]

---

[32]Robert Haveman and Paula Stephan, "The Domestic Program Congress Won't Cut," in Raymond E. Wolfinger (ed.), *Readings on Congress* (Englewood Cliffs, N.J.: Prentice-Hall, 1971): 367–70.

[33]*National Journal* (December 16, 1972): 1932–33.

Congress can use the threat of investigative hearings to influence the policy decisions of an agency. Only the threat of negative publicity from hearings in both the House and Senate seems to have moved the Food and Drug Administration to refuse certification in 1969 for a drug called Panalba manufactured by a major pharmaceutical company. Until the impact of that threat was considered, the FDA seemed disposed to go along with the company and the representative from the company's district.[34]

Opponents of bureaucratic policies can also simply keep the offending bureaucrats in the limelight and direct their criticism and those of hostile lobbies and (maybe) of the press toward them. In 1981 this was part of the strategy of the chairman of the House Interior Committee, Morris Udall (D-Ariz.) in dealing with the secretary of the Interior, James G. Watt. Udall and Watt were poles apart on policy: Udall was closely allied with various conservationist and environmentalist efforts and Watt, in Udall's view, was the leader of the irresponsible "rape, pillage, and burn" view of public lands and resources. Watt, of course, viewed his own efforts to maximize use of public lands for many purposes—including the extraction of resources—as responsible stewardship and Udall's views as hopelessly restrictive. The two men (and their respective allies) clashed repeatedly in public. Udall kept the public spotlight on Watt (although Watt also seemed to relish the spotlight). By early 1982 Udall's tactics had not been completely successful: Watt was still pursuing policies Udall found abhorrent. However, Watt had postponed expanded oil and gas leasing on public lands for a year, perhaps partially as a result of the public focus Udall (and other opponents both in Congress and in the environmentalist movement) had kept on what Watt was going to do.

Another instance of the "spotlight" strategy used by congressional committees occurred in 1984, when the House Government Operations Committee held hearings and issued a report on the enforcement activities of the Office of Surface Mining (OSM) in the Department of the Interior. This was the agency responsible for implementing the federal strip-mining law that had been enacted after a long struggle in 1977. The committee majority was appalled by what they considered to be non-enforcement, law enforcement, and even sabotage of the intent of the law. OSM responded with some additional enforcement activity.[35]

---

[34]Nadel, *The Politics of Consumer Protection,* 77–78.
[35]See Ripley and Franklin, *Policy Implementation and Bureaucracy,* 156–63.

# CONGRESSIONAL-BUREAUCRATIC RELATIONS: A SUMMARY ASSESSMENT

The analysis in this chapter may suggest that conflict is unimportant in the policy-making process of the national government. That is not the case. But there is a great amount of cooperation between Congress and the bureaucracy and it is in good measure based on mutual self-interest. There is nothing insidious about this cooperation; most prolonged human relationships are characterized by the desire for relative harmony and calm. Harmony and calm may produce either beneficial or useless public policy. However, the same may also be said for conflict.

Occasional conflict has the merit of raising questions about the status quo in any specific policy area. The resolution of the conflict may ultimately result in little movement away from that status quo, but at least its content is examined. Occasionally, substantial departures from the status quo follow major conflict. For example, a number of the policy innovations of the mid-1960s (the New Frontier and Great Society measures such as basic federal aid to elementary and secondary education, medical care for the aged, and several poverty programs) came after extended periods of conflict over similar or related proposals for the preceding years.

A superficial consideration of congressional-bureaucratic relations suggests that Congress dominates the bureaucracy. This is not the case. Congressional influence is substantial, but in many areas the powerful members choose not to exercise it. In addition, even in those cases in which a few members or subcommittees do seek to exercise their influence they may win some skirmishes or battles only to lose the war of overall policy direction. This can happen when the president and presidency lend the full weight of their support to a particular part of the bureaucracy under attack. This kind of support by the presidency occurs infrequently, but when it is used it is often effective because the weapons are very powerful: the impounding of large amounts of money that Congress has appropriated for specific purposes, the withholding of vital information from Congress under the claim of "executive privilege," and the taking of initiatives while Congress is out of session.

At root, the predominance of incentives for both bureaucrats and members of Congress to maintain good relations with each other so that the trading of valued resources is not disrupted also loads the legislative process in favor of the status quo. Habits and patterns of personal interaction and thought about public policy develop and become firmly entrenched. Participants hesitate to stray very far from policies that are known to command widespread support, regardless of their true value or the nature of their impact on American society. Disruptive forces such as visionary or aggressive presidents or major party upheavals can and do alter this situation, but they are the exception and not the rule. Not all policy change is minute or slow-moving, but most of it is. This situation may result in either "good" or "bad" policy; it certainly results in familiar policy.

Despite considerable talk in Congress about increased oversight of executive branch activities and bureaucratic performance, the dice are loaded against sustained oversight. There is little political payoff either in Washington or at home for senators and representatives who are aggressive overseers. There may be negative outcomes in the form of a less cooperative bureaucracy when the member is pursuing interests particularly close to his or her heart. In addition to the political disincentives for vigorous pursuit of oversight by Congress there is also the fact that the very broad delegations of power Congress has given the bureaucracy over the years, particularly beginning in the 1930s, makes oversight very difficult. There are often no standards in the legislation against which to measure performance, even in a rough sense.[36] Even when abuses have become publicly evident, as in the case of the intelligence agencies in the 1970s, it takes Congress considerable time to decide it wants to get involved in oversight.[37]

Sustained oversight by Congress is not a natural activity. Coordinated oversight might, in theory, provide some policy integration. The much more natural stance for Congress is either nonexistent or sporadic and disjointed oversight, which in turn contributes to policy fragmentation.

[36]Peter Woll, *American Bureaucracy*, 2nd ed. (New York: Norton, 1977).
[37]See John T. Elliff, "Congress and the Intelligence Community," in Dodd and Oppenheimer, (eds.) *Congress Reconsidered*, 193–206. See also Harry Howe Ransom, "Congress and the Intelligence Agencies," in Harvey C. Mansfield, Sr. (ed.), *Congress against the President*, Vol. 32, no. 1 of Proceedings of The Academy of Political Science (1975): 153–66.

# IV

## Congressional Influence Over American Public Policy

# 11

## Access

We have now examined the nature of Congress and both the internal and external environments in which Congress functions. Throughout, we have been primarily concerned with developing two themes. First, Congress is an integral and important part of the policy-making machinery in the United States. Second, it is a fragmented institution that usually produces fragmented policy. In chapters 11 and 12 we focus exclusively on congressional influence over American public policy.

A close look at the concept of legislative responsiveness identifies four components: policy responsiveness, service responsiveness, allocation responsiveness, and symbolic responsiveness.[1] Policy responsiveness involves legislative action on major substantive issues. Service responsiveness involves the provision by the legislature or its members of "particularized benefits" for individual constituents or constituency

[1] Heinz Eulau and Paul D. Karps, "The Puzzle of Representation: Specifying Components of Responsiveness," *Legislative Studies Quarterly* 2 (1977): 233–54. Quotations are taken from page 241.

groups. Allocation responsiveness involves legislative provision of general tangible benefits for constituencies, often in the form of public works and often labeled "pork barrel." Finally, symbolic responsiveness involves "public gestures" by the legislature intended to "create a sense of trust and support in the relationship between representative and represented."

We have dealt, in varying ways, with all of these elements of responsiveness in preceding chapters. In these final two chapters we will focus primarily on policy responsiveness and occasionally on symbolic responsiveness.

In examining responsiveness, particularly policy responsiveness, two central questions about congressional policy influence are worth pursuing. First, what explains variations in the amount of congressional influence? Second, what is the impact of influence wielded by Congress? The first question will be the focus of the present chapter. The second question will be treated in the next chapter.

In broad terms, the amount of congressional influence over policy-making is a function of the nature of congressional access to policy and program decisions. Congress does not have equal potential for developing influence in all cases because congressional access varies, depending on the type of policy under consideration and at different points in the sequence of policy making. Fortunately, there are patterns to the variance of congressional access.

The present chapter is organized around six broad generalizations:

1. The predominance of fragmentation in Congress sets some general limits on both access and impact.
2. The fluctuating popular standing of Congress as an institution serves only as a spur to some congressional policy activity, although it pushes in no specific substantive direction.
3. Congress systematically has more access to policy making at some stages of the policy process than at others.
4. The different parts of Congress have predictably different degrees of access to influencing policy statements in generically different policy areas.
5. The degree of centralization in the internal distribution of influence in Congress is systematically related to the promotion of specific values in congressional deliberations: thoroughness, representativeness, and responsibility.
6. The way in which Congress shapes its relations with the executive branch determines in large part how effective and responsive it will be in addressing public needs.

# THE BROAD CONSEQUENCES OF FRAGMENTATION

Three major consequences of fragmentation help shape congressional access to and impact on public policy.

First, fragmentation helps produce stable policy. Significant changes in policies and programs are difficult to achieve. The structure of Congress itself leads to the expectation that only small changes will occur in policies at any given time. Congress is imbedded in a policy system that most of the time is weighted toward some close variant of the existing situation. In short, "policy innovation is the exception, not the rule."[2]

This situation does not mean that Congress is powerless. It is, after all, a mark of considerable power that Congress can much of the time play a pivotal role in helping prevent major change, even when there are strong forces pushing for that change. Nor is this situation universal or inevitable. In some substantive areas, for at least short periods of time, Congress has been innovative and has promoted substantial policy change.

In 1981 some observers jumped to a premature conclusion that the "Reagan revolution" meant that Congress was following the president's lead in dismantling the accretions of policies and programs that had built up for almost 50 years. To be sure, the president and Congress slowed the rate of growth of some programs in the domestic area, absolutely cut a few domestic programs, and considerably accelerated the rate of growth in the defense area. But, after 1981 "normal" pressures leading to more stable policy were abundantly evident; 1981 represented an atypical experience.

A second major consequence of a high degree of fragmentation is that those engaged in debate over issues seek to define domestic policies as distributive if possible and foreign and defense policies as structural if possible. These types of policies are the easiest to deal with in political terms because everyone can appear to "win" and nobody "loses." Protective regulatory, redistributive, and even strategic policy all require clear winners and losers. Politicians would rather avoid those choices if possible.

A third major consequence of fragmentation in Congress is that

[2]Leroy N. Rieselbach, "Congress and Policy Change: Issues, Answers, and Prospects," in Gerald C. Wright, Jr., Leroy N. Rieselbach, and Lawrence C. Dodd (eds.), *Congress and Policy Change* (New York: Agathon Press, 1986): 280.

there is only minimal and sporadic concern with overseeing bureaucratic performance. In those policy areas in which subgovernments
are dominant, "oversight" simply means talking with like-minded
people in the bureaucracy on a routine basis to make sure that no
major deviations are occurring in policies and programs that the
members of the subgovernment have long since ratified. Simultaneously, the members of the subgovernment worry about the possible
intrusion of outsiders such as the president or department secretary
or a party leader in Congress or a public-interest group. They seek to
prevent or offset such intrusions. When such activities are the focus
of interaction between Congress and the bureaucracy, oversight in the
sense of monitoring or evaluation of government programs is obviously beside the point.


## THE POPULAR STANDING OF CONGRESS

When asked, people usually have an opinion about Congress as an
institution. That opinion is often not deeply held, because much of the
time Congress is simply not visible to a lot of people.[3] There is not a
great deal of news about Congress contained in most newspapers or
on television. This is especially true when one compares news about
the president to news about Congress. Congress is an extremely complex institution (as readers of this volume should know by now!) and
coverage of more than the most superficial aspects of it is rare in
anything read or heard by the general public. The many-headedness
of Congress militates against clear coverage.[4]

Public opinion about congressional performance fluctuates a great
deal. For example, between 1963 and 1985 the Harris survey asked a
sample of the general public almost every year (and several times in
some years) about the kind of job Congress was doing.[5] During those
years the favorable responses varied from a low of 20 percent to a high

[3]See Glenn R. Parker, "A Note on the Impact and Saliency of Congress," *American Politics Quarterly* 4 (1976): 413–21.
[4]See Robert O. Blanchard (ed.), *Congress and the News Media* (New York: Hastings House, 1974); and Max M. Kampelman, "Congress, the Media, and the President," in Mansfield (ed.), *Congress against the President,* 85–97.
[5]The Harris questions were worded: "How would you rate the job Congress is doing . . .—excellent, pretty good, only fair, or poor?" In the text the term "favorable responses" refers to excellent and pretty good ratings combined. The term "unfavorable responses" refers to fair and poor ratings combined.

For a summary of Harris and Gallup data on congressional popularity since 1939 see Glenn R. Parker, "Some Themes in Congressional Unpopularity," *American Journal of Political Science* 21 (1977): 93–109.

of 64 percent. The unfavorable responses varied from a high of 79 percent to a low of 26 percent. In 1985 positive opinion had climbed to about 50 percent, the highest level since 1964 and 1965. The rating of Congress as an institution is responsive to specific events and is also highly correlated with the general attitude toward and trust in government held by the public at any specific time.[6]

An examination of the Harris data on Congress since 1963 and of Gallup data on public opinion about Congress from 1939 to 1958 reveals two central facts. First, rarely do favorable responses reach as high as 50 percent of the public. Second, opinion fluctuates rapidly in both directions, not in gradual trends. Congress, as an institution, is held in reasonably low esteem by the public. However, the instability of opinion suggests that the public does not think about Congress continuously. Opinion about Congress reflects general opinion of political events of the present moment. For example, in 1964 and 1965 the government in general seemed to be working well. Many new programs were being created. President Lyndon Johnson won an overwhelming victory in the 1964 presidential election. Vietnam was not yet a major political worry. When asked about Congress under these conditions the public responded favorably, and Congress received the highest positive rating for the five decades for which data have been collected. By contrast, in 1980 only 20 percent of those polled gave Congress a positive rating. This view coincided with increased public perceptions of ineptitude on the part of President Jimmy Carter, revelations of corruption in Congress coming from the Abscam operation, a high rate of inflation, and growing frustration over the Iranian hostage situation.

Even though the public has been generally negative about Congress as an institution since the mid-1960s it has, at the same time, had generally favorable opinions about individual members. The high rate of re-election discussed in Chapter 3 attests to this opinion. The public evaluates the institution and the individuals in it on different grounds.[7] The institution is rated on its performance in such areas as domestic policy, the character of relations with the president, and the perceived pace and "style" of its legislative activity. Individual members, how-

---

[6]For a good summary of data on various aspects of public trust in government since 1958 see Herbert B. Asher, *Presidential Elections and American Politics,* 4th ed. (Chicago: Dorsey, 1988): 18–24.

[7]See Glenn R. Parker and Roger H. Davidson, "Why Do Americans Love Their Congressmen So Much More Than Their Congress?" *Legislative Studies Quarterly* 4 (1979): 53–61; and Timothy E. Cook, "Legislature vs. Legislator: A Note on the Paradox of Congressional Support," *Legislative Studies Quarterly* 4 (1979): 43–52.

ever, are not judged very often on policy considerations but are instead judged largely on the basis of personal attributes and their service to their constituents. In some senses individual members are perceived as local officials because that is where they are seen and where constituent services get rendered. The institution itself is, of course, viewed as a national institution.

In the long run, the most important implication of the public's estimation of Congress may be in terms of the kinds of individuals who are attracted to a career in Congress. The very best individuals might not be much interested in seeking membership in a body that is, over a long time period, held in low esteem. Year-to-year fluctuations are not so dangerous from this standpoint, but long periods of low public evaluation of congressional performance are.

## ACCESS AND THE STAGES OF POLICY-MAKING

There are many ways to try to comprehend a phenomenon as complex as the policy process in the American national government. A short discussion of stages in that process is introduced here in order to pinpoint those activities in which Congress is likely to have the most access.

Three different broad stages of policy activity lead to broadly defined policy products. The first stage in the process is one of *agenda setting.* Those topics to which the government gives its attention are on the agenda of government. This is the stage of problem identification. Since even a government as large and active as that of the United States cannot pay attention to all potential problems, there is constant definition and redefinition of what is on the agenda. There is also constant shifting of priorities of what problems should receive how much attention from which actors and institutions.

In agenda setting the impetus for change generally comes from external events or the president. But many actors and institutions, including members of Congress, can compete for getting items on the agenda.[8] Congress as an institution, given its fragmented and multi-headed nature, rarely speaks with one voice about new items that

[8]See Charles O. Jones, "A New President, A Different Congress, A Maturing Agenda," in Lester M. Salamon and Michael S. Lund (eds.), *The Reagan Presidency and the Governing of America* (Washington, D.C.: Urban Institute, 1984): 261–87; John W. Kingdon, *Agendas, Alternatives, and Public Policies* (Boston: Little, Brown, 1984); Barbara Sinclair, "Agenda, Policy, and Alignment Change from Coolidge to Reagan," in Lawrence C. Dodd and Bruce I. Oppenheimer (eds.), *Congress Reconsidered,* 3rd ed. (Washington, D.C.: Congressional Quarterly, 1985): 291–314; and Nelson W. Polsby, *Political Innovation in America: The Politics of Policy Initiation* (New Haven, Conn.: Yale University Press, 1984).

should be added to the governmental agenda. However, active and visible individual members and groups of members of both houses participate in the complex and often confusing process by which issues emerge somehow "certified" as being on the agenda, regardless of the relative weight of the individual problems. In the 1960s members of Congress were among the leading figures in the country in pushing a number of safety issues onto the agenda—auto, mine, and workplace safety in general.[9] In the mid-1970s members of Congress added their voices to the chorus in helping identify a number of aspects of energy as being a central problem requiring concerted attention. A number of members of Congress also helped call attention—through publicity—to the newly discovered national problem of child pornography in 1977. Similarly, members of Congress, including—most dramatically—Senator Paula Hawkins (R–Fla.), got involved in putting child abuse in general on the agenda. Many members of Congress got involved in the early 1980s in making "industrial policy" an agenda item (although it faded quickly and then resurfaced—again with congressional prodding—as "competitiveness"). Similarly, many members kept agricultural economic issues (specifically, an agricultural depression much more severe than general problems in the economy) on the agenda in the 1980s.

A member of Congress insistent on an agenda item is best advised to become genuinely expert and then to use all available public occasions (especially when the media are in attendance) to publicize the issue and the necessity of public attention to it. In the early and mid-1980s Senator Bill Bradley (D-N.J.) followed this route in pushing major tax revision onto the public agenda even when virtually no one thought serious change had much chance of success. Senators Phil Gramm (R-Texas). Warren Rudman (R-N.H.), and Ernest Hollings (D-S.C.) undertook the same activities effectively in drumming up support for the necessity of putting serious budget balancing on the congressional agenda during the same period of time.

No major domestic item comes onto the public agenda without congressional participation. In many instances, members of the House and Senate are the prime movers in moving an issue onto the agenda.

The second major stage in the policy process is that of policy formulation and legitimation. Once an item is on the agenda, then presumably there will be pressures from both inside and outside of

---

[9]For discussion of the safety examples plus a broader discussion of agenda setting in the Senate see Jack L. Walker, "Setting the Agenda in the U.S. Senate: A Theory of Problem Selection," *British Journal of Political Science* 7 (1977): 423–45. On child-abuse agenda building see Barbara J. Nelson, *Making an Issue of Child Abuse: Political Agenda Setting for Social Problems* (Chicago: University of Chicago Press, 1984).

**Table 11–1.** Potential Access of Principal Institutional Actors to Policy
Formulation and Legitimation Activities

| | INSTITUTIONAL ACTOR | | | INTEREST GROUPS |
|---|---|---|---|---|
| ACTIVITY | CONGRESS | PRESIDENCY | BUREAUCRACY | |
| Information collection, analysis, and dissemination | X | X | XXX | X |
| Alternative development and selection | XX | XX | XX | X |
| Advocacy | XX | XXX | XX | XX |
| Formal decisions | XXX | XXX | — | — |

XXX = primary access
XX = considerable access
X = some access
— = little or no access

government to do something about it. Policy formulation is the development of a proposed alternative for what should be done. Legitimation involves the ratification and possible amendment of that choice
in its details. The products of these activities are policy statements.
Congress is a major participant in the policy formulation and legitimation process. The passage of any major statute represents the culmina-
tion of formulation and legitimation activities. Constitutionally, Congress has to participate in a major way in the decisions leading up to
such passage.

There are a number of specific activities that go on during the
formulation and legitimation of policy statements: (1) the collection,
analysis, and dissemination of information; (2) the development and
selection of policy alternatives; (3) advocacy of the most widely supported alternative or alternatives; and (4) final formal decisions (in
statutory form). The access of Congress to formulation and legitimation overall is best thought of in terms of varying degrees of access to
those specific activities. Table 11–1 summarizes the potential access of
the principal institutional actors to these four activities. The table
suggests that the bureaucracy is particularly important in information
collection, analysis, and dissemination activities and helps narrow the
range of what is considered possible even before formal alternative
development and selection begins.[10] All of the major institutional
actors play a role in both alternative development and selection and

[10]Congressional staff collect, analyze, and disseminate a great deal of information. How much
the individual members can absorb or use varies from individual to individual but is clearly
limited. As one sophisticated and experienced Senate subcommittee staff director put it to the
author in discussing information relevant to development of a major draft bill in late 1981, "Up
here we need single numbers, not necessarily accurate ones."

# THE PASSAGE OF SOUTH AFRICAN SANCTIONS, 1986

In imposing economic sanctions against South Africa in 1986, Congress was responding simultaneously to a strategic foreign policy issue as well as to domestic concerns about the moral issue of apartheid. Congress also decisively seized the U.S. leadership initiative, which President Reagan had been reluctant to do himself. Instead he had actively opposed sanctions.

Almost no public attention was focused on South Africa prior to the end of 1984. The State Department's policy of "constructive engagement," in place since 1981, relied on limited and incremental diplomatic efforts to work with the existing South African governmental structure. By 1985 the failure of that low-key approach was evident, as multiple events converged:

- Civil rights and political leaders protested apartheid in front of the South African embassy, willingly being arrested; newscasts covered these demonstrations extensively.
- Bishop Desmond Tutu, a black South African and an articulate anti-apartheid spokesman, received the Nobel Peace Prize in December 1984. Tutu's extensive tour of the U.S. in 1985 was widely covered by the press, as was his plea to Congress to pressure the South African government to negotiate with black groups.
- Violence in South Africa by both the government and activist black groups increased, inspired by both racial and political injustices. Telecasts brought the violence and the grievances into American homes nightly.
- The House and Senate passed bills imposing restrained sanctions in 1985 but did not complete action. President Reagan adopted very mild sanctions in an Executive Order to forestall stiffer congressional legislation.

Public awareness of the repression by the South African government grew throughout 1985 and 1986, and as it did the pressure within Congress increased to take a stand against apartheid. In the words of Rep. Stephen Solarz (D-N.Y.): "If we are going to stand up against repression in Central America and terrorism in the Middle East, then I think it is time to stand up against racism in South Africa." The symbolic value of congressional action on the international and the domestic stages was also a significant incentive. Rep. Lynn Martin (R-Ill.) said "The vote matters not because of what it says about South Africa. It matters more because of what it says about America."

In June 1986, the House Democrats took Republican leaders by surprise, abruptly substituting a very tough bill that imposed a virtually total trade embargo offered by Rep. Ronald Dellums (D-Cal.) for the more moderate bill originally introduced by Rep. William Gray (D-Pa.). (The previous year, a similar substitute had been resoundingly defeated.) Republicans, feeling the bill's extreme nature would doom it to failure in the Senate [Rep. Mark Siljander [R-Mich.] called it the "kiss of death" for sanctions], cooked their own goose. The bill passed the House on a voice vote. The public impact raised dramatically the threshold of what was permissible to propose in dealing with the South African question.

In the Senate, Richard Lugar (R-Ind.), previously a staunch supporter of the president, engineered and shepherded a sanctions bill through the Foreign Relations Committee he chaired and the full chamber in July and August. Dismayed by the president's refusal to dissociate himself from the Pretoria government and to embrace more visibly the cause of South African blacks, Lugar deserted the president and steered the bill around attempts by opponents and energetic supporters to amend it. Lugar's goal was to maintain a bipartisan vote large enough to withstand the expected presidential veto, and he succeeded—the final vote was 84 to 14: almost guaranteed veto-proof. Lugar turned his efforts to the House, where he successfully convinced the leadership and the black caucus to accept the Senate bill without a conference. The possibility of a lengthy conference or a deadlock persuaded House members to agree, albeit reluctantly. They viewed a moderate bill as preferable to no bill.

The president was opposed to any sanctions, even the more moderate ones in the Senate version, and he vetoed the bill on September 26. Both houses had more than ample votes to override, and the outcome was not really in doubt. The House vote was 313 to 83, the Senate vote 78 to 21. The president's lobbying efforts were restrained, recognizing that the situation was virtually unwinnable. In defeat, the president was gracious, claiming (somewhat disingenuously) that his disagreement with Congress was not over ends but over means. But house Minority Leader Robert Michel (R-Ill.) was more realistic, saying "to put it in its mildest terms, the administration has been less than brilliant in handling this issue." In the face of presidential foot-dragging, Congress sent a strong signal to Americans and to the rest of the world that the U.S. would not support racial and political injustice in South Africa. Exercising a strong role in strategic foreign policy, Congress also sent a strong message to the president about leadership and about its access to major policy issues.

in advocacy, with the president playing a particularly important advocacy role when he chooses. The formal decision stage, since it ultimately requires action on statutes or amendments to statutes, is the province of both Congress and the president.

The third stage is program implementation. Once a policy statement has been made, then numerous decisions about the details of what should be done to implement it have to be made. The products of this stage are policy actions. Implementation is enormously important in the overall transmission of policies to intended beneficiaries. Bureaucracies have the most responsibility for this stage. Congressional participation in implementation is minimal and sporadic and usually consists of isolated interventions by individual members or, occasionally, subcommittees.[11]

A secondary product of implementation is the impact of the policies on society. Theoretically, both the program implementation itself and the impact of that implementation on target groups and on society in general should be evaluated in order that informed decisions can be made about the future. In principle, Congress should play a major role in that evaluation. In fact, very little systematic evaluation of either implementation or impact occurs with congressional participation. Incentives for members of Congress do not work in favor of oversight. If oversight is used to encompass the notion of evaluation, the same disincentives for systematic program evaluation exist. Congressional "evaluation" tends to consist of judgments based on political considerations, anecdotes about the benefits conferred by programs or individuals ("Minnie Jones' hearing was saved by medicare."), and gut feelings and intuitions. Some have argued this is inevitably the case. Others have argued that more systematic evaluation by Congress is possible.[12]

Figure II-1 summarizes the principal policy stages and policy products in the American national government and also indicates the general nature of congressional access to each stage. The arrows indicate the usual flow of activity. The "decisions about the future" stage is a way of indicating that the cycle can be re-entered at earlier stages. Like any graphic presentation of a messy process, this all appears quite tidy. Reality is, of course, considerably less structured.

## ACCESS AND TYPES OF POLICY

One of the major policy consequences of fragmentation in Congress is that most domestic issues are defined as distributive—that is, providing primarily subsidy for private activity. Three other types of domestic policy were previously identified: competitive regulatory

---

[11]For some examples of congressional interventions in implementation and for a general statement about the relative importance of all actors, including Congress, in implementation see Randall B. Ripley and Grace A. Franklin, *Policy Implementation and Bureaucracy,* 2nd ed. (Chicago: Dorsey, 1986).

[12]For a number of treatments of this question see the articles by James A. Thurber, Allen Shick, Robert H. Haveman, Charles O. Jones, Alton Frye, Andrew S. Carron, and Roger H. Davidson in *Policy Analysis* 2 (1976): 197–323; the articles by Randall B. Ripley, Charles O. Jones, Frederick O'R. Hayes, and Richard Royce in *Policymaking Role of Leadership in the Senate,* a compilation of papers prepared for the Commission on the Operation of the Senate (Washington: U.S. Government Printing Office, 1976); and Daniel A. Dreyfus, "The Limitations of Policy Research in Congressional Decisionmaking," *Policy Studies Journal* 4 (1976): 269–74.

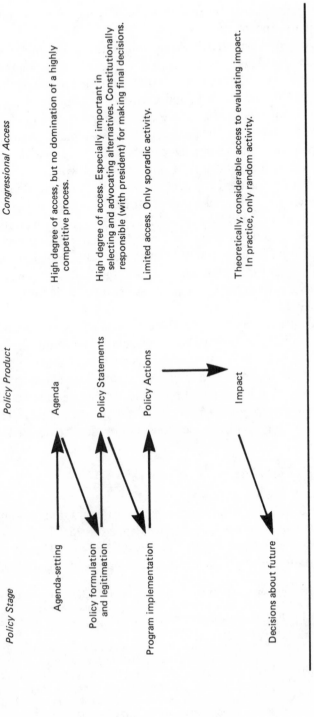

**Figure 11–1.** Congressional Access to Policy Stages and Policy Products

*Policy Stage*

Agenda-setting

Policy formulation
and legitimation

Program implementation

Decisions about future

*Policy Product*

Agenda

Policy Statements

Policy Actions

Impact

*Congressional Access*

High degree of access, but no domination of a highly competitive process.

High degree of access. Especially important in selecting and advocating alternatives. Constitutionally responsible (with president) for making final decisions.

Limited access. Only sporadic activity.

Theoretically, considerable access to evaluating impact. In practice, only random activity.

(which looks a great deal like distributive policy in many senses), protective regulatory, and redistributive.

Congress has different degrees of access to these different kinds of domestic policy. Congress also has different degrees of access to different kinds of foreign and defense policy. There are three principal types of foreign and defense decisions: structural, strategic, and crisis. Structural policies and programs aim primarily at procuring, locating, and organizing military personnel and materiel, presumably within the confines and guidelines of previously determined strategic decisions. This is basically a subsidizing activity, and structural foreign and defense policy resembles distributive domestic policy in terms of the political relationships generated. Examples of such policies and programs include sales of arms to foreign countries, weapons systems decisions (do we or don't we develop a B-1 bomber?), decisions about the size of the reserve military forces, a program to send surplus farm commodities overseas, and the placement, expansion, or contraction of military bases in the United States.

Strategic policies and programs are designed to assert and implement in broad terms the basic stance of the United States toward other nations, both in military terms and in terms of foreign policy. Foreign trade, foreign aid, the location and size of U.S. troop contingents stationed abroad, decisions about the basic mix of military forces, immigration policies, and decisions about involvement in specific military-political situations abroad (Vietnam, Cambodia, the Mideast, Rhodesia, Angola, El Salvador, Nicaragua, Libya, and the Persian Gulf) all serve as examples.

Crisis policies are short-run responses to immediate problems that are perceived to be serious for the United States, that have burst on policy-makers with little or no warning, and that seem to demand immediate action. Recent crisis decisions have involved the U.S. reaction to the placement of missiles in Cuba by the Soviet Union in 1962, the North Korean seizure of a U.S. Navy ship in 1968, the Cambodian seizure of a U.S. merchant marine ship in 1975, the Iranian seizure of U.S. hostages in 1979, and the seizure of other American hostages in the Mideast in the 1980s.

Different institutional actors in the policy-making process have different degrees of access to the formulation and legitimation of policy statements depending on the type of policy under consideration.[13] The principal contending actors are considered to be the presi-

---

[13]For considerable empirical evidence supporting this general statement, see Randall B. Ripley and Grace A. Franklin, *Congress, the Bureaucracy, and Public Policy,* 4th ed. (Chicago: Dorsey, 1987).

dent, presidency, and centralized bureaucracy (the Office of Management and Budget and presidential appointees scattered throughout the executive branch); bureaus and other subunits in the executive branch; Congress as a whole (symbolized by decision making on the floor of the House and Senate); the subcommittees of Congress in a disaggregated sense; and relevant portions of the private sector (the definition of which varies from policy type to policy type). Table II-2 summarizes the relative degree of access for each of these five sets of actors to each of the seven types of policy (four domestic and three foreign and defense). The last column indicates the most important multi-actor relationship in making policy determinations for each type of policy.

Several general statements emerge from an inspection of Table II-2. First, three patterns are identical—those for distributive domestic policy, competitive regulatory policy, and structural foreign and defense policy. Second, no one actor or combination of actors completely dominates decision making leading to policy statements. Third, the private sector in various incarnations is important in all policy areas except crisis. Most policy is made with significant input from and, usually, at least grudging acquiescence of the most directly affected portions of the private sector. In those three policy areas in which the classic triangular subgovernments dominate, the private sector is generally enthusiastic about supporting government policies and programs that emerge.

## ACCESS AND THE INTERNAL DISTRIBUTION OF INFLUENCE

Congress strives to achieve two objectives (both with ties to re-election prospects for incumbents): a responsiveness to national problems and the maintenance of a central role in policy making. The way influence is distributed in the House and Senate has a profound effect on the degree to which these goals can be met. Ideally, the internal distribution of influence should promote the following conditions, all of which are important to a strong congressional policy-making role: ready access for members to the most important points in the legislative process, efficient procedures that allow a relatively steady stream of output, and a moderately high degree of institutional stability.

These conditions in turn affect a set of values that influence congressional responsiveness to public needs; thoroughness, representativeness, and responsibility. *Thoroughness* is present in congressional actions if the major aspects of a problem are identified and appraised and

**Table 11–2.** Decision-Making Patterns for Different Types of Policy Statements

RELATIVE ACCESS OF:

| POLICY TYPE | PRESIDENT, PRESIDENCY, AND CENTRALIZED BUREAUCRACY | BUREAUS | CONGRESS | SUBCOMMITTEES | PRIVATE SECTOR | MOST IMPORTANT RELATIONSHIP IN DETERMINING DECISIONS |
|---|---|---|---|---|---|---|
| Distributive (domestic) | Low | High | Low (supports subcommittees) | High | High (the subsidized) | Subgovernment of subcommittee-bureau-interest groups representing the subsidized |
| Competitive regulatory (domestic) | Low | High | Low (supports subcommittees) | High | High (the competitors for regulated benefits) | Subgovernment, as above |
| Protective regulatory (domestic) | Moderately high | Moderate | Moderately high | Moderate | Moderately high (the regulated interests) | Presidency-Congress-regulated interests |
| Redistributive (domestic) | High | Moderately Low | High | Moderately low | High (peak associations representing clusters of interest groups) | Presidency-Congress-Peak associations |
| Structural (foreign and defense) | Low | High | Low (supports subcommittees) | High | High (the subsidized) | Subgovernment, as above |
| Strategic (foreign and defense) | High | Low | High (often responsive to executive) | Low | Moderate (interest groups, corporations) | Presidency-Congress |
| Crisis (foreign and defense) | High | Low | Low | Low | Low | Internal to the presidency |

the major alternative solutions to the problem are also identified and appraised. *Representativeness* is present if the main contending interests are heard and weighed during the decision-making process. *Responsibility* is present if the agents who have the most influence in making decisions are readily visible. Where responsibility is lacking, arbitrary action is more likely to be invisible and undetected.

The distribution of influence in the House and Senate involves a variety of traditions and units within the institution: party leaders, committees and subcommittees and their chairpersons, prevailing norms, and socialization patterns. It is the members of Congress as individuals who finally determine how Congress will operate. The distribution of influence is not the result of any single individual's efforts but is affected by the behavior and decisions of a variety of individuals. For example, a subcommittee chairperson who takes an aggressive role in running his or her subcommittee or party leaders who work diligently to achieve party unity on roll call voting help shape broader and longer lasting patterns of influence distribution.

The distribution of influence in the House and Senate is subject to varying degrees of centralization. In a centralized distribution, control is exercised by influential and aggressive central party leaders and committee chairpersons who are loyal to those leaders and who have considerable authority in their respective committees and use that authority to pursue outcomes desired by the leaders. Individual senators and representatives are oriented toward their party and possess only limited personal influence.

In a decentralized distribution, party leaders are at most only moderately aggressive and influential, while standing committee chairpersons and subcommittee chairpersons are largely independent from party leaders and tend to be relatively influential in their own committees in pursuit of outcomes defined with little concern for what the party leaders want. Individual members are also influential within the specific committees and subcommittees on which they sit.

A classic case of centralized distribution existed in the period during the first few years of Woodrow Wilson's presidency (1913 and 1914). The majority leaders in both houses—Oscar W. Underwood in the House and John W. Kern in the Senate—guided their respective caucuses in making sure that the most important bills emerging from the standing committees had their approval and the support of the majority of Democrats. Committee chairpersons worked closely with these leaders in shaping details of bills so that they would be true to the general policy positions taken by the leaders and by the caucuses. Individual members had their major policy impact through their participation in the party caucus, through loyal support of the positions that emerged from the caucus, and through bills that came from the standing committees that were in accord with caucus directions. The personalities of Wilson, Underwood, and Kern all lent themselves to these arrangements. More important, Wilson and the Democrats had come to power after making specific policy pledges to the electorate, pledges that a number of influential citizens wanted to see redeemed. The capture of the White House in the 1912 election was made possible primarily by a three-way race in which the normal Republican vote was divided between incumbent President William Howard Taft and former President Theodore Roosevelt running as a Progressive. Wilson, therefore, had extra incentive to be productive so as to stand a chance of winning re-election in 1916.

A strong pattern of decentralization was dominant in both houses during most of the 1940s and 1950s (with the partial exception of the two Republican-controlled Congresses in 1947–48 and 1953–54). Despite the presence of Sam Rayburn as Speaker of the House during the entire period and Lyndon Johnson as majority leader of the Senate during the latter part of the period, only some committee chairmen were consistently concerned with the policy preferences of those energetic and resourceful leaders. Rayburn and Johnson seemed so resourceful because they had to exercise considerable wile to have any substantive impact on the products that emerged from the standing committees.[14] Conservative-dominated committees regularly ignored their preferences and produced legislation unacceptable to the leaders. But—given the number of Republicans and conservative southern Democrats in Congress at the time—those Conservative bills often passed both in committee and on the floor.

In the One Hundredth Congress (1987–88) the distribution of influence in the House and Senate is mixed. Elements of centralization (especially in the House) are present; so are major elements of decentralization, particularly to subcommittees. In the House, Speaker Wright and his closest associates are aggressive but are also confronted by a number of subcommittee chairpersons who are equally aggressive and may insist on taking independent policy positions. In the Senate, Majority Leader Byrd is active, but not as aggressive as Wright in pushing specific policies. Subcommittee chairpersons are fairly autonomous in their various jurisdictions. In both houses, most full committee chairpersons are quite constrained.

---

[14]For two insightful personal appreciations of the style of leadership exercised by Rayburn and Johnson see the chapters by D. B. Hardeman (on Rayburn) and Ralph K. Huitt (on Johnson) in William S. Livingston, Lawrence C. Dodd, and Richard L. Schott (eds.), *The Presidency and the Congress* (Austin, Texas: Lyndon B. Johnson School of Public Affairs and Lyndon B. Johnson Library, 1979).

A high degree of decentralization is the "natural" state of Congress in that the structure and norms of both houses emphasize independent action on the part of individual members that often gets translated into support for "strong" committees or subcommittees and "weak" leaders. However, there is nothing inevitable about the dominance of decentralization. Some members argue that there is more genuine independence in working with aggressive central party leaders than in working more immediately under both the thumb and gaze of domineering committee or subcommittee chairpersons. There is constant ferment in Congress about the proper ratio of powers that should be allocated to and exercised by party leaders, caucuses, and standing committees and subcommittees. Judging by the last 75 years it seems safest to predict that the forces favoring increased centralization will lose more than they will win; but it is not accurate to say that that has been a uniform outcome during those 75 years or that it will be a uniform outcome in the future.

Different values are served by differing distributions of influence. *Thoroughness* of consideration seems to be most likely at the decentralized end of the spectrum and least likely at the centralized end. As decentralization increases, more members of the House and Senate increase both their substantive expertise and their degree of specialization. This means that virtually all members of the Senate and most members of the House have the potential of becoming expert on some legislative matter. They are aided by a relatively large number of knowledgeable and independently important staff members. There is more chance that thorough examination will take place under such conditions than when the committees are merely doing the bidding of the party leaders, without independent contributions from individual members or staff members.

*Representativeness* of the greatest number of interests is also most likely to occur in a situation of decentralization of influence and least likely to occur in a situation in which influence is centralized. With influence highly fragmented, many interests have a chance to ally themselves with a key subcommittee or individual senator or representative or staff member, and thus become effectively represented. In a highly centralized situation the interests that are close to the party leaders are represented, but competing interests may not be.

If *representativeness* is considered in a second sense, however—that of weighing competing interests—it may be facilitated more by a centralized distribution of influence than by a decentralized distribution. Since political parties have to agree to compromises between interests in order to attract broad electoral support, the centralized situation may lead to a weighing of competing interests before matters reach the Senate and House floors. Similarly, since an important subcommittee chairperson does not necessarily have to weigh competing interests and because his or her judgment, in the form of a bill, usually passes on the floor, only one interest may dominate a specific, relatively small area of public policy. Perhaps, in the matter of representativeness, when both number of interests and the weighing of competing interests are considered, responsiveness to national problems is best promoted by a situation in which the standing committees dominate their subcommittees, thus preventing the subcommittees from becoming autonomous satrapies.

*Responsibility* is most likely in a highly centralized situation and least likely in a highly decentralized one. In the former situation the party leader or leaders, along with the president, can be held responsible for what the Senate and House do legislatively. These leaders may be arbitrary, but the arbitrariness is highly visible. When decentralization is the norm, however, it is often impossible to assign responsibility in any meaningful sense.

In short, no single distribution of influence maximizes all of the values of *thoroughness, representativeness* in both senses, and *responsibility* simultaneously. High decentralization seems most likely to provide thorough consideration and action. High centralization seems most likely to provide responsible consideration and action. And some mid-point between the two extremes seems most likely to provide representative consideration and action.

## ACCESS AND THE CHARACTER OF RELATIONS WITH THE EXECUTIVE

The way Congress shapes its relations with the executive determines in large part not only how effective it will be in day-to-day duties, but also its effectiveness in policy-making in general and its responsiveness to broad public needs. A variety of factors help determine the level of cooperation between Congress and the president. These include: the party label of the president and majority parties in the House and the Senate; how leadership is defined by the president and congressional leaders; personal styles of the people in both institutions; the skill with which resources are used; and the willingness to compromise.

Congress is composed of a large and diverse group of individuals, and most of the time these individuals, alone and in groups, differ in their goals for Congress. It is possible, however, for a sizeable majority of the members to articulate and pursue (with varying degree of consciousness) broad institutional goals. Pursuit of these broad goals enables Congress to have specific kinds of impact on the substance of public policy.

Three alternative goals seem particularly relevant in affecting the substance of public policy. The first is to *maximize support for the substantive program of the president.* The second is to *maximize the independent influence of Congress on positive policy actions by the government.* The third is *to maximize ability of Congress to limit governmental innovation and to restrain the increase in governmental activity.* [15]

The way in which Congress performs its functions of lawmaking, oversight of administration, education of the public, and representation will help determine which goal or goals are in fact being sought. If, as is often the case, Congress consciously chooses no single goal and no single mode of performing its functions, then bits and pieces of all three goals will in fact be pursued simultaneously.

## Maximum Support for the Program of the President

If Congress seeks this goal it should perform its lawmaking functioning by enacting whatever legislative proposals the president submits or supports. It should perform its oversight function very generally, if at all, in the cases of agencies and programs that appear to have presidential approval. The president may, however, be concerned about the activities of some of the agencies and programs theoretically under his control and might welcome careful congressional scrutiny to help him influence matters that otherwise might be independent of any real checks. In these cases the president can make clear to various congressional committees those programs and agencies that he wants overseen and Congress can assist him in this way.

Congress should perform its public education function by propagandizing in favor of presidential proposals before enactment and on behalf of presidential performance after enactment. It should perform its representation function by concentrating on narrow activities (casework for individuals and corporations and division of federal

[15]For a good argument for maximum congressional support for the president see James MacGregor Burns, *The Deadlock of Democracy* (Englewood Cliffs, N.J.: Prentice-Hall, 1963). For a good argument for maximum independent congressional influence see Theodore J. Lowi, "Congressional Reform: A New Time, Place and Manner," in Theodore J. Lowi and Randall B. Ripley (eds.), *Legislative Politics U.S.A.*, 3rd ed. (Boston: Little, Brown, 1973). For a good argument for maximum congressional restraint on governmental activity see James Burnham, *Congress and the American Tradition* (Chicago: Regnery, 1959).

"goodies") in order to avoid conflict with the executive branch on broader questions—except in those few cases in which the president might view such conflict as beneficial to his program.

## Maximum Independent Influence on Positive Policy Positions

If Congress seeks this goal it should perform its lawmaking function by including explicit standards for administering new programs in all legislation it enacts. Congress can demand that the executive branch include such standards in draft legislation, it can add such standards by amending bills coming from the executive branch, and it can include them in bills initiated in Congress. Placing a termination date on all legislation would also help propel Congress toward the goal of maximum independent influence.

Congress should perform its oversight function by examining the role of specific federal agencies and programs in meeting or not meeting broad national needs. This form of oversight can uncover new areas and problems in which legislation is needed. Oversight to meet the goal of maximizing independent congressional impact should insist on rigorous adherence by executive branch agencies to the standards of performance included in the statutes authorizing the programs administered by those agencies. This form of oversight should also insist that agencies develop their own rigorous standards for evaluating performance and relative degrees of success or failure. Congressional committee members and staff members could themselves help in the development of such standards.

Congress should perform its public education function by selecting specific substantive areas in which efforts to stimulate public attention and support should be concentrated. Congress has little impact as a collectivity when it tries to educate the public on every side of every issue simultaneously. But if there is some genuine consensus, either bipartisan or at least on the part of the majority party in Congress, on which issues need special and constant attention, then Congress— through its most visible members—can educate at least the attentive part of the public.

Finally, Congress should perform its representation function by concentrating considerable attention on questions of national concern such as the federal responsibility in relation to racial equality or environmental quality. For maximum impact, such activity should be limited to only a few subject areas. If virtually every issue is claimed to involve matters of profound principle and the national good, the impact of the claim becomes diluted. Naturally, Congress would also continue the narrower kinds of representation (casework for individuals and corporations and division of federal largesse) and these are perfectly proper activities as long as they do not conflict with a focus on a limited number of broad-based proposals and questions reflecting the central problems of American society.

### Limited Governmental Innovation and Restraint of Increase in Governmental Activity

If Congress seeks this goal it should perform its lawmaking function very sparingly, restricting the number of new laws enacted. Those that are enacted should contain provisions guaranteeing continued tight congressional control. Similar provisions should be added to existing legislation. It should perform its oversight function by constantly involving itself in the details of the administration of programs. Relationships with key bureaucrats and interest-group representatives for purposes of maintaining the status quo in a wide range of programs should be cultivated and maintained.

Congress should perform its public education function by warning about asserted dangers of big government such as invasion of privacy or too much spending. Simultaneously, selective public education efforts should be undertaken to support existing specific programs. Finally, Congress should perform its *representation* function by concentrating exclusively on casework and the division of federal benefits.

### SUMMARY

Three central points should stand out in this chapter. First, Congress has the capacity for being influential over policy decisions because it has generally good access to the processes by which decisions are made. Second, that access is not undifferentiated—it is predictably greater under some conditions and it is predictably smaller under other conditions. Third, Congress as an institution has considerable choice about how it chooses to use the access it undoubtedly has. Neither the institution nor the individual members are caught in a situation in which their behavior is simply determined by outside influences. They have considerable latitude for determining their own potential for impact on policy despite important pressures and constraints built into the normal way of doing business in Congress.

# 12

# Impact

In the previous chapter we saw that, despite the fragmentation of the institution, Congress has a number of major points of access to policy decisions. As we turn from the notion of access to the notion of impact we will examine the following general propositions:

1. Congress is at its most influential and most comfortable when dealing with policies issue by issue (micro policy). However, beginning in 1981 macro-level policy questions focused on fiscal matters—taxing, spending, and deficits—have become dominant. Congressional action in this broad realm overshadows its performance in virtually all micro-level policy areas in the 1980s.
2. Congress and the executive branch tend to interact in one of four general ways on policy questions: executive dominance, joint program development, Congressional dominance, or stalemate.
3. Congress has had important programmatic impacts in the domestic arena, but the nature and degree of impact and the substantive direction of that impact have all varied by issue and over time.
4. Congress is often overshadowed by the executive branch in the

areas of foreign and defense policy, but it still has an important, even if sporadic, impact in these areas.

5. "Reform" of internal congressional procedures undertaken by the House and Senate is best thought of simply as change. Some changes are desirable in and of themselves. However, few specific changes are self-evidently good and no set of changes can reasonably be expected to negate permanently the nature of the congressional proclivity for fragmentation.

## MICRO POLICY, MACRO POLICY, AND THE BUDGET PROCESS

Most members of Congress are at their happiest when dealing with policies issue by issue. Much of the time tradeoffs are not needed in order to pass a large number of diverse micro policies. Coalitions have to be built to pass individual policies. But the more difficult task of building coalitions that encompass a variety of policies can be avoided. Emphasis on micro policies implies that limits on spending cannot be overly rigid and that budget discipline in Congress can be relatively lax.

From time to time Congress has, however, tried to impose some budgetary discipline on itself. It has engaged in such behavior, in two quite distinct periods, since 1974. Between 1974 and 1981 the congressional focus was on the nature of the budget process and resulted in the creation of a new process and new institutions (the budget committees in both houses and the Congressional Budget Office). This process and these institutions matured and found their places in the congressional scheme of things from 1975 through 1981, a period in which there was no sense of panic about the size of the federal deficit considered either annually or cumulatively. Following the watershed budget and tax decisions of 1981, the deficit—both annual and cumulative—ballooned. Panic, at least rhetorical, which became routinized as deficit-mania, ensued and continued through the 1980s. The deficit became the single overriding domestic issue on the congressional agenda. Again, now with a greater sense of urgency but also with a greater sense of helplessness, Congress sought self-discipline. Sections follow that analyze each of these periods.

### The Revised Budget Process, 1974–1981

The most visible and far-reaching procedural change made by Congress in the 1970s that was presumed to have potential for important changes in its impact on public policy was the establishment of a new budget process and related institutions.[1] This change was made by law in 1974 and implemented in 1975 on an experimental basis for decisions pertaining to fiscal year 1976 and on a permanent basis thereafter. When examined closely, the new process underscores a theme of this book: procedures are important but the preferences and behavior of important actors are much more important in determining the substantive outcome of decision processes. The budget process has a rationality of its own and offers the machinery for decision making. But the needs inside Congress and among actors who interact with Congress do not let machinery dictate processes of bargaining and compromise. In a fragmented Congress forces are present to make sure that important programs and privileged pockets for some of those programs will be maintained. In principle, the budget process offers some centralizing or integrating possibilities. In practice, there are great tensions between these possibilities and the large number of decentralizing or fragmenting tendencies. Appropriations committees, for example, find ways of thwarting some of the Budget Committee initiatives. So do some of the authorizing committees. Some items are placed "off-budget" in part as a way to keep decisions fragmented and to protect specific programs.

Budgeting is a large-scale enterprise in Congress. Five broad activities are primarily budgetary: establishing budget totals, making decisions about how much money to authorize for individual programs, making decisions about how much money to appropriate for individual programs, making decisions about taxes (revenue), and overseeing the carrying out of the budget (budget execution).[2] Table 12-1 arrays those types of decisions in terms of the key congressional actors involved, the types of congressional actions that are taken, and the duration of those actions. In any given year, there may also be addi-

---

[1] The literature on the congressional budget process by political scientists and other observers is vast. For some of the best analysis see the following: John W. Ellwood, "The Great Exception: The Congressional Budget Process in an Age of Decentralization," in Lawrence C. Dodd and Bruce I. Oppenheimer (eds.), *Congress Reconsidered*, 3rd ed. (Washington, D.C.: Congressional Quarterly, 1985): 315–42; Joel Havemann, *Congress and the Budget* (Bloomington, Indiana: Indiana University Press, 1978); Dennis S. Ippolito, *Congressional Spending* (Ithaca, N.Y.: Cornell University Press, 1981); Lance T. LeLoup, *Budgetary Politics*, 3rd ed. (Brunswick, Ohio: King's Court, 1986); LeLoup, *The Fiscal Congress: Legislative Control of the Budget* (Westport, Conn.: Greenwood Press, 1980); Paul E. Peterson, "The New Politics of Deficits," in John E. Chubb and Paul E. Peterson (eds.), *The New Direction in American Politics* (Washington, D.C.: Brookings, 1985): 365–97; Allen Schick (ed.), *Making Economic Policy in Congress* (Washington, D.C.: American Enterprise Institute, 1983); and W. Thomas Wander, F. Ted Hebert, and Gary W. Copeland (eds.), *Congressional Budgeting: Politics, Process, and Power* (Baltimore, Md.: Johns Hopkins University Press, 1984).

[2] LeLoup, *The Fiscal Congress,* Chapter 1.

**Table 12–1.** Congressional Budgetary Decisions

| CONGRESSIONAL BUDGET DECISION | KEY CONGRESSIONAL ACTORS | TYPE OF CONGRESSIONAL ACTION | PREDOMINANT DURATION OF ACTIONS |
|---|---|---|---|
| (1) Budget totals | Budget committees ——— Congressional Budget Office (CBO) | Concurrent resolutions on the budget | Annual |
| (2) Authorizations | Authorizing committees (standing committees) | Legislative authorizations ——— Entitlements | Annual ——— Multiyear ——— Indefinite |
| (3) Appropriations | Appropriation committees | Individual appropriation bills | Annual |
| (4) Revenues | House Ways and Means Committee ——— Senate Finance Committee | Permanent tax code changes ——— Surcharges, rebates | Annual ——— Indefinite |
| (3) Oversight and review | Appropriations committees ——— Authorizing committees ——— CBO ——— General Accounting Office (GAO) | Appropriation and authorization hearings ——— Program evaluation ——— Audits | Periodic |

SOURCE: *Adapted from Lance T. LeLoup,* The Fiscal Congress: Legislative Control of the Budget *(Westport, Conn.: Greenwood Press, 1980): 13.* Contributions in Political Science, No. 47. Copyright © 1980 by Lance T. LeLoup. Permission granted by author and publisher.

tions because of missed deadlines. For example, continuing resolutions allow continued government spending when appropriations deadlines are missed, as they frequently are. The central point of the table is clear: budgeting is complex, actors are many, types of action are diverse, and the period on which different types of actions have a major impact varies from case to case. The complex budgetary involvement of Congress is a ready-made formula for fragmentation *unless* a strong counterpressure—especially in the form of the will of a sizable majority of the members—is present. That will is rare and usually has not been present in the period since the creation of the budget process, even in the 1980s when deficits grew rapidly.

All of the details of the budget process need not be recounted here. The important institutions that were created were the budget committees in the two houses and the Congressional Budget Office. The former were given adequate staffing and considerable formal powers that allowed them to engage in bargaining with other standing committees. The latter added important staff competence to the congressional institution, as discussed in Chapter 7.

Two new processes were set up. One dealt with the presidential power to impound (that is, not to spend) money appropriated by Congress. The procedures included in the 1974 law severely restrict that power and give Congress the final say on whether money will or will not be spent. The second process set up a new budget timetable and also made Congress adopt overall spending and revenue goals and then adjust specific spending measures within the limits of those goals. Table 12-2 summarizes the congressional budget timetable as revised in 1985. Before 1986 many of the deadlines were slightly later. Congress, of course, can and does miss its own deadlines.

Even though Table 12-2 gives the impression of predictable and "rational" proceeding, neither the chronology nor the form of the "rationality" used in any given year has necessarily been the same as in any other year. Each year has seen its own variations. Those need not be detailed here. The process has survived some perilous moments on the floor of Congress, particularly in the House. In the spring of 1977, for example, the House defeated the first budget resolution. But the budget committee went back to work and produced a resolution acceptable to the majority the second time around. During the Ford and Carter years the House was the more dangerous host for the new process because it proceeded on a partisan basis. The Senate proceeded in a much more bipartisan mode. In 1981 new partisan stress came to the Senate too, fostered by the Republican takeover of the Senate, new

**Table 12–2.** Congressional Budget Timetable, 1986 and After

| REQUIRED ACTION | DATE |
| --- | --- |
| President submits budget | 1st Monday after January 3 |
| House and Senate authorizing committees submit views and estimates to Budget committees | February 25 |
| Congressional Budget Office submits report to Budget committees | February 15 |
| Budget committees report first concurrent resolution to respective chambers | April 1 |
| Congress adopts first concurrent resolution | April 15 |
| Congress completes action on reconciliation legislation | June 15 |
| Fiscal Year begins | October 1 |

ranking members on the committee from both parties, and the general budget stance of President Reagan, including his use of the reconciliation procedure in the 1974 law to foster the aims of his administration.

Reconciliation was used in both 1980 and 1981 as a way to allow Congress to consider all presidential recommendations in a single bill relatively early in the process rather than at the end.[3] The law allows for this variation. The 1980 and 1981 versions were also different from each other. In principle, reconciliation allows for more central decision making than other variations. However, it is not immune to bargaining and compromise. It needs some powerful central force—such as only the president can supply—to make it work.

The reconciliation process forces changes in substantive law driven by the need to make budget numbers come out even. The budget committees have authority over the numbers; the other committees of Congress have jurisdiction over the other substantive provisions of law. The latter are, however, heavily influenced by the decisions of the former. An aggressive president, such as Reagan in 1981, if he can get favorable action from the budget committees, can also achieve a great many changes in substantive law simultaneously. If the House and Senate back their budget committees they can force the other standing committees to make substantive changes.

The elaborate decisions that must be made and bargains that must be struck mean that the president and his aides, the party leaders, and a raft of committee leaders must all be involved. Indeed, a very large proportion of the members of both houses must be involved directly. In 1981, for example, 72 of the 100 senators and 208 of the 435 representatives were on the conference committee to produce the final reconciliation bill. The conference committee did its work in 55 different subgroups.

The reconciliation process is not equally well-suited for all substantive decisions. For example, it seems useful in dealing with entitlement programs but not useful for dealing with defense spending, because that money goes through "normal" annual authorizations and appropriations. Above all, the reconciliation process is hard to use because it forces Congress to make "zero-sum" choices: that is, tradeoffs between visible reductions in one program and visible increases in another or between visible reductions in one program and stability in

---

[3] On the reconciliation process in general—as well as for details on 1980 and 1981—see Allen Schick, *Reconciliation and the Congressional Budget Process* (Washington, D.C.: American Enterprise Institute, 1981). On 1981 see also Norman J. Ornstein (ed.), *President and Congress: Assessing Reagan's First Year* (Washington, D.C.: American Enterprise Institute, 1982).

another or (in a fat year) between increases in one program and stability or lesser increases in another. In reconciliation, a fixed pot of money is divided. That runs contrary to the congressional preference for structuring decision making so that everyone can appear to win or at least do pretty well simultaneously. Reconciliation is a tool for integration; normal congressional habits and preferences are for fragmentation. Tension over sustained use of reconciliation is inevitable, although the outcome can vary from year to year.

What general conclusions about the impact of the congressional budget process from 1975 through 1981 seem reasonable? It did not deliver much in the way of substantive impact. However, the process itself provided several variations that could, when will was present on the part of members and perhaps on the part of a president, contribute to more integrated policy making. A careful student of the process, Lance LeLoup, summarized the situation quite well as of 1980:

Those who hoped for drastic cuts in spending were disappointed; those who hoped to see national priorities restructured were disappointed. . . .

The policy impact of budget reform has been relatively slight. Some savings have been realized, but the relative allocation within the budget has been more stable than in the decade that preceded it. It would be difficult to make a case that the budget would have looked significantly different without the procedural changes in Congress. Yet this is not a critical indictment of the reforms. . . . Congress has institutionalized a set of procedures which increase their decision-making capability and their power in national politics. . . .

The complex decisions on authorizations, appropriations, entitlements, and taxes are better integrated than before. . . . As pressures build to cut spending and balance the budget, the means to accomplish these goals in the 1980s are in place. Conversely, an activist majority in Congress could once again expand the federal sector or establish other new policy directions. The budget process is important not for its own sake, or for the policy changes it has already made, but for the changes it might facilitate in the future.[4]

## Deficits and Macro Policy, 1981 and After

The spending and taxing decisions of 1981 produced several major changes with important ramifications for succeeding years:

[4]LeLoup, *The Fiscal Congress,* 157–58.

1. Those decisions demonstrated the potential for large-scale policy change in a relatively short period of time. Macro-policy change became more than a theory. Micro-policy decisions continued, but could be set partially within the context of broader change. Not all policy moved by small increments, though that tendency remained powerful. The inevitable tension between macro-level policy and micro-level policy affected outcomes. But, significantly, a macro focus had not been familiar to Congress for many years.
2. Those decisions displayed the basic policy commitments of Ronald Reagan that would remain in place for the rest of his presidency: cut most domestic spending, especially for social programs; increase defense spending; decrease tax revenue coming to the federal government.
3. The concrete decisions of 1981—to make very modest savings in the area of domestic spending (in part, because a great deal of that spending was based on entitlements over which only marginal immediate changes in spending levels could be effected); to increase defense spending considerably (a trend that had begun in 1978); and to reduce federal revenues dramatically through a major tax bill—helped create an immediate and unprecedented (at least for peacetime) rapid growth in the federal deficit. The deficit problem appeared on the scene immediately after the 1981 decisions and flourished throughout the rest of the 1980s, leaving both president and Congress groping for "answers."

After 1981 the question of deficit reduction came to overshadow most other policy concerns. From 1982 through the rest of the Reagan years, specific events in the broad fiscal arena (spending, taxing, deficit-reduction attempts) varied from year to year, but the sense of confusion and frustration remained. The major specific events from 1982 through early 1988 were:

1. The passage of the 1982 tax bill, which reversed some of the 1981 tax decisions and increased government revenues, but not enough to make a serious dent in the deficit.
2. The passage of the Gramm-Rudman-Hollings deficit-reduction bill in 1985. This was followed by a Supreme Court decision eviscerating part of the prescribed process for achieving deficit reduction. More important, it was followed by an evident lack of will on the part of both the executive and legislative branches to implement the Gramm-Rudman-Hollings deficit-reduction targets. In 1987, when some members of Congress tried to find new teeth to put into

Gramm-Rudman-Hollings, the effort failed, even though a relatively toothless revision was passed.

3. The passage of a major tax revision in 1986 that made many changes in the tax code but, critically, raised no new revenue (it was "revenue-neutral").

# CONGRESS, THE PRESIDENT, AND BUDGET POLITICS, 1987

BY JONATHAN FUERBRINGER

Debates in the House and the Senate over an amendment to reinvigorate the budget-balancing law are turning traditional fiscal politics upside down. Democrats are demanding more reduction of the Federal deficit while Republicans are asking for less.

To the astonishment of people with long memories, an original sponsor of the budget-balancing law, Senator Phil Gramm, Republican of Texas, last week opposed an amendment backed by several Democrats that would have required spending cuts or revenue increases totaling $36 billion in the budget for the fiscal year 1988, which begins this Oct. 1. Mr. Gramm's alternative, which passed, could require no more than $26 billion, and possibly much less.

In the House, Republican leaders have endorsed a plan that would limit any automatic spending cut under the law to only $18 billion.

The chairman of the House Budget Committee, William H. Gray 3d of Pennsylvania, said, "This proves what we suspected all along, that Republicans are not serious about deficit control while President Reagan is in office."

As a result, Democrats, especially in the House, now think they can

succeed where they have failed in the past in saddling Mr. Reagan with the responsibility for the nation's deficit problems.

The Democrat-Republican role reversal is a twist in this year's budget battle, which will drag on into the fall and maybe as long as Thanksgiving or Christmas. The drive to cut the deficit is now ensnared in a web of competing strategies.

Among Democrats, there is an effort to put pressure on the President to compromise on his antagonism to tax increases and to spotlight what they see as his refusal to deal with the deficit. But not all Democrats have agreed on how to do this.

Republicans, on the other hand, are trying to protect the President from tax increases and deeper reductions in his military budget in his last year and a half in office. To do this, they are willing to put off some major decisions on reducing the deficit until after the 1988 Presidential election.

On both sides, the stakes in the budget game have changed.

For Democrats, the new element is their endorsement of tax increases—$19.3 billion in 1988 and $64 billion over three years. In the last two years, Democratic leaders in the House opposed any tax increases. This made them reluctant to push for large cuts in the deficit because that would bring reductions in popular domestic programs.

But now the aim is to force the President to accept tax increases by threatening him with automatic spending cuts that would make deep reductions in his military budget. With tax increases to reduce the deficit, Democrats would not have to worry so much about having to cut domestic programs.

Some Democrats are worrying about the next President, who they hope will be a Democrat. The more that is done in the last two years of the Reagan Administration to reduce the deficit, they reason, the easier the task for the new President. They would also prefer that tax increases occur on Mr. Reagan's watch.

Republicans in the House and the Senate are concerned that the Democratic push for deficit reduction will result in cuts in the military budget, which has borne the brunt of deficit reduction the last two years. They also want to reduce the pressure for tax increases, to which the President is viscerally opposed.

This week the new politics of the budget is in full sway as House and Senate negotiators try to reach a compromise on the proposal to fix the budget-balancing law by adding a mechanism for making widespread spending cuts automatically when the budget does not meet the law's deficit targets. The new device would replace the mechanism the Supreme Court ruled unconstitutional last summer. Under the proposal, half of the spending cuts would be in the Pentagon budget.

The Democratic-controlled Senate last week approved a new mechanism that fits the Republican strategy because it would allow the White House and Congress to put off major decisions on taxes and the deficit until after the 1988 election. Led by the chairman of the Senate Budget Committee, Lawton Chiles of Florida, the Democrats had to concede. They were split among themselves and could not approve a new mechanism without Republican votes.

In the House, the Democrats were still divided. One group, led by the chairman of the House Ways and Means Committee, Representative Dan Rostenkowski of Illinois, wanted an automatic spending cut mechanism like that approved in the Senate. The big difference is they wanted to require a bigger cut in the deficit this year and before the new President is inaugurated in 1989.

Another group, led by the majority leader, Representative Thomas S. Foley of Washington, favored a plan to shift to the President the political blame for not reducing the deficit. Instead of making the spending cuts to reduce the deficit automatic, this proposal would force the President to choose between approving the cuts or vetoing them. The Democrats could then pin the results on him.

The first group believes that automatic spending cuts are the only chance to force the President to compromise on tax increases. They also want the automatic cuts as political cover for tax increases, allowing them to tell constituents they had to raise taxes to avoid sharp spending cuts.

The second group, in effect, has decided that the President cannot be put in a trap. Although he has been severely damaged politically by the Iran-contra affair, he is still politically potent on the budget and, especially, tax increases. They don't think he will compromise on taxes, and they are worried about the effect of the automatic spending cuts on domestic programs.

Today, as House and Senate negotiators began meeting to try to work out a compromise, it appeared that the Democrats who favor the automatic mechanism were going to prevail, opening the possibility of reaching an agreement by the end of the week, when Congress is due to start its summer recess.

On a 267 to 156 vote, the House endorsed a nonbinding resolution urging the conferees to include an automatic mechanism. Voting for the resolution were Republicans and many conservative Democrats who like the automatic mechanism because it forces action on the deficit even if Congress and the White House are deadlocked. The Republicans, who sponsored the resolution, side-stepped the question of how much deficit reduction to require.

After the vote, Mr. Foley said he was ready to drop his proposal and accept an automatic spending cut mechanism. But he said the conferees would have to decide the exact amount of deficit reduction.

Summing up, Representative Leon E. Panetta, Democrat of California, said, "The Democrats are moving toward some kind of tough trigger," the automatic spending cut mechanism.

"The more squeals that come out of the White House, the more inclination there is to put this together," he added.

What generalizations can be made about congressional involvement in the macro world of spending, taxing, and the deficit from 1982 through early 1988?

First, some of the details of specific programmatic outcomes have not changed dramatically during this period, both because of ingrained political patterns and also because of the constraints of previous legislation dictating a variety of mandatory spending, especially for entitlement programs in the social welfare area. For example, when spending in Fiscal 1982 (the first year in which Reagan's preferences had an impact) is compared with spending in Fiscal 1986 in *constant dollars* (with the effect of inflation removed) most of the major categories of spending on payments to individuals have increased substantially: 20 percent for education, training, employment, and social services; 18 percent for health; 31 percent for medicare; and 11 percent for social security. When spending in those same categories for Fiscal 1986 is compared to spending for Fiscal 1976, again in constant dollars, the changes are even larger: 77 percent for education, training, employment, and social services; 37 percent for health; 135 percent for medicare; and 45 percent for social security. These are not trivial items. They amounted to almost $305 billion in Fiscal 1986, well over 30 percent of all federal outlays and almost 43 percent of all federal outlays outside of the national defense field.

However, despite continued spending growth, some important perceptions of the basic decision-making choices and the nature of conflict in making them have changed, at least for the time being. A leading scholar of budgeting offers a perceptive comment:

> Priority decisions—budgeting at the macro level—have increasingly dominated budgetary politics as Congress and the president struggle to control broad revenue and spending aggregates over multi-year periods. While program and operation decisions—budgeting at the micro level— remain critical, they have increasingly been subject to top-down constraints. The basic conceptualization of budgeting has gradually shifted from a cycle of incremental executive requests and legislative actions to a complex series of political responses to short-term economic changes and projections of relatively inflexible long-term trends in outlays and revenues.[5]

Second, President Reagan set the broad "context for congressional choice" with his actions in 1981.[6] That basic context continued throughout his presidency even though the administration itself became less likely to get all it wanted and more sporadic and less skillful in pursuing its specific ends.

Third, Congress remained basically reactive to presidential proposals rather than initiatory in the macro-policy area. An astute observer of American politics caught this basic fact and put it in the perspective of post-World War II budgeting in general:

> The weight and significance of each of these (budgetary) institutions vary with time and circumstance. In the 1940s and 1950s great authority was ceded to the House Appropriations Committee, within which a bipartisan conservative coalition exercised fiscal constraints. Since the budget reforms of the early 1970s, the Budget committees in the House and Senate have gained influence. But the most stable force has been the control of the fiscal agenda by the institutionalized presidency. Throughout the postwar period Congress has operated within a budget framework initially specified by the president, who (with the help of the OMB, the Treasury, and the Council of Economic Advisers) is best able to construct an overall

---

[5]LeLoup, *Budgetary Politics,* iv–v.
[6]The quoted phrase is from Charles O. Jones, "A New President, A Different Congress, A Maturing Agenda," in Lester M. Salamon and Michael S. Lund (eds.), *The Reagan Presidency and the Governing of America* (Washington, D.C.: The Urban Institute, 1984): 286.

national fiscal policy. However much Congress may modify the details of that policy, it seems to have accepted the executive's prerogative to define the budget's general contours.[7]

Fourth, the Gramm-Rudman-Hollings bill, which ostensibly set firm goals for reducing the annual deficit to zero by 1991 (1993 in the revised statute passed in late 1987) *and* provided machinery that would not let the goals be missed, is more symbol than reality. The basic institutional relationships and policy preferences of individual and institutional actors will find a way to express themselves. Gramm-Rudman-Hollings is a constant reminder of the deficit problem but in no way does it solve the problem. The existence of the statute (in either its original form or in the 1987 revision) does not force the hard political and economic choices that would, in fact, reduce the deficit. As Representative Leon Panetta (D-Cal.) put it in early 1987: "You can build whatever kind of system you want, but the bottom line is still politics and guts."[8]

Fifth, complexity prevails as individual decisions get made. The basic decision-making necessity is that Congress and the executive branch must still reach compromises regardless of the specific details of the institutional processes. The complexity means that the details of arriving at those compromises can take months and a great deal of give and take. Two brief examples make the central point.

In 1985 and 1986 it took eight months for what became the Fiscal Year 1986 Reconciliation (or Deficit-Reduction) Act to get final approval from Congress. The House passed its version of the bill, which came from many different committees, on October 31, 1985. The Senate did the same on November 14. The conference committee included 240 members who met in 31 different groups over a two-week period and reached agreement by December 19. Between that date and March 20, 1986, the bill went back and forth between the two chambers nine different times. Each house made five different decisions on the floor and only the last two allowed the bill to be forwarded to the president for signature.[9]

The adoption of the Fiscal Year 1987 budget followed its own complex path between February 5, 1986, when President Reagan pro-

---

[7]Peterson, "The New Politics of Deficits," 379. On the changing place of the Appropriations Committees see Lawrence J. Haas, "Blame the Appropriators," *National Journal* (August 8, 1987): 2025–29.
[8]Quoted in Jonathan Rauch, "Is it Really Working?" *National Journal* (January 31, 1987): 248.
[9]Even the succinct *Congressional Quarterly Weekly Report* took 19 pages to summarize this story in its issue of April 5, 1986, 751–68.

# ADOPTION OF THE FISCAL YEAR 1987 BUDGET

(ALL DATES IN CALENDAR 1986)

Feb. 5: President Reagan proposed his budget for FY 1987: outlays of $994 billion and revenues of $850.4 billion, leaving a deficit of $143.6 billion, meeting the Gramm-Rudman target of $144 billion deficit for 1987. The budget called for a 12 percent increase in defense spending, and deficit reductions of $38 billion.

Feb. 26: The Congressional Budget Office (CBO) claimed that President Reagan's budget deficit projections were too low by $15 billion, but the Office of Management and Budget (OMB) claimed that his figures were correct.

March 6: The Senate Budget Committee voted down the president's budget by a vote of 16 to 6, objecting to the heavy increase in defense spending and cuts in social spending. However, Democrats and Republicans agreed to make deficit reduction the prime goal of the 1987 budget.

March 17: The House of Representatives voted down the president's budget by a vote of 12 to 312 with most Republicans voting "present." The Republicans argued that the vote was a tactic on the part of the Democrats to embarrass the president.

March 19: The Senate Budget Committee reported a FY 1987 budget by a vote of 13 to 9 that called for $18.7 billion in new taxes and slashed $25 billion from the president's defense increase. The budget passed by the committee also included spending cuts of $14.4 billion in domestic spending,

and met the Gramm-Rudman target of $144 billion.

April 15: The deadline passed for Congress to have adopted a budget resolution for FY 1987; it had not done so.

May 2: The Senate passed its version of the FY 1987 budget by a 70 to 25 vote. Its budget called for outlays of $1 trillion and revenues of $857 billion, leaving a deficit of $143 billion, which would meet the Gramm-Rudman target. The budget called for $10.7 billion in new taxes, cut $19 billion from President Reagan's defense request, and spared most of the programs that Reagan wished to cut.

May 8: The House Budget Committee passed a budget resolution with a deficit of $137 billion on outlays of $994 billion and revenues of $857 billion. The resolution slashed $35 billion from Reagan's defense buildup, and cut domestic programs 2.5 percent on average.

May 15: The House by a vote of 245 to 179 passed the FY 1987 budget resolution, which provided for a deficit of $137 billion, $7 billion less than the Senate's budget. The House budget proposed $10.7 billion in revenue increases, and held defense to $285 billion, keeping defense spending under inflation in increase.

June 13: Senators offered a proposal to the House-Senate Conference Committee to freeze all spending at 1986 levels unless President Reagan agreed to new taxes for defense spending and deficit reduction. The conference committee worked on the Senate-passed budget.

June 26: The House passed the Senate bill by a vote of 333 to 43, and the Senate passed it by voice vote the same day. The budget proposed outlays of $995 billion, revenues of $852.4 billion, and a deficit of $142.6 billion. The budget also included new revenues of $3.5 billion, a defense budget of $292 billion, and freezes or cuts in most domestic spending.

July 31: The Senate Budget Committee reported its reconciliation bill, and the House Budget Committee reported its own bill. However, both fell short of the savings needed to reach the Gramm-Rudman deficit target.

Sept. 15: House, Senate, and administration negotiators agreed on a package of deficit-reduction measures in order to speed up passage of the reconciliation bills.

Sept. 20: The Senate voted 88 to 7 to pass the Senate bill containing $12.6 billion in deficit reduction.

Sept. 24: The House voted 309 to 106 to pass its bill containing $15.2 billion in deficit reduction.

Oct. 17: Both chambers passed a $576 billion spending measure that would allow the government to continue operating. The House-Senate Conference Report cut $30 billion from Reagan's defense request, and left most domestic spending intact. Congress also passed the budget reconciliation bill that left a FY 1987 deficit of $151 billion, which fell within the $10 billion range of $144 billion Gramm-Rudman target, a provision in the Gramm-Rudman law.

Oct. 30: President Reagan signed the continuing resolution into law as part of the 1987 budget. The FY 1987 Budget contained provisions to sell government assets in order to meet deficit targets.

posed his budget and October 30, 1986, when he could sign a bill agreed on by both houses.

## BROAD PATTERNS OF CONGRESSIONAL INTERACTION WITH THE EXECUTIVE BRANCH

Congress, because of both its constitutional position and the activity of its members, is involved in one way or another in every area of policy in which the federal government is active. But the nature of congressional activity varies from issue to issue and from time to time. Generalizations that Congress is losing power to the president and has been since the beginning of the twentieth century may make exciting rhetoric but reveal almost nothing about the nature of congressional involvement in policy making. The reality of congressional involvement is much more complicated and cannot be caught in a facile general statement.

There are four analytical models that are useful in understanding congressional involvement in policy making. Congress never follows a single model at any given time. Rather it usually is involved in all four models simultaneously in different issue areas. It may be that trends develop in specific areas—that is, with Congress consistently moving from one model to another one—but any comprehensive generalization about the trend of congressional involvement is bound to be so general that most important variations will be obscured.

The first model can be labeled *executive dominance.* In this model the principal source of initiation for legislative ideas comes from the executive branch. The executive, usually the president on major matters, sets the agenda for Congress to consider. Congressional participation in shaping the details of specific programs is generally low. Not only does the executive serve as the principal source of initiation but it also produces the details of proposals, which are, for the most part, ratified by Congress. Congress simply legitimizes what the executive proposes. There is a final legislative product that is broadly acceptable to both the executive branch (which gets what it wants without much change) and Congress (which seems quite content to approve the details of what the executive wants).

There are a number of easy generalizations in the literature that the whole of foreign policy and defense policy are typified by the executive dominance model. More careful examination, however, suggests that this generalization is only selectively true. The original proposal for a "war on poverty" in 1963–64 through programs such as community action, the job corps, the neighborhood youth corps, and Headstart provides a closer fit to the executive dominance model, as does the budget reconciliation bill in 1981 and the tax bill in 1981.

The second model is *joint program development.* In this model the principal source of legislative initiative can be either the executive branch or Congress or it can be a joint initiative either coordinated and planned or fortuitous and unplanned. Both the executive and Congress are heavily involved in decisions about details. There may be some conflict over these details but there is also a high degree of willingness both within Congress and the executive to compromise so a final product broadly acceptable to both can emerge.

A great variety of matters in the economic field—the 1986 tax bill for example—seem to fit this model reasonably well. Additional examples include the "depressed areas" programs (Area Redevelopment and Economic Development) of the 1960s, the Model Cities program of the late 1960s, the Job Training Partnership Act of 1982, and the major farm bill in 1985.

The third model is *congressional dominance.* In this model the principal source of initiation comes from within Congress; congressional involvement in shaping details is high. The executive branch in this case is willing to participate in the shaping of details in only a marginal way. The executive is also willing at least to acquiesce to the congressional initiative and decisions on details and may even be eager to embrace the congressional solution. Whatever the motivation and whatever the degree of eagerness, a final legislative product emerges because the important individuals in the two branches reach some form of agreement.

In recent years policies and programs relating to atomic energy, strip-mining control, consumer protection, air pollution, water pollution, the tax bill of 1982, the immigration bill of 1986, South African Sanctions in 1986, and highway construction in 1987 all fit this model because of aggressive members of Congress with decided policy views and institutional positions from which to push those views successfully.

The fourth model is *stalemate.* In this model there may be initiative in either branch, or there may be competing initiatives undertaken simultaneously in both branches. Both branches also get heavily involved in the attempt to shape details, but their simultaneous efforts run counter to each other. Finally, all of this activity bears no immediate fruit because neither side is willing to yield to the views of the other or even to compromise to reach some mutually agreeable solution.

The controversy over the supersonic transport (SST) in the early 1970s fits this model. The executive branch was pushing federal funding for the development of the SST and Congress was balking. As a result some initial funds were spent but the entire project was finally cancelled. Welfare reform in many administrations, including Reagan's, also provides an example, as do proposals for national health insurance, controlling hospital costs, and forging a coherent energy policy in the Carter years. The lack of a tax bill in 1985, the failure of genuine deficit reduction in the 1980s, and the failure of "enterprise-zone" legislation throughout the Reagan years serve as additional examples.

Oftentimes debate in an area will fit the stalemate model for several years and then a different model will finally apply as some form of compromise is reached. For example, in the late 1950s a large number of areas fit this model: aid to education, area redevelopment, medicare, and manpower development and training. But in the 1960s agreement was reached and measures passed. In the Reagan administration, major tax reform moved from stalemate in 1985 to joint-program development and passage in 1986, a major farm bill moved from stalemate throughout the Reagan first term to joint-program development and passage in 1985, and job training moved from stalemate in 1981 (when the administration wanted no Federal program to replace the Comprehensive Employment and Training Act) to joint-program development and passage in 1982. In general, the same policy area can move between any combination of models over time. It is far too simple to think of a single dimension of presidential "strength" or "weakness" as explaining patterns of relative influence over all policy.

Table 12–3 summarizes the models of congressional involvement in policy-making.


## DOMESTIC PROGRAM DEVELOPMENT

Congress is always important in the shaping of domestic policy. The total domestic agenda of the government at any given time becomes, automatically, the congressional agenda. In the pages that follow, thumbnail sketches of some recent congressional involvement in five broad domestic-policy areas are presented. The point of these sketches is not to summarize policy developments for their own sake. No attempt is made to tell complete stories or bring them up to the minute. Rather, the sketches are meant to give some additional glimpses of the dynamics involved as Congress helps determine the content of domestic policy in the United States.

**Table 12–3.** Models of Congressional Involvement in Policy-Making

| MODEL | PRINCIPAL SOURCE OF INITIATION | DEGREE OF CONGRESSIONAL PARTICIPATION IN SHAPING DETAILS | DEGREE OF EXECUTIVE PARTICIPATION IN SHAPING DETAILS | FINAL LEGISLATIVE PRODUCT |
|---|---|---|---|---|
| Executive dominance | Executive | Low | High | Yes |
| Joint program development | Executive or Congress or both | High | High | Yes |
| Congressional dominance | Congress | High | Low | Yes |
| Stalemate | Executive or Congress or both | High | High | No |

## Economic Policy[10]

Congress is heavily involved in specific policy and program decisions affecting the domestic economy. The usual model is joint program development.

Despite its important role in individual programs, it is virtually impossible for Congress to develop and implement an overall economic policy of its own. Almost inevitably, this task must fall to the president and his top advisers, who set general economic goals and strategies in the annual budget message and economic report and monitor performance in light of those goals on a continual basis.

Congress also contributes to the more general debate through the work of two joint committees: the Joint Economic Committee and the Joint Committee on Taxation. But these committees cannot perform a consolidating function in lieu of presidential activity.

A specific example of an economic policy issue that moved from a stalemate model to joint program development model is provided by what became the Area Redevelopment Act.[11] In the 1950s Senator Paul Douglas, an Illinois Democrat, began to build a coalition in favor of giving special federal aid to economically depressed areas of the country. Gradually that coalition became a majority in Congress, and Douglas's bill passed. President Eisenhower, however, vetoed the bill containing the program and Congress did not override the veto (stalemate). When a Democrat became president the new administration and the congressional supporters reached agreement on details and the bill passed (joint development). After the administrators of the original program had committed some fatal blunders, a new liaison effort between congressional supporters and the executive branch produced a revised program and a renamed agency (joint development).

An example of an economic measure that began with congressional initiative and then became a matter of joint development is provided by the Humphrey-Hawkins full-employment bill (named for Senator Hubert H. Humphrey, Minnesota Democrat, and Representative

[10]See Ralph K. Huitt, "Congressional Organization and Operations in the Field of Money and Credit," in Commission on Money and Credit, *Fiscal and Debt Management Policies* (Englewood Cliffs, N.J.: Prentice-Hall, 1963): 399–495; and Harvey C. Mansfield, "The Congress and Economic Policy," in David B. Truman (ed.), *The Congress and America's Future* (Englewood Cliffs, N.J.: Prentice-Hall, 1965): 121–49.

[11]See Randall B. Ripley, *The Politics of Economic and Human Resource Development* (Indianapolis: Bobbs-Merrill, 1972): Chapter 2; Roger Davidson, *Coalition-Building for Depressed Area Bills: 1955–1965,* Inter-University Case Program no. 103 (Indianapolis: Bobbs-Merrill, 1966); and Sar A. Levitan, *Federal Aid to Depressed Areas* (Baltimore: The Johns Hopkins University Press, 1964).

Augustus F. Hawkins, California Democrat, its primary sponsors). The bill was introduced in 1974 and called for mandatory measures to reduce unemployment to 3 percent within eighteen months. The bill made no headway while Republicans Nixon and Ford were still president. However, in late 1977 President Carter worked out a compromise with congressional sponsors and they jointly endorsed a new version that set a 4 percent unemployment goal within five years. The compromise bill authorized new programs but did not require their use in reaching the goal. As watered down, even before the presidency reverted to the Republicans after the 1980 election, the bill was merely symbolic and had no concrete programmatic reality. Joint development in this case helped produce a general policy statement that had no practical results.

Another example of congressional initiative that produced a primarily symbolic statement was the Gramm-Rudman-Hollings Act in 1985. The White House participated in the sense of keeping the public spotlight on what the president asserted was the responsibility of Congress for deficits. Congress produced machinery, goals, and a timetable it hoped would lead to a deficit reduction to zero by 1991. But the machinery was partially damaged by a Supreme Court decision in mid-1986. The replacement statute Congress provided in late 1987 remained mainly symbolic. Congressional determination and resolve to reduce the deficit could not be created by machinery, goals, and timetables.

## Human-Resource Development Policy[12]

In the 1960s and 1970s the federal government became increasingly involved in efforts to alleviate the effects of poverty and to develop human resources. This involvement took many different specific forms. Some of the programs were generated in a fashion much like the model of executive dominance. This was true of the development and passage of the Economic Opportunity Act (EOA) of 1964 as well as the Model Cities program. Other parts of the specific programs,

---

[12]For a wealth of detail on policy development in this broad area see Donald C. Baumer and Carl E. Van Horn, *The Politics of Unemployment* (Washington, D.C.: Congressional Quarterly, 1984); Grace A. Franklin and Randall B. Ripley, *CETA: Politics and Policy, 1973–1982* (Knoxville, Tenn.: University of Tennessee Press, 1984); Sar A. Levitan, *The Great Society's Poor Law* (Baltimore, Md.: Johns Hopkins University Press, 1969); Levitan and Robert Taggart, *The Promise of Greatness* (Cambridge, Mass.: Harvard University Press, 1976); Robert D. Plotnick and Felicity Skidmore, *Progress against Poverty: A Review of the 1964–1974 Decade* (New York: Academic Press, 1975); and Ripley, *The Politics of Economic and Human Resource Development.*

however, were generated through joint development. The Appalachia program of 1964 is an example of such development. It also involved state and local officials as initiators.

But even in programs like EOA and Model Cities, in which the immediate initiative came from the executive branch, there had been a prior history of at least sporadic (and unsuccessful) congressional initiative. For very different reasons, for example, both liberal and conservative critics of urban renewal had laid some of the groundwork for the Model Cities program. Likewise, Democrats in the 1950s had taken a variety of initiatives—for a Youth Conservation Corps, for example—that were absorbed by the executive branch in its fashioning of the Economic Opportunity Act.

In the Nixon-Ford years, stalemate occurred on most aspects of human-resource development policy, for the simple reason that the Republican presidents and the large majority of the Democrats in Congress disagreed about what was needed. The compromises that were reached were primarily in the form of parceling out monies for human-resource development activities to states and localities. Presidents Nixon and Ford and congressional Republicans liked this solution because it was in accord with their general ideological preference for less federal government and more state and local autonomy. Congressional Democrats went along because it was the principal way to save some large chunks of tax revenue for use in human-resource development activities, given the power of the presidential veto to thwart most of their initiatives.

In the area of federally funded employment and training programs, the decades of the 1960s, 1970s, and 1980s saw a continuing change of operative models of program development. In the 1960s, a large number of specific "categorical" programs emerged, often primarily at the insistence of the executive branch in the beginning of the decade. By the mid-1960s members of Congress were also helping develop additional programs in this general area of providing training for those unemployed and disadvantaged in other ways in the labor market.

By the time Richard Nixon became president in 1969 there was general agreement that the categorical programs (which involved direct contracts between the federal government and thousands of local service delivery agents) had become inefficient for a variety of reasons. But it took almost five years of stalemate before Nixon and the Democratic Congress could agree on a compromise with which they both could live: the Comprehensive Employment and Training Act of 1973 (CETA). This compromise increased federal spending but shifted considerable responsibility for implementation to local governments.

A pattern of joint program development continued under President Carter in 1978 when CETA was amended in some major ways during its required reauthorization. The arrival of Ronald Reagan as president promised another period of stalemate. The new administration both favored the death of CETA and its nonreplacement by any federal effort in the employment and training area. However, congressional initiative from members of both political parties would not be stilled and eventually resulted, in 1982, in the Job Training Partnership Act (JTPA). This act reduced spending, further limited the federal role beyond the provision of money, and increased the role of the private sector. But, in many ways, it represented continuity with efforts begun in 1962.

## Educational Policy

After World War II, Congress enacted a great number of education laws. There is a popular misconception that, until the major educational legislation of the Johnson administration in the mid-1960s, which was impressive in both scope and magnitude, all federal aid to education proposals had been stalemated. This is true of general aid to elementary and secondary education but is untrue in other fields. In the pre-1965 period, for example, the federal government provided aid to higher education through various "G.I. bills" for ex-servicemen, subsidies for college dorms, and the National Defense Education Act. Elementary and secondary education also received aid from the NDEA as well as from an extensive program of aid to school districts that were considered to be "federally impacted" because the proximity of large federal installations increased the school-age population. These various measures emerged in large part on the basis of joint program development. The major Johnson accomplishments—particularly the Elementary and Secondary Education Act of 1965—were also developed jointly.[13]

In the first six Reagan years, educational policy was a frequent battleground between the administration and Congress. Stalemate often resulted. However, a large bipartisan coalition in Congress succeeded in 1986 in passing a higher education bill that extended major programs for five years, well beyond the end of the Reagan presidency. The bill was so popular in Congress it was "veto-proof." It passed in final form by 385 to 25 in the House and by voice vote in the Senate.

[13]See Eugene Eidenberg and Roy D. Morey, *An Act of Congress* (New York: Norton, 1969).

In order to get these kinds of majorities the bill contained some provisions not opposed by the administration, which allowed even conservative Republicans to support the bill.

Reagan's first preference was to cut aid to education, including higher education, dramatically. His proposals, however, went nowhere in legislative form and had success only when the administration could act without further legislation. The long and complicated coalition building throughout the Ninety-ninth Congress (1985-86) produced a final higher education bill in September 1986 that rejected the Reagan desire to cut funding and renewed the most popular aid programs for college students: Pell Grants and Guaranteed Student Loans. The total authorization contained in the bill was for about $10 billion annually, with the two major programs accounting for about 70 percent of the authorized spending. The moderates and liberals in Congress also succeeded in increasing loan-limit amounts and extended eligibility to students enrolled for less than half time. In order to obtain conservative support, however, Congress kept the stress on loans rather than on grants (liberals claimed more grants were necessary for the poorest students). It also tightened many eligibility restrictions in order to focus more on the truly needy, although, at the same time, it limited the discretion of the Secretary of Education in writing the "needs analysis" rules. Congress demonstrated the ability to continue a major domestic program initiative in the face of hostility from the executive branch.

## Science Policy[14]

Science policy is really a collection of discrete policies. In the post-World War II period, Congress has been sporadically important in some scientific areas. Some specific policies, as in the field of atomic energy, have been the product of joint development. Other policies and programs have essentially been executive-branch programs in which there has been congressional input. The creation of the National Science Foundation serves as a good example.

Examples of congressional leadership, sometimes verging on dominance, are afforded by some specific areas of health research and the space program.

Science policy could be dominated by the executive in principle, but

[14]Sanford A. Lakoff, "Congress and National Science Policy," *Political Science Quarterly* 89 (1974): 589–611.

in practice congressional input has been and is likely to be very important from time to time. The reasons for this are at least threefold: the president is not always well staffed to deal with science policy across the board; Congress has some pockets of genuine staff expertise in scientific areas (the Office of Technology Assessment also gives Congress additional strength); and even where congressional expertise is lacking, members of Congress will not usually think of "science policy" as something either separate or sacred. If "science policy" has to do with the location of a costly government facility, such as an accelerator for atomic particles or a super-conductor, members are likely to see the decision as another locational-distributive issue, not as a matter involving the treatment and development of something abstract called "science." In 1987, in yet another iteration of this point of view, members of Congress eagerly sought the location of a huge and costly underground nuclear accelerator in their district. The provision of the facility was "science policy"; its location involved familiar congressional pork-barrel politics.

## Energy Policy[15]

Before the "energy crisis" of the early 1970s there seemed only occasional realization by anyone in either the executive branch or Congress that there should be some overall plans for coping with what, in retrospect, was an inevitable shortage of at least some forms of energy, especially those based on petroleum products.

Once the realization broke on the country in the form of closed gas stations, a lowered speed limit, soaring energy prices, and closed, unheated schools and factories, there was a flurry of activity in the executive branch and in Congress to deal with the problems.

By the late 1980s no comprehensive energy policy had emerged. Presidents Nixon, Ford, and Carter had all made proposals (quite different from each other) and various individuals and committees in Congress also made proposals. There were disagreements among various proposals from all sources and there were also major congressio-

[15]See Charles O. Jones and Randall Strahan, "The Effect of Energy Politics on Congressional and Executive Organization in the 1970s," *Legislative Studies Quarterly* 10 (1985): 151–79; Bruce I. Oppenheimer, "Congress and the New Obstructionism: Developing an Energy Program," in Lawrence C. Dodd and Oppenheimer (eds.), *Congress Reconsidered,* 2nd ed. (Washington, D.C.: Congressional Quarterly, 1981): Chapter 12; Oppenheimer, "Policy Effects of U.S. House Reform: Decentralization and the Capacity to Resolve Energy Issues," *Legislative Studies Quarterly* 5 (1980): 5–30; and John G. Stewart, "Central Policy Organs in Congress," in Harvey C. Mansfield, Sr. (ed.), *Congress against the President* (New York: Academy of Political Science, 1975).

nal-presidential disagreements. But the whole period of ferment, despite its confused nature, can best be characterized as frustrated and partial attempts at joint policy development, with substantial elements of stalemate. The jointness of the work did not produce a coherent single package. However, congressional behavior in the mid-1970s—especially in 1975 and again in 1977—showed considerable institutional imagination as congressional leaders put together *ad hoc* machinery to overcome the normal institutional fragmentation that had long afflicted the energy field. The effort at comprehensiveness did not fail because of defective congressional machinery (for example, too many committees that could not agree with each other). Rather, policy disagreement finally brought the efforts to their knees.

The effort to develop comprehensive energy policy became moot with the coming to the presidency of Ronald Reagan. He and his administration showed no interest. Congressional interest in such an effort simultaneously became almost invisible.

## FOREIGN AND DEFENSE POLICY

In some ways Congress plays second fiddle to the executive branch in the realms of foreign and defense policy. But its role is vital and has become more so during the last several decades, especially after both public and congressional disenchantment with the Vietnam War. The following sections give brief overviews of the congressional role in foreign policy, in defense policy, and in relation to the War Powers Act, which deals with key aspects of both foreign and defense policy.

### Foreign Policy

Until recently, one of the most common generalizations in both scholarly and popular literature on Congress was that the executive branch, especially the president, had completely overshadowed Congress in foreign-policy matters and that the president took all major initiatives in foreign affairs without any opposition.[16] Like most simple generalizations, this one failed to portray a complicated relationship accurately.

---

[16]For statements of this position see Aaron Wildavsky, "The Two Presidencies," in Wildavsky (ed.), *The Presidency* (Boston, Little, Brown, 1969): 230–43; and James A. Robinson, *Congress and Foreign Policy-Making* (Homewood, Illinois: Dorsey, 1967, revised ed.).

In many ways the model of executive dominance may well have described a period from roughly 1955 to roughly 1965.[17] Before the mid-1950s Congress was heavily involved in the post-World War II foreign-policy initiatives of the United States: the United Nations, the Marshall Plan and other foreign aid, and NATO. Members of the House and Senate were involved in the early planning of these initiatives and consideration of them by Congress was comprehensive. In recent years Congress has again become more assertive—particularly in reaction to Vietnam and the power of the president to wage an undeclared war—but also on other questions, such as arms sales, intervention in rebel movements against foreign governments, attempts to recover hostages, foreign aid, foreign intelligence activities, and export of nuclear materials and technology.

For approximately ten years (1955–1965) Congress did not raise major objections to the expansion of presidential influence. Congress was willing to pass resolutions that gave the president virtually a unilateral right to use American troops almost anywhere in the world if he deemed such action to be wise and in the national interest. The last resolution of this sort was the later-repealed Gulf of Tonkin Resolution passed in 1964. Even in this period of congressional passivity, however, Congress had major influence in the creation of the Development Loan Fund in 1957 and the International Development Association in 1958.[18] These were new facets of the foreign-aid program stressing loans and grants to underdeveloped nations for economic purposes only.

Presidential influence on roll call voting in Congress is stronger in the area of "international involvement" than in any other. In four other areas: government management, social welfare, agricultural assistance, and civil liberties, his influence on roll call voting is virtually absent.[19]

A study concluding that the president predominates on foreign

[17]For material supporting this thesis that congressional impotence in foreign affairs was mainly limited to one identifiable period of time in the late 1950s and early 1960s see Ronald C. Moe and Steven C. Teel, "Congress as Policy-Maker: A Necessary Reappraisal," in Moe (ed.), *Congress and the President* (New York: Goodyear, 1971); John F. Manley, "The Rise of Congress in Foreign Policy-Making," *Annals of the American Academy of Political and Social Science* 337 (1971): 60–70; Holbert N. Carroll, *The House of Representatives and Foreign Affairs* rev. ed. (Boston: Little, Brown, 1966); and Edward A. Kolodziej, "Congress and Foreign Policy: The Nixon Years," in Mansfield (ed.), *Congress against the President*: 167–79.

[18]See David A. Baldwin, "Congressional Initiative in Foreign Policy," *Journal of Politics* 28 (1966): 754–73.

[19]For an analysis of these patterns of presidential influence on voting on the five dimensions see Aage R. Clausen, *How Congressmen Decide* (New York: St. Martin's, 1973), especially Chapter 8.

policy also reported a number of cases in which congressional influence was predominant and a few cases in which the initiative was congressional (six of twenty-two cases were found to have been initiated by Congress).[20] Another study, based on a survey of a large number of cases, noted that in many areas congressional participation was vigorous, although not dominant. This was true in regard to the role of the Senate in treaty-making (the Japanese Peace Treaty of 1952, the North Atlantic Treaty, and the United Nations Charter are cited as examples) and the role of the House Appropriations Committee in a number of foreign policy areas. In addition, Congress was found to dominate "many areas of foreign policy which in themselves appear to be peripheral. Collectively, however, they constitute a major portion of U.S. foreign policy. For example, Congress is generally credited with dominant influence over decisions on economic-aid policy, military assistance, agricultural-surplus disposal, and the locations of facilities, to name only a few. In addition, immigration and tariff policies are generally considered part of foreign policy and there is considerable evidence to indicate that Congress remains a major actor in these fields."[21]

Congress became noticeably more aggressive and self-assertive on foreign policy matters during the late 1960s and especially in the 1970s.[22] Congressional assertiveness continued into the 1980s and was fueled anew by the Iran-contra hearings in 1987. This self-assertiveness reached a peak in some ways, at least in terms of widespread public visibility, during the attempts by Congress to curb and then end the war in Indochina, particularly after Richard Nixon had become president. But the self-assertiveness was not solely or even primarily a product of hostility to Mr. Nixon as a person or of a Democratic Congress to a Republican president. The same self-assertiveness continued in congressional dealings with Presidents Ford, Carter and Reagan. Foreign aid, foreign economic policy, arms sales, support for

[20]Robinson, *Congress and Foreign Policy-Making,* 65.
[21]Moe and Teel, "Congress as Policy-Maker," 49.
[22]See Cecil V. Crabb, Jr., and Pat M. Holt, *Invitation to Struggle: Congress, the President and Foreign Policy,* 2nd ed. (Washington, D.C.: Congressional Quarterly, 1984); I.M. Destler, "Executive-Congressional Conflict in Foreign Policy: Explaining It, Coping with It," in Lawrence C. Dodd and Bruce I. Oppenheimer (eds.), *Congress Reconsidered,* 3rd ed. (Washington, D.C.: Congressional Quarterly, 1985): 343–63; Thomas M. Franck and Edward Weisband, *Foreign Policy by Congress* (New York: Oxford University Press, 1979); Robert A. Pastor, *Congress and the Politics of U.S. Foreign Economic Policy* (Berkeley, California: University of California Press, 1980); John Rourke, *Congress and the Presidency in U.S. Foreign Policymaking: A Study of Interaction and Influence, 1945–1982* (Boulder, Colorado: Westview Press, 1983); and James L. Sundquist, *The Decline and Resurgence of Congress* (Washington, D.C.: Brookings, 1981): Chapter 10.

foreign rebels, and foreign-intelligence activities all came under increasing congressional scrutiny. Joint development, often with considerable antagonism between the executive and legislative branches, was widely used, eagerly by Congress and begrudgingly by presidents. Sometimes the antagonism led to stalemate. Partisanship is often a consideration in foreign policy-making (despite the myth of bipartisanship) and is particularly in evidence in the strategic area, which contains the issues that must promote continuing institutional tensions between president and Congress. Partisanship reinforces normal disagreements based on the differing perspectives of the legislative and executive institutions.[23]

In the first Reagan year the president got permission, narrowly, to sell the AWACS plane to Saudi Arabia. He also got a foreign-aid appropriations bill—the first president to do so in three years. Prohibitions on aid to Pakistan, Chile, and Argentina were lifted by Congress at presidential request. However, Congress added new restrictions on aid to countries embroiled in controversy over human rights or nuclear proliferation. Congress placed restrictions on aid to El Salvador and refused to lift the prohibition of aid to supposedly pro-western forces in Angola. A number of reporting requirements were added to the president's responsibilities even in areas in which he got a good part of what he wanted.

In subsequent Reagan years, sale of weapons to the Mideast (Saudi Arabia, Jordan, Iran) remained a topic of much interest to Congress. Congress continued oversight of the agencies engaged in foreign intelligence, especially the Central Intelligence Agency, often with tart-tongued reminders that the agency was responsible for keeping the intelligence committees of Congress informed of what was happening. The subject of aid to rebels in several locations was constantly on the congressional agenda, nowhere more continuously or controversially than in the case of the contras seeking to oust the Sandinista government in Nicaragua. Foreign economic policy, with its major domestic ramifications, is always on the congressional agenda, especially in an era when U.S. trade deficits were large and growing and were linked to the collapse or serious shrinkage of some key American industries. Congress took the lead in producing a major immigration bill in 1986.

A balanced conclusion about the relative positions of the president and Congress in foreign-policy making must recognize that the partic-

---

[23]Randall B. Ripley, "Congressional Partisanship and Bipartisanship in U.S. Foreign Policy," in Louis W. Koenig, James C. Hsiung, and King-yuh Chang (eds.), *Congress, the Presidency, and the Taiwan Relations Act* (New York: Praeger, 1985): 63–84.

ipants have different capabilities that enable each to perform some things better than the other. The president has some natural advantages that allow him to dominate certain aspects of foreign policy. His greater ability to act rapidly and flexibly and his superior information sources are assets in diplomacy. Imagine, for instance, the likelihood of the multi-headed Congress arranging and successfully executing a re-opening of ties with China, an accomplishment that President Nixon and his foreign advisor, Henry Kissinger, managed with apparent ease in 1972. The enormous press coverage inherent in such foreign-policy coups as the China thaw lends a great deal of support to the misconception of the president's ability to dominate all foreign affairs. Or try to picture Congress—with its contending views, individuals, and factions—taking the initiative in promoting accord between Egypt and Israel, an initiative successfully taken by President Carter. Or imagine Congress negotiating an arms limitation treaties with the Soviet Union, an executive activity that met with some success in 1987 and continues to be pursued in 1988.

Foreign-policy spectaculars such as the resumption of contact with China or the Camp David agreements between Israel and Egypt are rare events. Much policy-making in foreign affairs is without glamor. Routine matters may receive little or no press coverage, which results in low public visibility, but they are important to the total foreign-policy picture. In these less visible areas, congressional involvement is likely to be high. Work on the details of trade policy, foreign aid, and immigration policy, though slow and tedious, is important to shaping overall U.S. policy toward much of the world. Congress has considerable influence in these fields.

## Defense Policy

Congress is often written off entirely in the defense field. But closer analysis reveals substantial congressional impact. As in the case of foreign policy, a facile generalization about the total power of the executive is not accurate.

On the one hand, there is good evidence that particularly in the late 1950s and early 1960s individual members did not consider the broad aspects of defense policy when they were called on to make decisions about that policy. For example, the Armed Services Committees often were more concerned about "real estate" decisions (the location or closing of military facilities) than about defense policy writ large. Members in general felt technically incompetent to challenge the judgment of military personnel.[24] At the institutional level, Congress did not usually make major cuts in the overall defense budget proposed by the president. It looked "mostly at the details of defense spending but rarely at the big picture."[25]

A closer examination of defense budgets in the 1960s shows that congressional impact was substantial. The key to understanding the nature of congressional impact is to disaggregate the budget into its component parts.[26] Although congressional impact on the overall budget figures for the Department of Defense appeared to be limited, when the budget was split into four categories—personnel; operations and maintenance; procurement; and research, development, testing, and evaluation—a more precise view of congressional impact became evident. Congress made only small changes in the areas of personnel and operations and maintenance, and these areas accounted for over half of the budget. There was, however, considerable congressional activity in the areas of procurement and research, development, testing, and evaluation.

Data for the 1970s and 1980s show that Congress has continued to have some marginal impact on defense budgets and has continued to focus on procurement and research, development, testing, and evaluation in making its changes.

In addition to the systematic congressional impact on defense budgets, Congress also makes individual budget decisions about major defense items that are important. In recent years one of the most publicized decisions has involved the B-1 bomber. In 1977 Congress decided to go along with the scuttling of the project proposed by President Carter. Congress had stalled during the Ford administration (which supported the B-1) and thus gave Carter the latitude to put building the new plane on ice. By 1978 the project appeared dead. In 1981, however, Congress changed its mood and supported President Reagan's proposal to revive the B-1. It is now operational, although the finished product has some serious problems. Congressional involvement in making decisions on other specific weapons has also been substantial. Beginning midway through the first Reagan term, Con-

[24]Lewis A. Dexter, "Congressmen and the Making of Military Policy," in Raymond E. Wolfinger (ed.), *Readings on Congress* (Englewood Cliffs: Prentice Hall, 1971): 371–87.

[25]See Douglas M. Fox, "Congress and U.S. Military Service Budgets in the Post-War Period: A Research Note," *Midwest Journal of Political Science* 15 (1971): 382–93; and Robert J. Art, "Congress and the Defense Budget: Enhancing Policy Oversight," *Political Science Quarterly* 100 (1985): 227–48. The quotation is from Art, 227.

[26]Arnold Kanter, "Congress and the Defense Budget: 1960–1970," *American Political Science Review* 66 (1972): 129–43.

gress also dealt continuously with various aspects of the authorization of and funding for the complicated pieces of the defense package known as the Strategic Defense Initiative (or, more popularly, "Star Wars"). Congress helped change the amount, nature, and timing of some parts of this package, which was at the top of the Reagan administration's defense agenda.

## The War Powers Act

A special instance of both foreign and defense policy was the passage of the War Powers Act over a Nixon veto in late 1973. At the time it was heralded as a major preventative against U.S. involvement in another situation like Vietnam. Looked at from the perspective of 15 years later, it appears to be primarily a symbol of congressional insistence that Congress has the ultimate power to declare war coupled with acquiescence to the practical realities of the modern world. These suggest that a president may sometimes have to use force and commit troops without the opportunity for congressional action or even consultation with members of Congress.

There has been a great deal of constitutional and theoretical debate about the meaning of the act. Perhaps more important, there has now been some experience with relatively small crises that show the vagueness of the statute and the power of the president to interpret the law as he sees fit. In a speech in April 1977, former President Ford voiced his opposition to the act and also discussed his experiences as president.[27] He identified six events during his presidency that might have come under the provisions of the War Powers Act: the evacuation of U.S. citizens from three locations in Indo-China in the spring of 1975; the rescue of the U.S. freighter, *Mayaguez,* in May 1975; and two evacuation operations in Lebanon in June 1976. Ford asserted he did not believe the act applied to any of these cases. Some congressional critics had thought otherwise at the time. But, in fact, as events unfold rapidly, the president clearly has the upper hand on what he does and does not do. Congressional criticism can be forthcoming afterward, and a president may pay a political price in terms of loss of support

[27]Gerald R. Ford, "The War Powers Resolution," speech delivered April 11, 1977, at the University of Kentucky, published by the American Enterprise Institute (Washington, D.C., 1977) as Reprint No. 69. See also Sundquist, *The Decline and Resurgence of Congress,* Chapter 9; Franck and Weisband, *Foreign Policy by Congress,* Chapter 3; and Daniel Paul Franklin, "War Powers in the Modern Context," *Congress and the Presidency* 14 (Spring 1987): 77–92.

in Congress for differences of opinion. But there is very little Congress can do in the short run if the president and the majority opinion in Congress differ on the applicability of the act in any given situation.

Ford also made it clear that even the consultation provisions in the act (which simply urge consultation of congressional leaders by the president) were difficult to implement:

> Once the consultation process began, the inherent weakness of the War Powers Resolution from a practical standpoint was conclusively demonstrated.
>
> When the evacuation of DaNang [in South Vietnam] was forced upon us during the Congress's Easter recess, not one of the key bipartisan leaders of the Congress was in Washington.
>
> Without mentioning names, here is where we found the leaders of Congress: two were in Mexico, three were in Greece, one was in the Middle East, one was in Europe, and two were in the People's Republic of China. The rest we found in twelve widely scattered states of the Union.
>
> This, one might say, is an unfair example, since the Congress was in recess. But it must be remembered that critical world events, especially military operations, seldom wait for the Congress to meet. In fact, most of what goes on in the world happens in the middle of the night, Washington time.
>
> On June 18, 1976, we began the first evacuation of American citizens from the civil war in Lebanon. The Congress was not in recess, but it had adjourned for the day.
>
> As telephone calls were made, we discovered, among other things, that one member of Congress had an unlisted number which his press secretary refused to divulge. After trying and failing to reach another member of Congress, we were told by his assistant that the congressman did not need to be reached.
>
> We tried so hard to reach a third member of Congress that our resourceful White House operators had the local police leave a note on the congressman's beach cottage door: "Please call the White House."

In April 1980, when President Carter ordered a commando raid in an attempt to rescue the hostages being held at the American embassy in Teheran, Iran (the raid failed) he chose not to consult Congress. After the details of the raid were revealed, congressional opinion was divided on whether the War Powers Act required consultation or not. No clearly dominant view emerged.

In the Reagan years, various events involving U.S. troops—the dispatch of military advisers to El Salvador in 1981, the sending of marines to Lebanon in 1982, the invasion of Grenada in 1983, the air strike against Libya in 1986, U.S. naval escorts for oil tankers in the Persian Gulf in 1987—all raised questions about the meaning of the War Powers Act. There was some public debate by various officials after each of these events. The upshot was continued lack of clarity on the precise meaning of the Act with the continued reality that presidents could generally act first and square themselves with Congress afterwards, at least in these fairly marginal and small-sized events. A major test of the act—which would involve sending sizable numbers of American ground troops—has not yet emerged.

The most accurate conclusion about the War Powers Act—although hardly comforting—is that it remains an unclear and probably ineffective congressional attempt to control warmaking powers. Needless to say, there are no automatic formulas, given modern technology that allows mass destruction to be ordered and occur within minutes, that can preserve congressional power in all contingencies.

## "REFORM" OF CONGRESS[28]

### Institutional Stability, Change, and the Ambiguity of "Reform"

Members of the House and Senate are faced with a choice between supporting institutional stability in Congress or striving for institutional change. This differs from the choice of change or stability in the substance of specific governmental policies. There are, however, ties between degree of institutional stability, degree of policy stability, and relative impact of Congress on the substance of policy. Increased institutional stability can both strengthen and weaken the ability of Congress to have important substantive effects.

Members of Congress interested in maximizing the policy impact of the institution face a dilemma. On the one hand, the institutional stability and organization possible under relatively stable conditions are likely to be necessary if Congress is to have major policy input of its own rather than depending on the executive branch for all direction and details. On the other hand, stability also breeds substantive policy

---

[28]For interesting treatments of different aspects of recent reforms, both actual and proposed, see Roger H. Davidson and Walter J. Oleszek, *Congress Against Itself* (Bloomington, Indiana: Indiana University Press, 1977); Leroy N. Rieselbach, *Congressional Reform* (Washington, D.C.: Congressional Quarterly, 1986); James L. Sundquist, *The Decline and Resurgence of Congress* (Washington, D.C.: Brookings, 1981); and Susan Welch and John G. Peters (eds.), *Legislative Reform and Public Policy* (New York: Praeger, 1977).

conservatism and tends to stifle innovation. In theory, a stable organization may be the most likely to have a large policy impact but in fact may become moribund, allowing competing organizations such as the Executive Office of the President or various parts of the bureaucracy to acquire policy initiative by default. Despite the claim that "reform" can cure congressional ineffectiveness, there is no pat answer to this dilemma. Both change and stability may promote either congressional potency or impotence. The advantages and disadvantages of either course have to be weighed again and again in specific situations.

"Reform" can push in many different directions. Some changes labeled as reforms can serve fragmentation. Some changes can serve integration. There is no simple correspondence between being a "reformer" and promoting specific policy values. The relationship is complex and needs to be assessed with respect to specific proposed or actual changes. It also needs to be remembered that the same "reform" may serve different values at different times. For example, depriving the Speaker of the House of a number of powers in 1910–11 was supposed to be serving "liberal" policy values. Creating some additional powers for the Speaker in the 1970s was also supposed to serve "liberal" values. Ralph Huitt, a long-time and highly perceptive student of Congress, provides the best summary statement about the links between institutional "reform" and policy values: "Structural and procedural devices give little assurance of permanent rectitude."[29]

In the mid-1970s there were contradictory strains of deliberate change in both the House and Senate, particularly the former. One strain served primarily to disperse power among individual members—what might be called a "democratizing" strain. The other strain served primarily to centralize power in order to enhance the power of Congress as an institution. Examples of the former are changes enhancing the power of subcommittees in relation to parent committees, dispersing subcommittee chairmanships more widely, and ensuring virtually all members of having at least some highly desirable committee and subcommittee assignments. Examples of the latter include the creation of a new budgetary process in a 1974 statute, the passage of the War Powers Act in 1973, and strengthening the hand of the Speaker. Some changes have pushed in both directions simultaneously. For example, moves to make the House Democratic caucus (composed of all Democratic members of the House) more powerful were democratizing in that they gave individual members a vote over party policy. But they also had some centralizing potential to the

[29]Ralph K. Huitt, "Congress: Retrospect and Prospect," *Journal of Politics* 38 (1976): 227.

extent that the caucus could be dominated by the party leaders. Overall, the reforms of the 1970s resulted in greater internal openness and accountability but did not affect the high level of policy fragmentation.[30]

## Congressional Performance and "Reform"

"How to Reform Congress" is a favorite parlor game played by large numbers of people, many of whom have little knowledge of the institution they seek to reform. Many who pay any attention to the institution at all feel they know what is wrong with it and have one or more quick fixes for the ailments they see. The standard criticisms of Congress revolve around charges that it is unresponsive, inefficient, and does not uphold high ethical standards for behavior by its members. Usually one or more remedies are proposed. Most of these remedies turn out to be fairly mechanical and may or may not have any relationship to the problem toward which they are allegedly aimed.

Most outsiders promote reform packages that the proponents assert will cure the problems they allege to be rampant in Congress, whether they be problems of unresponsiveness, inefficiency, or dishonesty or some combination of such problems. Favorite prescriptions over the years have focused on such items as eliminating seniority for selecting committee chairpersons, disclosing personal financial worth and holdings of members, strengthening conflict of interest laws, setting a retirement age for members, increasing staff, installing computers to allow for greater storage and recovery of information, and changing specific rules of procedure such as that allowing filibusters in the Senate. Rarely are these prescriptions analyzed to see if they can reasonably be expected to cure the problems identified. And rarely are additional consequences projected and analyzed.

Insiders to Congress—the members themselves—also promote "reform" from time to time. They are sometimes successful. Even they have problems in predicting all of the consequences of the reforms they adopt.

In general, "reform" is best understood as change, in this case deliberately sought. Many changes in a complex setting produce unintended or unexpected consequences as well as some of the anticipated results. For example, the holding of power in the House by the few

---

[30]This conclusion is supported in detail by a thoughtful analysis in Leroy N. Rieselbach, *Congressional Reform* (Washington, D.C.: Congressional Quarterly, 1986).

was successfully broken up by the reforms of the 1970s. But the seeming near-anarchy produced by subcommittee government was not to everyone's taste either, even those who supported the reforms but had not foreseen all of the consequences.

The perspective on "reform" that is offered here is not meant to deny the utility and necessity of some reforms. There are always aspects of congressional life and behavior that can profit by change; and the public does, in fact, stand to gain by some changes. But Congress is an extremely complex institution, and some changes billed as reforms may not have any effect at all on the problem that has been identified, and some may have unforeseen effects that are not necessarily desirable. While some changes effectively address problems that have been identified, there is nothing automatic or easy about the matching of changes with problems.

Several general points about change and reform in Congress underscore this perspective. First, the same reform may be viewed very differently by different individuals. For example, senior members and junior members may view changes in the seniority system quite differently, for the obvious reason that one group has something to lose and the other group presumably has something to gain. However, proposed changes in seniority are rarely debated in such straightforward self-interest terms. Instead the debate takes on a highly moralistic tone both in Congress and outside.

A lot of what is billed as reform primarily represents jockeying for position by individuals or by ideological blocks. Such reforms, if adopted, may have the desired impact in the short run. But in the long run they may be used in the service of interests and values quite distasteful to the original reformers. The classic case of changes used primarily in the service of values different from those originally served involves the position of the Speaker of the House. In 1910–11 the progressives in the House revolted against Speaker Joseph Cannon and stripped him (and succeeding Speakers) of many powers. These reforms were undertaken expressly to aid progressive legislative causes. But within a few years it became clear that the weakening of the speakership fostered the development of virtually autonomous committee chairpersons who, for the most part, came to use their power for relatively conservative purposes. By the 1960s and 1970s the liberals in Congress took the lead in restoring some powers to the Speaker so that he could effectively lead the liberal forces against the more conservatively oriented committee and subcommittee chairpersons.

Second, "reform movements" often embrace contradictory goals simultaneously. In the 1970s in the House, for example, the reformers simultaneously sought to strengthen the position of the subcommittees (and individual members on those subcommittees), the position of the Speaker, and the power of the Democratic caucus. In many ways these institutions are competitors for power. They can work together, but the reforms did not really address the problem of how to promote cooperation. Instead, the changes aimed at maximizing the potential impact and autonomy of each of them simultaneously.

Third, some matters are worth policing and changing for their own sake, although the precise nature of the most desirable state of affairs is not usually self-evident. The whole area of honesty and ethics is one in which high standards should be set and upheld. However, there is legitimate debate over the specific measures designed to define and implement those standards. By and large, the impact of Congress on most public policy most of the time will not be affected by changes in standards, codes of ethics, limits on outside income, disclosure of personal financial information, and like measures. To be sure, the influence of foreign governments that attempt to buy influence may be reduced. The most obvious conflicts of interest that are exposed may inhibit certain kinds of preferential legislative treatment for specific interests. But "better policy" is not likely to emerge overnight (or ever) solely because senators and representatives have to be honest in their personal financial dealings and report those publicly. Such requirements are good in themselves if properly drawn and at least may help lay the groundwork for more public acceptance of Congress as an institution populated by honest folk.

Fourth, the most important reforms and changes are those that increase or decrease the access of Congress institutionally to critical leverage points in the policy process and will, over the long run, increase or diminish the institution's capacity for making a substantive impact.

We need to realize, however, that Congress has only limited control over its own access to policy-making. In Chapter 1, in the discussion of supporting conditions for relatively high degrees of institutional integration and relatively high fragmentation, only two major conditions (out of twelve discussed) were identified as manipulable to any significant degree by Congress itself: the nature of committee organization and the nature of party organization in Congress. The other conditions are largely givens with which Congress must work and to which Congress must adjust.

However, within the areas in which Congress does have room for maneuver, specifically in relation to committee, subcommittee, and party leadership organization and powers, changes can be important in affecting the potential for institutional impact on policy. An observer of Congress should be particularly alert to changes in those areas.

Fifth, "reform" in the classic sense (that is, focused around prescriptions about matters such as seniority, ethics, retirement age, and specific rules) is usually not central to the quality of congressional performance and the nature of congressional impact on policy. Much more central is the will of the members of the House and Senate. The machinery of Congress is not inherently deficient. The links with the public are not deficient. The electoral system is not deficient. The ties with the other organs of government are not deficient. What may be deficient is resolve on the part of a sufficient number of members to make the machinery, the ties to other publics and agencies, and the "system" work. It can work when that resolve is present. But the willingness to experiment consciously with internal structures and arrangements and the willingness to take stands that might at least temporarily be unpopular with a mass public, an elite public, or other officials are critical in determining potency.

In a general sense this book ends on a "reformist" note: a hope that members of the House and Senate will not relax with set patterns of thinking and doing but will instead seek new patterns, even within the confines of existing congressional institutions. The institutions allow for both stagnation and innovation; the critical question is how the people responsible for making the institutions function behave. There are no permanent solutions to making Congress a body that arrives at responsive and intelligent decisions about matters affecting the citizens of the nation. But in a dynamic setting such as that surrounding Congress, adjustments and changes to afford at least temporary solutions to perceived problems can be important in determining both the standing of the national legislature and the kind of policy it helps produce.

# Selected Bibliography

The amount of writing on Congress is vast. The following bibliography is selective and omits a lot of good literature. It is intended as a guide for readers who want to explore further the topics treated in this volume. A number of items included are not cited in the footnotes. The bibliography is organized along the line of the book. Parts 1 through 8 correspond to the topics covered in Chapters 1 through 8. Part 9 of the bibliography encompasses the concerns of both Chapters 9 and 10. Part 10 of the bibliography covers both Chapters 11 and 12. Some of the items cited are useful for several purposes but each item is listed only once. The bibliography does not include comprehensive textbooks or volumes composed of previously published material.

Two recent major volumes should also be called to the attention of the reader who wants to explore the literature on Congress further. One is a major bibliography: Robert U. Goehlert and John R. Sayre, *The United States Congress: A Bibliography* (New York: The Free Press, 1982). The other is a major set of literature reviews. Its scope is broader than Congress but contains an assessment of much of the scholarly literature on Congress: Gerhard Loewenberg, Samuel C. Patterson, and Malcolm E. Jewell (eds.), *Handbook of Legislative Research* (Cambridge, Mass.: Harvard University Press, 1985).

## 1. THE NATURE OF CONGRESS

American Political Science Association, "Toward a More Responsible Two-Party System," *American Political Science Review* 44 (1950), supplement. A classic statement of the case for reform inside Congress in order to enhance "party responsibility." Written by a committee chaired by E.E. Schattschneider, a perceptive student of American politics.

Bolling, Richard, *House Out of Order* (New York: Dutton, 1965). A reformist analysis of the

House by an important liberal Democrat from Missouri, who retired in 1982 after 34 years in the House.

Burnham, James, *Congress and the American Tradition* (Chicago: Regnery, 1959). A conservative view of the proper role of Congress: i.e., to stop executive expansion of governmental activities.

Burns, James MacGregor, *The Deadlock of Democracy* (Englewood Cliffs, N.J.: Prentice-Hall, 1963). A liberal attack on Congress for being unresponsive to national needs, especially as interpreted by the president.

Cater, Douglas, *Power in Washington* (New York: Random House, 1964). Primarily a study of subgovernments in action.

Clapp, Charles L., *The Congressman* (Washington: Brookings, 1963). A report and commentary on interviews with and discussions by about fifty members of the House in 1959. Good material on relations with constituents and interest groups, the impact of party leadership, and the working of committees.

*Congressional Quarterly.* Publications of this Washington-based organization are indispensable for the student of the post-World War II Congress. Especially useful are the weekly reports it has issued since 1945, the yearly almanacs, its *Guide to the Congress of the United States* (1982, 3rd ed.) and *Congress and the Nation* (volume 1 covers politics and policy from 1945 through 1964; subsequent volumes each cover four years coinciding with presidential terms).

Davidson, Roger H. and Walter J. Oleszek, *Congress against Itself* (Bloomington, Indiana: Indiana University Press, 1977). A careful analysis of the attempt by the House in 1973–1974 to restructure its committee system.

de Grazia, Alfred (ed.), *Congress: The First Branch of Government* (Garden City, N.Y.,: Doubleday Anchor Books, 1967). Twelve original essays on topics such as oversight, decision making, liaison, information systems, and congressional handling of the budget.

Dexter, Lewis A., *The Sociology and Politics of Congress* (Chicago: Rand McNally, 1969). A collection of essays by one of the most original students of Congress. Especially useful on elections and relations with constituents and interest groups.

Dodd, Lawrence C. and Bruce I. Oppenheimer (eds.), *Congress Reconsidered* (Washington, D.C.: Congressional Quarterly, 1985, 3rd ed.). A collection of original papers focusing on the contemporary Congress.

Huitt, Ralph K. and Robert L. Peabody, *Congress: Two Decades of Analysis* (New York: Harper & Row, 1969). Part I of this book is a long and very useful essay by Peabody summarizing and evaluating the literature on Congress. Part II is a collection of articles by Huitt, one of the pioneers of modern congressional research. These articles include his classic studies of Lyndon Johnson as a Senate Majority Leader and William Proxmire as a maverick senator.

Mann, Thomas E. and Norman J. Ornstein (eds.), *The New Congress* (Washington, D.C.: American Enterprise Institute, 1981). A collection of essays assessing various aspects of both changed and unchanged congressional behavior in the 1970s.

Mayhew, David R., *Congress: The Electoral Connection* (New Haven: Yale University Press, 1974). An essay that attempts to link most congressional behavior to the single, central fact that the members are elected.

Miller, Clem, *Member of the House* (New York: Scribner's, 1962). Insightful letters from a California representative to his constituents. Good material on House procedure, the workload of a representative, the impact of party in the House, and relations with interest groups.

*National Journal.* This Washington-based publication comes out weekly and is focused on policy developments. Excellent material on executive-congressional relations. Some material on the internal workings of Congress.

Ornstein, Norman J., *Congress in Change: Evolution and Reform* (New York: Praeger, 1975). A collection of mostly original papers focusing on change in Congress both throughout its history and primarily in the early 1970s.

Saloma, John S. III, *Congress and the New Politics* (Boston: Little, Brown, 1969). An analysis of congressional capabilities and performance. Useful material on workload, relations with constituents, and relations with the executive branch.

Tacheron, Donald G. and Morris K. Udall, *The Job of the Congressman* (Indianapolis: Bobbs-Merrill, 1966). Intended as a manual for new representatives. Also contains much basic information useful to the student of the House.

## 2. CONGRESSIONAL DEVELOPMENT

Alexander, DeAlva S., *History and Procedure of the House of Representatives* (Boston: Houghton Mifflin, 1916). Still an important work on the House.

Baker, Richard A., *The United States Senate: A Historical Bibliography* (Washington: U.S. Government Printing Office, 1977). A comprehensive bibliography on the Senate, with special attention to historical materials, including biographies of senators.

Blaine, James G., *Twenty Years of Congress,* 2 vols., (Norwich, Conn.: Henry Bill Publishing Co., 1884–86). Memoirs of the period between 1800 and 1880 by an important Speaker of the House.

Chiu, Chang-wei, *The Speaker of the House of Representatives Since 1896* (New York: Columbia University Press, 1928). A standard work on the Speakership during a period of transition.

Clark, Champ, *My Quarter Century of American Politics,* 2 vols., (New York: Harper, 1920). Insightful memoirs of a long-time member who was a Speaker of the House.

Dunn, Arthur W., *From Harrison to Harding,* 2 vols., (New York: Putnam's, 1922). Memoirs of a journalist that contain much valuable material on Congress and congressional-executive relations during the period.

Farrand, Max, *The Framing of the Constitution of the United States* (New Haven: Yale University Press, 1913). Indispensable source for understanding the original vision of the role of Congress (and the alternative visions that were rejected).

Follett, Mary P., *The Speaker of the House of Representatives* (New York: Longmans, Green and Co., 1896). An excellent treatment of the speakership in the nineteenth century.

Galloway, George B., *History of the United States House of Representatives* (New York: Crowell, 1962). An "official" history of the House; brief, but useful. Also available as House Document No. 246, Eighty-seventh Congress, First Session (1962).

Gwinn, William R., *Uncle Joe Cannon, Archfoe of Insurgency* (New York: Bookman Associates, 1957). A useful biography of Speaker Cannon.

Hamilton, Alexander, John Jay, and James Madison, *The Federalist* (New York: Random House, n.d.). Contains a number of papers explaining the founders' notion of how Congress would function in the total political system.

Haynes, George H., *The Senate of the United States,* 2 vols., (Boston: Houghton Mifflin, 1938). A standard history of the Senate.

Huntington, Samuel P., "Congressional Responses to the Twentieth Century," in David B. Truman (ed.), *The Congress and America's Future* (Englewood Cliffs, N.J.: Prentice-Hall, 1973, 2nd ed.). A reformist analysis of House development.

MacNeil, Neil, *Forge of Democracy: The House of Representatives* (New York: McKay, 1963). Summarizes much of the anecdotal material on the House. Contains a good bibliography.

Patterson, James T., *Congressional Conservatism and the New Deal* (Lexington: University of Kentucky Press, 1968). A study of executive-legislative relations and internal congressional politics from 1933 to 1939. Explores the rise of the "conservative coalition" of Republicans and southern Democrats.

Polsby, Nelson W., "Institutionalization in the U.S. House of Representatives," *American Political Science Review* 62 (1968): 144–168. Explores and documents the growing stability of the House in the twentieth century.

Price, H. Douglas, "Congress and the Evolution of Legislative 'Professionalism'," in Norman J. Ornstein (ed.), *Congress in Change: Evolution and Reform* (New York: Praeger, 1975): 2–23. Examines various aspects of the "professionalization" of the congressional career.

Price, H. Douglas, "The Congressional Career—Then and Now," in Nelson W. Polsby (ed.), *Congressional Behavior* (New York: Random House, 1971). Contrasts the instability of nineteenth century congressional membership with the stability of twentieth century membership.

Rothman, David J., *Politics and Power in the United States Senate, 1869–1901* (Cambridge: Harvard University Press, 1966). An excellent account of the evolution of the Senate from chaos to party government.

Stephenson, Nathaniel W., *Nelson W. Aldrich: A Leader in American Politics* (New York: Scribner's, 1930). Fine biography of the most important Republican leader in the Senate in the late nineteenth and early twentieth centuries.

Wilson, Woodrow, *Congressional Government* (New York: Meridian, 1956). This classic interpretation of Congress was first published in 1885 and still contains many valid observations.

Young, James S., *The Washington Community, 1800–1828* (New York: Columbia University Press, 1966). A fascinating study of the national government in its youth. Rich material on Congress of the period.


## 3. CONGRESSIONAL ELECTIONS

Cummings, Milton C., Jr., *Congressmen and the Electorate* (New York: Free Press, 1966). A study of the relationship between voting for president and voting for House members.

Fishel, Jeff, *Party and Opposition* (New York: McKay, 1973). A study of all the challengers for House seats in the 1964 election and of the subsequent six years in the careers of those who won.

Hacker, Andrew, *Congressional Districting* (Washington: Brookings, 1964, revised ed.). A brief, but thorough treatment of the subject.

Hinckley, Barbara, *Congressional Elections* (Washington, D.C.: Congressional Quarterly Press, 1981). A thorough summary and assessment of what political scientists do and do not know about congressional elections.

Jacobson, Gary C., *Money in Congressional Elections* (New Haven: Yale University Press, 1980). A thorough examination of campaign finance in the 1970s.

Jacobson, Gary C., *The Politics of Congressional Elections* (Boston: Little, Brown, 1987, 2nd ed.). A clear analysis of the nature and consequences of congressional elections.

Jacobson, Gary C. and Samuel Kernell, *Strategy and Choice in Congressional Elections* (New Haven: Yale University Press, 1981). An argument that congressional candidates and their prime backers provide a link between the national political context and local voters.

Jones, Charles O., *Every Second Year* (Washington: Brookings, 1967). A study of the effect of the two-year term for House members and of the consequences of various alternative proposals.

Mann, Thomas E., *Unsafe at Any Margin: Interpreting Congressional Elections* (Washington, D.C.: American Enterprise Institute, 1978). A treatment of congressional elections focusing on the local and disaggregated nature of them.

Price, H. Douglas, "The Electoral Arena," in David B. Truman (ed.), *The Congress and America's Future,* 2nd ed. (Englewood Cliffs, N.J.: Prentice-Hall, 1973). An examination of changing electoral patterns and practices in the twentieth century.


## 4. CONGRESSIONAL DECISION-MAKING

Clausen, Aage R., *How Congressmen Decide* (New York: St. Martin's, 1973). A study of five substantive dimensions of voting in the House and Senate.

Fenno, Richard F., Jr., "The Internal Distribution of Influence: The House," in David B. Truman (ed.), *The Congress and America's Future,* 2nd ed. (Englewood Cliffs, N.J.: Prentice-Hall, 1973). A summary assessment of how things get done in the House.

Froman, Lewis A., Jr., *The Congressional Process* (Boston: Little, Brown, 1967). A discussion of the use and impact of the rules in the House and Senate.

Huitt, Ralph K., "The Internal Distribution of Influence: The Senate," in David B. Truman (ed.), *The Congress and America's Future,* 2nd ed. (Englewood Cliffs, N.J.: Prentice-Hall, 1973). A summary assessment of how things get done in the Senate.

Kingdon, John W., *Congressmen's Voting Decisions,* 2nd ed. (New York: Harper and Row, 1981). An analysis, based largely on interviews, of how members of the House make up their minds on floor voting.

Matthews, Donald R., *U.S. Senators and Their World* (Chapel Hill: University of North Carolina Press, 1960). An analysis of decision making in the Senate in the 1940s and 1950s.

Matthews, Donald R. and James A. Stimson, *Yeas and Nays: Normal Decision-Making in the U.S. House of Representatives* (New York: Wiley, 1975). A study of cue-giving and cue-taking in the House of Representatives as an explanation of decision making.

Mayhew, David R., *Party Loyalty Among Congressmen* (Cambridge: Harvard University Press, 1966). A roll call study that shows that Democrats support each other's interests better than do Republicans.

Oleszek, Walter J., *Congressional Procedures and the Policy Process* (Washington, D.C.: Congressional Quarterly Press, 1984, 2nd ed.). A careful study, by a specialist with the Congressional Research Service of the Library of Congress, of the content of House and Senate rules and their impact on the substance of legislation.

Ripley, Randall B., *Power in the Senate* (New York: St. Martin's, 1969). Focused on decision-making in the Senate in the 1960s. Also has some material on Senate history.

Turner, Julius and Edward V. Schneier, Jr., *Party and Constituency: Pressures on Congress* (Baltimore: The Johns Hopkins Press, 1970, revised ed.). A classic roll call analysis of the comparative importance of party and constituency for scattered congresses between 1921 and 1967.

## 5. COMMITTEES AND SUBCOMMITTEES

Fenno, Richard F., Jr., *Congressmen in Committees* (Boston: Little, Brown, 1973). A comparative study of the workings of six House committees.

Fenno, Richard F., Jr., *The Power of the Purse* (Boston: Little, Brown, 1966). A long and valuable study of appropriations politics, focused primarily on the House Appropriations Committee.

Goodwin, George Jr., *The Little Legislatures* (Amherst: University of Massachusetts Press, 1970). A brief, but thorough treatment of committees.

Hinckley, Barbara, *The Seniority System in Congress* (Bloomington: Indiana University Press, 1971). A thorough analysis of seniority in Congress that concludes that its policy impact is quite limited.

McConachie, Lauros, *Congressional Committees* (New York: Crowell, 1898). A classic work on the development of standing committees.

McGown, Ada C., *The Congressional Conference Committee* (New York: Columbia University Press, 1927). An early and still useful treatment of conference committees.

Manley, John F., *The Politics of Finance* (Boston: Little, Brown, 1970). A perceptive study of the House Ways and Means Committee.

Matsunaga, Spark M. and Ping Chen, *Rulemakers of the House* (Urbana, Illinois: University of Illinois Press, 1976). A thorough study of the House Rules Committee.

Murphy, James T., "Political Parties and Porkbarrel: Party Conflict and Cooperation in House Public Works Committee Decision Making," *American Political Science Review* 68 (1974): 169–85. A study that focuses on the highly partisan nature of the House Public Works Committee.

Parker, Glenn R. and Suzanne L. Parker, *Factions in House Committees* (Knoxville, Tenn.: University of Tennessee Press, 1985). A careful examination of voting in House committees from 1973 through 1980.

Robinson, James A., *The House Rules Committee* (Indianapolis: Bobbs-Merrill, 1963). An examination of the functions and internal politics of this important committee.

Smith, Steven S. and Christopher J. Deering, *Committees in Congress* (Washington, D.C.: Congressional Quarterly Press, 1984). A thorough overview of congressional committees.

Steiner, Gilbert Y., *The Congressional Conference Committee* (Urbana: University of Illinois Press, 1951). Analyzes conference committee behavior in the 1930s and 1940s.

Vogler, David J., *The Third House* (Evanston: Northwestern University Press, 1971). Analyzes conference committee behavior in the 1950s and 1960s.

## 6. PARTY LEADERSHIP

Bolling, Richard, *Power in the House* (New York: Dutton, 1968). A history of party leadership in the House with proposals for reform in the direction of responsible party government. Written by a representative from Missouri from 1949 through 1982.

Brown, George R., *The Leadership of Congress* (Indianapolis: Bobbs-Merrill, 1922). A very perceptive account of party leadership in the first two decades of the twentieth century.

Evans, Rowland and Robert Novak, *Lyndon B. Johnson: The Exercise of Power* (New York: New American Library, 1966). Contains a long and perceptive account of Johnson as Democratic floor leader in the Senate.

Hasbrouck, Paul D., *Party Government in the House of Representatives* (New York: Macmillan, 1927). A first-rate study of the development of party leadership in the House.

Jones, Charles O., *The Minority Party in Congress* (Boston: Little, Brown, 1970). A perceptive analysis of the role of the minority party in Congress with special attention to party leadership.

Nelson, Garrison, "Partisan Patterns of House Leadership Change, 1789–1977," *American Political Science Review* 71 (1977): 918–39. Concludes that "the two parties differ significantly in their patterns of House leadership change."

Peabody, Robert L., *Leadership in Congress* (Boston: Little, Brown, 1976). A study of leadership stability and change from 1955 through 1974.

Ripley, Randall B., *Majority Party Leadership in Congress* (Boston: Little, Brown, 1969). An analysis of party leadership and leader-president relations based on data from ten Congresses in the twentieth century.

Ripley, Randall B., *Party Leaders in the House of Representatives* (Washington: Brookings, 1967). An analysis that includes some attention to historical development and a focus on leadership in the early 1960s.

Sinclair, Barbara, *Majority Leadership in the U.S. House* (Baltimore, Md.: Johns Hopkins University Press, 1983). A careful examination of the Democratic leadership in the House from 1977 through 1981.

Stewart, John G., "Two Strategies of Leadership: Johnson and Mansfield," in Nelson W. Polsby (ed.), *Congressional Behavior* (New York: Random House, 1971). A comparison of the contrasting styles of these two Senate Democratic leaders.

Waldman, Sidney, "Majority Leadership in the House of Representatives," *Political Science Quarterly* 95 (1980): 373–393. A careful look at aspects of leadership in the reformed House based largely on interviews with leaders, members, and staff in the 94th (1975–76) and 95th (1977–78) Congresses.

## 7. OTHER INTERNAL INFLUENCES

Born, Richard, "Cue-Taking within State Party Delegations in the U.S. House of Representatives," *Journal of Politics* 38 (1976): 71–94. An argument that the importance of state party cues has been exaggerated in other studies.

Butler, Warren H., "Administering Congress: The Role of the Staff," *Public Administration Review* 26 (1966): 3–12. A brief description of the place of congressional staff.

Clausen, Aage R., "State Party Influence on Congressional Party Decisions," *Midwest Journal of Political Science* 16 (1972): 77–101. A roll call analysis that shows the strong influence of state party delegations.

Deckard, Barbara, "State Party Delegations in the United States House of Representatives—An Analysis of Group Action," *Polity* 5 (1973): 311–34. An attempt to explain delegation cohesiveness and its relation to alliance behavior.

Deckard, Barbara, "State Party Delegations in the U.S. House of Representatives—A Comparative Study of Group Cohesion," *Journal of Politics* 34 (1972): 199–222. An analysis based on interviews.

Ferber, Mark F., "The Formation of the Democratic Study Group," in Nelson W. Polsby (ed.), *Congressional Behavior* (New York: Random House, 1971). An examination of the conditions that led to the creation of the DSG and its early functioning.

Fiellin, Alan, "The Functions of Informal Groups in Legislative Institutions," *Journal of Politics* 24 (1962): 72–91. A study of the New York Democrats in the House.

Fox, Harrison W., Jr., and Susan Webb Hammond, *Congressional Staffs: The Invisible Force in American Lawmaking* (New York: Free Press, 1977). A thorough analysis of the functioning and impact of congressional staff.

Henry, Charles P., "Legitimizing Race in Congressional Politics," *American Politics Quarterly* 5 (1977): 149–76. A study of the Congressional Black Caucus in the House of Representatives.

Kofmehl, Kenneth, *Professional Staffs of Congress,* 3rd ed. (West Lafayette, Indiana: Purdue University Press, 1977). A description of congressional staffs that omits only personal staffs for members of the House.

Malbin, Michael J., *Unelected Representatives: Congressional Staff and the Future of Representative Government* (New York: Basic Books, 1980). An assessment of the influence of staff that argues that it is too dominant and thereby endangers the "deliberative" nature of Congress.

Manley, John F., "Congressional Staff and Public Policy-Making: The Joint Committee on Internal Revenue Taxation," *Journal of Politics* 30 (1968): 1046–67. An excellent case study of the policy impact of one committee staff.

Patterson, Samuel C., "The Professional Staffs of Congressional Committees," *Administrative Science Quarterly* 15 (1970): 22–37. A concise, but thorough discussion of committee staffs.

Stevens, Arthur G., Jr., Arthur H. Miller, and Thomas E. Mann, "Mobilization of Liberal Strength in the House, 1955–1970: The Democratic Study Group," *American Political Science Review* 68 (1974): 667–81. A study of the origins and functioning of the Democratic Study Group in the House.

Stevens, Arthur C., Jr., Daniel P. Mulhollan, and Paul S. Rundquist, "U.S. Congressional Structure and Representation: The Role of Informal Groups," *Legislative Studies Quarterly* 6 (1981): 415–37. An analysis of the impact of the expansion of informal groups in Congress on the structure of the institution, with special attention to the expanded opportunities for representation of constituent interests afforded by these groups.

Truman, David B., "The State Delegation and the Structure of Voting in the United States House of Representatives," *American Political Science Review* 50 (1956): 1023–45. An early roll call study that seeks to isolate the impact of state delegations.

## 8. CONGRESS, INTEREST GROUPS, AND CONSTITUENTS

Bauer, Raymond A., Ithiel de Sola Pool, and Lewis A. Dexter, *American Business and Public Policy* (New York: Atherton, 1963). A case study of a decade of reciprocal trade legislation that concludes that interest groups and constituents had only limited influence.

Davidson, Roger H., *The Role of the Congressman* (New York: Pegasus, 1969). An analysis of the distribution of self-perceived roles, including those relating to representation of constituents and attitudes toward interest groups.

Dexter, Lewis A., *How Organizations Are Represented in Washington* (Indianapolis: Bobbs-Merrill, 1969). A rich source for understanding the subtleties of relations between lobbyists and Congress.

Eulau, Heinz and Paul D. Karps, "The Puzzle of Representation: Specifying Components of Responsiveness," *Legislative Studies Quarterly* 2 (1977): 233–54. An insightful analysis of the different meanings of representation and responsiveness in legislatures.

Fenno, Richard F., Jr., *Home Style: House Members in Their Districts* (Boston: Little, Brown, 1978). An insightful and provocative study of what House members do "back home."

Hayes, Michael T., *Lobbyists and Legislators: A Theory of Political Markets* (New Brunswick, N.J.: Rutgers University Press, 1981). A major effort to state the varying relationship between lobbyists and legislators in theoretical terms that challenges "conventional wisdom" about the relationship.

Milbrath, Lester W., *The Washington Lobbyists* (Chicago: Rand McNally, 1963). A general study of Washington lobbyists that contains much material on their relations with Congress.

Parker, Glenn R., *Homeward Bound: Explaining Changes in Congressional Behavior* (Pittsburgh, Pa.: University of Pittsburgh Press, 1986). An analysis of growing attention to constituencies on the part of members of Congress.

Schlozman, Kay Lehman and John T. Tierney, *Organized Interests and American Democracy* (New York: Harper and Row, 1986). A major empirically-based analysis of interest groups in Washington that includes some attention to their interaction with Congress.

## 9. RELATIONS WITH THE PRESIDENT, PRESIDENCY, AND BUREAUCRACY

Aberbach, Joel D. and Bert A. Rockman, "The Overlapping Worlds of American Federal Executives and Congressmen," *British Journal of Political Science* 7 (1977): 23–47. A study that suggests that the belief systems of bureaucrats and members of Congress are not very different.

Chamberlain, Lawrence H., *The President, Congress and Legislation* (New York: Columbia University Press, 1946). Short studies of major legislation passed by Congress for over half a century. Assessments are made of the relative influence of Congress and the executive branch.

Davidson, Roger H., "Breaking Up Those 'Cozy Triangles': An Impossible Dream?," in Susan Welch and John G. Peters (eds.), *Legislative Reform and Public Policy* (New York: Praeger, 1977): 30–53. An exploratory essay on how the influence of subgovernments might be reduced.

Edwards, George C. III, *Presidential Influence in Congress* (San Francisco: Freeman, 1980). An analysis of presidential influence in Congress focusing on the Eisenhower through Carter period and using quantitative measures where available.

Fiorina, Morris P., *Congress: Keystone of the Washington Establishment* (New Haven: Yale University Press, 1977). An argument that members of Congress help perpetuate their own tenure in office by publicly berating bureaucracy and privately cooperating with bureaucrats.

Holtzman, Abraham, *Legislative Liaison* (Chicago: Rand McNally, 1970). A study of White House and departmental liaison efforts. Especially strong on the Kennedy presidency.

Jones, Charles O., *The Trusteeship-Presidency: Jimmy Carter and the United States Congress* (Baton Rouge, La.: Louisiana State University Press, 1988). A thorough analysis of relations between President Carter and Congress.

King, Anthony (ed.), *Both Ends of the Avenue: The Presidency, the Executive Branch, and Congress in the 1980s* (Washington, D.C.: American Enterprise Institute, 1983). A collection of good original papers on various aspects of executive-legislative relations.

Mansfield, Harvey C., Sr. (ed.), *Congress against the President,* Proceedings of the Academy of Political Science 32 (1975). A collection of original papers exploring a number of aspects of presidential-congressional relations.

Moe, Ronald C. and Steven C. Teel, "Congress as Policy-Maker: A Necessary Reappraisal." *Political Science Quarterly* 85 (1970): 443–70. An updating of Chamberlain's work that reaches the same conclusion: Congress is an influential partner in the policy process and is not subservient to the president and bureaucracy.

Neustadt, Richard E., "Politicians and Bureaucrats," in David B. Truman (ed.), *The Congress and America's Future* (Englewood Cliffs, N.J.: Prentice-Hall, 1973, 2nd ed.). An examination of the tripartite relationship between members of Congress, the president, and bureaucrats. Argues that the former two have common interests different from those of the bureaucrats.

Neustadt, Richard E., "Presidency and Legislation: The Growth of Central Clearance," *American Political Science Review* 48 (1954): 641–71. A discussion of growing control by the Executive Office of the President over legislative proposals coming from the bureaucracy.

Neustadt, Richard E., "Presidency and Legislation: Planning the President's Program," *American Political Science Review* 49 (1955): 980–1021. A discussion of the evolution of the "program of the president."

Ogul, Morris S., *Congress Oversees the Bureaucracy: Studies in Legislative Supervision* (Pittsburgh: University of Pittsburgh Press, 1976). A general consideration of oversight with some detailed case examples.

Pipe, G. Russell, "Congressional Liaison: The Executive Branch Consolidates Its Relations with Congress," *Public Administration Review* 26 (1966): 14–24. A description of the size and scope of departmental liaison efforts.

Ripley, Randall B., *Kennedy and Congress* (Morristown, N.J.: General Learning Press, 1972). A case study of congressional-presidential relations in 1961–1963.

Ripley, Randall B. and Grace A. Franklin, *Congress, the Bureaucracy, and Public Policy* (Chicago: Dorsey Press, 1987, 4th ed.). An analysis of the impact of congressional-bureaucratic relations on the formulation and passage of different types of policies.

Robinson, James A., *Congress and Foreign Policy Making,* rev. ed. (Homewood, Ill.: Dorsey, 1967). An intensive study, based in part on interviews, of executive-legislative relations in the area of foreign policy.

Sundquist, James L., *The Decline and Resurgence of Congress* (Washington, D.C.: Brookings, 1981). A major study of congressional-executive relations, with special attention to congressional "resurgence" in the 1970s.

Wildavsky, Aaron, *The New Politics of the Budgetary Process* (Glenview, Ill.: Scott, Foresman, 1988). A general treatment of budgeting that contrasts "old style" budgeting and budgeting in the 1980s.

## 10. CONGRESS AND POLICY

Bailey, Stephen K., *Congress Makes a Law* (New York: Vintage, 1964). A classic case study of the passage of the Employment Act of 1946.

Clausen, Aage R. and Carl E. Van Horn, "The Congressional Response to a Decade of Change: 1963–1972," *Journal of Politics* 39 (1977): 624–66. A study that explores the conditions for change or stability in the policy orientations of individual members.

Dahl, Robert A., *Congress and Foreign Policy* (New York: Harcourt, Brace, 1950). A thoughtful early study of the foreign policy role of Congress.

Eidenberg, Eugene and Roy D. Morey, *An Act of Congress* (New York: Norton, 1969). A case study of the passage of the Elementary and Secondary Education Act of 1965.

Ferejohn, John A., *Pork Barrel Politics: Rivers and Harbors Legislation, 1947–1968* (Stanford, California: Stanford University Press, 1974). A careful study of congressional handling of rivers and harbors legislation for 20 years, with some general explanation of how Congress handles distributive policies.

Franck, Thomas M. and Edward Weisband, *Foreign Policy by Congress* (New York: Oxford University Press, 1979). A careful study of the dramatic increase in congressional power in foreign affairs in the 1970s and the consequences—both positive and negative—of that increase.

Jewell, Malcolm, *Senatorial Politics and Foreign Policy* (Lexington: University of Kentucky Press, 1962). A detailed study of Senate activity in the foreign policy area.

Kolodziej, Edward A., *The Uncommon Defense and Congress, 1945–1963* (Columbus: The Ohio State University Press, 1966). A detailed study of the congressional role in defense policy.

LeLoup, Lance T., *Budgetary Politics* (Brunswick, Ohio: King's Court, 1986, 3rd ed.). A well-crafted general analysis of the current budget process and its politics that puts the congressional role in perspective.

LeLoup, Lance T., *The Fiscal Congress: Legislative Control of the Budget* (Westport, Conn.:

Greenwood Press, 1980). A comprehensive, but moderate-sized, analysis of the development, politics, and consequences of the congressional budget process adopted in 1974.

Morgan, Donald G., *Congress and the Constitution* (Cambridge: Harvard University Press, 1966). Includes ten case studies of congressional action on matters involving constitutional questions from 1818 through 1964. Urges that Congress not rely on the Supreme Court for constitutional wisdom but arrive at independent decisions instead.

Munger, Frank J. and Richard F. Fenno, Jr., *National Politics and Federal Aid to Education* (Syracuse: Syracuse University Press, 1962). A careful analysis of the congressional role in federal aid to education legislation—both successful and unsuccessful.

Pastor, Robert A., *Congress and the Politics of U.S. Foreign Economic Policy, 1929–1976* (Berkeley: University of California Press, 1980). A careful analysis of the role of Congress in foreign economic policy for almost half a century.

Redman, Eric, *The Dance of Legislation* (New York: Simon and Shuster, 1973). A well-told story of the passage of the Emergency Health Personnel Act of 1970.

Reid, T. R., *Congressional Odyssey: The Saga of a Senate Bill* (San Francisco: Freeman, 1980). A good book by a reporter for the *Washington Post* in the "a bill becomes a law" genre. It focuses on what became a waterway user charges statute.

Rieselbach, Leroy N., *Congressional Reform* (Washington, D.C.: Congressional Quarterly, 1986). A brief, insightful overview of recent reform activity in Congress by a long-time student of congressional reform.

Schick, Allen (ed.). *Making Economic Policy in Congress* (Washington, D.C.: American Enterprise Institute, 1983). Nine insightful papers on aspects of congressional action with regard to matters such as spending, taxing, redistribution, trade policy, and regulatory policy.

Sundquist, James L., *Politics and Policy* (Washington: Brookings, 1968). A detailed study of domestic policy making and the interaction between Congress and the executive branch from 1953 through 1966. Argues that most of the successful Democratic initiatives of the 1960s were developed in Congress in the 1950s during the Eisenhower administration.

Wright, Gerald C., Jr., Leroy N. Rieselbach, and Lawrence C. Dodd (eds.), *Congress and Policy Change* (New York: Agathon, 1986). Contains ten papers that explore many aspects of policy change and explanations for those changes.

# Index